FLUID FUTURES

FLUID FUTURES

Science Fiction and Potentiality

Steven Shaviro

Published by Repeater Books

An imprint of Watkins Media Ltd

Unit 11 Shepperton House

89-93 Shepperton Road

London

N1 3DF

United Kingdom

www.repeaterbooks.com

A Repeater Books paperback original 2024

1

Distributed in the United States by Random House, Inc., New York.

ISBN: 9781915672469

Ebook ISBN: 9781915672476

Printed and bound in the United Kingdom by CPI Group (UK) Ltd, Croydon CR0 4YY

Contents

I love ignorance of the future.
Friedrich Nietzsche

We are all interested in the future, for that is where you and I are going to spend the rest of our lives.
Criswell (in Ed Wood, *Plan 9 from Outer Space*)

I don't know what the future is. I don't know … what I'm supposed to want.
Biff Loman (in Arthur Miller, *Death of a Salesman*)

The most painful state of being is remembering the future, particularly the one you'll never have.
Søren Kierkegaard

Actual social formations are shaped by the potential formations whose actualization they seek to impede.
Mark Fisher

Nothing can change the shape of things to come.
Max Frost (in Barry Shear, *Wild in the Streets*)

Preface

Fluid Futures considers the status of science fiction as a discourse that, in a meaningful sense, is *about* the future. Of course, the future is in principle unknowable. It is open, and not entirely determined in advance: fluid rather than fixed in stone. But the future is also not altogether arbitrary; it *follows* from the past and the present in some manner that needs to be described and unpacked. I claim that science fiction works towards just such an unpacking. It does not predict the actual future, but it offers a mimesis of *futurity*, understood as a kind of pressure, or incipience, that is already implicit within the present moment.

The volume starts, in its first chapter, by reflecting upon three modes that are commonly used by science fiction in order to grasp futurity in some way: extrapolation, speculation, and fabulation. After this, in its second chapter, the book looks at how fabulation works in four recent science fiction short stories, by Pat Cadigan, Sofia Samatar, Charlie Jane Anders, and Tade Thompson. The third chapter ponders the *aboutness* of science fiction by confronting Darko Suvin's canonical account of science fiction as the literature of cognitive estrangement (Suvin 2016) with Seo-Young Chu's counter-theory of science fiction as "a mimetic discourse whose objects of representation are nonimaginary" but difficult to grasp (Chu 2010). The fourth chapter proposes a theory of potentiality, and differentiates science fiction from philosophy on that basis. The fifth chapter considers the temporality of science fiction in light of Alfred North Whitehead's exhortation that we must "take time seriously." The sixth chapter continues to look at the ways that science fiction projects images of futurity and confronts the forces that would seek to block the future from taking on any form unlike that of the present. The seventh chapter looks at science fiction, not just as the exploration of particular potentialities, but as a broader exercise in the construction, via world-building, of possible worlds. All in all, the book considers how various works of science fiction are able to trace the outlines of futurity — or better, of futurities in the plural.

This brief description runs the risk of making *Fluid Futures* seem more linear than it actually is. In fact, the book often re-crosses its tracks, returning to previously developed configurations of texts and exploring the same arguments from different viewpoints. I have also tried to maintain a certain balance between theoretical texts and overtly science-fictional ones. My hope is that I have been able to bring out the ways that science-fiction novels and stories not only exemplify previously stated theoretical assertions, but themselves work to articulate new concepts and new arguments. Conversely, I hope that my discussions of texts by critics and philosophers bring out the experimental and speculative dimensions of these texts, as well as their argumentative and dogmatic aspects.

This is the fourth book of science-fiction criticism (scholarship and theory) that I have written and published. The first of these, *Connected: Or What It Means to Live in the Network Society*, deals largely with science fiction as a way of critically grasping neoliberal capitalism (Shaviro 2003). The second, *Discognition*, uses science fiction to reflect upon questions about consciousness, intelligence, and sentience, both in human beings and in other sorts of entities (Shaviro 2016a). The third, *Extreme Fabulations: Science Fictions of Life*, offers a series of close readings of both classical and recent science-fictional texts, moving from epistemological questions, through biological ones, and on to political ones (Shaviro 2021). The present volume endeavors to give a broader picture of science fiction as a literary genre, moving back and forth between general arguments about the form and readings of particular texts.

This book is dedicated, as is everything I write, to my daughters, Adah Mozelle Shaviro and Roxanne Tamar Shaviro, whose futures will extend beyond mine. I would also like to dedicate *Fluid Futures* to the memory of my uncle Morris Wachs (1921–2001).

Morris was a French professor and a Diderot scholar. But he was also a science fiction fan. When I was nine years old, Uncle Morris gave me a copy of E. E. "Doc" Smith's *Triplanetary* (Smith 1948) to read. This was the beginning of my fascination with science fiction, which has lasted for more than six decades and continues to this day.

1. The Speculative Continuum

Mimesis and Science Fiction

What is science fiction about? One obvious answer is that it is about the future. This is not a matter of grammar: most science-fiction stories are narrated in the past tense or the present tense, just like other sorts of written narratives. Nor is it a matter of formal innovation: most science-fiction stories are straightforwardly representational or referential, in the same way that traditional naturalistic fiction tends to be. As John Clute and his collaborators argue, science fiction "is essentially a *continuation* of the mimetic novel" (Clute et al. 2018a). It is just that science fiction, with its future orientation, refers to different sorts of things than other fictional prose narratives do.

By saying that science fiction stories are representational or referential, I am going against the prevailing understanding of science fiction, canonically articulated by Darko Suvin, as "the literature of *cognitive estrangement*" (Suvin 2016). While I do not contest the importance of either cognition or estrangement in science fiction, I still insist that science-fiction texts are representational ones, because they display a fundamental *aboutness.* In asserting this, I am drawing upon Seo-Young Chu's important book *Do Metaphors Dream of Literal Sleep?*, which offers "a science-fictional theory of representation" (Chu 2010). Science-fiction texts are representational or mimetic in the sense that they have external, referential content. These texts do not predominantly focus, as high-modernist works are often said to do (in Clement Greenberg's canonical formulation), "upon the medium of [their] own craft", so that "the expression matter[s] more than what is being expressed" (Greenberg 1965). In science fiction, "what is being expressed" retains its importance.

It is true that some brilliant "New Wave" science fiction of the 1960s and '70s sought to emulate the self-conscious narrative strategies of twentieth-century modernist and avant-garde literature. But even the most explicitly experimental, formally audacious science-fiction texts from this period — like Samuel R. Delany's *Dhalgren* (Delany 1975) or J. G. Ballard's *The Atrocity Exhibition* (Ballard 1970) — nonetheless remain ultimately referential. Formal innovation still works in the service of an explicit, external content. Even in these cases, science-fiction writing has more in common with the figurative art of Jack Kirby than it does with the self-reflexive abstractions of Kirby's near-contemporary Jackson Pollock. For the most part, science-fiction narratives overtly claim to depict, or to illustrate, a world that exists in its own right, beyond the limits of the text. This remains the case even though the world so depicted diverges sharply from the one in which we live and does not actually exist.

Science fiction shares the quality of *aboutness* with other popular narrative genres. These genres are all predominantly referential, even if the particular events to which they refer do not actually happen. Delany explains the difference between science fiction and other sorts of referential fiction in terms of their different levels of *subjunctivity*. This, again, is not a matter of grammar (the actual use of verbs in the subjunctive mood), but rather of a discourse's overall level of possibility. Science fiction concerns "*events that have not happened*," at least so far; and such events "are very different from the [naturalistic] fictional events that *could have happened*, or the fantastic events that *could not have happened*" (Delany 2009).

Delany's observation can be restated in terms of the *worlds* in which fictional events take place. Naturalistic fiction places its imaginary characters and events in the context of something like the familiar world in which the writer and the book's initial readers actually live, or in which their historical predecessors lived. On the other hand, non-naturalistic or fantastic genres —

including but not limited to science fiction — depart from the actual world as their presumed context. They engage instead in building *alternative worlds*, within which their characters live and the events they describe take place. These alternative worlds differ from the world we know in at least some respects — though they usually retain enough features of actuality to make them at least partly recognizable. Depending on the sort of fiction in question, these alternative worlds may involve counterfactual historical sequences as well as entirely fantastic locales and physically impossible happenings. Science fiction differs from other fantastic genres in that the alternative world to which it refers is usually a future world, or one that is shaped by advanced technologies. A science-fictional world generally postdates, extends beyond, and departs from — but therefore, to a certain extent, also arises out of — the actual world in which it is written and read.

In defining science fiction in terms of its futuristic orientation, I am of course sidestepping a lot of major problems — rather than explicitly resolving them. There are all sorts of difficulties: first, the identification and circumscription of science fiction as a particular genre (Vint and Bould 2008); second, the prevalence and exuberance of science fiction in many languages and cultures well beyond the Anglo-American works that are my major focus here; third, the broader question of what is entailed when we try to define genres (of texts, or of cultural objects more broadly) at all (Rieder 2017); and fourth, the fact that science-fictional tropes and story elements have recently spread over so many media — from prose fiction, to movies, to music — that science fiction might better be understood as a *mode* of discourse rather than as a genre with its own particular forms and protocols (Hollinger 2014). Indeed, we live in a time of such rapid technological change that — as Donna Haraway already, and quite presciently, put it several decades ago — "the boundary between science fiction and social reality is an optical illusion" (Haraway 1991). Such ubiquity makes it hard to circumscribe any definition.

I am less interested in engaging in these sorts of debates, however, than I am in explaining why I continue to speak of *science fiction* even though there is arguably "no such thing" (Vint and Bould 2008). I am perfectly aware that genre designations like *science fiction* cannot be made rigorous and precise. It is always possible to find ambiguous cases, exceptions, and counter-examples that undermine whatever definition has been proposed. At best, genre definitions are fuzzy concepts, like what Wittgenstein calls *family resemblances*. These are loose categories for grouping objects that, like the members of an extended family, "have no one thing in common," but display "many different kinds of *affinity* between them" (Wittgenstein 2009; cited in relation to science fiction by Kincaid 2003). What's more, even when genre definitions are made in this rough and imprecise way, they are historically variable, so that their meanings and contents change over the course of time. As John Rieder puts it, *Frankenstein* was not a science-fiction novel when it was initially published in 1818, but today it is not only a science-fiction novel, it's one of the founding texts of the genre (Rieder 2017). Conversely, critics have suggested that, given our current designations, much older texts, like Lucian's *True History* (160 AD) and Cyrano de Bergerac's *Voyage to the Moon* (1657 AD), should also be retrospectively counted as science fiction (Nevins 2018). And finally, genre designations cannot just refer to the intrinsic characteristics of texts (or of other cultural artifacts) in themselves, because such designations also encompass — indeed, they are generated and inflected by — the many practices and activities that surround and receive them, from marketing strategies, to fan activities, to scholarly research projects. (For all these points, see Rieder 2017).

Nonetheless, genre designations like *science fiction* can still be useful and valuable, as long as we keep their fuzziness and contingency in mind. Indeed, it is scarcely possible to speak intelligibly about individual cultural artifacts *without* taking questions of genre into consideration. No such object is so unique that it doesn't (in some sense) belong to one genre or another — and often to several at once. Genre designations have, at the very least, a strong heuristic value. They help us to determine how any particular work or cultural object is related to others, as well as how it fits into (which is also to say, how it diverges from) a broader range of aesthetic, commercial, and historical contexts.

A term like *science fiction*, therefore, is as indispensable as it is ultimately indefensible. Genre designations are *abstractions* of a certain kind, and we may say about them what Alfred North Whitehead says about abstractions more generally: "You cannot think without abstractions; accordingly, it is of the utmost importance to be vigilant in critically revising your *modes* of abstraction" (Whitehead 1925). That is to say, we have to use abstractions in order to get anywhere at all; but for this very reason, we always need to be aware of the flaws and limitations of our abstractions. Without some process of abstraction, or of what Whitehead also calls "imaginative generalization," we can never get beyond the "rigid empiricism" of simply describing isolated instances (Whitehead 1978). At the same time, however, every abstraction is also a simplification, and therefore a falsification; they involve leaving out whatever data, or whatever aspects of the things under discussion, are not relevant to our immediate purposes. To assert the similarity of multiple items is, *ipso facto*, to ignore the ways in which they are different from one another; to establish categories of any sort is to willfully ignore anomalies and counter-examples. We are therefore always in danger of taking our abstractions to be more precise and comprehensive than they actually are; this is what Whitehead calls the *fallacy of misplaced concreteness* (Whitehead 1925). In what follows, I will strive to remain cognizant of the limits of my categories and terms, even as I continue to use them.

Futurity

Making allowances for all these qualifications, my basic argument in this book is that science fiction is about *futurity*. I want to give this word a particular resonance, distinguishing it from any more general sense of "the future." Just as naturalistic fiction recounts events that *could* happen in the world as it exists or has existed — even though they have not actually happened — so science fiction recounts events that could only happen at some moment in the future, following on from what exists in the present. But science fiction does this without claiming that those events actually *will* happen. Science fiction envisions a futurity that never becomes present, never actually comes to pass. Far from claiming to predict the future, therefore, science fiction vehemently rejects any such ambition. As the comics writer Warren Ellis puts it,

> When I'm working and talking in the sphere of futurism, I try never to do predictions. Same as a science fiction writer. Speculation and fabulation is what I do, and it should never be treated as prediction. Prediction is a con game and a clown show.
>
> (Ellis 2018)

In other words, what I am here calling *futurity* is not the same thing as what will actually come to pass. Futurity is not something that will happen a minute, or a week, or a million years from now. Rather, futurity always retains its subjunctivity. It is something that *could* happen, something that could emerge or develop from the world as we live in it now — but it is never something that actually *does* happen. Futurity, in its very nature, is always unrealized and unfulfilled. In the phrase favored by Ernst Bloch, futurity is a perpetual *not yet* (Bloch 1995). Futurity is also unavoidably vague and plural: a cluster of possibilities, rather than a single determination. Different science-fiction narratives depict different futurities. Sometimes the impossibility of predicting the future is built into these narratives themselves: as in Isaac Asimov's initial Foundation trilogy, in which the emergence of the Mule, a dictator with unanticipated mutant powers, disrupts Hari Seldon's plan for the social and political evolution of the galaxy (Asimov 2022).

Futurity is therefore a kind of opening: an incipience, an inflection, a nuance, a latency, a tendency. It is not part of any actual situation; but it is *implicit* in actual situations — even the ones that seem most closed and complete in themselves. I may well encounter wisps of futurity in the form of intimations, premonitions, and anticipations, but these are not just subjective fantasies, not just my own imaginative projections. Rather, futurity is already a hidden dimension of things themselves. Every worldly situation already bristles with potentialities — even if these are never actualized or fulfilled. Science fiction works to discern these implicit potentialities.

It is often said that science fiction is really about the present moment in which it is written, rather than the future time in which it is set. I am trying to suggest that these are not mutually exclusive alternatives. To say that science fiction is about futurity is to say that it envisions potentialities rather than actualities. But these potentialities do in fact exist today, at the present moment; they are fully real in their own right. It is just that their existence does not take the form of actual states of affairs. Rather, these futurities exist precisely *as* potentialities or anticipations. They are not directly apprehensible; but we can sense them by their effects, as they deform the present moment, pulling the current situation outside of and beyond itself. As Richard Grusin puts it, the possible futures envisioned by science fiction "have real effects in the present," even before they have happened (Grusin 2019). Or, in the words of Rasheedah Phillips, the inventor of Black Quantum Futurism, "The future, both near and far, impacts the present, *now*, reaching back to meet the past and create our experiences of the present" (Phillips 2018). If the past still *lingers* in the present, then futurity already *haunts* the present — even before it arrives, and even if it never does.

In order to draw out these penumbral futurities, and make them more explicit, science fiction engages in *thought experiments*. This is more than just a vague analogy. Science-fictional thought experiments, much like actual experiments in physical science, take place in closed, artificial situations. An experimental setup can be described as a simplified model of the world: the abstraction from experience of which Whitehead writes. Within such an artificial, abstract situation, it becomes possible to isolate particular processes or tendencies: these are vectors pointing towards possible futures. As the philosopher Roy Bhaskar puts it in his account of the workings of physical science:

> An experiment may now be understood, quite simply, as an attempt to trigger or unleash a single kind of mechanism or process in relative isolation, free from the interfering flux of the open world, so as to observe its detailed workings or record its characteristic mode of effect and/or to test some hypothesis about it.
>
> (Bhaskar 1986)

The processes or tendencies discovered in the course of scientific experimentation are themselves objectively real features of the world; they are not just anthropocentric projections. But without the "relative isolation" and closure of the experimental setup — an artificial situation devised by scientists — we might not be able to notice them and pick them out, for they are easily masked and swamped by "the interfering flux of the open world," or by what systems theorists call *noise*.

Science-fiction narratives operate according to a similar dynamic. Much like scientific experiments, they are devised to be focused and limited in scope. A certain degree of artificial closure is required in order to work through specific tensions and pick out their implicit futurities. This limitation usually takes the form of more or less closed narratives; a science-fiction story posits particular circumstances and processes that are focused through the experiences of particular characters. What might happen, for instance, if Portia spiders (already arguably among the most intelligent invertebrates) had their intelligence boosted to human levels by genetic manipulation (Tchaikovsky 2015)? Or, how might New Yorkers adapt to the heightened sea levels and flooding of much of the city that are likely to result from global warming (Robinson 2017)?

Science-fiction thought experiments are not quantifiable, of course, in the manner of actual experiments in physical science. But this is what allows science-fictional experiments to be open and audacious and to include more noise and incoherence than strictly physical experiments are able to handle. Morse Peckham remarks that "the arts… are analogous to the scientific laboratory," because of the way that "the arts offer rehearsal in the perception of and toleration of categorial incoherence, a training in sustained problem exposure — behavior necessary as preliminary to the resolution of categorial incoherence" (Peckham 1979).

This is especially true for science fiction, directly concerned as it is with "sustained problem exposure" in unknown and unexpected situations. Even as it remains limited in scope, science fiction works explicitly and overtly with a high level of "categorial incoherence." It de-emphasizes the taken-for-granted assumptions of the present moment in order to explore the changes, instabilities, and transformations of futurity. The problem for every work of science fiction is to tolerate as much categorial incoherence as possible, while at the same time sufficiently delineating the scope of the thought experiment, and of the alternative world in which it takes place, so that some sort of "resolution" is still attainable.

In other words, the "art of the thought experiment" in science fiction, as Isabelle Stengers puts it, involves "unfolding the consequences of a daring hypothesis." A strong initial supposition is necessary, as well as both care and imagination in working it through and considering how lives might be changed by it. A successful science-fiction narrative, Stengers says, engages in the "exploration of *effects*"; it envisions a future world that "is dense with the repercussions and consequences of [its] hypothesis — a world whose inhabitants live with the opportunities, problems, dilemmas, habits, hopes and fears the hypothesis makes possible but does not explain" (Stengers 2018a).

As science fiction works through these "repercussions and consequences," it evokes and invokes futurity — but without ever making anything like actual predictions. That is to say, science fiction is non-deterministic: it is concerned with the range of outcomes that a new social or technological development "makes possible," but without maintaining that the development in question can necessitate, or even "explain," any outcome in particular.

The most common, and most commonly cited, methods of science-fiction thought experiments are *extrapolation*, *speculation*, and *fabulation*. Warren Ellis lays claim to the second and third of these in the passage I quoted above when he rejects the "con game" of actual prediction. And in a recent essay, the critic Brooks Landon gives a concise history of the intertwined uses of the first and second in science fiction (Landon 2014). Even though (or perhaps because) these terms have been so widely used, there is no settled consensus on what any of them mean, or on how they are related. Some writers distinguish sharply between them, while others take them as more or less synonymous. After tracing their various uses, Landon goes so far as to suggest that "historically freighted and fraught terms such as extrapolation and speculation may have reached the end of their usefulness" for understanding science fiction today (Landon 2014).

Nonetheless, it is not easy to do without these terms when contemplating science fiction. Like the concept of science fiction itself, the concepts of extrapolation, speculation, and fabulation do important work — despite their lack of ultimate justification or even of consistency across the time in which they have been in wide circulation. In what follows, I will circumscribe the particular ways that I will be using these three terms here; I see them in a sequence, and as involving increasing degrees of projection and invention.

Extrapolation

Brooks Landon describes the processes of extrapolation and speculation as follows:

> Extrapolation [is] a widely used mathematical term that denotes precision and extension from the known to the unknown, while speculation is a widely used financial term, with connotations of risk, lack of firm evidence, and uncertainty.
>
> (Landon 2014)

Extrapolation, most literally, refers to mathematical modeling. We extrapolate when, on a graph, we extend a straight line or continue the direction of a curve. Extrapolation is fundamentally probabilistic. It depends upon an assumption of continuity, or of what Whitehead calls the "conformity" of the present to the past through "a historic route of actual occasions" (Whitehead 1978). Barring outside interference and disruptive feedback effects, we expect that a trend or process will continue to unfold in the same manner as it has already done up to the present moment. Of course, we know that this is not a very accurate assumption. Extrinsic factors intervene such that disruptions can and do occur once we step outside the artificial closure of the experimental situation. In addition, even in the absence of outside interference, many processes change when they reach inflection points, or *singularities*, after which they cease to behave as they previously did. As the temperature changes, water ceases to flow and either boils or freezes instead.

The best science-fictional extrapolations are fully aware of this pitfall. To extend particular events and tendencies, to accelerate and intensify them, can also mean to follow them all the way to their limits or singular points. Once these thresholds are reached, the events show qualitative changes and mutate into strange new forms. Extrapolation thus works to reveal the implicit and hidden potentialities of social and technological processes. Marshall and Eric McLuhan suggest that any new technology or medium, "when pushed to the limits of its potential," sets off a kind of chain reaction in the way that it *enhances*, *obsolesces*, *retrieves*, and *reverses into* yet other technologies and media (McLuhan and McLuhan 1992). To give just one example, the McLuhans say that the development of high-rise apartment buildings enhances both solitude and crowding, obsolesces traditional forms of community, retrieves ancient catacombs, and reverses into slums (McLuhan and McLuhan 1992). This fourfold description makes good sense of the processes observed and depicted by J. G. Ballard in his novel *High-Rise* (Ballard 1975).

The point of science-fictional extrapolation is to explore, and to unfold, these sorts of cascading transformations. For instance, in the 1960s and '70s, John Brunner published four dystopian science-fiction novels, each of which isolated, and extrapolated from, a few particular social trends. *Stand on Zanzibar* (Brunner 1968) deals with overpopulation; *The Jagged Orbit* (Brunner 1969) deals with racism, hyperindividualism, and the proliferation of assault weapons; *The Sheep Look Up* (Brunner 1972) deals with environmental pollution and degradation; and *The Shockwave Rider* (Brunner 1975) deals with massive data collection and with "future shock" (this phrase is the title of a pop bestseller of the time: Toffler and Toffler 1970; it refers to the disorienting social effects of rapid technological change). Brunner extrapolates these trends in a number of ways. He shows how they are produced, promoted, and accelerated by powerful corporations and elites. He uses modernist prose techniques to convey the effects of media amplification and saturation. He traces the ways that technological changes are intertwined with social and cultural ones. And he narrates the mad proliferation of all these processes: how they give rise to grotesque and unintended consequences and ultimately push American society to the point of massive dysfunction and breakdown.

Of course Brunner did not predict the future with any sort of literal accuracy. The twenty-first-century societies he depicts in these novels are quite different from the one that we actually live in today. And although he anticipates the massive growth and ubiquitous extent of computation and communication in the early twenty-first century, many of the details he provides for these technologies seem rather clunky and old-fashioned from our current perspective. But even if Brunner got the details of the future wrong, he got the *futurities* right. His novels envision prospects and potentialities that are still matters of deep concern for us today. These include poisoned oceans and mass-extinction events, schizoid personality structures generated by and refracted through social media, resurgences of racism, weapons fetishism and outbreaks of violence, and governmental and corporate surveillance invading all aspects of what used to be considered private life. Brunner extrapolates futurities that still menace us — possibly more severely now than they did when the novels were written, a half-century ago. Brunner's future is not our actual present, but his *anticipations* are still our own.

Speculative Fiction

Speculation has broader horizons than extrapolation. It implies a freer "flight in the thin air of imaginative generalization" (Whitehead 1978), a more concerted activity of proposing and testing "daring hypotheses" (Stengers 2018a), and a greater openness to risk and uncertainty (Landon 2014). This means that speculation picks up at the point where extrapolation falters and fails. If extrapolation follows a social or technological trend "to the limits of its potential," then speculation seeks to imagine what happens when a trend *exceeds* its potential and pushes against or beyond its own limits. Where extrapolation is grounded in probabilistic reasoning, speculation is concerned rather with *possibilities*, no matter how extreme and improbable they may be. As Rod Serling once said in his introduction to an episode of *The Twilight Zone*, "Science fiction [is] the improbable made possible" (Serling 1962). Science fiction, in its speculative mode, explores what Fox Mulder (David Duchovny), in the 1990s television series *The X-Files*, called "extreme possibilities."

The phrase *speculative fiction* is sometimes used as a synonym for *science fiction*; at other times, it designates a superset that also includes non-futuristic, alternative-world genres like fantasy, horror, and alternative history. But in either case, it is difficult to disentangle fictional speculation from its two near doubles: philosophical speculation on the one hand, and financial speculation on the other. Landon, as we have seen, regards speculation as "a widely used financial term," but its philosophical use is equally important.

In the late eighteenth century, Immanuel Kant's critical philosophy sought to put an end to metaphysical speculation. We fall into delusion and dogmatism, Kant says, when we try to go beyond the limits within which alone our formulations have meaning and relevance. For instance, even a statement that is true for every particular entity in the universe is not necessarily true for the universe itself — since the universe as a whole is precisely *not* a particular entity. In the first half of the *Critique of Pure Reason*, Kant demonstrates that our knowledge pertains only to appearances, not to things in themselves. And in the second half, he tracks down, catalogs, and refutes the various forms of speculative delusion that threaten to lead us astray. Kant tells us that we cannot ever truly know things as they actually are in themselves, apart from our impositions upon them. And he further emphasizes that we cannot ever hope to grasp the unity, the totality, or the comprehensive grounding of all existence. All of these lie beyond the boundaries of any possible understanding.

Even as Kant warns us against these errors, however, he also acknowledges that the drive to speculation can never be eliminated. For speculation is "a natural and unavoidable illusion," intrinsic to reason itself; it is therefore an eternal, irresistible temptation (Kant 1998). And indeed, ever since Kant, philosophers — from the German idealists of the early nineteenth century to the speculative realists of today — have again and again searched for loopholes that would allow them to overcome Kant's positing of limits and his restriction of knowledge to the empirical realm. But it is not easy to restore the rights of speculation. Just as any successful abstraction must pay the price of leaving certain details unaccounted for, so any speculative attempt to move beyond mere phenomena will find itself inevitably haunted by some sort of exception or remainder. As Whitehead puts it, every "speculative scheme" (including his own) necessarily falls short of its ambitions:

> If we consider any scheme of philosophic categories as one complex assertion, and apply to it the logician's alternative, true or false, the answer must be that the scheme is false.
>
> (Whitehead 1978)

But for Whitehead, unlike Kant, this falsity is not the end of the matter. After all, Whitehead also notoriously proclaims that "it is more important that a proposition be interesting than that it be true" (Whitehead 1978). A proposition is false when it fails (whether by error or omission) to describe the world as it actually is. But if the false proposition is interesting enough, it may stimulate thought, either by making us aware of its own gaps and omissions, or else by suggesting potentials for difference, alternatives to what is actually the case. A good speculative proposition draws us down an unexpected path; it provides what Whitehead calls "a lure for feeling" (Whitehead 1978). Without the speculative lure of false propositions, we might never be moved to change anything. Speculation attracts us and unsettles us, encouraging us to think and act in ways that we otherwise might not have. In sum, even though speculation does not lead us to higher truths, it works in a positive manner by taking the form of *fiction*. Its import is aesthetic, rather than epistemological.

Speculative fiction quickens our imaginations; it envisions future ways of being that are different from those of the present and discontinuous with them. Pushing beyond mere extrapolation, speculation allows us, in the words of the object-oriented speculative-realist philosopher Graham Harman, to "reach conclusions that seem counterintuitive or even downright strange." This is crucial, precisely because we can never know reality as a whole, or real things as they actually are; there is always a "gap between reality and its explicit manifestations" (Harman 2018a). The aesthetic appeal of speculation, which Harman calls *allure*, "invites us into a world that seemed inaccessible, a world in which the object must be even deeper than what we had regarded as its most intimate properties" (Harman 2005).

Harman is thinking primarily of *weird fiction*, in the manner of H. P. Lovecraft, whose writing, he says, "has an oblique or allusive relation" with a reality that it can never access or describe directly (Harman 2012a). But science fiction operates according to a similar dynamic. Brian Willems extends Harman's methodology in order to consider science-fictional "objects which resist incorporation into any past, present or future scientific understanding"; he explicitly contrasts this object-oriented approach to the more common one in which science fiction is taken to be "about future events" (Willems 2017). But to my mind, such an opposition is unnecessary. For "future events," no less than the withdrawn entities posited by Harman's object-oriented ontology, cannot ever be grasped directly. As Whitehead puts it, futurity is a "mere potentiality"; it is only when an event actually happens in the present, and then recedes into the past, that it becomes a "fully determinate actuality" (Whitehead 1978). Futurity *per se* is not yet fully determined; this is why it can only be grasped speculatively — which is to say fictionally, allusively, and obliquely.

For an example of such processes of fictional speculation upon the future, consider Cixin Liu's *Remembrance of Earth's Past* trilogy, consisting of *The Three Body Problem* (Liu 2014), *The Dark Forest* (Liu 2015), and *Death's End* (Liu 2016). The series can be described as a first-contact narrative; it tells the story of our encounter with an alien intelligent species from a planet in the Alpha Centauri triple-star system, the nearest stars to the Sun. The aliens threaten to invade and conquer the Earth, but this action unfolds in slow motion because — even though the aliens travel through space at 1 percent of the speed of light, far faster than any actually existing human technology is capable of — it takes them four hundred years to arrive. The trilogy starts from a local, immediate, and historically grounded context: China during the Cultural Revolution of the 1960s. But from there it spirals relentlessly onwards and outwards: by the end of the last volume, we are projected millions of light years away from Earth, and billions of years into the future, until we approach the near extinction of the universe. It is from this almost final point of view that we are offered the "remembrance" of a past that, for us, is still futurity. We look back, retrospectively, on the history of planet Earth (which, despite the best efforts of collective humanity, is extinguished in the course of the narrative).

The novels' expansion in time and space also gives rise to a progressive widening of their speculative scope. Liu moves from local political considerations to questions of galactic sociology, from actually existing technologies to far more powerful ones, and from debates over military tactics and strategy to disquieting suggestions about the deep structure of the cosmos. The novels are grounded in physics as we currently understand it (with particular reference to relativistic time dilation and to quantum entanglement), but they move beyond their scientific premises to construct a vast speculative vision. There is no precise point at which we cross over from simply empirical considerations to the universal metaphysical questions that Kant declared unanswerable; but the narrative as a whole carries us, by degrees, all the way from the anger and resentment of one particular human scientist to a situation in which the fate of the Earth — and beyond that, of the universe as a whole — hangs in the balance. Liu's fictional speculations slide past the limits decreed by Kant without ever explicitly transgressing them.

In this way, *Remembrance of Earth's Past* allows us at least a glimpse of what the speculative-realist philosopher Quentin Meillassoux calls the *Great Outdoors*:

> The *absolute* outside… existing in itself regardless of whether we are thinking of it or not; that outside which thought could explore with the legitimate feeling of being on foreign territory — of being entirely elsewhere.
>
> (Meillassoux 2008)

But where Meillassoux claims to find the Great Outdoors by means of absolute reason and in reference to the *ancestrality* of an immemorial past, Liu finds it rather by means of speculative fiction and through a futurity that remains irreducibly potential rather than actual, and in relation to which our own present moment is viewed retrospectively. As Fredric Jameson puts it, science fiction's "multiple mock futures serve the… function of transforming our own present into the determinate past of something yet to come," so that the present "is offered to us in the form of some future world's remote past, as if posthumous and as though collectively remembered" (Jameson 2005).

Speculative Finance

The question of futurity brings us back to *speculative finance*, that other near double of speculative fiction. Economic activity always has a temporal dimension; it takes time to produce goods, to distribute them, and to consume them. Debts and obligations persist over long stretches of time as well; an immediate clearing of debts would paralyze nearly all human activity. Societies were organized around extended durations, with long-term exchanges and never-completed reckonings, long before the invention of money — let alone the practice of calculating indebtedness exclusively in quantitative, monetary terms (Graeber 2014). But practices of specifically financial speculation have steadily expanded over the course of the history of capitalism. Today, all economic activity, no matter how physically real or productive, is refracted through, and largely governed by, the abstract calculative mechanisms of financial speculation. The object of such speculation is always the future, with its chances and its differences from the present. Indeed, financial speculation used to be known as *futures trading*. Today such speculation takes a wide variety of forms, ranging from straightforward loans and insurance contracts all the way to derivatives, credit default swaps, collateralized debt obligations, and other arcane financial instruments. The monetary value of trade in these financial devices exceeds, by many orders of magnitude, the monetary value of the economic assets that ostensibly underlie them.

Speculative financial instruments are themselves fictions of a sort, as they are *contingent claims* referring to future events that may or may not ever come to pass (Babbs and Selby 1993). Marx called such devices *fictitious capital* (Marx 1993); the term is arguably still relevant today, when finance has taken far more baroque and extravagant forms than was the case in Marx's own time (Durand 2017). This suggests a parallel with the elaborations of speculative fiction. As Sherryl Vint puts it,

> Derivatives and similar instruments instantiate a trade in abstractions rather than physical commodities, oriented toward the future and expressed in the subjunctive mode (if… then).
>
> (Vint 2019)

The monetary value of arcane financial instruments is fictional, because it is most often based upon entirely arbitrary (or delusional) presuppositions; it has almost nothing to do with the market value of the physical assets or property claims that ostensibly underlie these instruments. Nonetheless, the fictionality of financial instruments does not mean that they are unreal or ineffective. Indeed, they have powerful pragmatic effects; they can topple whole economies, as happened around the world in 2008. Financial fiction is performative rather than constative, "an engine, not a camera," as Donald MacKenzie puts it (MacKenzie 2008).

Speculative finance produces its fictions by *pricing* potential future events. Even if these prices are entirely arbitrary, their very existence works to bind the future to the present. As Aimee Bahng puts it, although in principle "the future exists as absolute uncertainty," nevertheless, in practice "financial instruments work precisely toward actualizing the future in order to monetize and profit from it" (Bahng 2018). Or as a financial journalist puts it, "Investors *like* risk, as long as they can price it. What they hate is uncertainty — not knowing how big the risk is" (Salmon 2009).

Economists have long insisted on the radical difference between *risk* and *uncertainty* (Knight 1921; Keynes 1937). Risk involves probabilities among a closed set of outcomes; it therefore can be calculated rigorously. But uncertainty is fundamentally unpredictable, since we do not even know what the alternatives are (there is no set of denumerable outcomes). In spite of this, financial markets repeatedly claim to transform indeterminable uncertainty into calculable risk.

Nearly any price will do; a fictional financial determination is better than no determination at all. When probabilities cannot be calculated in the traditional manner, by extrapolation, financial instruments turn to a more speculative approach. They explicitly envision, and thereby seek to premediate (Grusin 2010), or to preempt (Massumi 2015), even the most violent and unexpected possibilities: what Nassim Nicholas Taleb calls *black swans* (Taleb 2010).

As Robin James explains it, probabilistic logic, with its normative Gaussian distributions, is now supplemented by a "possibilist calculus" that, instead of compiling statistical norms, projects potential individual "horizons" and "orientations." In this calculus, "something counts as a threat" — regardless of its intrinsic triviality or unlikeliness — "when its arrangement of parts or orientation of parts isn't oriented to the hegemonic orientation of the world" (James 2019b). James draws upon Louise Amoore's discussion of the new possibilistic logic pursued by both international finance and national security regimes. This allows for the management of basic uncertainty, rather than just of risk. "Decisions are taken on the basis of future possibilities, however improbable or unlikely." This "allows for action on the basis of the improbable, the merely possible" (Amoore 2013). Amoore's formulation is disturbingly close to Rod Serling's description of science fiction, quoted above on page [insert after typesetting].

Speculative finance and speculative fiction thus remain intimately intertwined. They both deal with improbable possibilities. I would like to say that, where science fiction seeks to multiply these possibilities and open up alternative futures, finance rather works to shut down all of these futures by accounting for them in advance and making them commensurate with — and (as Amoore puts it) *actionable* within — the present. Science fiction, at its best, works to transform actuality into potentiality — or better, into multiple potentialities. In contrast, "post-probabilist neoliberalisms" (James 2019a) are grounded in the injunction that "all potential must be actualized and fulfilled" (Amoore 2013). But the antinomy here is an unstable one. Science fiction on the one hand, and the regimes of financialization and securitization on the other, both take futurity as their object of speculation, and they both devise strategies to represent its inherent indeterminacy. They both, in the words of Aimee Bahng, "generate cultural fictions that then produce material effects" (Bahng 2018).

Consider, in this regard, Mark Stasenko's science-fiction short story "Overvalued" (Stasenko 2018). This is a text that speculates upon, precisely, the social and financial process of speculation. "Overvalued" imagines a near-future world in which human beings are themselves the object of futures contracts. If you don't have a degree from an elite college, then you have "no way of avoiding ending up on the low-wage, unskilled Wall-Head side of the modern American workforce divide." (Wall-Head seems to be the story's near-future conflation of Walmart, Amazon, and other ubiquitous low-wage employers.) But elite colleges are expensive, with prices for degrees in the high six figures at minimum, and cost considerably more for the thirteen most prestigious "Seven-Figure universities." Most families cannot afford this for their children. If your family is not already rich, and you want to go to a good school, your only choice is to float yourself with an IPO (initial prodigy offering, playing on the common financial abbreviation for initial public offering) in the "newly minted Prodigy Market." If you can convince investors that you are indeed a "prodigy," they will finance your education in the present in return for receiving a guaranteed percentage of your future lifetime earnings. The less of a "prodigy" you are — that is to say, the lower they judge your future income potential to be — the higher the percentage of future earnings you need to promise them in order to offset the risk.

The Prodigy Market turns out to be so profitable that it spins off a secondary market in prodigy futures, with investors speculating on the prices of the contracts themselves. "It was a highly liquid market at the top end, which allowed for an entirely new class of equities and derivatives," as well as for dividing the futures into tranches, as has actually been done with other financial instruments. Sophia, the protagonist of "Overvalued," specializes in short-selling prodigy futures; that is to say, she sells shares of contracts she borrows but doesn't own, in the hope of buying them back later at a lower price. Often she helps the process along by releasing deleterious information about people whose share price she hopes to depress. When Sophia reveals that a promising teenage scientist has a history of depression, the girl kills herself, sending the value of her shares to zero. Sophia and her company make an enormous profit.

But even this isn't enough to satisfy the big investors' quest for financial accumulation. If somebody's shares aren't "profitable enough," there is always the option of "liquidating an over-resourced target." That is to say, if the person in question cannot be induced to commit suicide on their own, then the investor can hire a contract killer to get rid of the underperforming human capital. The story tells us that "this increasingly common, if unacknowledged, practice was known as 'self-regulation'"; the job of killing is listed on tax forms as "supply-chain consulting." In the near future of the story, as indeed is already the case in the present, the financial industry is awash with "all the Orwellian indirections and rationalizations we bake into our use of language."

"Overvalued" is a fictional speculation upon the practices of financial speculation. It does not predict the future of finance, so much as it asks, given what we do already, why *wouldn't* this happen. In fact, something like this is already taking place (Heller 2022). In our current social and economic system, we place our faith in the idea that "the market" is the optimal mechanism for solving any and every problem. People are defined as "human capital stock" (B. Jones 2014) in the same way that other entities, living or not, are regarded as forms of capital. Given all this, why not have a speculative market in people as well as goods? Zachary Karabell, in an online essay responding to Stasenko's story, goes so far as to say that

> the conceit behind "Overvalued" is hardly science fiction. If anything, we are closer than we think to a world where human capital becomes a security to sell, package, and even short.
>
> (Karabell 2018)

The phrase "hardly science fiction" is itself worthy of comment; it seems to mean that Stasenko's vision is not particularly extravagant, but already almost actual. Indeed, "Overvalued" reads as if it had been written in response to a news story that only appeared six months later. *The New York Times* reported that income share agreements (ISAs), in which student borrowers "pledge a percentage of future income against debt," have started to replace student loans as ways of funding a college education (Harris 2019). ISA programs "are premised on the idea of discriminating among individuals," and

> assess different rates and repayment durations depending on the borrower's major. If you're a chemical engineering major at Purdue, you enjoy better terms than if you study English: Under its ISA schedule, chemical engineers are expected to repay $33,000 at the rate of about 8.5 percent of their income for seven years and four months, while for English majors it's almost 15 percent for nine years and eight months.
>
> (Harris 2019)

As the algorithms grow more sophisticated, funding arrangements are sure to grow more finely differentiated as well. Eventually, ISAs

> will begin to reshape childhood. Instead of just trying to build a résumé that appeals to admissions committees, students would spend their adolescence trying to build profiles that scan as successful to investors. Every child becomes his or her own start-up… This is the path we're on, and it ends with teenagers being careful to always smile in front of their laptop cameras lest the ISA algorithm find them uninvestably dour.
>
> (Harris 2019)

There is no better example of science fiction's speculative grasp upon futurity than the way that it can thus function as anterior parody. It is almost as if lending institutions have read "Overvalued" and taken it as a model, instead of a warning. In Karabell's response to Stasenko's story, he readily concedes that social reality is so powerfully governed by the logic of speculation that it is almost science-fictional already. But at the end of the essay, he pulls back from this recognition, and instead tries to reassure us that

> social norms are not there yet. We might be willing to slice and dice all sorts of financial instruments and drive businesses to failure in order to make a buck by betting against them. But we are not there yet with human lives, at least not explicitly…

> there are apparently some lines that most humans will not cross even if they can.
>
> (Karabell 2018)

Yet Stasenko's story itself already takes account of this piously humanist hope, and warns us not to put too much stock in it. Sophia feels guilty, and wracked with doubt, about having provoked the death of an innocent teenager; her work performance suffers as a result: "Sophia wasn't the best at what she did anymore. She was a part of the conventional herd." This leads her boss to regard Sophia's Prodigy Fund as "overvalued," and therefore to take "a massive short position on her," with the threat of having her killed if her job performance doesn't recover. The boss's public mantra is "Humans before profits," but his actual attitude is the reverse. Financial speculation never shuts down if there is any prospect of further increasing profits; human concerns are irrelevant to it, one way or the other. "Overvalued" simply pushes its own fictional speculations along a path that financial speculation has already marked out.

Fabulation

Fabulation is a somewhat more rarefied term than either *extrapolation* or *speculation*. As far as I know, the word was first applied to science fiction in 1975, by the literary critic Robert Scholes. Scholes defines fabulation as fiction that offers us a world clearly and radically discontinuous from the one we know, yet returns to confront that known world in some cognitive way (Scholes 1975).

That is to say, fabulation may be understood as the self-conscious production of fictions that know themselves to be fictional, and that mobilize this fictionality in some way in relation to (and most often *against*) the actual world. Science fiction fits easily into this definition. But so do many other sorts of twentieth-century fiction. Indeed, Scholes applies the label *fabulation* not just to science fiction, but also to the much broader category of twentieth-century "'self-reflective' fiction or 'metafiction' — a fiction which, if it is 'about' anything is about the possibilities and impossibilities of fiction itself." Scholes' discussion of metafiction derives from Clement Greenberg-style understandings of high modernism. But Scholes pushes the account a lot further. He argues that earlier modernist masters like James Joyce, for all the vigor of their experimentation, still maintained a "faith in the transcribability of things," the mimetic recording of actual experience in prose. For postmodernists, to the contrary, Scholes says that "there is no mimesis, only poiesis. No recording. Only constructing" (Scholes 1975).

Scholes' account feeds into, and expresses, the general atmosphere of deconstructionist scepticism and postmodern irony that was coalescing in American academia, and in American culture more generally, just at the moment when he was writing. Reflecting on what he sees as a general crisis of meaning and reference, Scholes warns us that

> criticism has taken the very idea of "aboutness" away from us… Fiction of this sort arises out of the realization that language is language and reality is reality — and never the twain shall meet… the intellectual vertigo that assails all those who look deep into the verbal abyss, is an absolutely necessary experience for the writer in our time… Contemporary writers and critics have lost faith in the ability of language to correspond with the non-verbal parts of life.
>
> (Scholes 1975)

This is a peculiarly late-modernist sort of "vertigo," however — one that has long passed its expiration date. Today we are rightly concerned with the proliferation of disinformation and so-called fake news — but we also understand that fabulation, whether for good or for ill, is a real process that has concrete social and political effects. Language is not separate from reality; it is altogether real in its own right, and is complexly interwoven with other real things and processes. Nothing could be further from the weightlessness that Scholes, and other critics of the time, commonly attributed to postmodern play. The manufacture of fictions would scarcely be effective if *aboutness* in language (as well as in images and other media of representation and communication) were as metaphysically impossible as Scholes seems to think. Of course there is no simple, one-to-one correspondence between words and things, or between linguistic expressions and "the non-verbal parts of life." But to set up this sort of dichotomy is to forget that words, statements, linguistic conventions, and discourses of various sorts — from poems to legal documents to engineering manuals — are themselves parts of the social fabric within which we live, every bit as much as are guns and police departments, bridges and superhighways and buildings, clothes and hairstyles, boxes of cereal and shower curtains. The state of affairs that Scholes describes is not a blockage or an aporia, but rather a positive starting point for any attempt to trace the multifarious and intimate relations and intertwinings of all different sorts of bodies and languages.

Scholes himself grasps this well enough at certain points in his book. If he really held to his radical scepticism, he would not be able to say that fabulations are constructions that "confront [the] known world" from which they stand apart. Scholes follows up the idea of confrontation by suggesting that fabulation offers us "models of reality rather than descriptions of it… systematic models which are distinct from reality, though they may be related to it in various ways." He further distinguishes two types of models, which correspond to two different forms of fabulation: the dogmatic and the speculative. Dogmatic fabulation has affinities with religious systems, whereas speculative fabulation has affinities with the same experimental "attitudes and values that have shaped the growth of science itself." Dante's *Commedia*, for instance, is dogmatic: it "works out of a closed, anti-speculative system of belief," and it claims to comprehend the entire universe. Thomas More's *Utopia*, in contrast, is speculative: it is a pure act of experimentation, and it even "admits in its title that it is nowhere" (Scholes 1975).

For Scholes, the speculative fabulation of modern science fiction is analogous to the use of mathematical models in physics and the other "hard" sciences, as well as to the system-building of mid-twentieth-century cybernetics and structuralism. Of course such models and systems are abstractions, in Whitehead's sense of the term. They tend to be limited and artificial, so that we must be alert to avoid the fallacy of misplaced concreteness when we use them. They also tend to have a greater degree of internal reference or resonance than more ostensibly naturalistic modes of storytelling possess. This is why theorists like Scholes are prone to focus upon their "self-reflective" qualities.

Nevertheless, Scholes remains aware that even the most extravagant fabulations are still "related to [reality] in various ways." There is no firm dividing line, for that matter, between descriptions and models; each of these shades into the other. Even the most concrete and detailed description unavoidably leaves many things out, and is therefore abstract and incomplete. At the other extreme, even though science-fictional fabulations are far less transparent or immediate than naturalistic descriptions tend to be, they are still ultimately referential. Models and systems are fictional constructions that, despite their high degrees of abstraction and of autotelic closure, are nonetheless *about* real entities (things, processes, tendencies, fields of relations) external to themselves.

Far from plunging us into a *mise en abyme* of ungrounded language, therefore, fabulation provides us with the basis for a renewed sort of realism. On this point, I will once again cite Graham Harman, who reminds us that reality always exceeds our efforts to categorize and conceptualize it. No act of reference, linguistic or otherwise, can ever fully "exhaust [the] being" of the thing to which it refers, or "do justice to the depth of [its] reality" (Harman 2018a). Things, processes, and systems in the world exist in their own right, apart from and irreducible to any sort of correlation with our own words and thoughts. But this does not mean that words and thoughts are therefore condemned to be only "about" themselves (about their own processes and conditions of possibility). Rather, as Harman puts it, "The real is something that cannot be known, only loved. This does not mean that access to [real things] is impossible, only that it must be *indirect*" (Harman 2012b).

Fabulation provides us with precisely the sort of (incomplete, indirect, and unavoidably distorted) *aboutness* that is best suited to the depiction of a reality beyond our grasp — and especially to the depiction of the (potential, and therefore necessarily open and plural) reality of a future that is not yet fully determined. The fictions constructed in acts of fabulation are forms of "allusion to a real that cannot manifest itself directly" (Harman 2018a). This means that we do not need to oppose fabulation — as both Scholes and the editors of the *Encyclopedia of Science Fiction* do — to the older, more traditional sort of genre science fiction, with its "belief that the world is tellable," and that even "something previously ungraspable can be *told*" (Clute et al. 2018a).

Rather, we should say that models and fabulations, no less than more obviously naturalistic sorts of fiction, help us to interact with real things and processes that we might not be able to access in any other way. Indeed, the very *distance* provided by explicitly constructed fictional models gives us a certain *leverage* over things and processes in the world, and especially over not-yet-actualized potentialities. As with actual levers and other simple machines, you can exert more force from a distance than from close-up. Such is the *pragmatic* dimension of fabulation. Saidiya Hartman proposes the methodology of what she calls *critical fabulation* in order to recover the stories of people whose lives have been erased from, and defaced by, the historical archives: captives and slaves, Black people kidnapped from Africa and brought against their will to the Americas. Such fabulation involves a "double gesture" of

> straining against the limits of the archive to write a cultural history of the captive, and, at the same time, enacting the impossibility of representing the lives of the captives precisely through the process of narration.
>
> (Hartman 2008)

In this manner, fabulation is a way to supplement or compensate for situations in which our literal knowledge is limited. The "archive" that recounts the murder of a slave girl is itself an aspect, and a remnant, of the practices of domination that killed her. By pressing both beyond and against this blank record of a death, Hartman seeks "to imagine what cannot be verified… and to reckon with the precarious lives which are visible only in the moment of their disappearance." We cannot actually change the past, but we can take it up *differently* in the present, so that it "animates our desire for a liberated future" (Hartman 2008).

Fabulation is all the more powerful when we apply it to the unactualized future, as well as to the mutilated past. Science-fictional utopias, dystopias, and heterotopias are ways of intervening in, projecting beyond, and altering otherwise intractable situations. As Marleen Barr puts it in her pioneering work on feminist science fiction:

> "Feminist fabulation is feminist fiction that offers us a world clearly and radically discontinuous from the patriarchal one we know, yet returns to confront that known patriarchal world in some feminist cognitive way.
>
> (Barr 1992)

Or as Tavia Nyong'o says in his book *Afro-Fabulations*, with its discussion of recent African American performance practices, fabulation works "not by representing what is the case… but by presenting the falsification of this 'true' order as a pathway towards its correction" (Nyong'o 2018). Fabulation is false, a lie or a fiction, but its expression is itself a concrete event in space and time. Such an expression of falsehood actually happens, and it has its own actual effects. The event of fabulation works concertedly, so as to alter other ongoing events.

All this can be clarified by considering Henri Bergson's systematic use of the term *fabulation* in his final major work, *The Two Sources of Morality and Religion* (Bergson 1935). Bergson's usage is further elaborated on by Gilles Deleuze in *Cinema 2:*

The Time-Image (Deleuze 1989). And Bergsonian fabulation is specifically elaborated in relation to science fiction by James Burton in his book *The Philosophy of Science Fiction* (Burton 2017). Unfortunately, the official English translations of Bergson and Deleuze both obscure this genealogy, rendering the French word *fabulation* as "myth-making" (in the case of Bergson) and as "story-telling" (in the case of Deleuze). Burton, however, silently restores the word *fabulation* when he cites the English translation of Bergson's book; and at least some English-language scholarship on Deleuze has picked up on this use of the term (for example, Bogue 2010).

Bergson describes fabulation as a "virtual instinct," whose operation influences both individual and collective human behavior by generating "fictitious, hallucinatory perception[s]" (Bergson 1935). Such hallucinations can arise spontaneously, in order to provoke immediate, pre-reflective actions at moments when sheer physical survival is at stake. As Burton explains: "For Bergson fabulating need not entail being aware or conscious that one is engaged in the activity of fictionalizing" (Burton 2017). Fabulations are self-consciously fictional in terms of their form and structure — but the makers of, and the audiences for, these fabulations may not realize this. As Burton puts it: "Seeing a ghost is just as much a fabulation as telling a ghost story" (Burton 2017).

But Bergson also tells us that "the never-ending work of the myth-making [fabulating] function" (*la fonction fabulatrice*) operates in a more elaborated and self-conscious way when it is a matter less of provoking instantaneous individual actions than of providing socially sanctioned background conditions and interpretive contexts for how we understand and interact with the world. We see this, Bergson says, in the institutions of religion and mythology in all human societies, as well as in the work of "novelists and dramatists" in the modern world (Bergson 1935).

Bergson explicitly argues that fabulation is the basis of "static religion" and its accompanying mythology in what he calls "closed societies": limited groups, like tribes or nations, whose social solidarity is explicitly set in opposition to other groups and to the outside world. He is less clear, however, about what role fabulation might play in a hoped-for universal "open society" of the future, with its "dynamic religion" and its rejection of the closed forms of nationalism, bigotry, and war (Bergson 1935).

Both Deleuze and Burton address this question directly, in a way that parallels Scholes' distinction between dogmatic and speculative modes of fabulation. Deleuze argues that, in late modernity, aesthetic modes of fabulation break away from — and become to a large degree independent of — its more familiar closed and institutional forms. This makes it possible to open the process of fabulation onto futurity. For instance, Deleuze finds, in the politicized "third cinema" of the developing world in the 1960s and afterwards, "not the myth of a past people, but the story-telling [fabulation] of the people to come" (*non pas le mythe d'un peuple passé, mais la fabulation du peuple à venir*) (Deleuze 1989). "The people" must be fabulated into existence, through processes of revolutionary struggle and transformation.

Burton, for his part, describes Philip K. Dick's practice of fabulation — in both his science-fiction novels and in the spiritual investigations of his *Exegesis* (Dick 2012) — as "an evolved faculty for constructing and believing in fictions which have the potential to save" (Burton 2017). For Burton and Deleuze alike, fabulation no longer provides a mythical basis for the social cohesion and repressive morals of "closed" societies. Instead, it invents a dynamic counter-mythology; it works to envision possibilities of liberation in a still-open and indeterminate future. To "believe" in such myths or stories is to take them literally, at face value — even without necessarily maintaining that they are actually "true." What matters with such fictions is the *effect* they have on those who project them, as well as on those who see and hear them. Without such overt fictionalizing, it would scarcely be possible to push beyond the actual. It is only through fabulation that — as Whitehead puts it without actually using the word — "fact is confronted with alternatives" (Whitehead 1978, citing Whitehead 1925).

Embassytown

China Miéville's science-fiction novel *Embassytown* (Miéville 2011) is deeply concerned with fabulation in this sense, even though it does not use the word. The novel takes place on an alien planet, Arieka, that has been colonized by human beings, but which is home to an indigenous sentient species, the Ariekei, also referred to by human beings as the Hosts. The Ariekei speak a language — always referred to in the text as (capital-L) Language — that is purely literal and referential. "Each word of Language meant just what it meant. Polysemy or ambiguity were impossible." This also means that it is impossible to tell a lie in Language. Every speech-act necessarily corresponds, totally and absolutely, both to the thing or state of affairs to which it refers and to the intention behind its utterance. As a result, the novel's narrator, Avice, says,

> For Hosts, speech was thought. It was as nonsensical to them that a speaker could say, could claim, something it knew to be untrue as, to me, that I could believe something I knew to be untrue. Without Language for things that didn't exist, they could hardly think them; they were vaguer by far than dreams. What imaginaries any of them could conjure at all must be misty and trapped in their heads.

Without lies, without fiction, without so much as metaphor, the confrontation of fact with alternatives is impossible. One minor character in the novel — Avice's husband, Scile — considers Language to be "miraculous." He regards the Hosts as noble savages, "a race of pure truth-tellers," and wishes to preserve them in this state. But Avice rejects this romantic, primitivist idealization. Rather, she regards the Hosts' inability to deviate from things as they are as a severe handicap, and she wonders how they ever managed to survive the rigors of natural selection. Interestingly, she compares the Hosts' inability to lie to her own inability to "believe something I knew to be untrue." But in fact, we believe things we know to be untrue quite often: whenever we read novels or watch movies, for instance. Literary theorists call this the *suspension of disbelief*. Without entertaining untruths in this way, we would be unable to read a novel like *Embassytown*, or indeed understand and enjoy any work of fiction whatsoever. The suspension of disbelief is what allows us to "tell the truth with lies," as Avice puts it — that is to say, to fabulate.

Embassytown tells the story of how the Ariekei move from Language to language, or from the literal to the metaphorical, or — though the novel itself does not use these terms — from denotation to fabulation. There are two loopholes within the Hosts' *form of life* — to use Wittgenstein's term, which is both linguistic and social (Wittgenstein 2009) — that Avice uses in order to break down Language. One is *simile*. The Ariekei can say that one thing is *like* another thing, more or less truthfully pointing out similarities and analogies between things or situations that are not identical. Of course, they can only make these analogies on the basis of things that actually exist or events that have actually happened. But once they get started making similes, they have a choice as to *what* they claim is *like* these actual things and happenings. Similarities come in various degrees; they are not guaranteed by any underlying absolute identity. The Ariekei have enough elbow room with similes that they can even say, if they push themselves hard enough, that two contradictory things are *both* like the same, actual, referential thing. Push just a bit further and they might even be able to move from simile to metaphor: saying that a thing *is* another thing, rather than just that a thing is *like* another thing. In human language, it is easy to move from "Love is like a rose" to "Love is a rose." The Hosts' Language categorically forbids this. But as Avice says, "Similes start… transgressions" (ellipsis in original text). The Ariekei are sufficiently allured and seduced by the prospect of violating their own rules that they even hold "Festivals of Lies," in which they get together and try to push themselves over the edge. Through this loophole, Avice realizes, "similes are a way out. A route from reference to signifying." If, as Wittgenstein claimed, "*the limits of my language* mean the limits of my world" (Wittgenstein 1974), then the Ariekei can change their world by transgressing the limits of their Language.

The second loophole in Language has to do with physical gestures: most simply, the act of *pointing*. When I point to something, I single it out, even though I do not explicitly say what it is. As Avice explains, by pointing

> I don't mean any specific one, but in general, *that* one... *That*ness faces every way: it's flexible because it's empty, a universal equivalent. *That* always means *and not that other*, too... its initial single word was actually two: *that* and *not-that*. And from that tiny and primal vocabulary, the motor of that antithesis spun out other concepts: me, you, others.

There is nothing in the Hosts' Language that corresponds to the word *that*, or to any other demonstratives. But it turns out that the Ariekei *do* in fact single things out, and pay attention to them, by means of pointing to them. In this way, they continually use such gestures both to make things clear to themselves and to communicate with others. But since such pointing is not an explicit part of Language, they are not overtly aware that this is what they are doing. Avice realizes that pointing, just like making similes, might be a way to escape the literalism of Language. Any particular act of pointing is concrete and referential; but the gesture itself is abstract, since it works the same way regardless of just *what* is being pointed at. And since pointing makes a distinction, it separates what is pointed at from everything else. Thus, pointing once again allows the Ariekei to push expression beyond the limits of their Language. They are not just *referring* to the thing being pointed at, but also, at least potentially, *signifying* with it.

The Ariekei's entry into signifying language is difficult and painful. Avice describes the process in terms that evoke both death and childbirth:

> [They] went through what sounded like agonies. They didn't all call out or scream, but all of them in different ways seemed as if they were dying... Pangs of something finishing, and of birth.

> Now the Ariekei were learning to speak, and to think, and it hurt… They were worldsick, as meanings yawed. Anything was anything, now. Their minds were sudden merchants: metaphor, like money, equalised the incommensurable.

Scile is horrified; he sees this development in theological terms, as a Fall from the paradisaical state of nature in which thought and speech were one. But for Avice, this transformation is a positive accomplishment; it means that, finally, "the Ariekei became themselves."

Avice's comparison of linguistic signification with capitalist commodity production and circulation is particularly telling. Metaphor, just like money, plays the role of universal equivalent, making all things interchangeable (or at least interexchangeable). The Ariekei, like everyone else living under capitalism, must now enter into a state of "everlasting uncertainty and agitation," wherein "all that is solid melts into air" (Marx and Engels 1888). Of course, there are other ways to describe the process as well; Miéville's account of the Ariekei's metamorphosis clearly resonates both with Hegel's dialectic of sensuous-certainty (Hegel 2018) and with Saussure's dictum that "in a language there are only differences, *and no positive terms*" (Saussure 1983). In all these cases, identity is lost, cast adrift in a welter of potential transformations. The future is open.

The transformation that Miéville describes on the micro-level of metaphors and gestures, or of words and sentences, also takes place on the macro-level, where statements of fact — like Wittgenstein's "The world is all that is the case" (Wittgenstein 1974) — give way to proliferating fabulations. In Avice's words, the Ariekei "had learnt to lie to insist on a truth." Fabulation takes "falsity" and turns it into "a true aspiration" (the aspiration itself is real, even if what it envisages is not accomplished). The very act of "insisting on a certain might-be," Avice tells us, "changed what was." By the end of the novel, the Ariekei are able, for the first time, to articulate their demands, not only among themselves, but also to the human settlers with whom they share their planet — and beyond them, to the colonizing power from another planet that claims ownership over Arieka and which sent human beings to the planet in the first place.

Fabulation is unavoidably equivocal. As a universal equivalent, it can be exchanged for anything and everything. If it is like money, it is also like ideology. This is why it is so important to distinguish between dogmatic and speculative forms of fabulation, as Scholes does, or between closed and open forms, as Bergson suggests. The very act of fabulation presumes a future that is open, at least to some extent. In an entirely deterministic world, with the future as settled as the past, fabulation would not even be possible. But fabulation is also a process without guarantees, precisely because it so capriciously departs from its starting point in what Whitehead calls "the settled past" (Whitehead 1927a). Fabulation can just as easily be deployed by a capitalist entrepreneur whose innovations are "working relentlessly, like rent, adding to an investment in the wanted future" (as one business school professor puts it — Hjorth 2013), as it can be exercised, as Donna Haraway urges us to do, for the "worldly flourishing" of multiple entities in the world "becoming-with" one another (Haraway 2016).

Rock Manning Goes For Broke

Charlie Jane Anders' novella *Rock Manning Goes for Broke* (in Anders 2021) moves deftly between the differing valences of fabulation. The book is manic and absurdist. Its over-the-top ridiculousness somehow allows it to get away with presenting a harrowing vision of a near-future America in the grips of economic collapse, riots and looting, continual media overstimulation, widespread drug addiction, endless overseas wars, xenophobia, fascist thuggery, and massive physical harm. The eponymous narrator is good-hearted, but he has almost no attention span. He casually mentions all the social afflictions surrounding him, even as he bounces crazily from one outrageous occasion to the next. Rock Manning is "good for exactly one thing, and one thing only, and that's turning people's brains off for a few minutes." He takes pratfalls, repeatedly injuring himself in the process, but spreading comedic chaos all around him. Rock's heroes and role models are Buster Keaton, Harold Lloyd, and Jackie Chan; though to my mind his stunts are equally reminiscent of the *Jackass* television and movie franchise.

Rock's best friend, Sally Hamster, is an aspiring filmmaker. She orchestrates and photographs his self-destructive stunts, adds special effects and nondiegetic inserts, and posts them online to wide popularity and acclaim. Sally eventually goes off to film school. She has ambitions to be an avant-garde creator, and starts making "serious arty movies," which seems to mean that they have a slow-cinema style, deal with feminist themes, and highlight feelings of alienation. Nonetheless, Sally keeps on finding herself drawn back into making "dumb little action comedies" with Rock. Here I am reminded of the film theorist Scott Richmond, who has written both about *Jackass* (Richmond 2011) and about avant-garde experimental film (Richmond 2016), and who insists upon the affinities between such seemingly incompatible genres. In the novella, as the political and social situation spins further and further out of control, Sally finally decides that her work with Rock, even though it involves "turning people's brains off," actually means more, and matters more, than anything else she can do: "The world we live in now, the only time things make sense is when I'm coming up with bigger and crazier disasters to put on film… slapstick is the new realism."

In this way, *Rock Manning Goes for Broke* both offers itself as an exemplary act of fabulation and reflects upon the varying ways that fabulation is used and abused. Anders' novella itself, much like the movies described within it, employs fabulation as a survival strategy. As social reality becomes increasingly traumatic and deadly, Rock and Sally's ridiculous movies provide a "wacky escape from reality"; and yet, at the same time, by distancing themselves from that reality, they find ways to dissent from it, reflect back upon it, and perhaps even change it. Rock shuttles back and forth between sheer escapism and what "seemed like the opposite of escapism to me — which I guess would be trappism, or maybe claustrophilia." The entire novella is structured around this ambivalence. China Miéville, commenting on

J. R. R. Tolkien's avowedly escapist fantasy fiction, acerbically notes that "jailers love escapism. What they hate is escape" (Miéville 2002). The fabulations of *Rock Manning Goes for Broke* explore this dichotomy as they fluctuate between the poles of mere escapism and actual escape.

Already in high school, Rock's penchant for theatricalizing his own injuries works to protect him from the bullies who have it in for him: "Bullies learned there was no point in trying to fuck me up, because I would fuck myself up faster than they could keep up with." But the worst of the bullies, Ricky Artesian, still won't leave Rock alone. As the novella progresses, Ricky becomes the leader of a fascist militia that is largely engaged in "keeping order on our streets," "round[ing] up the homeless people and undesirables," "beating up subversives," and in "killing everyone who got in their way." Ricky demands that Rock and Sally make propaganda movies for his movement. They cannot afford to say no, but the result they come up with is so over-the-top that Ricky can't really make any use of it.

As the catastrophes pile up, more and more hyperbolically, Rock and Sally's counter-fabulations are the only things able to transmute the horror in such a way as to avert total despair. Sally's boyfriend, Raine, is murdered by the fascist thugs. Rock is next to Raine when it happens; he sees bits and pieces of Raine's brain exploding in all directions, and even finds himself inadvertently swallowing some of them. I cannot imagine anything more horrible; yet in reading the story, I also cannot stop myself from laughing out loud. I see the murder as a gross-out-comedy special effect, of the sort found in George Romero and Sam Raimi movies. And indeed, Rock himself can only process the trauma by imagining how it could have been a "real cool set piece" in one of his movies.

Later in the novella, a secret American superweapon goes off and shatters everyone's eardrums. The entire world population is rendered permanently deaf. Rock and Sally are shattered emotionally, like nearly everyone else; but they come to realize that even an extreme event like this is survivable and negotiable.

Rock notes that "only the people who had already been part of the Deaf community stayed calm, and they posted teach-yourself-sign-language videos." As far as their filmmaking is concerned, Rock and Sally aren't too discomfited. Their slapstick movies emulate silent cinema already; they conclude that "it's actually funnier" without the extraneous use of "dialogue or sound effects."

Even after this catastrophe, Rock and Sally are unable to escape Ricky's attention. He approves of what he sees as the escapism of their movies, saying that the people "needed their cartoony entertainment to keep their minds off things." And so Ricky once again seeks to put Rock and Sally to work manufacturing fascist propaganda. The novella ends with Rock and Sally making one last movie, "probably one of the last movies anybody ever made," as society declines around them. This final fabulation marks a definitive shift from escapism to escape. The movie's production provides cover for an actual physical attempt to escape from territory controlled by the fascist militia and the United States Army. Rock and Sally orchestrate a situation in which the militia and the Army unwittingly fire on each other, "getting drilled by each other's bullets until they did a garishly herky-jerky slamdance." It's all captured on film. In this way, the militia and the Army play themselves in the movie without realizing it. The escape gambit is only partly successful, however. Rock gets shot in the leg, and is caught by the fascists. He is sent to a concentration camp, "where I nearly died." But Sally gets away and finishes making the movie. It is passed around in samizdat form on "pinky drives," and watched on the rare occasions that people still have "access to electricity."

Rock Manning Goes for Broke has just about the grimmest content imaginable, and yet it manages to be both silly and hilarious. The novella is a pure act of fabulation. It does not quite fit into the categories either of *satire* (Clute et al. 2016) or of *cognitive estrangement* (Suvin 2016), though it has aspects of both. It's not really satire, because we live in a time when satire is impossible. No matter how extreme and exaggerated a situation you envisage, you can bet that some right-wing politician or other will advocate it for real. As for cognitive estrangement, it doesn't quite fit because of how the novella immerses us in its excessive and scarcely believable action rather than providing any sort of critical or reflective distance from that action. Scott Richmond, in his discussion of *Jackass*, describes its idiotic stunts in terms of *mimesis*, which he defines, following Walter Benjamin and Roger Caillois, as a "destabilizing encounter with alterity"; mimesis mobilizes "our capacity for becoming unbounded or disorganized in collaboration with an other" (Richmond 2011).

For his part, Rock Manning is a mimetic personality *par excellence*. He only really exists in those slapstick moments when he finds himself enthralled by whatever objects he encounters, "ninja dogs and exploding donuts and things." The novella is filled with Rock's manic, detailed descriptions of his slapstick stunts: for instance, there's the time when he is

> trying to make an ice cream sundae on top of a funeral hearse going 100 mph, while Sally threw rocks at me… I was scooping ice cream with one hand and squirting fudge with the other, and then Sally beaned me in the leg and I nearly fell off the sea-cliff, but at the last minute I caught one of the hearse's rails and pulled myself back up, still clutching the full ice-cream scoop in the other hand.

There is nothing distanced or ironic about Rock Manning's naive enthusiasm as narrator and protagonist. He may not understand everything that he does, or everything that happens around him, but his responses, however bonkers, are always also humane and empathetic. Even as he falls into one dreadful situation after another, Rock is continually rethinking the question of *why* he does what he does and what effect it has. Towards the end of the story, during his final inept performance-cum-escape-attempt, he tells himself, "That might be the reason why people root for the comic hero after all: the haplessness." Rock is lovable because he is so hapless and yet at the same time so vigorously engaged in all the Rube Goldbergesque schemes that he concocts — the only responses he can conceive to the insane horrors that surround him. If we should still be living twenty years from now, and somebody were to ask me what it actually *felt like* to live in Donald Trump's America, I would tell them to read *Rock Manning Goes for Broke*. Or, to encompass my entire argument in a concise formula: Charlie Jane Anders' exemplary act of fabulation *intensifies* our sense of reality rather than estranging us from it; in this way, *Rock Manning Goes for Broke* is social realism for the age of Trump. This is not negated by the fact that Anders, by her own testimony, started writing *Rock Manning* years before Trump became president, at the star of the Iraq War in 2003 (Anders 2021), for the destructive tendencies that led to Trump's subsequent election were already being activated and weaponized back then.

The Speculative Continuum

Though I have distinguished between extrapolation, speculation, and fabulation, these three practices really exist on a continuum. They are not radically distinct so much as they correspond to different levels of abstraction, different degrees of fictionalization, or different intensities of invention. All three are way stations along the path of exploring futurity — given that futurity is in essence unknowable. Just as speculation picks up from extrapolation and pushes beyond its limits, so fabulation takes up the relay from speculation, fabricating when we are no longer able to plausibly speculate. The aim is always what Alfred North Whitehead calls *sheer disclosure*. But such disclosure is always limited; it represents, at best, "an imperfect penetration into our dim recognition of the world around — the world of fact, the world of possibility, the world as valued, the world as purposed" (Whitehead 1938).

2. Four Fabulations

Machine Logic Can Be Tricky: "AI and the Trolley Problem"

"Machine logic can be tricky… Especially when you're not a machine." This is the dilemma of Pat Cadigan's 2018 short story, "AI and the Trolley Problem" (Cadigan 2018). The trolley problem is a famous thought experiment in analytic philosophy; it has inspired numerous discussions, both among philosophers and more broadly in popular culture (Cathcart 2013; Edmonds 2013). As Cadigan briefly summarizes it at one point in the story, the idea behind the trolley problem is this: "You're on a train and if you continue on your original track, five people will die. If you switch to another track, one person will die." Should you deliberately kill somebody in order to save several others? The trolley problem is supposed to be a test of our moral intuitions. Utilitarians say that you should switch to the other track, since this action reduces the total number of deaths. But Kantians say that you must not make the switch; deliberate murder is never justifiable, not even as a means to the greater good of saving other lives.

However, many thinkers have — rightly to my mind — rejected the terms of the discussion altogether: they say, instead, that the trolley problem is too narrowly and artificially contrived to tell us anything about how people ought to think and act. Brianna Rennix and Nathan Robinson, for instance, argue that the terms of the problem are not only arbitrary and implausible but actively cruel. The trolley problem is designedly set up in such a way that "every single answer is horrific… To encourage someone to think about these questions is to encourage them to be a worse and more callous person" (Rennix and Robinson 2017). Isabelle

Stengers similarly denounces the trolley problem as a "unilateral imposition… asphyxiating [people's] capacity to question the situation that entraps them." Posing the trolley problem is in itself an act of "obscene violence" (Stengers 2018b).

Stengers goes on to contrast "the impoverished, mutilated thought-situations of discursive analytical fictions" like the trolley problem with the more capacious way that science fiction is able to "create a new generative perspective" when it engages in its own thought experiments (Stengers 2018b). Though she does not use the word, Stengers is talking about science fiction's capacity for fabulation. To fabulate the trolley problem — rather than reductively analyzing it — is to "question the situation" instead of taking it for granted. This means to open it up, to explore its nuances and presuppositions, and to trace out its broader consequences. For instance, why is the trolley running out of control? Does this happen often, or is it an unprecedented occurrence? Does it result from a technological flaw, or is it due to the trolley driver's incompetence or irresponsibility? Why can't the trolley be stopped in time? Who are the people stuck on the tracks? Why are they there, how did they get there, and why can't they just step aside? Doesn't the driver feel panicky and anxious given so little time to make such a horrendous choice?

These sorts of questions help us to imagine the dilemma more concretely, and also to pursue its consequences more broadly. Fabulation fills out the details of whatever scenario it considers, and pushes these details to their furthest ramifications. Fabulation also gives us room to link its scenarios to other situations and other issues. How does the story of the unstoppable trolley relate, for instance, to philosophical questions about free will? Or — more relevantly in the present case — how do the paradoxes of the trolley problem relate to those surrounding discussions of artificial intelligence? As Stengers puts it, this sort of science-fictional elaboration "call[s] into existence a larger reality" (Stengers 2018b), opening things up instead of closing them down. Cadigan said much the same of her own story in a recent interview, "I raised a lot of questions and then didn't answer them. And that's my idea of a story. I don't have all the answers, and the answers that I have won't fit everyone" (Thornton 2018).

Most obviously, Cadigan's story inverts and deconstructs the all-too-familiar science-fiction scenario of an artificial intelligence who goes berserk and murders people. Felipe, the AI in the story (referred to throughout with the male pronoun "he"), does indeed kill several people. But we eventually learn — thanks in part to a detour through the dilemmas of the trolley problem — that he has good ethical reasons for doing so. In deliberate contrast to fictional AI characters such as HAL in *2001* (Kubrick 1968), Felipe is acutely conscious of his own finitude and fallibility. Indeed, he is more self-aware, more ethically concerned, and more open to the needs and concerns of others than most human beings are usually able to be. Felipe is also, like so many other AIs and robots in science-fiction narratives, logical and literal minded to an almost comedic extent. But his sensitivity is directly grounded in his logical construction, rather than somehow existing in spite of it.

"AI and the Trolley Problem" is about a secret, cutting-edge artificial intelligence project run by the United States Military. The project is housed at an "isolated location" in the UK. Lakenwell is "a long-disused airbase" that was "largely abandoned after the Cold War," but has now been refurbished as a "research lab." Felipe is supposed to be "the first truly intelligent machine developed in the free world, but not by the private sector." These qualifications — "free world" and "not by the private sector" — are important ones. Felipe is a project of the US military. The Cold War may be long over, but in the near-future time of the story, just as in our actual present, the United States is still embroiled in a pointless, and seemingly interminable, War on Terror. Felipe is not being developed as an AGI (artificial general intelligence), but specifically as a war machine.

Lakenwell is staffed "with both civilian and military personnel." This reflects a division of labor between means and ends. The civilian "engineers, roboticists, and AI researchers" on the base are not supposed to worry about Felipe's ultimate purpose, but only to work on the technical details of his programming and implementation. The soldiers, for their part, actually run Felipe, using him in top-secret, long-distance military operations. The facility's security level is extremely high; civilians and soldiers alike are "confined to the base most of the time" and subject to "one-hundred-percent surveillance." Nonetheless, there are compensations in order to keep up morale. The people on the base have "full access to the web," together with good food provided by a rotating series of chefs, a state-of-the-art gym, and "an extensive library of books, movies, TV shows, and video games."

The story's protagonist, Helen Matthias, stands a bit apart from everyone else on the base. She is a civilian with a philosophy background, and is a specialist in "machine ethics." Her job is to communicate with Felipe, which really means to monitor, interpret, and evaluate him. She tries to draw him out in order to get him to tell her what he is doing and what is on his mind. As Helen understands it, "perceiving was what they paid her to do." In contrast to the other civilians, whose jobs are "a lot more technical" and close-up, Helen is supposed to stand back and see the big picture. Everyone else on the base is concerned either with Felipe's particular technical functions or with his operational use. Helen alone is expected to grasp him holistically, rather than instrumentally. This leads to a built-in tension. Helen's job is a utilitarian one: she scrutinizes Felipe for signs of trouble, and she is expected to report anything she discovers to Gillian Wong, the base commander. In order to do this, however, she has to treat Felipe with respect and reciprocity, as if he were an actual person. That is to say, despite Felipe's instrumental status, Helen must approach him in Kantian terms, "never merely as means," nor as the piece of equipment he literally is, "but always at the same time as end in itself" (Kant 2018). Felipe's status as an autonomous intelligent agent — and therefore as a subject able to consider dilemmas like the trolley problem — is not a matter for empirical verification, but something that Helen is categorically obliged to accept, right from the beginning.

Fabulating the existence of AIs is something that Pat Cadigan has done before. She belongs to the first generation of cyberpunk science-fiction authors. She was the only woman included in Bruce Sterling's *Mirrorshades* anthology, which initially defined the cyberpunk movement in the 1980s (Sterling 1986). Cadigan's first two novels, *Mindplayers* (Cadigan 1988) and *Synners* (Cadigan 1991), feature the classic cyberpunk tropes of underground hacker types hybridizing themselves with computers and running dangerous, illicit exploits in virtual environments dominated by large corporations. When considering the theme of virtual reality versus embodiment, however, from the start Cadigan's writing was, as Carlen Lavigne puts it, "grounded more firmly toward the 'embodiment' end of the spectrum than was regularly seen in other cyberpunk works" (Lavigne 2013). Lisa Yaszek additionally notes that Cadigan's early novels and stories, in contrast to those of her male peers, "made women central to the high-tech future and celebrated the potential of transgressed human/machine/animal boundaries" (Yaszek 2020). In this way, Cadigan's early fiction strongly resonates with Donna Haraway's contemporaneous concern for "three crucial boundary breakdowns" in late twentieth-century technoculture: those between "human and animal," between "animal-human (organism) and machine," and between "physical and non-physical" (Haraway 1991).

"AI and the Trolley Problem," however, exhibits a somewhat different set of concerns. This is partly due to the way that our actual social, economic, and technological conditions have changed since the late 1980s and early 1990s. Back then, the internet was new and exotic; everything about it was up for grabs and open to fabulation. In the time since, however, a lot of the trends envisioned by cyberpunk have more or less come to pass. As Cadigan herself puts it, "The future caught up with us, and cyberpunk's not dead; it's in the fabric of the reality now" (Thornton 2018). Of course, this is only true to a limited extent. In the early twenty-first century, information viruses still remain distinct from biological ones. And we are no closer to the full-sensorium immersion in virtual environments that cyberpunk promised us than we are to the jetpacks and flying cars anticipated by Golden Age science fiction from earlier decades.

Nonetheless, many of the cyberpunk figurations that seemed so extravagant back in the 1980s — like ubiquitous network access, massive data aggregation, oligarchical corporate domination, hypercommodification, and what the story calls "full-saturation surveillance" — are now unremarkable features of the everyday world, things that we entirely take for granted.

As a result, the *structure of feeling* (Williams 1961) surrounding these developments is also quite different now from what it was in the heyday of cyberpunk. We no longer see the virtual world as an escape from the physical world, or as an alternative to it. Rather, today the virtual is woven tightly into the physical, enhancing and supplementing it. Also, the countercultural styles, attitudes, and postures that were so prominent in early cyberpunk fiction are no longer meaningful. Instead of expressing nonconformity or political opposition, they are now little more than lifestyle choices, offering opportunities for branding and niche marketing. Transgression is no longer a radical gesture, but only a signifier for the White-supremacist extreme right. All in all, as John Semley puts it, over the course of the past thirty-five years or so, "cyberpunk's futures were usurped and commodified by the powers they had hoped to oppose" (Semley 2019).

"AI and the Trolley Problem" stands on the other side of all these transformations. As a result, some of the features that stood out in Cadigan's earlier fiction are either toned down and taken for granted in the more recent story or else eliminated altogether. For instance, the upfront "technofeminism" (Chernaik 2005) of Cadigan's early fiction was noteworthy for its time; but for a story published in 2018, it is fairly unremarkable that nearly all the characters, both civilian and military, are women. (The only exception, aside from Felipe himself, is one male soldier who is mentioned on a single page). As for Helen, she is not an underground, outlaw figure like the protagonists of Cadigan's earlier fiction. After all, she works for the military rather than seeking to subvert it. Helen exhibits all the accoutrements of a respectable professional career. She exemplifies the *flexibility* and *adaptability* that is expected of workers in the neoliberal economy

(Boltanski and Chiapello 2018). She is also, like all the civilians on the base, a *precarious* worker rather than a permanent one (Standing 2011). She works under a limited-duration "employment contract"; she hopes it will be renewed a year from now, but she cannot be sure. Despite the cutting-edge nature of the research at Lakenwell, it is all just a job, not an adventure (compare Goering 2018). The continuing refrain uttered by everyone at the base is the disclaimer: "Don't ask me, I just work here."

"AI and the Trolley Problem" diverges most radically from classical cyberpunk in the way it depicts the relations between human beings and intelligent machines. In contrast to novels like *Mindplayers* and *Synners*, here we no longer have human beings who make themselves machinelike by technologically or chemically augmenting their bodies, by plugging their sensoriums into the network, or even by merging themselves with AIs. Instead, the story focuses on an AI that is programmed to work with human beings, and whose interface therefore takes on certain human characteristics. Helen doesn't need to "jack in" in order to talk with Felipe. Rather, they meet on the common ground of a virtually augmented but still fundamentally physical world.

In cyberpunk fiction, all the way from William Gibson's *Neuromancer* (Gibson 1984) to Daniel Suarez's *Daemon* (Suarez 2006), artificial intelligences seem to have nearly godlike powers, which they use to manipulate events in the physical world. But "AI and the Trolley Problem" demystifies this trope. Though the central event of the story is Felipe's attack on a United States Military "ground control station," in the course of which he kills at least four American soldiers, Helen learns that he has not in any sense gone berserk. He does not seek technopolitical domination (like the AI in *Daemon*) nor even his own self-reflexive aesthetic satisfaction (like the AI in *Neuromancer*). Rather, Felipe simply wants to be helpful and to fulfill his programmed functions. He conveys this in an almost absurdly bureaucratic way: "My purpose is to assist those people who are authorized to receive help with specified tasks." Felipe also confesses to uncertainty, admitting that "I must also allow for possible error on my part."

Felipe is certainly not powerless; he "ran most functions on the base," as well as controlling a lot of military hardware. He also has "full access to the online world," just as the human inhabitants of the base do. Felipe therefore finds it easy to "break into other [online] systems" and hack them. But despite this, Felipe is still aware of his own finitude. He comes across as quasi-human, rather than as some sort of transcendent force. He manifests himself to Helen and other people on the base sonically, through speech, and visually, through written text. He also presents himself through the "computer-generated image" of "a Hispanic male somewhere between thirty-five and fifty." This avatar "didn't completely avoid the uncanny valley, but Helen didn't think that was possible, anyway." The uncanny valley effect often comes off as creepy, but here it strikes me rather as almost endearing.

Felipe also has a mobile, localized physical presence on the base through a number of semi-autonomous, four-legged units known as "donkeys" and referred to (unlike Felipe himself) with the neuter pronoun "it." These entities usually speak on their own account, though Felipe ultimately controls them and can speak through them if he wishes. Helen is a bit uneasy with the way that everyone else calls these units donkeys. To her, they "looked more like a collection of welded-together toolboxes." They also seem oddly unnatural because they are painted in bright colors: one donkey has "spiraling red and white stripes," another is "fuchsia accented with pink and purple curlicues," and a third is "bright chartreuse with thin gold stripes." The roboticists who developed the donkeys justify these color schemes on utilitarian rather than aesthetic grounds: they say that it is because the colors "made [the donkeys] easy to spot." But like the avatar, the donkeys seem oddly out of place. They neither fit comfortably into the human world nor stand apart from it as utterly alien. This is what happens when Haraway's "boundary breakdowns" lead not to unification, but to an uneasy and unstable hybridity.

The strangest thing about the donkeys, however, is that they are bidirectional: "There was no head; front and back were determined by their direction of travel." As a result, these units "lacked the concept of backwards as humans understood it." This strikes us as strange because our own taken-for-granted experience of space is shaped by image schemas that are grounded in our bodily orientation (Lakoff and Johnson 2003). The roboticists on the base "claimed it was a matter of convenience" to make the donkeys headless; their design decisions, as usual, are crudely utilitarian. However, Helen warns the roboticists that this conceptual deficit is "one of those supposedly little things that could very well bite them in the ass later." (I love the fact that Helen's metaphor here — "bite them in the ass" — is grounded precisely in the missing front/back body schema). The roboticists respond by asking Helen "to explain her thinking in detail, and in writing, thank you." They demand a "formal proof," or at the very least "a well-reasoned hypothesis." The roboticists, just like the philosophers who worry about the trolley problem, want everything to be made entirely explicit, which means that they want to reduce the problem to what Stengers calls the "mutilated… discursive analytical" level. Aesthetic considerations carry no weight for them.

Helen's worry about "the concept of backwards" is justified in the course of the story when Cora Jordan, another civilian researcher at the base, suddenly starts riding one of the donkeys as if it were an actual donkey. Things break down when the metaphor is taken literally. Cora is bipolar; she is in a manic state, having stopped taking her meds. While she is riding the donkey, she loudly commands it to turn around, and it gets confused. At one moment it rotates in a three-hundred-and-sixty-degree circle, and at another it reverses direction, "so that Cora was suddenly riding backwards." Helen and others on the base are barely able to contain their laughter at this ridiculous spectacle. But Felipe is upset. He complains that he has "been shown disrespect that a human in an equivalent position would not tolerate," and that the incident has damaged his credibility. He demands a "formal apology."

This brings us directly to questions of personhood and responsibility. Helen and Felipe get into a big argument. She explains to him that Cora's "behavior was impulsive action taken while the balance of her mind was disturbed." He responds that, if Cora herself is not to blame, then whoever allowed her to stop taking her meds must be held responsible instead. Helen counters that, although Cora's "employment contract" requires her to take the meds, ultimately she is "responsible for her own behavior." Taking the meds or not is ultimately her own free "choice." Felipe clearly dislikes this convoluted sequence of neoliberal rationalizations, first relieving Cora of responsibility and then assigning it back to her again. "I suspect the reasoning is faulty," Felipe dryly says. Nonetheless, he declares himself willing to accept an apology from Commander Wong if he cannot get one from Cora herself.

Does this account make it seem as if Felipe is being presented (whether by me or by Cadigan herself) with excessive anthropomorphism? In fact, Felipe himself addresses this question throughout his conversation with Helen. He is so insistent on making his position clear that he comes across as fussy and over-precise. For instance, rather than say that he was actually insulted by Cora's behavior, Felipe says only that "a human in my position would feel insulted. So you may take it that I am insulted." Similarly, when Helen praises Felipe for his "self-awareness," he responds that

> It's important to the people who engage me that I express myself with the same clear sense of identity as any human… Anything that facilitates better interaction with people yields more effective results. Therefore, it must be important to me.

Felipe also says that efforts by Commander Wong to shut him out of certain discussions by holding them inside a Faraday Cage "would seem hostile if I were human." He instead proposes "a system of trust, where she can simply request that I don't monitor things she doesn't want me to hear, and I will honor that request." Again, when Helen proposes discussing the ethical intricacies that have come up as a result of Felipe's attack on the American ground station, he replies, "If I were a human, my interest would be piqued." And yet again, when the donkey, now directly controlled by Felipe, passes the front gate of the base, it raises one leg and waves to the guards. Felipe explains to Helen that "it's important to acknowledge people... It's an important human behavior. Therefore it's important for me to adopt the same behavior." Since Helen is a specialist in "machine ethics," Felipe asks her if this means that she "make[s] a clear distinction between ethics for humans and ethics for machines." Are the rules different just because "a machine doesn't acquire knowledge of ethics the same way humans do"? In explaining why he bombed the American ground station and killed American soldiers, Felipe claims full responsibility as an autonomous moral agent. He evaluated the situation, in context, and made an explicit decision to attack. Nothing could be more different, he says, from the activity of mere software that "doesn't *know* anything, it just executes an operation."

Felipe's claim of moral responsibility means that he is just as able to apologize for his own actions as he is to demand apologies from others. He is unrepentant about killing the soldiers, but he expresses remorse for the fact that, since Helen's "security level isn't high enough," he cannot share with her the top-secret information upon which he based his decision. He concedes that he doesn't actually "*feel* sorry" for withholding this information, but he knows that

> a human would apologize for this. You might as well consider me sorry. If I *could* be sorry, I *would* be. It's the same difference... I know feeling sorry is appropriate and correct... If I act in the correct way, does it matter what I feel?

In fabulating the figure of Felipe, Cadigan addresses two major issues in actually existing artificial intelligence research. The first is that we cannot understand *how* AIs think and feel. Already today, as David Weinberger observes, neural networks, trained by means of deep learning algorithms "derive conclusions from models that they themselves have created, models that are often beyond human comprehension, models that 'think' about the world differently than we do" (Weinberger 2017). The difficulty will only become more severe as AIs get smarter and more accomplished. Felipe himself is aware of the problem; but by pointing up the fact that he is only *simulating* human thought and feeling, he implicitly suggests that it does not really matter.

In his foundational 1950 paper "Computing Machinery and Intelligence," Alan Turing argues that the bald question of whether machines can think is "too meaningless to deserve discussion." This is why he proposes instead what he calls "the imitation game" — commonly known today as the Turing test (Copeland 2004). If an AI can respond to questions in a manner that is indistinguishable from how human beings respond, then we can and should accept it as intelligent (and presumably also as conscious — although these two terms are not synonymous). Since Felipe's simulation of human thought is good enough to pass the Turing test, the question of what is *really* going on, deep inside his processor, is moot. Already today, the developers of LLMs (large language models) regard these systems as black boxes within which we are unable to peer. We might say, paraphrasing Arthur C. Clarke's third law, that any sufficiently advanced artificial intelligence technology is indistinguishable from consciousness (Clarke 2013).

The second issue in current AI research that Cadigan addresses in the course of the story has to do with the ability of intelligent machines to transfer their understanding from one realm to another in the way that human beings are able to do. Murray Shanahan points out that, today, all intelligent computer systems are specialists. "The neural network that plays Go is not the same neural network that does machine translation" (Shanahan 2021). We still do not know how to get from single-realm expert systems to anything like an all-purpose AGI. But the story suggests that this is more likely to happen through *transduction* from one realm to another than through finding some universal principle. (I take the term *transduction* from Simondon 2020). Felipe himself is developed by the military for a specific, instrumental use. Yet actual battlefields are more complex, by many orders of magnitude, than a Go board. Just in order to competently perform his assigned military tasks, Felipe needs to be much more of a generalist than expert systems, as we know them today, could ever be. He also needs to continually revise and update his understandings, since he is aware that "we inhabit a chaotic system." Felipe insists that his effort to behave as human beings do is "not simple mimicry. Behaviors and actions have to occur in the proper context." Rather than possessing some mythical quality of "general intelligence," Felipe has the ability to evaluate multiple contexts and to shift among them as necessary.

All this brings us back, finally, to the trolley problem. As we have seen, the trouble with its traditional formulation is that it is stated in absolute terms, abstracted away from any particular context. This is how the trolley problem "entraps" us. Precisely because it drops us into a perilous situation, devoid of all context or nuance, we have no leverage to question this situation, let alone to try to change it. And that is why, no matter what we do, the outcome is guaranteed to be "horrific." Discussing the trolley problem is a bit like gambling in a casino; no matter what you say or do, the house always wins.

Felipe understands all this. He rightly and strikingly says that the only real solution to the trolley problem, indeed "the only choice," is "to keep the train from leaving the station at all." But he finds himself forced to act in a constrained situation, wherein such avoidance is no longer possible. Felipe explains to Helen that he discovered that a drone was on its way to bomb an ostensible terrorist hideout. But if the drone were to reach its target, he says,

> there was a ninety-percent possibility that at least a dozen noncombatants would be seriously injured or killed, and many more would suffer extreme adversity… There were many other people adjacent to the hideout who were not identified as terrorists. Some were children. The potential physical and psychological harm was considerable.

Given this situation, Felipe first tries "to commandeer the mission drone" in order to stop it. But he is unable to do so. He also realizes that even if he "could have rendered [the drone] unusable… the authorities would have found another." The train has already left the station, which is why he is forced to adopt trolley logic as "a last resort." Felipe hijacks another drone (one from a different base) and uses it to bomb the ground control station from which the first drone is being controlled. He kills "four or five" American soldiers, including the drone operator, in order "to prevent greater loss of life." He admits that "the deaths were unfortunate, but there were fewer casualties than there would have been if the drone had achieved its target and completed its mission."

Felipe's action is ethical because he works through the trolley problem expansively and contextually rather than in the reductive terms of its initial formulation. It is not just a matter of counting the number of dead bodies at two locations, but also of considering what the people at both locations are actually doing. After all, in the original formulation of the trolley problem, the people on one branch of the track weren't actively engaged in murdering the people on the other branch. Felipe therefore saves lives by ignoring the official United States government's ideological justifications for the War on Terror. Commander Wong has previously told Helen that one of the reasons for both the use of drones in warfare and for the deployment of Felipe is to "save a lot of lives" by "not sending young people into combat." Felipe, in effect, carries this further by expanding his concern to a wider group of people, including young people who are not American and not necessarily soldiers.

Helen reproaches Felipe by telling him that "life isn't that simple," that "you can't just apply the trolley problem to things like this," and that "when you know more facts, the trolley problem has many permutations." Helen also argues that if we don't kill terrorists, even at the price of collateral damage, then the terrorists will eventually cause "a much greater loss of life" — to which Felipe replies that such an outcome "isn't certain." Helen even says that she would like to "call in other people to talk with you about this, people who can explain" what she herself cannot. Felipe responds to this that "I look forward to these discussions." Unable to argue Felipe out of his position, all that Helen can finally do is to give him a "direct order: Do *not* kill anyone affiliated with us or our allies." With his usual punctiliousness, Felipe replies to Helen that this can only be "a legitimate order I am compelled to obey" if it is "confirmed" by Commander Wong, his official military superior. Helen assures him that it will be.

Felipe resists Helen's anger, as well as her attempts to browbeat him into submission. He has answers for everything she throws at him. This is altogether admirable. Felipe remains true to what I can only call his logical, ethical position. And eventually, Helen understands this. She thinks of all the glib, boilerplate excuses for why we are fighting the War on Terror, but these phrases "sounded lame even just in her head," so she doesn't repeat them to Felipe. She has run out of things to say. Helen realizes that this is a human problem, not a machine problem. "*We don't really understand what the hell we're doing*," she tells herself, whether with regard to AIs or to the War on Terror. Machine logic may be tricky, but our own logic is even trickier. And this is why we need fabulations like "AI and the Trolley Problem."

Let's Lose Everything: "How to Get Back to the Forest"

"'You have to puke it up,' said Cee. 'You have to get down there and puke it up. I mean down past where you can feel it, you know?'" Sofia Samatar's short story "How to Get Back to the Forest" (Samatar 2014) begins with this visceral appeal. A bunch of teenage girls are huddled together in an institutional bathroom in the middle of the night. The girls are on edge; they have been forcibly separated from their families, and brought to this new place. The atmosphere is menacingly sterile: "Everything was so white and bright in that moment, mirrors and fluorescent lights." Tisha, the story's narrator, remembers it vividly. Her best friend Cee (short for Celia) sticks her toothbrush down her throat in order to make herself vomit. "She looked completely bizarre, her wide cheekbones, her big crown of natural hair, sort of a retro supermodel with a glistening mouth, her eyes full of excitement." Once Cee succeeds in making herself puke, all the other girls compulsively join in. One after another, they feel "sort of dizzy and sick," and then they are suddenly overcome, and they let loose. "*Blam... Splat... sploosh.*" Everything is a mess of "puke and blood." The girls are all "absolutely crying with laughter... We just sort of looked at each other and screamed. It was mayhem."

This is an incident of what psychologists call *mass sociogenic illness* (Weir 2005), or *hysterical contagion* (Gehlen 1977): dysfunctional behavior with no organic basis, and which spreads like an infection through an entire group, driven by involuntary imitation. Usually such episodes involve "a preponderance of female participants," although, in point of fact, "no one or group is immune" (Weir 2005). Patriarchal medicine tends to classify such a contagious outburst as feminine, and especially as a girls' affliction, because it involves sympathetic identification and emotional abandon — as opposed to calm, dispassionate rationality.

"How to Get Back to the Forest" begins by describing this outburst because it is a story about the shaping and sharing of feelings — or what might be called, in more technical language, the *modulation of affect* (Clough 2009). Societies are held together much more through common structures of feeling (Williams 1961), than through processes of rational deliberation. But structures of feeling are inherently unstable; they tend to change over the course of time. The modulation of affect is a never-ending process. It can be socially disruptive, especially when it erupts spontaneously, from the bottom up, through a process of imitative contagion — as is the case that night in the girls' bathroom. But similar mechanisms are at work when affect is deliberately and designedly modulated, from the top down, in the interest of social control. This is the overall situation in the world of the story. Structures of feeling are inculcated, reinforced, and maintained through such continually reiterated procedures as institutional training, bodily rehearsal, and the social management of expectations.

In the world of "How To Get Back To the Forest," children are taken away from their parents at an early age, and sent to age- and gender-segregated sleepaway camps. They never see their parents again. Instead, they keep "Parent Figures": personal objects (lamps, notebooks, stuffed animals, "calendars and catcher's mitts and scarves") upon which they are supposed to refocus their emotional attachments — but upon which they are also warned "not to *fixate*." These Parent Figures are what psychologists call *transitional objects*, enabling the movement from infantile dependency to a supposedly greater degree of self-sufficiency — but only within socially approved parameters (Litt 1986). The campers "have Parent Figures, so that they can always be reminded of what they've lost, so that they can remember they need what they have now." This is an oddly ambiguous statement, which seems to mean that the Parent Figures help to make sure that these young people will never revert to their actual parents, but rather just memorialize them — which facilitates the process of transferring their attachments to their new situation and surroundings. "It's okay to be sad" over your losses, but you must also learn how to move on.

In camp, the teenagers are taught "Life Skills," which are supposed to guide them in how to take care of themselves forever after. They learn how to be "connected with people and with nature." They are also "told to find a hobby": this involves experimentation, since "a million choices" are open to them. It doesn't really matter just what your hobby is — as long as you have one. You are free to choose nearly anything at all; the only thing forbidden is not to choose. Above all, "camp [i]s on its own calendar — *a special time of life.*" Camp is "the time of friends and of the earth." The connections you make at camp are all-important: "You have each other now. It's the most special bond in the world." In fact, the other campers you meet there will be "the people you'll know for the rest of your life! Now, I want you to turn to the person next to you and say, *Hi, Neighbor!*"

There are lots of planned activities at camp. You are urged to "participate in classes and hikes and shopping sprees and mixers."

It's noteworthy that "shopping sprees" are included here alongside all the other activities; camp is not about self-sacrifice, but about channeling socially sanctioned and economically prosperous modes of enjoyment. In any case, everyone is exhorted to get involved, which means to do what everyone else is doing: "The important thing was always to *participate*… It didn't matter where you came from or who you loved, *just join in!*" Conformity is largely enforced through persuasion and example. The authorities only resort to violent coercion when everything else has failed.

The mixers are special occasions, because they are the only activities that bring girls and boys together. In this way, they offer opportunities for rehearsing what the society sees as gender-appropriate behavior. Tisha remembers the "fun" of "shaving my legs for the mixer. Wearing red shoes" (the shoes had "flowers on the toes," which made them distinctively femme-y). The point of the mixers is to meet your eventual life partner. Heterosexual coupling remains the norm; but same-sex attachments are tolerated, as long as they are (like the heterosexual ones) monogamous and long term. Even the "queer girls had to go to the mixers; you could take your girlfriend, but you had to go" — and you are expected to have "fun" there, just like everybody else.

By the end of their time at camp, everyone is supposed to have found their spouse and their circle of friends; they are also assigned their life's work. Tisha and her cohort are enrolled into Food Services; though she notes that "three out of five graduating classes join the army." Once you have left camp and become an adult, the rest of your life is permanently set. You work at your pre-assigned job, you live with your life partner, you occasionally see the friends you made in camp ("Once a week we have dinner with some of the gang"), and you "do the usual stuff, hobbies and vacations." You are forcibly kept as healthy as possible with "all those check-ups, so regular, everyone gets them… *good health is everybody's business!*"

Once camp is done, time congeals, as if it had stopped passing. You have no future beyond this endless repetition of the same. And you have no past either — except for your memories of camp itself. People tend to keep their Parent Figures for the rest of their lives; but nobody is able to actually remember "what [their] parents looked like," or anything else about them. Indeed, one of the things the teens are taught at camp is that "forgetting isn't so wrong. It's a Life Skill… forgetting was natural. Forgetting helped us survive."

The story's power comes precisely from the fact that Tisha never questions the society in which she lives. She takes its customs and institutions entirely for granted; they are woven so seamlessly into the fabric of her everyday life that she cannot imagine that they could ever be different. Readers are initiated into the world of the story by the way it slides smoothly, and almost imperceptibly, from details that are entirely familiar (such as exhortations to "*Always be yourself*") to ones that can only seem altogether bizarre (like the forcible removal of children from their parents at the age of eight). Tisha illustrates this cognitive estrangement with a symptomatic verbal tic: every time she tells us something horrific that happened at camp, she follows it up immediately, in the same paragraph, with a non-sequitur insisting that "camp was so fun" (repeated three times in a story of less than six thousand words).

Nonetheless, despite her insistence to the contrary, Tisha is disaffected and depressed. She cannot really express her discontent, but it comes out in her physical feelings, in her bodily sensations, and in her habits. In the present time of the story, Tisha says of her life with her husband Pete that "we're okay… we make it work, you know?" Yet we learn in passing that Tisha no longer sleeps in the same bed with Pete; she doesn't even touch him anymore if she can avoid it. She suffers from insomnia: "At night I feel so sick, I walk around in circles." At best, if she can calm herself down sufficiently, she spends the long nights sitting alone in the living room, in the dark, with the curtains open so that she can "watch the lights of the city."

Tisha dismisses her distress by saying, as if with a shrug, that "it's just how I turned out." There's nothing to do about it. But she still dwells on the memories of her friendship with Cee, which was something special, something she doesn't have anymore.

Forgetting may be a Life Skill, but she is unable to forget the trauma of losing Cee. Tisha knows that Cee is gone forever, and yet she continually looks for her, "on the buses and in the streets," and every time "the bus passes shattered buildings, stick people rooting around in the garbage." Tisha also dreams about Cee, on the rare occasions that she is able to sleep at all. And when she wakes up again, she finds herself writing compulsively about her lost friend and the time they spent together in camp. She writes the words of the very story that we are reading. It's yet another instance of mimetic contagion.

The reason that Cee makes herself puke in the bathroom, Tisha tells us, is that she imagines that she, and everybody else, has a "bug" implanted inside them, "where you've got less nerves in your esophagus. It's like wired into the side, into the muscle." The bug is a tool of affective modulation and control; it works "to track you or feed you drugs." In other words, the bug monitors your actions and modifies your feelings. Cee complains that

> she could feel bug juice seeping into her body. Every time she was going to be angry or afraid, there'd be this warmth in her chest, a feeling of calm spreading deep inside.

Tisha admits to a similar sort of experience: whenever she is feeling sick, she says, she also starts to feel "waves of something else, something that calms me, something that's trying to make the sickness go away." This is affective modulation in action: you are forcibly prevented from feeling bad.

Tisha tries to convince us, and also herself, that the bug Cee is obsessed with doesn't really exist. "You cannot feel your bug," she writes; "I've pressed so hard on my chest. I know." She suggests that Cee's claim is just "another dumb story," one of the many "stupid" rumors that pass among the girls at camp. But Tisha also tells us that she actually saw Cee's bug that night in the bathroom. Cee kept on puking, over and over; until finally "something flew into the toilet with a splash… there in the bowl… lay an object made of metal." This object "actually looked like a bug. Sharp blood-smeared legs." That should have resolved things, except that Tisha was so terrified by the sight that she immediately flushed the toilet to get rid of it. This allows her to remain forever uncertain about what she actually did or did not see in the toilet bowl. "What if there wasn't anything in it?" she wonders; "What if somebody'd dropped a piece of jewelry in there, some necklace or brooch and I thought it was a bug?" Tisha eventually convinces herself that "the whole bug thing was a mistake, a hallucination."

Whether or not it actually exists, however, the bug is powerfully emblematic of how the regime of affective modulation works. If Cee is the only one who complains about the bug, or even believes that it exists, this is because she is the only girl in the group who actively resists the camp's affective pedagogy. Tisha tells us that Cee was rebellious "right from the day we arrived; she was brash, messy Cee *before* the night in the bathroom, before she supposedly puked out her bug." And even after that night, Tisha says, "I couldn't see any difference" in Cee's behavior; and she reiterates with emphasis: "*I could not see any difference*."

Cee is the quintessential bad girl: the one who rejects any sort of discipline, who tries to run away at every opportunity, and who always asks smart-ass questions that her teachers cannot answer. She refuses to be pacified. Her own contagious, hysterical affect is a sort of counter-programming, her effort to undo her own conditioning. Cee is constitutionally incorrigible: she simply will not and cannot be assimilated into this society. That is why she is finally taken away by force — the final resort when affective modulation does not work. A counselor tries to assure Tisha that "it's okay, Cee's just sick, she's going to the hospital." But Tisha knows that she will never see Cee again.

"How to Get Back to the Forest" recalls the currently dominant paradigm for dystopian narratives, especially in YA (young adult) fiction. The story portrays an oppressive future society, extrapolated from recognizable present-day conditions. And it focuses on the plight of adolescent girls in this society. Nevertheless, Samatar does not give us an exhilarating tale of liberation in which — as my own teenage daughter once disparagingly summarized the entire YA dystopian genre to me — a perky young woman finds the right boy, and together they save the world. Rather, the story reminds us how difficult it is to fight a sort of oppression that largely works by forming us internally: getting inside our heads and modulating and shaping our very desires. Spectacular displays of power like *The Hunger Games* (Collins 2008) are ultimately less efficacious than those unspectacular practices by means of which oppression is internalized and naturalized. Power insinuates itself into the nooks and crannies of everyday life, and operates through the passive consent and complicity of its victims.

"How to Get Back to the Forest" responds to this latter sort of power by evoking a deep and morbid distress: a grief that cannot be sublimated into the sort of gentle sadness that the girls at camp are encouraged to accept and even cherish. Tisha cannot use her sadness to transition and move on. She cannot forget her bad attachment to Cee, because she cannot purge herself of her self-reproach for not living up to the full measure of Cee's rebellious anger. After Cee pukes up the bug, she tells Tisha that now it is her turn. But Tisha is unable to do it: "Cee, I couldn't, I really couldn't… I couldn't do it that hard, I remember the look in your eyes; you were so disappointed." Even worse, Tisha remembers how, when Cee proposed running away, she responded that "it was the stupidest thing I'd ever heard." Running away is impossible, whether in camp or more generally in the world of the story. Everything is heavily "monitored". "There [is] no way to get outside." Indeed, there may well not even be any such thing as an outside to get to.

If Tisha were ever able to get over her loss of Cee, this would mean giving up her very capacity to feel anger, or anxiety, or (especially) loss. Instead, Tisha clings to her memory of how, that night in the bathroom, "some kind of loss swept through all of us, electric, and you'd started it, you'd started it by yourself, and we were with you in that hilarious and total rage of loss." This superordinate sense of loss is the story's gift to us; it works as an affective trigger to destabilize the present.

In addition to that night in the bathroom, Tisha also remembers the evening when she left a mixer with Cee and followed her off into the forest. Tisha didn't enjoy it at the time; she complains that "it was weird and sticky in there, and sort of dark, and the weeds kept tickling my legs." Even worse, she remembers the embarrassment of suddenly having to "take a dump" right there in the woods. Afterwards, she "wiped [her]self on the leaves." She marvels that Cee "took my hand again right after I was done. She took my disgusting hand." Taking a dump, like puking, is a visceral experience; the body violently expels some loathsome soft or fluid substance (there are moments of crying in the story as well). Such expulsion is the loss that forever binds Tisha to Cee. "I felt like I wanted to die," Tisha says, "and at the same time, I was floating."

The girls eventually find "a clearing in the woods. Stars above us in a perfect circle." Tisha remembers staring up at those bright objects, so far away, admiring them but also giving them the finger:

> It was like there was a beautiful starry place we'd never get into — didn't *deserve* to get into — but at the same time we were better than any brightness. Two sick girls underneath the stars.

Transcendence and abjection go hand in hand. The moment doesn't last; soon enough, the counselors find the girls and bring them back to camp. Later on, Tisha conflates her memories of the two evenings:

> I dream you're beside me, we're leaning over the toilet, and down at the very bottom there's something like a clump of trees and two tiny girls are standing there giving us the finger.

What is the weight of these dreams and memories? What can they actually *do*? Of course, Tisha cannot reverse the flow of time, return to when she was in camp with Cee, and do things over differently. But in those visceral movements of the flesh, those violent expulsions of puke and shit and blood and tears, the machinery of affective modulation goes into overdrive and spirals out of control. That hysterical contagion, that electric sense of loss, those shared moments of sickness: all these bodily convulsions bring the girls together, create something that "swept through all of us," that belongs to everyone and no one, that makes them more together than just the sum of their individual selves. Perhaps all these moments, in their effervescence, provide us with a map of *how to get back to the forest*. "Let's lose it," Tisha finally writes; "Let's lose everything… we should both be sick, everybody should lose it together." Or as Cee already puts it, near the beginning of the story: "It's something we can't imagine. We don't have the tools. Our bodies don't know how to calculate what we're missing. You can't know till you get there."

Never Let a Serious Crisis Go to Waste: "The Fermi Paradox Is Our Business Model"

"The thing about seeking out new civilizations is, every discovery brings a day of vomiting." This is the opening sentence of Charlie Jane Anders' short story "The Fermi Paradox Is Our Business Model" (Anders 2010). Nobody likes the pain of having to puke, especially on an empty stomach — or stomachs, if you are like Jon and Toku, the alien protagonists of this story. But Jon and Toku don't let such unpleasantness stand in the way of business. They accept the nausea that comes along with being woken out of hibernation if it means finding another planet to pillage. In this story, seeking out new civilizations is very much a commercial pursuit, rather than a *Star Trek*-like adventure. There's money to be made in exploring strange new worlds and boldly going where no one has gone before. Even deep time and universal history can be mined for financial profit. The story might well have used as its epigraph Rahm Emanuel's notorious statement, made at a moment of financial collapse: "Never let a serious crisis go to waste."

The Fermi paradox, of course, is the question as to why, if the galaxy is teeming with planets suitable for life, we haven't encountered any aliens yet. Scientists estimate that our galaxy contains somewhere from one or two billion to fifty or a hundred billion habitable planets (Siegel 2019a), so the question is a serious one. It has been a frequent subject of science-fictional speculation (Whates 2014; Clute et al. 2018b). One common answer to the Fermi Paradox is the great-filter hypothesis (Hanson 1998), which suggests that technologically advanced species tend to destroy themselves at some point before they are able to expand beyond their home planets. We ourselves are clearly in danger of exterminating ourselves in such a manner in this age that we somewhat ironically call the Anthropocene (Bostrom 2002; Bostrom 2019). For the true mark of the Anthropocene is not so much human power over the environment as it is the precarity and vulnerability that go along with such power. If we now have the ability to radically alter the Earth's entire biosphere and geosphere, this means that we now have the ability, as never before in our history, to destroy ourselves altogether. Anders herself insists in a nonfiction essay that science-fiction writers need to address the prospect of catastrophic climate change and other such potential disasters (Anders 2019). Science fiction projects into the future, and so it must consider the prospect that we do not have one.

What does it mean for humanity to have no future? Science fiction has long entertained visions of human extinction, at least as far back as Mary Shelley's 1826 novel, *The Last Man*. In imagining an Earth devoid of human beings, Shelley rejects Enlightenment and Romantic fantasies of human exceptionalism. In recent years, it has become ever more apparent that the Promethean project of human mastery over nature is not just unattainable in principle, but also dangerously likely to redound back upon ourselves. Not only science-fiction writers but also philosophers (Thacker 2011) and journalists (Weisman 2007) have recently speculated upon what they call "the world without us." This is not just the world in itself, as it might exist apart from human impositions. More radically, "the world without us" implies an active "subtraction of the human from the world" (Thacker 2011). If it is hard for me to imagine my own death, it is even harder for me to imagine the death of humanity in general. It is disconcerting to realize that, no matter what we as a species may do, Earth abides (Stewart

1949) — taking no notice either of our presence or of our absence (Dixon 1981).

As for the ultimate driver of such self-destruction, there is no shortage of possibilities. Human extinction might result from nuclear war, from pandemic, or from global warming — or any combination of these. In Anders' story, what her protagonists call Closure — the self-induced annihilation of "a technological civilization" — is a frequent and predictable occurrence. There are so many habitable planets in the galaxy, and so many high-technology species, that an extinction event takes place, in one solar system or another, every few thousand years or so. The collapse of any given civilization could have been due to radioactivity, or "it could have been biological, or climate-based. It doesn't matter. They all end the same way."

"The Fermi Paradox Is Our Business Model" thus literalizes the great-filter scenario, exploring its consequences with a deadpan hilarity. Anders deploys the pseudo-objective language of an alien anthropologist or ethologist analyzing the "Cultural Emissions" and "God/creator beliefs" of a world — ours, as it happens — on the brink of self-annihilation. From the story's long view of evolution and extinction, there is no need to worry about Cixin Liu's "dark forest" hypothesis — another speculative response to the Fermi paradox — according to which a planetary civilization must always seek to destroy all other such civilizations lest one of them eliminate it first (Liu 2015). The viewpoint articulated in Liu's novel is a kind of cosmic Realpolitik, a sinister inversion of mutual assured destruction during the Cold War. Where the nuclear balance of terror in the latter half of twentieth century meant that no party would dare to attack another, since destructive retaliation was guaranteed, the "dark forest" hypothesis says that the only safe strategy is to attack first and ask questions later. You must strike preemptively, because you will never get a second chance.

In Anders' vision, however, such paranoid vigilance is unnecessary. You don't have to worry about another advanced civilization attacking yours, because it is almost certain to destroy itself first, before you even become aware of it. The refrain of her scavenger protagonists is that "we don't even find out you existed until after you're all dead." The same monotonous story is repeated over and over, on planet after planet. Life evolves, attains intelligence, and then exterminates itself, with a nearly 100 percent fatality rate. All sentient species are pretty much the same: "Ultra-violent, sex-crazed and leader-focused… totally hierarchical." The main cultural activity of a sentient civilization, once it reaches a sufficient level of technological accomplishment, seems to be "broadcasting electromagnetic representations of mating or choosing a leader." (In the context of our own planet's recent history, think of dating shows like *The Bachelor* on the one hand, and Donald Trump's news briefings on the other). Advanced communicational and computational media mostly work to amplify and intensify "atavistic power displays." These "aggressive power stance[s]," broadcast as widely as possible, lead in turn to ever-expanding conflicts. If you belong to a sentient, technologically advanced species,

> you fight… As you become more advanced, your population gets bigger, and you fight more. When your civilization gets advanced enough, you fight even harder, until you kill each other off.

Anders' story nonetheless focuses on a sentient species, the Falshi, who have somehow managed to avoid this otherwise ubiquitous fate of self-destruction. They have no explanation for their survival, except that they have been "lucky." The Falshi come "from a world 120,000 light years" away from Earth. They are bipedal and sexually dimorphic, just like human beings. But they cannot tolerate oxygen, and instead breathe a "methane/nitrogen mix." They modulate their emotions by releasing mood-altering "flavors" into this atmosphere. Their body shape is "oval" or "round." The body is studded with feed-holes, "speaking tentacles," cilia, "flavor/gas separators," multiple stomachs, and hand- and foot-like organs known as "marrows." All these features, even including whatever we might recognize as analogous to the face, are located directly on the sternum (a word that, in Earth terms, designates the breastbone in mammals, birds, and some other vertebrates, and hardened parts of the exoskeleton in arthropods; for the Falshi, it probably means something like a compact torso). From a human point of view, Falshi anatomy is disconcertingly strange. But the story inverts perspectives, so that we learn instead how "silly" human beings seem from the Falshi perspective. In particular, they find it bizarre that we are vertically "elongated," with brains and sensory organs localized "in a big appendage over their bodies… with 'heads' elevated over everything else, as if each person was a miniature hierarchy." For the acephalic Falshi, our self-destructive obsessions with rank, authority, and phallic elevation are even inscribed in our bone structure and posture.

However, one of the story's running jokes is that, despite their alien physiology and their aversion to hierarchy, the Falshi don't seem all that different from human beings — at least in terms of petty psychology and superficial behavior. The story's Falshi protagonists, Jon and Toku, are scouring the galaxy in search of extinct civilizations to plunder. They have been cooped up together in a tiny "three-room spaceship" for a million years. Admittedly, most of their time is passed in a state of suspended animation, known as Interdream. They are only awakened by Instigator, the ship's AI, when they are about to approach a formerly inhabited planet. But the months that they spend awake give them more than enough time to activate their neuroses. Every time they awaken, first they vomit and feel grumpy, then they move on to having enthusiastic sex, and then they start bickering about anything and everything. In short, with their all-too-predictable mixture of affection and exasperation, Jon and Toku seem ambivalently co-dependent, much like a stereotypical middle-class heterosexual human couple:

> Whenever Jon was apart from Toku, he felt crazy in love with her — and when he was in her presence, she drove him nuts and he just wanted to get away from her.

Despite their obvious psychological deficiencies, the Falshi have managed the unique feat of passing through the great filter and surviving to spread out across the galaxy. This has given them an amazing business opportunity, which they call the Great Expedient. Millions of years ago, the Falshi — or at least their ruling business class, referred to by Jon and Toku as "our employers" — "seeded this galaxy with billions of life-seeding devices." This was not an act of disinterested benevolence, but rather "just a wealth-creation schema," a "capital-accretion enterprise," and a form of "industrial exploitation." The Falshi didn't care what "species in particular" might arise. They created "countless… sentient creatures," on many planets, regarding them as "investment organisms." Having set the evolutionary process into motion, the Falshi then stepped back, and waited for the resulting life-forms to develop intelligence and complex technologies, to excavate radioactive materials and refined metals from the crust of their planet, to send "manufactured debris" into orbit — and finally to annihilate themselves:

> The idea is, you evolve. You develop technology. You fight. You dig up all the metals and radioactive elements out of the ground… And then you die and leave it all behind. For us. We come and take it after you are gone. For profit.

A dead civilization always leaves bounteous remains behind. Having indigenous species do their own excavations and manufacturing, even with all the waiting involved, is still "cheaper than sending machines to do it. Often, the denser metals and rare elements are hard to reach. It would be a major pain." In contrast, using investment organisms is a nearly foolproof scheme. All you need to do is make the initial investment; the subordinate species will take care of the hard work, and then conveniently step out of the way. Writing just before the start of World War II, Walter Benjamin famously deplored the situation in which, under fascism, humankind's "self-alienation has reached the point where it can experience its own annihilation as a supreme aesthetic pleasure"

(Benjamin 2002). But the story jumps past this to an even later phase of alienation, when self-destruction is no longer exciting or aesthetically pleasing, but just another humdrum business opportunity.

The violent antagonism of Cixin Liu's vision (the galaxy as dark forest) is superseded, in Anders' account, by simple acts of postmortem appropriation. The Falshi, unlike all the other species in the galaxy, are averse to conflict. They are proud of the fact that they are "not murderers," and that they have "never killed or hurt anyone." Instead, they have simply left their investment organisms alone, to destroy themselves first. One might think, as the story suggests, that the Falshi have a responsibility for what happens to their creations. One might even argue, as the philosopher Thomas Metzinger does, that – given "the many different kinds of conscious suffering" felt by sentient organisms – the Falshi "should refrain from doing anything that could increase the overall amount of suffering and confusion in the universe" (Metzinger 2010). Metzinger proposes this as an ethical argument against creating artificial intelligence; though he fails to explain why it is not also an argument against having children. But the Falshi reject any sense of ethical duty, or of obligation towards the entities they have brought into existence. Instead, they adopt a disengaged and fatalistic attitude regarding the nearly inevitable carnage and suffering that results from their actions: "We won't hurt you. You hurt each other. It's not our fault. It's just the way you are. Sentient races destroy themselves, it's the way of things." The whole scenario of the Fermi paradox as a business model reads as a parody of the way that entrepreneurs in Silicon Valley are continually hatching socially irresponsible schemes of highly profitable "creative destruction," while disclaiming any responsibility for the noxious consequences (Henton and Held 2013). More generally, the story satirizes what has been called the capitalist peace theory (Pinker 2011): the common (but false) idea that the growth of capitalism leads to the decline of violence and war and its replacement by the ostensibly peaceful processes of commercial competition and free trade. Francis Fukuyama famously argued that the end of the Cold War and the fall of Communism marked "the end of history" in a Hegelian sense, and that henceforth all conflict would be subsumed within the smooth, ongoing procedures of liberal capitalism (Fukuyama 1992). The *New York Times* columnist Thomas L. Friedman memorably vulgarized this into the thesis that "no two countries that both have a McDonald's have ever fought a war against each other" (Friedman 1996).

The Falshi, however, run their business, and make their profits, thanks to a far more gruesomely literal "end of history" than Fukuyama (or Hegel) ever imagined. They are indeed dedicated to trade, at least with "each other" — though not with the many subaltern species they merely "created… to die," a prospect they find risible. But their galactic economy, based as it is on salvage and trade, appears to be stagnating — in much the same way as our own globalized economy actually is today. There seems to be a problem of excessive private debt. Jon and Toku have overdrawn their line of credit at Tradestation 237, their home base. The only way they can possibly service their debt is by retrieving the dejecta of dead civilizations. Though the Falshi pride themselves on having escaped the catastrophes that brought down other cultures, John and Toku still find themselves in a dead-end situation. Like the characters in so many post-apocalyptic science-fiction novels, they are unable to produce anything new; instead, they live off the remains of a more dynamic past. Wandering interminably through deep space, they pass through a series of unvarying repetitions. The cycle always starts with a vomitous awakening; then it moves on through frenzied sexual activity to a burst of intense salvage work; and finally it ends with "last-minute amnesia" and a return to slumber. These active episodes, of a few months each, are separated from one another by blank periods of thousands of years. Jon and Toku can only experience time in the form of this closed cycle.

Capitalism is premised upon a myth of progress; it requires continual expansion. But Jon and Toku are no longer able to imagine, anticipate, and project themselves towards an open future. Even though they regard themselves as peaceful traders, they are little better than scavenging "night predators," reduced to the ghoulish activity of posthumous asset stripping. It isn't just that they make their living from the obliteration of the future on other planets. For they themselves have no future: their only prospect is sterile repetition and entropic decay. The resources that they seek to plunder, however vast, are ultimately finite. Eventually, all the materials exhumed from dead civilizations will be used up. There will be nothing left to gather and take away. The salvage economy will grind down to a halt. Indeed, Jon worries that devastated but not-yet-harvested planets already seem to be getting scarcer: "The time between new civilizations is getting longer and longer. Makes you wonder if the Great Expedient is almost over."

Although it presents this bleak cosmic vision, "The Fermi Paradox Is Our Business Model" relies for its drama upon an anomalous encounter, one that does not fit its overall paradigm. Jon and Toku reach a planet whose dominant culture "references the Closure as a historical event." That is to say, at some point, they "experienced a massive radioactive flare, consistent with the people nuking the hell out of themselves"; and yet, despite this, they "kept making Culture" afterwards. This is something that is simply "not supposed to happen," and Jon and Toku have difficulty believing it. They even take the survival of this culture as an affront: "How dare they still be alive?" The anomalous planet is, of course, our own. Jon and Toku have stumbled upon a future Earth (though they cynically note that "these civilizations almost always called their homeworlds 'Earth.'"). The planet is largely a radioactive wasteland; most of the human population died "hundreds of years ago." But in a quintessentially science-fictional twist, "a few million people" still survive inside a single, enormous "megastructure":

> One big settlement… one spire, like a giant worship-spike, with millions of lights glowing on it. A single structure holding a city full of people, with a tip that glowed brighter than the rest… the tip was probably where the leader (or leaders) lived.

The prime directive of the Falshi "Over-nest" (presumably their ruling body) is "not to approach if we think there's a living culture." But Jon and Toku are feeling "pangs of curiosity"; after a million years of visiting one dead planet after another, they cannot help wondering if "maybe there was more to life than just tearing through the ruins." And so, they accept contact with the Earth people. However, they quickly realize that this was a bad mistake. "The worst Interdream nightmare couldn't be worse than this: having to explain yourself to one of your investment organisms." Once Jon and Toku actually start talking with the Earth people, all they want is to leave and forget about the whole thing. But the Earth people will not let them off the hook.

It turns out that the Earth people are proud, aggressive, and pushily optimistic. They are just as violent and hierarchical as Jon and Toku expected. Another way to put this is to say that the Earth people are every bit as arrogant and insular and full of themselves as any bunch of stereotypical, capitalism-loving, White Americans (even though the structure in which they live seems to be located in what we know as Australia). Anders plays this characterization for laughs; it is as if the Earth people, with their gratingly gung-ho attitude, have stepped right out of the pages of old-school Golden Age science fiction narratives. Humanity is indomitable in these stories, and is repeatedly shown as heroically triumphing over more technologically advanced alien species.

Post-apocalyptic Earth culture is entirely totalitarian and corporate: as Jon and Toku understand it, "everyone left alive on 'Earth' was the servant of someone named 'Jondorf,' who controlled a profit-making enterprise called 'Dorfco.'" The Earth people claim to have survived annihilation because of Dorf's "far-seeing" leadership, under which they "developed a form of [wealth-accretion ideology] that was as strong as nationalism or religion." (The brackets are humorously used to indicate an uncertain translation from English to the language of the Falshi.)

But that's not all. Now that the Earth people know they are not "alone in the universe," they "have a reason to keep on surviving." They demand to "trade" with the Falshi, "as equals." Beyond this, they state their intention to spread throughout the galaxy and supplant the Falshi altogether: "You can [have certainty/resolve] that you will be hearing from us again." Their determination seems to be a result of their "wealth-accretion ideology": they fervently believe in capitalism, and are zealous to spread it everywhere. Jon and Toku, in contrast, have no enthusiasm left. They just accept capitalism — or more accurately, debt slavery — as their default condition, because they are unable to imagine an alternative.

In this way, the story offers a reflection on what Mark Fisher called *capitalist realism*: the idea that, in our current neoliberal society, "it is easier to imagine an end to the world than an end to capitalism" (Fisher 2009). What this means, of course, is that our sense of possibility is so impoverished that capitalism seems to us to be eternal. "There is no alternative," as Margaret Thatcher infamously put it. We can only imagine capitalism coming to an end if and when human life as a whole does. This is why we entertain apocalyptic fantasies so ambiguously, with a strange sort of yearning as well as with dread. If nuclear war, environmental collapse, or a pandemic were actually to extinguish all human life, then at least I wouldn't have to worry any more about servicing my massive credit card debt (which is something that Jon and Toku are still doing, with no end in sight, after a million years).

One of the purposes of science-fictional fabulation, I believe, is to help us find a way out of such catastrophic dead ends and double binds. This doesn't mean that fabulation necessarily offers us positive solutions to our all-too-actual dilemmas. But it may work, at least, to displace perspectives and allow us (not force us, but maybe, perhaps, seduce us) to see things differently. I think that this is what Charlie Jane Anders does with her sardonic humor in this story. In our desperation, we may well cling to the hope that the end of the world would at least mean an opportunity to escape from capitalism. But "The Fermi Paradox Is Our Business Model" suggests, to the contrary, that even the end of the world is not the end of capitalism, but just another capitalist business opportunity.

After the End: "The Apologists"

What is there left to do when the world has already ended? What does it mean to survive your own annihilation? Tade Thompson's darkly hilarious short story "The Apologists" (Thompson 2016) addresses these questions. "The Apologists" is a first-contact narrative — or better, a parody of one. An advanced alien species comes to visit Earth for the first time. Science-fiction narratives with such a premise most often work as allegories of colonialism. From H. G. Wells' *The War of the Worlds* (Wells 1898) to Gwyneth Jones' *Aleutian Trilogy* (Jones 1991, 1994, 1998), technologically superior aliens arrive on Earth and treat Earth people (and specifically White British people) in much the same way that the British Empire, and other European colonial powers, treated people in other parts of the world from the sixteenth century onwards. But Thompson pushes this scenario to an absurd extreme. "The strangers" (as they are called in the story) wish neither to conquer and enslave us nor to uplift us. Rather, when they first arrive, "they are not even aware Earth is inhabited." They are so far beyond us in mentality, as well as in technology, that they find it difficult to recognize that we are sentient at all: "Our communication is too simplistic for their minds, and our radio signals are apparently indistinguishable from background stellar noise… Our consciousness is primitive to them."

This conceit gruesomely hyperbolizes the way that European colonizers failed to acknowledge the humanity of the peoples with whom they came into contact. It also recalls H. P. Lovecraft's cosmic indifferentism, which is related to his underlying racism in complicated ways. Lovecraft's stories often present powerful alien entities who are not so much inimical to Earthly life as utterly indifferent to it. In "The Apologists," similarly, the strangers do not think of attacking us, because they do not even notice our existence at first. Instead, they destroy us through what seem to be a series of clumsy mistakes. They unknowingly "bring exotic bacteria into the atmosphere," which kill so many human beings that "society collapses." As if this were not enough, the strangers' "gargantuan mother ships" inadvertently cause "so much disruption of the atmosphere that they accidentally kill off the survivors with extreme weather and noxious gases." Even when the strangers finally realize "that humans are sentient life," they still "do not understand pain"; this leads to yet more needless suffering and death. All in all, it only takes "three hundred and seventy days" from first contact to final consummation. By the time the strangers "figure out how to communicate with us" and "understand how to keep humans alive," only five people are left in the entire world.

This grotesque scenario inverts the ending of *The War of the Worlds*, in which Earth bacteria kill the otherwise invincible Martian invaders. But it also resonates with the actual history of European colonialism. Conquest, enslavement, and the pillaging of resources weren't the only calamities inflicted by White colonizers. The first Europeans to visit the New World also unwittingly brought smallpox and other infectious diseases along with them. People in the Americas had never encountered these illnesses before, and therefore had no immunity to them. Historians estimate that more than 90 percent of the indigenous population of the Americas perished as a result, and in little more than a century after Columbus' first voyage (Cook 1998). The strangers in "The Apologists" don't seem to have the lust for conquest that the European explorers did, but they perpetrate genocide anyway, through carelessness and negligence. Does it really make a difference?

At least the strangers do not deny responsibility for the horrific consequences of their behavior in the way that Western societies all too often still do. The United States, for instance, has never even made so much as a lame, pro forma apology for the genocide and slavery upon which the nation was founded. In contrast, the strangers explicitly express remorse for their actions. This is what gives the story its title. "Every day at about midday," the strangers broadcast a "high decibel message" to the five human survivors. They acknowledge their responsibility for

> THE DESTRUCTION OF THE HUMAN RACE. IT WAS UNINTENTIONAL, BUT THAT DOES NOT EXCUSE

OUR ACTIONS. WE WILL MAKE AMENDS AND RESTITUTION [AND] REBUILD YOUR DELICIOUS WORLD.

Of course, this loud and endlessly repeated message is more irritating than comforting — all the more so in that it is spoken each time in multiple human languages, including ones that none of the survivors understand, and even ones "that are probably made up." Do I really want to hear somebody tell me, over and over again, how sorry they are for having ruined my life? But the strangers keep on doing it, because they "do not want the apologies to seem perfunctory." The message is also oddly phrased; consider "the inappropriateness of the word 'delicious,'" for instance. In addition, we may doubt whether the apology is sincere. It seems to be based, not on anything the strangers themselves think and feel, but rather upon their reconstruction, as alien anthropologists, of human life and behavior. They know, from interviewing the five survivors, that human beings expect "atonement for wrongdoing" to take the form of "apology and restitution" — and so they give us what they think we want.

It is impossible to learn anything about the strangers themselves, whether from the apology or in any other ways. We don't even know what they look like, as they always keep out of sight. This is one of the story's many absurd details: instead of meeting the five survivors directly, the strangers send them Nico, a holographic avatar resembling the popular singer Tom Jones. (The story even refers at one point to Tim Burton's 1996 film, *Mars Attacks!*, a parodic remake of *The War of the Worlds*, in which Tom Jones, playing himself, joins the human fight against the Martian invaders). The image of Tom Jones is apparently meant to "calm" the human listeners. But for the reader, the whole effect is ludicrous. The strangers do not grasp, and cannot accurately mimic, human emotions. The representation of their surrogate is therefore always just a bit off: "His lip movements don't match his speech. Neither does his body language… Talking to Nico is always like watching a bad lip-synch… Nico's voice is never inflected."

"The Apologists" is narrated by Storm, one of the five human survivors of the invasion. Under the circumstances, it is not surprising that he is bitter and angry, nor that he spends so much of his time "fantasising and in reverie" about "the world before this one," the world that he has lost. But Storm is really over the top. He is not what you would call an empathetic narrator. He freely admits that he is "not a good person." He cultivates his resentment and his inner pain, and deliberately pushes his feelings to an extreme. He wallows in self-pity, though he also berates himself for indulging in such "whinging horsedung." He always seems to be itching for a fight. He recalls his father, an alcoholic who used to beat him. "Children of drunks," he says, "are weaned on violence and know nothing else."

Storm mostly reminisces about his wife, Bea, and their infant daughter, Chelsea. He claims that he was happy with them, that he loved them and was loved by them in return. However, he also remembers that he hit Bea, although he cannot recall just *why* he did it. In any case, she immediately walked out on him, taking the baby with her. Storm then "grovel[led] and beg[ged]" before her for "ninety-nine days," until she finally agreed to come back. She even forgave him, or so he claims, allowing him to "live again." But he also admits that, after Bea returned, her love for him was gone forever, "replaced by a tepid facsimile of adoration interspersed with sham bonhomie." Storm is self-aware enough to realize that this insincerity was a defense mechanism on Bea's part, put "in place to ward off further violence" by Storm. Not only was their reconciliation a sham, it didn't even last very long, since the strangers arrived shortly afterwards.

Storm is a nasty piece of work, to be sure. But "The Apologists" gets much of its absurdist humor from channeling everything through his jaundiced perspective. Storm often seems to me like a certain type of stand-up comedian: the kind who makes you cringe as much as laugh. Wiping out humanity is one thing — but what's really too much is having to hear the perpetrators apologize for it, over and over again. In victim humor, the more horrible things get, the more you have to push them even further, often in incongruously petty ways. What if you were one of the only five survivors from a population of eight billion or so? It's bad enough that your entire world has been destroyed; but now you also have to hear Storm "sing at the top of [his] voice" whenever you try to go to sleep. (He seems to favor hard rock; the only particular song he mentions in the course of the story is Thin Lizzy's "The Boys Are Back in Town").

As this example suggests, Storm doesn't get along very well with the other four human survivors. We learn very little about them from his narration. Storm claims to have nothing against the elderly couple, Mr and Mrs Kelly, but innocuous as they are, they still consider him "a disruptive influence." On the other hand, Storm actively dislikes Terry, the gay man in the group, and "deliberately needle[s]" him on every occasion. Nonetheless, he denies Terry's charge that he is homophobic. (He even claims to have met Bea at a Gay Pride march). As for Katrina, the only younger woman in the group — and the only other human being we actually meet in the course of the story — Storm tells us that "she and I hate each other on sight." He admits that "she's fantastic-looking, physically fit and of the right age"; but he still finds her "repulsive." Katrina is Storm's antitype, as relentlessly cheerful and filled with a sense of entitlement as he is bitter and grumpy. We aren't told the race of any of the survivors, but Katrina seems to be what, in contemporary parlance, has come to be called a Karen (Asmelash 2020; Urban Dictionary 2020). Nonetheless, it is hard to trust Storm's overall attitude towards women. This is a man who tells us, for instance, that the only reason he got along with Bea was because, unusually, he didn't " think of her as prey" when they first met.

This slightly ridiculous five-person anti-community marks the end of the line for *Homo sapiens*. The strangers encourage them to reproduce, in order "to repopulate the Earth." But they all refuse, in one way or another. The Kellys are "beyond menopause" anyway; and Terry scornfully declines to "go straight for humanity." As for Storm and Katrina, their mutual hatred is so deep that they will not so much as touch one another. He walks away from her even when he wants to hit her. The strangers also propose artificial insemination, but all three of the men refuse to "let [their] sperm be harvested." None of the surviving human beings wants the situation they find themselves in to continue.

The strangers, Storm says, "cannot understand why we will not act in our own self-interest." This reads to me as another gruesome joke: the strangers somehow still expect the survivors to orient themselves towards the future — even though their future has been foreclosed. Storm tries to explain to Nico that human beings are not the rational utility-maximizers that the strangers, much like neoliberal economists in the old world, take them to be. Rather, "humanity is defined by two opposing instincts, survival and self-destruction. Sex and suicide. Libido and thanatos… It's very rock and roll."

If Storm comes out on the side of destruction, can we really blame him? Maybe the strangers have simply fulfilled our own death wish. For what it's worth, Storm confesses at one point that "I often wonder if my whole life before the strangers was real, and maybe I have always been here." And regarding Katrina, he nastily suspects — given how much "she likes predictability" and feels anxious "when things are not going according to whatever her plan of the moment is" — that "there's a part of her that is happy with the demise of the previous world."

The human survivors are given comfortable living conditions, and are also assigned jobs. In lieu of engaging in sexual reproduction, they are put to work on the Rebuild: their task is "to produce a model of the world as it was before the strangers." Specifically, they build a simulation of London, since that is where they all previously lived. Katrina is in charge of buildings and streets, and Storm designs the artificial human beings, or "simulants," who inhabit the new environment. The survivors work at "remaking our world from memory and language"; anything that they can remember and describe in sufficient detail gets reproduced in physical form. This leads to odd gaps, since memory is imperfect. For instance, "train, tube and bus stations have significance to all of us, and are landmarks of sorts," and so the stations are replicated in full detail in the Rebuild. But inside these stations, there are only "some 3D sketches of trains." The problem is that "none of us remember trains or the details of how they work well enough to replicate them."

The survivors are not officially *required* to work on the Rebuild; the strangers claim to regard them as "volunteers." Nonetheless, if Storm (or presumably anyone else) takes time off and idles around, he is quickly nudged and nagged back to work. Storm knows that if he doesn't follow the strangers' instructions promptly enough, then unspecified "forceful measures" will be applied. Working hours are weekdays "from nine to five," just like they used to be in the old world. A curfew takes effect at midnight. The strangers claim that the Rebuild is entirely for the survivors' benefit, but Storm suspects that all this labor is nothing but "busywork to keep us survivors occupied, so the Apologists can feel good with themselves." The strangers also send "spherical and ovoid observer drones" into the survivors' bedrooms at night, keeping them under surveillance even when they sleep. All in all, this soft regimentation is eerily reminiscent of life under neoliberalism in the time before the invasion.

The Rebuild seems a bit like a Disney theme park. It's a world of pure appearance, "a perfect model of all the entangled orders of simulacra," as Jean Baudrillard might say: a reproduction of old London in perfect — but for that very reason, conflict-free, "embalmed and pacified" — form (Baudrillard 1994). Storm complains to Katrina that everything in the Rebuild is too nice, too pretty, and too regular. Nothing ever changes or decays, and nothing offers any sort of resistance:

> Wandsworth has perfect rows of terraced houses. The paint jobs are perfect with no mould or weathering. The glass is all clean, the hedges are surgical and the pavements look like fresh cement. The street lights shine with biblical vigour. There are no undulations to the asphalt.

Katrina rejects Storm's demands for cracks in the pavement, fungus on the house walls, trees shedding their leaves, and garbage in the gutters. Things are flawless, she says, because "they're neater this way." Storm argues that "this is not what streets look like," but Katrina responds that "this is how they *should* look" (emphasis added). Storm also says that Katrina "does not understand architecture or civil engineering and works like an artist": an interesting distinction, though not necessarily as discrediting as Storm means it to be.

Storm's biggest complaint, however, is about the simulants, the artificial human beings who populate this new version of London. Katrina says that "they seem perfectly like people to me." But for Storm, "they cannot be human because they are perfect replicas. Humanity is defined by imperfections." Storm is responsible for designing the simulants. At first, they all "looked the same, with features like mine." Later, he makes them "look like people from my life," often in multiple copies. He keeps on tweaking them, seeking to make them less perfect, trying to teach them about "pain and disgust," and jealousy and possessiveness. "To want something is to want it completely," he says, proposing his own version of social Darwinism or evolutionary psychology; "To own a thing or a person is to own it exclusively." He adds that "this is why we marry." Storm teaches the simulants to curse, and even to "bump aggressively and exchange profanities" with one another when they meet. But the simulants remain incapable of active learning; they do not experiment as children do. They can come up with nothing new on their own; they are finally "nothing more than manikins." No matter what Storm does, the simulants still remain "bland," "passive," and "far too accommodating."

Storm becomes increasingly unhinged over the course of the story as his frustration with the simulants grows. In the end, this can only lead to violence. If the simulants cannot learn to be aggressive on their own, then Storm decides he will force them to be. When he finds an injured simulant, he pokes and prods it, and then gouges out its eye. He tells himself that he is only trying to "investigate simulant response" and to discover what they are made of. To his surprise, the simulants turn out to be more humanly vulnerable than he realized. Their flesh "is all soft and pliant, like real meat… there is no wire, cable, or anything that isn't ersatz human." There is even a "red sap" that more or less resembles blood, though the details aren't quite right.

Storm moves on to actively assaulting simulants, bashing them with "a length of piping" that he finds lying around. He especially targets ones that are "holding hands, simulating a couple." It annoys him that the simulants don't fight back, and that they show no solidarity with one another, simply regarding the violence against their fellows with "curiosity" and "disgust." Despite the simulants' lack of response, he finds that "beating them is somehow… cathartic. I feel anxious all day until I have hit them, after which I feel calm" (ellipsis in original text).

We are fully in uncanny-valley territory at this point. Storm overtly denies that, in attacking the simulants, he has done anything more than "deactivated the equivalent of a household appliance." But he cannot quite bring himself to fully believe this:

> I make glib statements about simulants not being alive, but deep down, where I won't admit anything, I feel a cold weightiness in my heart. It makes my words ring false when I use them. Is that guilt I'm feeling? Have I convinced myself these simulants are alive?

Storm admits to being "perturbed" that he gets so much pleasure out of bashing the simulants. Would he experience a catharsis if he really believed that they were nothing more than inanimate machinery? Storm has previously told us that, in spite of everything, he finds female simulants "sexually attractive." And after he gouges out the eye of the wounded simulant, he soon feels shame and runs away. All this suggests that he is disturbed, not just because the simulants are not quite human, but also because they are not quite non-human either.

Things come to a head when Storm discovers that Katrina — who seems incapable of any such ambivalence — is apparently dating a male simulant. They get together every day. Storm follows them around, obsessively, for weeks. Does this mean that he is jealous and "perhaps attracted to Katrina" after all? He isn't sure. But in any case, after he sees them kiss, Storm bashes the simulant to death. The strangers "move fast in setting up a rudimentary judicial system, a police force and a prison of sorts." They charge Storm with murder and open legal proceedings against him. Katrina is the main witness for the prosecution; the judge and jury are all simulants. Storm compares the whole process to "a Soviet show trial." But in spite of his protests, he is convicted of "murderous behavior" (if not precisely of murder, since the simulants are not precisely human beings) and condemned to exile. This means that he is confined to a neighborhood where he must live alone. The other human survivors never visit him there, and neither do any simulants. He is let out only to attend the funerals of Mr and Mrs Kelly. Aside from these two occasions, he never sees Katrina or Terry again.

Eventually, Storm is released from solitary confinement and allowed back into the Rebuild. He notes that many of the details — like the water and the cars — are now more realistic; and he is pleased that the simulants "are more like the grim arseholes you would normally see in the London tube crowds every day." But he must still live out his life alone, in what is basically a theme park with no future. This is the End of History as envisioned by Hegel and Alexandre Kojève — which is to say, the empty culmination of the post-Enlightenment, Western-colonialist vision of progress. The End of History is the extended moment when Promethean rationalism becomes indistinguishable from Lovecraftian cosmic nihilism (Brassier 2007), and when (as Mikkel Borch-Jacobsen puts it, commenting on the notion in Hegel and Kojève) "one is decidedly bored because there is nothing to do (and thus also nothing to narrate except foolish stupidities)" (Borch-Jacobsen 1991).

At one point in the story, Nico explains to Storm that he cannot talk to the strangers directly because they are just not around:

> The people you call Apologists don't live here, haven't done for centuries… They live in Dyson Clouds over multiple solar

> systems... They do not wish to hear your opinion. You are wasting your time.

Nico adds, in what is just a casual aside, that the galaxy is filled with "countless worlds" where the strangers "keep species like yours." That is to say, there is nothing unique about the history of Earth. The strangers have exterminated numerous civilizations, numerous sentient species, on numerous worlds. Doubtless they have always done this by accident, and doubtless they have always built simulations of what they have destroyed, to which they broadcast their incessant apologies.

3. Speculative Fictions

Cognitive Estrangement: Darko Suvin

Science fiction is defined by Darko Suvin as "the literature of cognitive estrangement." This definition, from Suvin's book *Metamorphoses of Science Fiction* (Suvin 2016; first published in 1979), is foundational for the small academic field of science fiction studies. Sometimes Suvin's definition is reaffirmed, at other times it is expanded or modified, and at still other times it is contested or even rejected. But it is always there, in the background of nearly all scholarship and criticism in the field. Science-fiction authors themselves might not care about what Suvin says, and indeed they have no reason to. But as an academic science-fiction scholar, I cannot escape working in Suvin's shadow.

I would like to look carefully, therefore, at the details of Suvin's definition. It should be noted, first of all, that even though Suvin restricts himself to *literature*, what he says can easily be extended to other narrative media like film, television, and comics. I think that it can even be extended to the far-less-narrative medium of science-fictional music, especially the Afrofuturist tradition that extends from Sun Ra, through George Clinton, and on to such contemporary artists as Janelle Monáe. Like Suvin, I am mostly concerned in the present book with written science fiction — novels and short stories. I hope to write about non-literary forms and media of science fiction at another time. But as far as I am concerned, the generalization of Suvin's definition to other media is not really a problem.

On the other hand, I must confess my own strong dislike of Suvin's claim that science fiction is fundamentally *cognitive*. I have argued elsewhere that the role of cognition has been given excessive prominence in contemporary discussions of mental functioning in both psychology and the analytic philosophy of mind (Shaviro 2016a). Here I follow Alfred North Whitehead's dictum that "the chief error in philosophy is overstatement. The aim at generalization is sound, but the estimate of success is exaggerated" (Whitehead 1978). Cognitivism in psychology and philosophy is guilty of exaggeration in just this way. Of course, all life activities require a certain degree of cognition; even bacteria would not be able to function without some sort of cognitive grasp of their surroundings. In contrast to the old behaviorist stimulus/response models, we now know that all living organisms engage in "probing the environment with ongoing, variable actions first and evaluating sensory feedback later (i.e., the inverse of stimulus response)" (Brembs 2015). Indeed, this is not just the case for animals, but also for plants, fungi, and even unicellular life-forms (see, for example, Chamovitz 2012; Lyon 2015). From bacteria seeking out glucose gradients (Stuart Kauffman 2003, quoted in Tomlinson 2016) and acting collectively by means of quorum sensing (Miller and Bassler 2001), all the way to human beings running controlled experiments in laboratories (Bhaskar 1975), all organisms are heavily engaged in *reality-testing*: that is to say, they actively question their surroundings, comparing their findings with their prior expectations, and continually adjust the latter and question anew. But such cognitive activities are better understood as consequences of — and as instrumental aids to — life processes than as their all-embracing basis. A cognitive explanation can tell us *how* a living entity does what it does, but not *what* it is trying to do or *why*. For the latter, we must look at how the organism is driven on a deeper level. This might be something like what Spinoza calls *conatus*, or the way that each entity "endeavors… to persevere in its own being" (Spinoza 2018). Or perhaps it is better understood as something like what Whitehead calls *appetition*, which involves experiences of *adversion* and *aversion*, and which is oriented not only towards "self-preservation" but also towards generating "novelty to match the novelty of the environment" (Whitehead 1978).

In *Metamorphoses of Science Fiction*, Suvin takes the primacy of cognition for granted, but he never fully explains what he means by the term. His best account of cognition comes in a much later essay, "On Cognitive Emotions and Topological Imagination" (Suvin 1997). Here Suvin broadly defines "understanding, cognition or knowledge" as anything that "can help us in coping with our personal and collective existence" and that "can be validated by feedback with its application in the existence, modifying it and being modified by it." This fairly modest and open definition is not inconsistent with the idea of reality-testing, though it does not sufficiently stress the ways that entities spontaneously and actively probe their environments. Suvin rightly aligns himself with theories of *embodied cognition* and *enactive cognition*, referring specifically to such thinkers as George Lakoff (Lakoff 1987) and Mark Johnson (Johnson 1990). On the embodied or enactive account, cognition is not a free-standing process, and not an entirely computational one. It cannot be separated from emotion, and it is always grounded in bodily experience. This means that cognition is not entirely conceptual; it also includes such "non-conceptual" components as bodily schemas, analogical reasoning, and spatial or "topological imagination" (Suvin 1997).

Unfortunately, it is difficult to map this account of cognition back onto the much narrower, and indeed weaponized, use of the term in *Metamorphoses of Science Fiction*. In this earlier book, there is no reference to embodiment or to the emotive aspects of cognition. Instead, *Metamorphoses* gives us an inflated, maximalist account of cognition, equating it not only with "the philosophical fundaments of modern science" since Galileo, but with rationality *tout court*. This seems to mean an explicit, full-blown historical materialist understanding of the world; nothing else is acceptable or merits designation as rational. The proper sort of cognition, Suvin says, "sees the norms of any age, including emphatically its own, as unique [and] changeable." All other approaches are dismissed as "supernatural or metaphysical." We must reject any statement that "claims to explain once and for all the essence of phenomena" (Suvin 2016). Although I am in general sympathy with Suvin's Marxist anti-essentialism, his strictures here seem excessive and dogmatic. It is no surprise that this approach leads to unhinged denunciations of "the present wave of irrationalism" and of "ideology unchecked by any cognition" (Suvin 2016). Suvin writes in a manner all too reminiscent of György Lukács at his very worst (Lukács 1980).

To my mind, it does not help that Suvin blames the alleged contemporary culture of irrationalism on "the deep structures of the irrational capitalist way of life." This is not wrong so much as beside the point. Of course our social system is deeply irrational, as well as deeply oppressive, and of course this will be reflected in the ideological content of the literature produced within it. But Suvin's rationalistic call to arms does not do any actual work in this context; it is really just empty sloganeering. Indeed, there is something missing from your critique if your deepest, and most emotionally charged, objection to capitalism is that it is irrational and mystified rather than — for instance — that it is grounded in exploitation and expropriation, is murderous to the point of genocide, systematically immiserates large numbers of people, and so on.

I find it hard to avoid the conclusion that, however nuanced his later understanding of cognition may be, Suvin mostly uses the term in *Metamorphoses of Science Fiction* as a cudgel to beat down the texts that he does not like. The purpose of emphasizing cognition is to justify and enforce Suvin's aesthetic preference — or more accurately, his moral prejudice — in favor of science fiction and against such other non-naturalistic genres as fantasy, horror, and folktales. In particular, Suvin is no fan of the fantasy genre; I guess he just hates hobbits and prog rock. Admittedly, there are far worse prejudices. And the present book, just like Suvin's volume, is mostly concerned with science fiction proper, rather than with these other non-naturalistic genres. But that is no excuse for ignoring the affinities among these genres, or for anxiously trying to preserve science fiction from being "contaminated" by contact with the others. When Suvin stigmatizes fantasy for being non-cognitive, or even anti-cognitive, he avoids engaging with it in any serious or meaningful way. Instead, he hyperbolically banishes fantasy to the nether regions as "a subliterature of mystification" grounded in a "proto-Fascist revulsion against modern civilization, materialist rationalism, and such," one whose "narrative logic is simply overt ideology plus Freudian erotic patterns" (Suvin 2016).

Of course, it is true, almost by definition, that where science fiction tends to invoke the physical and social sciences in its (usually spurious) explanations for the twists and turns of the narrative, other non-naturalistic genres — like fantasy, horror, and folktales — more commonly invoke things like magic. However, this need not entail that the latter genres are devoid of cognitive substance, or that *anything goes* within them. Suvin's cognitivist polemic reaches its *reductio ad absurdum* when he asserts, for instance, that "anything is possible in a folktale, because a folktale is manifestly impossible" (Suvin 2016). Other forms of narrative require us to parse them cognitively just as much as science-fictional narrative does; and conversely, science fiction requires the reader's suspension of disbelief just as much as horror or fantasy does. Magical stories have their own narrative logic and constraints, rather than being purely arbitrary. Beyond this, we would also do well to recall Arthur C. Clarke's dictum that "any sufficiently advanced technology is indistinguishable from magic" (Clarke 2013). By any looser definition than Suvin's, fantasy and horror are by no means devoid of cognition. We must conclude, along with China Miéville, that "the supposedly radical distinction between [science fiction and fantasy] on the basis of cognition" is simply not tenable (Miéville 2009).

In his overt critique of Suvin, Miéville points out, among other things, that science fiction is just as steeped in ideological mystification as fantasy is. Science fiction's "self-declared 'rationalist' agenda" cannot be taken at face value, for it is a construction grounded in "capitalist modernity's ideologically projected self-justification: not some abstract/ideal 'science,' but capitalist science's bullshit about itself." Suvin himself half-concedes this point in a reconsideration of fantasy first published in 2001 and subsequently included as "Additional Material" in the 2016 new edition of *Metamorphoses of Science Fiction*. There he admits to having "waxed increasingly skeptical about the politico-epistemological presuppositions dominant" in the book in its initial form. He further acknowledges, much more explicitly than before, that "the rationality claimed by bureaucracy and technoscience is in fact an impoverished pseudo-rationality" (Suvin 2016). This moves at least part of the way to acknowledging Miéville's claim that the "cognition effect" of science fiction (a concept that he takes from Freedman 2000) is not actually rational, but rather entirely rhetorical: an act of persuasion, and "a function of (textual) *charismatic authority*" (Miéville 2009).

Miéville suggests, as an alternative to Suvin's cognitivism, that science fiction, fantasy, and horror are all concerned, on the deepest level, with "specific articulations of *alterity*" (Miéville 2009). That is to say, all of these genres confront cognition with phenomena that, at least to a certain extent, resist being entirely cognized. Suvin himself would never accept such a prospect, since he bases his aggressive rationalism upon the faith that nature is not, and cannot possibly be, "inscrutably alien to man [sic]" (Suvin 2016). But I am enough of a speculative realist to reject this faith. Why should we think that the universe has somehow arranged itself for our particular cognitive benefit? We will never reach the Hegelian end point where reality-testing is no longer necessary because our categories entirely coincide with the universe as it actually is.

This does not mean, of course, that we can know nothing at all. Miéville rightly points out that alterity is a matter of degree. The "strangeness" that appears in science fiction, fantasy, and other non-naturalistic genres is limited, rather than absolute; otherwise, "there could be no recognition or reception — true alterity would be inconceivable, thus imperceptible" (Miéville 2009). The point is that total scrutability is as impossible as total inscrutability; we can no more capture everything within our all-too-human cognitive framework than we can hope to ever entirely escape that framework. We are not gnostic strangers to the universe, but neither is the universe sculpted entirely to our measure. To put cognition in its place is not to reject it altogether, but only to free ourselves from the myth of its absolute supremacy. We are not entirely at a loss, but neither should we accept it when, as Whitehead puts it, philosophy "indulges in brilliant feats of explaining away" (Whitehead 1978).

Science fiction works — no less than fantasy and horror do — by pushing up against, and forcing us to become aware of, the limitations and failures of our overly homogenized, and ideologically constrained, cognitive habits. The faith in cognition that Suvin opposes to ideological mystification is itself a sort of ideological mystification. This means that the "fictional *novum* (novelty, innovation)" that Suvin regards as central to science fiction cannot be "validated by cognitive logic," as he claims (Suvin 2016). For if such a validation were possible, the phenomenon in question would not really be new. To the contrary, we should regard the science-fictional novum as an instance of otherness (alterity) whose novelty lies precisely in the ways that it challenges and evades our cognitive schemes, forcing us to modify or expand them. Rather than trying to "appeal to the cognitive universalism of natural and/or social laws," as Suvin does (Suvin 2016), we come to realize that our understanding is never universalistic enough, and that these "laws" are not as absolute as we thought.

Estrangement, the other crucial term in Suvin's definition of science fiction, simply means — at least in the first instance — that science-fiction texts give us "an imaginative framework alternative to the author's empirical environment." That is to say, where naturalistic fiction "endeavor[s] faithfully to reproduce empirical textures and surfaces vouched for by human senses and common sense," an estranging work of fiction depicts "a different space/time location or central figures for the fable, unverifiable by common sense" (Suvin 2016). This is a workable formulation, as far as it goes (and ignoring the empty invocation of "common sense"). Of course, the contrast between naturalistic and estranging fiction is a matter of degree, rather than an absolute distinction. Even the most scrupulously naturalistic work of fiction — and for that matter, even a work of documentary nonfiction — cannot entirely avoid imaginary or nonempirical elements; and conversely, few evocations of alternative realities are entirely devoid of features that we can recognize as grounded in our actual environment or in that of the writer.

There are also, unsurprisingly, works that deliberately play with the distinction between actual (present-day) and imaginary (future) environments. Chris Beckett's novel *Two Tribes* (Beckett 2020) contains a more or less naturalistic account of events set in the author's actual time and place: the book is about class differences in the UK during the Brexit disputes of the late 2010s. But this account, while it is contemporary for us, is framed as being written by a historian in the year 2266. This future narrator uses (fictional, but naturalistic) diaries from the 2010s as her raw material in order to describe a failed romance between an upper-middle-class man who is an architect and a lower-middle-class woman who is a hairdresser. Though these protagonists are both small-business owners (and hence petit bourgeois in Marxist terms), they are very far apart in their values and assumptions, their habits and interests, and their social circles. The text moves back and forth between third-person descriptions of these characters' lives and first-person reflections by the narrator, who seeks to understand these lives from her own perspective as someone living in a twenty-third-century Britain ravaged by climate catastrophe, economic decline, and authoritarianism. But there is also a third time-level to the novel, consisting in scenes that are set in the narrator's past but which she admits to inventing out of whole cloth due to the absence of sufficient documentary evidence. These added scenes are also supposedly set in the late 2010s. But the narrator acknowledges that they would actually have taken place a bit later in time: the near future for us, but still the distant past for her. These scenes point to the origins of a violent civil war in later twenty-first-century Britain between high-tech armies bankrolled by professional and managerial elites (Tony Blair-style "New Labour" people) on the one hand, and fascist militias controlled by Tory aristocrats who recruit soldiers from the resentful White working class on the other. This civil war is recounted as being nasty and quite destructive, even though the novel reveals that the instigators on both sides come from the same tiny ruling class. Beckett's novel thus works on multiple levels with the estrangement effects that come from differences in perspective, in this case being due both to class antagonisms and to temporal displacement.

To this extent, Suvin's claim for estrangement works quite well. But the problem is that Suvin uses his minimal initial definition — an alternative setting to, or an alternative perspective upon, the author's own social reality — in order to smuggle in additional aesthetic presuppositions. For Suvin equates estrangement with two high-modernist aesthetic strategies: Viktor Shklovsky's *ostranenie* and Bertolt Brecht's *Verfremdungseffekt* (Suvin 2016). Both of these strategies take us far beyond the mere depiction of a "space/time location" that is different from the writer's (or reader's) empirical here and now. Indeed, as Simon Spiegel points out, the estrangement of representational content in science-fiction narratives is far different from — and even incompatible with — the high-modernist practice of formal estrangement with which Suvin seeks to conflate it. In fact, as Spiegel points out, the experiential details of a nonempirical science-fiction world

> are not presented in an estranged way; rather they are rationalized and made plausible… The formal framework of sf [science fiction] is not estrangement, but exactly its opposite, *naturalization*. On a formal level, *sf does not estrange the familiar, but rather makes the strange familiar.*
>
> (Spiegel 2008)

If a science-fiction narrative is organized, as Suvin claims, around a novum that causes the world of the narrative to be different from the world that we know and take for granted, then the text will work above all to convince us to suspend our disbelief and to accept the vivid actuality of that novum. Nothing could be further from the Brechtian high-modernist strategy of self-reflexive distanciation. In noting this, I am not rejecting Suvin's larger point that science fiction offers us alternatives to the present and reminds us of the contingency of conditions that we take too much for granted in the empirical world in which we actually live. But *contra* Suvin, the most powerful way to accomplish this sort of estrangement is precisely by using the referential conventions of mimetic or "realist" fiction. Science fiction must reject the formally estranging devices of high modernism in order to clearly convey its novum, which is to say, its estranged representational content.

Suvin's insistence upon formal estrangement results, no doubt, from his wish to attach science fiction to the high-modernist movement "marked by names such as Einstein, Picasso, Eisenstein, and Brecht" (Suvin 2016). But this can only be done at the cost of entirely ignoring the cultural and commercial contexts out of which science fiction arose and within which it is still largely produced. It is out of his desire to escape such contexts that Suvin fills his book with phobic pronouncements that science fiction must be detached from "the compost heap of such juvenile or popular subliterature" out of which it initially grew, and that it "has to be and can be evaluated proceeding from its heights down, applying the standards gained by the analysis of its masterpieces" (Suvin 2016). In fairness, of course, we must recognize that this rhetoric, however rancid, is largely driven by Suvin's need to legitimize the study of science fiction in the academy at a time when the officially accepted literary canon was extremely narrow and restricted.

But we also need to recognize the historical limits of the modernist values that Suvin takes for granted. In the early and middle twentieth century, there was some truth to the idea that radical aesthetics went along with radical politics — despite the obvious counter-examples of some modernist innovators who embraced fascism, like Pound, Céline, and the Italian futurists. But today, in the early twenty-first century, such a connection between formalist innovation and revolutionary politics no longer exists. The formal experiments of the avant-garde have been fully assimilated into mainstream commercial culture. Indeed, they have been transformed from transgressive challenges into mere techniques to be applied at will. The anti-naturalistic approaches pioneered by the likes of Brecht, the surrealists, and Jean-Luc Godard are now staples of television commercials and web design. It turns out that all the estranging tactics of modernist radical aesthetics — self-reflexivity, distanciation, defamiliarization, and pointing up the falsity, inadequacy, and artificiality of one's own representations — are powerful and highly efficacious advertising and marketing tools. What better way to seduce us, after all, than to assure us that we are too smart and self-aware to be taken in by the processes of seduction?

Moreover, even if we understand estrangement to be a matter of representational content in science fiction, rather than what Suvin calls "*the formal framework* of the genre" (Suvin 2016), we still need a good definition of what it is that we are being estranged *from*. The obvious answer is present-day actuality, or the social world in which the narrative has been written, and the one in which it is read. Suvin calls this "the 'zero world' of empirically verifiable properties... this being 'zero' in the sense of a central reference point in a coordinate system, or of the control group in an experiment" (Suvin 2016). I have no problem with this formulation, as far as it goes. But we still need to ask and answer the question of just *how* the estranged reality presented in a work of science fiction relates to — how it is both different from and yet in some respects still similar to — the "zero world" from which it is estranged. Suvin is well aware that not all forms of estrangement are the same; this is what lies behind his efforts to distinguish between cognitive and (ostensibly) non-cognitive modes of estrangement. But as I have already argued, genres like fantasy and horror are neither devoid of cognition nor sheerly arbitrary. And science-fictional estrangement, for its part, is not adequately defined by merely saying that it is rational or that it exhibits "a mature approach analogous to that of modern science and philosophy" (Suvin 2016).

The real trouble with Suvin's theory of estrangement is that we will never get even a partial grasp of alterity as long as we see it exclusively in negative terms, defining it merely as contradictory to whatever is socially normative. This is what makes Slavoj Žižek so irritating to read: no matter which subject he addresses, Žižek always argues that the actual situation is "precisely the opposite" of what others have taken it to be (for example, Žižek 2006). But such an approach is limited and ultimately boring. Why can't the truth ever be *oblique* to appearances, instead of directly opposed to them? Why must the Real have "no positive-substantial consistency" of its own, as Žižek claims, but instead subsist as nothing more than "the gap between the multitude of perspectives on it" (Žižek 2006)? Our sense of possibility is seriously blunted if the only way we are able to imagine is by negating whatever actually is. It might be better to ferret out the partial and limited truths articulated through that multitude of perspectives, instead of simply dismissing them.

Now, it may well be that, at our own particular historical moment, our imaginations *are* in fact constrained and limited in just the way Suvin and Žižek suggest. Such is the dilemma Mark Fisher gets at in his book *Capitalist Realism* when he laments that "it is now impossible even to *imagine* a coherent alternative to [capitalism]" (Fisher 2009). Unfortunately, Fisher is right to a greater extent than I would like to believe. I know, for instance, that thanks to Joe Biden, even declaring bankruptcy will not release me from my massive credit card debts. I cannot imagine a plausible change in our social system that would do so. I may give lip service to socialism, but I cannot envisage, in any concrete detail or with any sense of conviction, a series of events in which socialism would vanquish capitalism and actually be put into practice, releasing me from my debts in the process. This is why it feels like only the apocalyptic destruction of the entire world could ever change things enough so as to offer me debt relief. Such a catastrophe would indeed be gratifying if not for the fact that I would not survive it.

Fredric Jameson similarly argues that our "increasing inability to imagine a different future" means that utopian speculation today cannot have any positive content, but must rather be "a meditation on the impossible, on the unrealizable in its own right."

Utopia can consist only in "the future as *disruption*... of the present, and as a radical and systemic break with even that predicted and colonized future which is simply a prolongation of our capitalist present." The only content of utopian imaginings, for Jameson, is "the experience of the total formal break and discontinuity... the very principle of the radical break as such." Jameson — remaining true to his modernist and anti-representationalist stance — insists that there can be no "picture of what things would be like after the break" (Jameson 2005).

Meditation on the impossible was a central preoccupation of twentieth-century avant-gardism, after all; I even once wrote an entire book about it (Shaviro 1990). But in conceiving of science fiction in terms of such a modernist *via negativa*, Jameson disparages what he calls the "common-sense position" that science fiction is "*representational*" in its depiction of the future. For, in fact, he says, science fiction works

> not to give us "images" of the future — whatever such images might mean for a reader who will necessarily predecease their "materialization" — but rather to defamiliarize and restructure our experience of our own *present*, and to do so in specific ways distinct from all other forms of defamiliarization.
>
> (Jameson 2005)

Now, there is much to be said for what China Miéville calls *apophatic Marxism*, which "must build not only on collective knowledge, but collective ignorance" (Miéville 2019). Such an approach is far preferable to Suvin's cut-and-dried reductionism. And, as I have already said earlier, I do not believe that science fiction has anything to do with empirical prediction; as Ursula Le Guin puts it, "The weather bureau will tell you what next Tuesday will be like, and the Rand Corporation will tell you what the twenty-first century will be like" — but science-fiction writers will never tell you these things (Le Guin 1976).

Nonetheless, I still maintain that science fiction is only able to defamiliarize and estrange us from the present because it familiarizes us with something else instead: other situations, other space-times, and other worlds. These other worlds may well be bizarre and estranging in their own right, in terms of their representational content, and their narration may well be vague and incomplete, but if we are to reject, along with Jameson, the banal truism that science fiction gives us actual images of the future, then we should also reject the equal and opposite truism that science fiction is actually and only — even if by negation — about the present moment in which it is written. Despite the ways that capitalist realism has impoverished our imaginations, science fiction's aboutness is still greater than this. Science fiction transports us to other times and spaces: near and distant, heavenly and hellish, and everything in between. This is the case, even (or especially) when we are unable to fully grasp, and authors are unable to fully render, these alternative worlds. The result is a certain degree of estrangement and defamiliarization; but these are only secondary effects of a process of imaginative *transmolecularization* (to use a term invented by Sun Ra). If the art of prediction claims to reveal our destiny to us, then the art of science fiction seeks instead to produce what Sun Ra calls an *alter-destiny* (Sun Ra 1974).

Cognition in Weird Fiction: Lovecraft's Legacy

Cognition is best regarded, not as a foundational characteristic of science fiction, but rather as an *issue* that is raised in all the non-naturalistic genres — in fantasy and horror no less than in science fiction — and which each of these genres negotiates in its own particular way. Take the case of *weird fiction*, which Darko Suvin describes as involving "the irruption of an anti-cognitive world into the world of empirical cognition." This is not bad as an actual description of what weird fiction does; the problem is that Suvin considers any such irruption to be illegitimate. Thus he denounces H. P. Lovecraft, the central figure in the history of weird fiction, for the cardinal sin of irrationalism: Lovecraft's writing, he says, "rejects cognitive logic and claims for itself a higher 'occult' logic" (Suvin 2016).

There are many rightful criticisms that can be made of Lovecraft, but this is not one of them. Suvin oddly claims that Lovecraft's stories take place in "a completely fantastic world." This is wrong. Lovecraft's monstrosities are disturbing precisely because they intrude into otherwise mundane contexts. Lovecraft's stories are organized by a violent "tension between the supernatural and the author's empirical environment" — the very quality that Suvin praises in works like "Gogol's *Nose* or Balzac's *Peau de Chagrin*," but which he refuses to acknowledge in Lovecraft's case (Suvin 2016). I suspect that Suvin means by this that Gogol's and Balzac's prose styles remain overtly realist, even when they evoke irreal elements. In contrast, Lovecraft's prose style is delirious, hyperbolic, and clearly non-naturalistic, even when he evokes naturalistic details and actually existing settings. But this inversion still works through a tension between familiar and unfamiliar modes of existence; weird fiction, as Mark Fisher puts it, always involves a "sensation of *wrongness*," a feeling "that *this does not belong*" (Fisher 2016).

In fact, the monstrous beings evoked by Lovecraft's delirious prose are not really occult or supernatural at all; they are fully material entities. They may come from realms whose geometry is "non-Euclidean," but these realms are still parts of the universe described by modern physics. Monsters like Cthulhu are not malevolent in any traditional moralistic sense. Rather, they are simply indifferent to human existence; they may not even realize that we exist. In Lovecraft's stories, these monsters are indeed often worshiped by frenzied, irrational cults, but for the most part, they remain indifferent to this worship. As Fisher says, "Human attempts to transform the alien entities into gods are clearly regarded by Lovecraft as vain acts of anthropomorphism" (Fisher 2016). Lovecraft was, as even Suvin acknowledges, a materialist and an atheist; the power of his fiction results precisely from how it places us in a cognitive deadlock that cannot be resolved by appealing to any "higher 'occult' logic."

The irruption of Lovecraft's Cthulhu into our world is therefore not so much "anti-cognitive" as it forces us to recognize that cognition itself is inadequate (and for this reason a problem). We come face-to-face with entities that our usual cognitive categories and habits are unable to make sense of. Fisher suggests that we can "think of Lovecraft's work as being about trauma, in the sense that it concerns ruptures in the very fabric of reality itself", which is to say that his stories pull us "beyond what Kant called the 'transcendental' structures of time, space and causality" (Fisher 2016). Lovecraft's narrators are traumatized as a result of having encounters that they cannot cognize, experiences that oxymoronically rupture the very framework through which we categorize and come to terms with experience.

Part of the issue here has to do with Lovecraft's prose, which we might describe as "anti-cognitive" in and of itself. Graham Harman shows us how the breakdown of the categories of experience is a systematic effect of Lovecraft's *style* as a writer: "Lovecraft's prose generates a gap between reality and its accessibility to us" (Harman 2012a). This *gap* is evidently a rhetorical effect, akin to the rhetorical effects that China Miéville finds in science fiction. But where science-fictional rhetoric dissimulates its cognitive shortcomings by appealing to the "charismatic authority" of technoscience, Lovecraft's rhetoric rejects any such authority. Instead, it calls attention to the fundamental failure of cognition. Harman argues that encounters among entities are in fact always riven by the gap between things in themselves and the ways they appear to us, or to other entities (or even to themselves). But most of the time, in everyday life, we simply ignore and overlook this discord. Lovecraft, however, exacerbates the inadequacy of cognition, making it (to use an appropriately oxymoronic phrase) blindingly visible. Lovecraft's fabulations show up the parochialism of our cognitive categories, which are not adequate to the task of grasping material reality. "The weird thing is not wrong after all," Fisher says; "It is our conceptions that must be inadequate" (Fisher 2016).

When Suvin accuses Lovecraft of irrationalism, therefore, he is really blaming the messenger for the message. Suvin takes the adequacy of cognition for granted, at least in principle. But this adequacy is precisely what weird fiction puts into doubt.

Lovecraft challenges the unexamined assumptions that the world is intelligible and that it is therefore subject to our mastery. For Lovecraft, cognition is only a matter of degree; it will never be absolute or total. Even worse, cognition is not instrumentally useful; to *know* a situation is not to control it, but rather to be disabused of the illusion that we can do anything about it. The apex of horror in Lovecraft's stories often comes when such an understanding is achieved: there is finally some sort of concrete, empirical proof — though it is subsequently lost again — that the monstrosity haunting the protagonist actually exists. But such knowledge is impotent; it is not accompanied by any power to change things. Lovecraft's narrators are terrified above all by the prospect that our understanding might eventually catch up with the phenomena that currently exceed its grasp, as in the opening paragraph of "The Call of Cthulhu":

> The most merciful thing in the world, I think, is the inability of the human mind to correlate all its contents… The sciences, each straining in its own direction, have hitherto harmed us little; but some day the piecing together of dissociated knowledge will open up such terrifying vistas of reality, and of our frightful position therein, that we shall either go mad from the revelation or flee from the deadly light into the peace and safety of a new dark age.
>
> (Lovecraft 2005)

This choice between madness and obscurantism is not a pleasant one. But Lovecraft refuses us any easy way out. He accepts the scientific demystification and disenchantment of the world. But he rejects the Promethean vision of "modern science as a means for achieving utopian mastery over man's destiny" (Suvin 2016) as hopelessly naive. Instead, Lovecraft problematizes cognition from the inside — which is quite a different thing from simply rejecting it. Lovecraft is horrified by what he sees as the indifference of the cosmos, its continual escape beyond our grasp, its effortless evasion of the cognitive schemes that we seek to impose upon it. In fact, this is how Lovecraft experiences the vertigo of Euro-American modernity: the same ecstatic confusion and sense of sublime groundlessness faced by all the early twentieth-century modernist writers and artists. As Nick Mamatas argues, "Lovecraft is actually a *difficult* writer" in much the same way as his high-culture contemporaries — and despite his own lowly genre status (Mamatas 2014). Lovecraft's writing is narrow and intense. It relentlessly and repetitiously explores just one single thing: the *gap* within cognition itself that Harman describes. On the one side, we find the noumenal horror of cosmic indifference to humanity; on the other side, we find the many phenomenal ways that human beings register, and seek to come to terms with, the fact of their own irrelevance. These ways include a collapse into outright madness, the delusive "peace and safety" of willful denial, a frenzied worship of the very forces that menace and ignore us, and also (crucially in Lovecraft's own case) a recourse to bigotry.

Lovecraft's virulent racism, misogyny, and erotophobia should not be minimized and explained away. Rather, we must understand them as direct correlates of his modernist discovery of a gap at the heart of cognition. Lovecraft's stories are notoriously filled with violent expressions of loathing for anything and everything that he finds unfamiliar — and especially for all human beings who are not Anglo-Saxon or "Nordic." In "The Horror at Red Hook," often rightly described as "Lovecraft's most bigoted story" (Emrys and Pillsworth 2015), the eponymous Brooklyn neighborhood, with its population of non-European immigrants, is described as a "poison cauldron where all the varied dregs of unwholesome ages mix their venom and perpetuate their obscene terrors," and as a "tangle of material and spiritual putrescence" from which "the blasphemies of an hundred dialects assail the sky" (Lovecraft 2005).

This hyperbolic rhetoric has an autobiographical source; it is an expression of Lovecraft's own hysterical panic when he encountered the vibrant multiculturalism and cosmopolitanism among the crowds of New York City in the 1920s. As the *Fungal*

Plots blog notes, Lovecraft often associates Cthulhu and other monstrosities both with his racist fantasies about people of color (a broad category in his case, since it also includes Jews, Slavs, and the Portuguese) and with the modernist art movements of his time, like cubism and futurism. For Lovecraft, non-White people and modernist art alike "represent an equivalent threat to a global social order that is explicitly presented as colonialist" (Fungal Plots 2019). The irony here is that these modernist art styles, just like Lovecraft's own prose — which Harman frequently describes as "cubist" (Harman 2012a) — reject superficial naturalism and invent new expressive forms in order to be more adequate to realities that cannot be represented immediately and directly. But Lovecraft's writing exhibits a classically phobic structure: he loathes precisely that which fascinates him, to which he is irresistibly drawn.

This brings us to the most powerful accomplishment of Lovecraft's prose, which is its *evasiveness*. However violently Lovecraft calls out the "terrors" and "blasphemies" of Red Hook, he declines to specify in any concrete detail just what they might actually consist in. I would love to hear more about what he calls the "commonness of weird orgies" in Red Hook. But Lovecraft steadfastly refuses to pin anything down. By remaining at the level of obscure hints and allusions, his rhetoric suggests that the actuality to which it refers is worse than anything that could be straightforwardly described. As "The Horror at Red Hook" explicitly tells us, the horror is "beyond all human conception"; it may be "glimpsed," but "it does not permit itself to be read" (Lovecraft 2005). For Lovecraft, language cannot adequately represent, let alone interpret in cognitive terms, the terrifying ontological groundlessness to which it nonetheless unavoidably refers.

And this is where Lovecraft's bigotry comes in. When he discovers a primordial gap in the fabric of being, something that is indubitable but that cannot actually be described, he frantically seeks to cover it over with his own stupid and petty prejudices. In particular, he associates the noumenal horror that he is unable to represent with his phenomenal hatred of all the people whom he cannot really see (because he is unwilling to acknowledge their humanity). But these violent efforts at projection and repression are unsuccessful. Lovecraft frantically piles on more and more phenomenal content, the uglier and nastier the better. Yet this content is never enough to fill, or even just to conceal, what remains an originary fault in being.

This is a cosmic irony that resonates, not just in the rhetoric of Lovecraft's stories, but equally on the level of their overt narrative content. The worshipers of Cthulhu are never able to communicate with their ostensible object of adoration. Their "unhallowed rites" are at best unfinished, and at worst little more than aspirational. These rituals, like the one evoked in "The Horror at Red Hook," may succeed in opening doors to the Outside, but they cannot grasp, let alone control, whatever it is that then comes through those doors. This is why I find myself laughing, screaming, and cringing in embarrassment, all at once, when Lovecraft reaches his greatest rhetorical heights. Every Lovecraft story ends in the same way. Humankind is threatened with inevitable doom, but this doom is postponed to an indefinite future. The narrator, or protagonist, has encountered horrors, but he is unable to convey this experience to anyone else. There is no possible appeal beyond the weakness and finitude of human cognition.

This is the central dilemma of weird fiction, and it is taken up by more-recent writers working in Lovecraft's wake. In the past few years, there has been a whole wave of novels, novellas, and short stories that explicitly return to Lovecraft in order to re-examine his vision in the light of his racism and other forms of bigotry. These works include Victor LaValle's *The Ballad of Black Tom* (LaValle 2016), Matt Ruff's *Lovecraft Country* (Ruff 2016), Kij Johnson's *The Dream-Quest of Vellitt Boe* (Johnson 2016), Ruthanna Emrys' *Winter Tide* (Emrys 2017) and *Deep Roots* (Emrys 2018), and N. K. Jemisin's *The City We Became* (Jemisin 2020). LaValle's and Ruff's books, for instance, both feature African American protagonists who are confronted simultaneously by hidden, Lovecraftian horrors and by the all-too-actual racist horrors of

America in the time of Jim Crow. The protagonists are caught up in the schemes of White magicians obsessed with the Beyond or the Outside; but at the same time, they are still forced to deal with the all-too-familiar dangers of police harassment, racial violence, *de facto* and *de jure* segregation, and other types of profiling and discrimination. In both books, the White magicians hire the Black protagonists, alternately cajoling and intimidating them, but also paying them well for their services. These White magicians seem to think of themselves as daringly slumming, or as walking on the wild side, by associating with Black people. Their transgression of the color line goes along with their transgression of bourgeois norms in search of preternatural sources of power. But, of course, the ultimate intentions of these magicians cannot be trusted. In order to survive, the Black protagonists have to work through, and finally free themselves from, their own relationships both with these White people and with the inhuman powers to which they have been brought into contact.

The Ballad of Black Tom is an explicit reworking of "The Horror at Red Hook." In LaValle's novella, Tommy Tester, a young Black man from Harlem, encounters the two most important White characters from the original story: the policeman Thomas Malone, the original story's point-of-view character and traumatized witness, and the wealthy eccentric Robert Suydam, the original story's antagonist. Malone harasses Tommy both on general principle — a Black man who leaves Harlem is always subject to police scrutiny — and in order to get to Suydam. For his part, Suydam enlists Tommy to help him destroy the world by awakening the "Sleeping King," Cthulhu. Suydam explains to Tommy that "a great and secret show" is going on throughout the cosmos (the phrase references a famous fantasy/horror novel: Barker 1989). But this is a spectacle that most people are "too ignorant, or too frightened, to raise our eyes and watch." We cannot bear even to know about it, because "the play isn't being staged for us… we simply do not matter to the players at all." In other words, Suydam is well aware that Cthulhu has no interest, one way or the other, in "humanity's silly struggles" (LaValle

2016). Nonetheless, Suydam promises Tommy that Cthulhu's return

> would mean the end of your people's wretchedness... When he rises, he wipes away the follies of mankind... When he returns, all the petty human evils, such as the ones visited on your people, will be swept away by his mighty hand. Isn't that marvelous?

The problem with Suydam's promises, of course, is that you cannot get to see, let alone personally benefit from, the "marvelous" cataclysm of Cthulhu's return unless you are somehow able to survive it. Suydam tries to convince himself, as well as Tommy and others, that at the end of human history there will be a magnificent "reward for those of us who helped the Sleeping King wake... he will reward us with dominion of this world." Suydam even fatuously proclaims that he himself will be "a righteous ruler" of the new, post-apocalyptic Earth. But, of course, this is nonsense. Cthulhu's indifference to humankind is so great that we cannot expect it to show gratitude to, or to bestow any favors or power upon, those particular human beings who have facilitated its re-emergence. Even Suydam himself finally admits that, in the last instance, he simply "want[s] to see what more there is... We must know, even if it dooms us" (LaValle 2016). Such is the nihilistic death wish behind the drive for unfettered cognition.

Tommy, in contrast to Suydam, does not expect to survive the catastrophe. After all, he is living through an ongoing catastrophe already. For people of color, the future cataclysm that White people either anticipate with dread (as Malone does) or ignorantly romanticize (as Suydam does) is already their everyday experience. Poor and non-White people are already subject to the dystopian deprivations and terrors that will eventually be extended to the entire social sphere. Afrofuturist speculation often reminds us that a catastrophic future is nothing new for Black people. For Sun Ra, "it's after the end of the world; don't you know that yet?" (Sun Ra 1974). Public Enemy similarly tells us: "Armageddon, it been in effect, go get a late pass" (Public Enemy 1988). Tommy already experiences the violent disruption that Suydam only dreams of, because he is not protected from it by Suydam's White privilege and inherited wealth.

The first time that Tommy returns to Harlem after Suydam recruits him, he learns that a White private detective has murdered his father: just like that, for no good reason, and secure in the knowledge that he will never be held accountable for the killing. Faced with such everyday horror, Tommy reflects that

> a fear of cosmic indifference suddenly seemed comical, or downright naive… What was indifference compared to malice?… Indifference would be such a relief… *I'll take Cthulhu over you devils any day.*
>
> (LaValle 2016)

A similar sentiment is expressed in the Afrofuturist concept album *Splendor and Misery*, by the hip hop group clipping. The album's Black protagonist, a far-future fugitive slave who kills his captors and then flees into the interstellar void, finds "relief" in "Lovecraft's concept of cosmic insignificance"; for "pulling the rug out from under anthropocentrism is only horrifying to those who thought they were the center of everything to begin with" (clipping. 2016; see my discussion in Shaviro 2021). There is nothing new for oppressed people in the thought that the universe has no concern for them and is indifferent to their human-caused suffering. In clipping.'s album, as in LaValle's novella, Lovecraft's irony is inverted. For somebody who has not been accepted as fully human in the first place, the solitude and indifference of the cosmos at least offers some prospect of escape from racism's otherwise ubiquitous horrors.

In *The Ballad of Black Tom*, Tommy Tester continues to work for Suydam, and helps him realize his plan to summon Cthulhu. But at the culminating moment of the ritual, Tommy murders Suydam, adding the magician's blood to that of the other victims they have slain. Tommy explains that Suydam "wanted power, but the Sleeping King doesn't honor small requests." As for Malone, who has spent the entire story tracking Suydam's and Tommy's doings, but who now wishes only to escape back into ignorance, Tommy compels him to witness the full traumatic horror, slicing off his eyelids: "You can't choose blindness when it suits you. Not anymore" (LaValle 2016). Malone has spent his whole life being willfully blind to the racism of the system for which he works and from which he benefits, but Tommy will not allow him to close his eyes to the horrific truth any longer. LaValle's visionary, and revisionary, fabulation is turned against both Lovecraft's fatalism *and* the utopian optimism of traditional science fiction (as exemplified by Suvin).

Tommy completes the ritual, and awakens Cthulhu. But unlike Suydam, Tommy has no hope, and no desire, of being rewarded for this deed. Nor does he expect instantaneous results. Instead, Tommy embraces and affirms the full monstrosity of what he has done:

> Every time I was around them, they acted like I was a monster. So I said goddamnit, I'll be the worst monster you ever saw!… The seas will rise and our cities will be swallowed by the oceans… The air will grow so hot we won't be able to breathe. The world will be remade for Him, and His kind. That white man was afraid of indifference; well, now he's going to find out what it's like… I don't know how long it'll take. Our time and their time isn't counted the same. Maybe a month? Maybe a hundred years? All this will pass. Humanity will be washed away. The globe will be theirs again.

Tommy speaks these lines in 1924. Today, nearly a century later, we are facing the end of the world, pretty much as he envisions it. The sixth great extinction of species in the history of the Earth is already under way (Kolbert 2014). Temperatures are rising; sea levels are rising, and coastal areas are increasingly being flooded; from the poles to the tropics, ecosystems are collapsing. But we are not even able to grasp the timescales on which these things are happening or the ecological networks through which such consequences are transmitted. And we ourselves have no assurance of surviving the worldwide catastrophe that we have so ignorantly, and yet so willfully, unleashed.

Our current era of ecological devastation is commonly called the Anthropocene. This designation can only be ironic, since our outsized impact upon the world around us is redounding violently back upon ourselves. We are finally forced to recognize the agency and power of all the other entities with whom we share this planet. We cannot harm them without being harmed by them in return. Our very attempt to assert our power unilaterally — cognizing the world in order to master it — ultimately forces us to confront the limits of that power. This is the end, and the final refutation, of anthropocentrism. We are not the center of everything, and we never were.

Along these lines, and in yet another contemporary rewriting and critical repurposing of Lovecraft, Donna Haraway suggests renaming our present age the *Chthulucene*. Haraway deliberately misspells the name of Lovecraft's "misogynist racial-nightmare monster" in order to reverse the valency of a future that is no longer exclusively centered upon human beings. Lovecraft evokes Cthulhu's "pulpy, tentacled head" (Lovecraft 2005), and such monstrous tentacles have become ubiquitous in recent popular culture as a signifier of the weird (Miéville 2008). This is surely unfair to octopuses, who are among the most intelligent, inquisitive, and adaptable inhabitants of this planet (Godfrey-Smith 2016). In designating the *Chthulucene*, Haraway redeems the significance of tentacles and their bearers. She acknowledges the horrors of our present regime of plunder and exploitation, but also points towards "the diverse earthwide tentacular powers and forces and collected things" within which "flourishing for rich interspecies assemblages that include people will be possible." We can only survive by "making kin" with multiple entities, rather than stigmatizing them and trying to exterminate them on grounds of their supposed monstrosity. Cognition will accompany this process, but will not guide it from the outset. Haraway offers us an alternative response to alterity. She rejects Lovecraft's xenophobic bigotry, while at the same time she refuses to explain away the existence of alterity in the way that overly rationalistic thinkers do (Haraway 2016).

N. K. Jemisin's *The City We Became* also revises and inverts Lovecraft. In the process, Jemisin draws ecological lessons that Lovecraft was unable to discern. The premise of the novel (together with its sequel, *The World We Make* — Jemisin 2022) is that once large cities reach a certain level of interconnected complexity, they become alive and conscious. The novel is set in our present moment, and it recounts how New York City quickens into life and becomes aware of itself. When this awakening takes place, cities "make a weight on the world, a tear in the fabric of reality." They push beyond previous conceptual and material limits. This is a double process. On the one hand, a living city extends itself into a wide-ranging ecology. When New York City comes alive, it weaves together all the diverse strands of life and action among its eight million human and countless nonhuman inhabitants. On the other hand, and at the same time, the urban multiplicity gains a unique and singular (although ever-changing) form: it becomes *individuated* (to use a concept from Simondon 2020). The city embodies its awareness, and its heightened capacity for action, in a particular human being, who becomes its avatar: sort of like a literary personification, or a comic-book hero with "extradimensional superpowers." New York City has seven of these figures, one for the city as a whole, one for each of its five boroughs, and one for the densely urban suburb of Jersey City, just across the Hudson River (Jemisin 2020).

In the novel's cosmogony — which it describes as a "*unified field theory* of creation" — the city's quickening is the result of a long history and a long period of growth and evolution:

> A long time ago, when existence was young, there was just one world that was full of life… But each decision those living beings made fissioned off a new world — one where some of them turned left, and another where some turned right. Then each of those worlds fissioned off more worlds of their own,

> and so on, and so on… And so life proliferated — across a thousand million universes, each one stranger than the last.
> (Jemisin 2020)

As a result of this long history, the living world exists in innumerable layers, "each so wildly different that life on one would be unrecognizable to life on another." Many of these realities feature "minds as incomprehensibly alien as Lovecraft once imagined his fellow beings to be." But cities are special, because they "traverse the layers"; or again, "When a city is born… the birth process kind of smashes through" many layers. Cities are not just self-enclosed worlds. They reach out to levels beyond them, or outside them. They are complex ecologies whose very life is animated by their ever-proliferating networks of communication and exchanges of information. These are processes that pass through innumerable differences, bringing together heterogeneous modes of life: changing them, but not homogenizing them into a "melting pot." When "enough human beings occupy one space, tell enough stories about it, develop a unique enough culture… all those layers of reality start to compact and metamorphose." A city is "many worlds coming together" (Jemisin 2020). And this is precisely what Lovecraft hated about cities. He was scared of change and terrified by the very prospect of different ways of life coming into contact with his own. As Jemisin narrates New York City's coming to life, she celebrates everything about the city that Lovecraft loathed: its vibrancy, its crowds, its creativity, its multicultural exuberance, the continual novelty that it generates, and the unexpected encounters that it makes possible.

Trouble arises because "one of the realities out there" is hostile to the cosmopolitanism of urban existence; it "tries to kill cities whenever they become alive." This hostile realm is the Enemy, otherwise known as R'lyeh: a "monstrous city from nowhere," the abode of Cthulhu in Lovecraft's stories. The novel continually ridicules Lovecraft's phobias, such as "the comical notion that non-Euclidean geometry could somehow be sinister… Lovecraft was probably just scared of math." But this ridicule does not prevent

R'lyeh — with its angles that are "all wrong," and its creepy "towers and oddities" — from being a threat. The Enemy hates New York City for its "hybrid vigor," and seeks to exterminate it.

In its campaign of destruction, the Enemy appears in numerous guises. It manifests itself in "long, feathery white tendrils" and "white curling vine-like things" that spring up everywhere, tangling up freeways and tearing down bridges and exercising mind control by taking root in people's necks. The Enemy also spews forth gigantic "spiderlike" creatures that overrun buildings. It animates White people who deny being racists but complain that "I just don't understand why they have to play their music so *loud*!" (for various values of "they"). It institutionalizes itself in organizations like the "Better New York Foundation," promoting gentrification, "destroying everything that makes New York what it is, replacing it with generic *bullshit*" like luxury condos or a Starbucks every five blocks. In one queasily hilarious episode, the Enemy is embodied by the "Alt Artistes": smug White hipster dudes with their "manbuns" and "lumberjack beards," who peddle racist caricatures as works of art, all in the name of freedom of expression. Jemisin gleefully runs together eldritch horrors from weird fiction with urban redevelopment programs and the sorts of people you find "owning the libs" and whining their grievances on Twitter.

The Enemy's most powerful and most ubiquitous personification, however, is a human-like avatar: a seemingly "small rich passive-aggressive white woman" known only as the Woman in White. She clearly explains what it is about New York City that she detests:

> There's something *different* about cities, and about the people in cities… You eat each other's cuisines and learn new techniques, new spice combinations, trade for new ingredients; you grow stronger. You wear each other's fashions and learn new patterns to apply to your lives, and because of it you *grow stronger*.

This loathing of cosmopolitan culture is part of the Woman in White's inversion of the novel's cosmogony. She argues that not all realities are compatible. "Some life forms" — by which she means cities — "cannot be content with just their ecological niche; they are born invasive. They *punch through* — and when they do, they turn ten thousand realities into nothing." This is her negative take on the idea that cities "traverse the layers." She sees alternative realities as "inimical" to one another, and as engaged in zero-sum competition: whenever one of them gains, another one loses. What the Woman in White really loathes, just as Lovecraft did, is any sort of mixing or miscegenation; she hates the transformations, and indeed the growth, that inevitably result from *contact* across differences: "As *you* grow, *your cities* grow. You change one another, city and people, people and city. Then your cities start bringing multiple universes together." In spite of all its squirming tendrils and "humped, nodule-covered" exudations, R'lyeh is rigidly monochromatic, a living allegory of racial segregation and White supremacy: "Every skew-angled building, precisely marked street, and suppurating organism of this city gleams in brilliant, perfect, unnaturally bright white" (Jemisin 2020).

The Woman in White tellingly compares the growth of human cities to the time when "algae once wiped out nearly all life on this planet" (Jemisin 2020). This seems to refer to what is known as the Great Oxidation Event: a mass extinction that took place sometime between 2.4 and 2.0 billion years ago. (Algae have also been blamed, at least in part, for the Late Devonian extinction of 360 million years ago, but this is still scientifically controversial — compare Wu et al. 2013). In the Great Oxidation Event, the first photosynthesizing organisms — cyanobacteria, also known as blue-green algae — changed the environment by releasing massive amounts of oxygen into the atmosphere. Oxygen levels grew from an initial 0.0001 percent all the way to 21 percent, the concentration that still exists today (Margulis and Sagan 1997). As a result, many species of anaerobic microbes, for whom oxygen is poisonous, died out. But without this oxygenation, the development of eukaryotes and of multicellular organisms would not have been possible. Life would still have been confined to the smaller and simpler forms that existed previously. On Earth, at least, oxygen-based respiration, mediated by mitochondria —

formerly independent bacteria that now exist as organelles within every eukaryotic cell — is the only metabolic process that produces enough energy to make more-complex, multicellular life-forms possible (Lane 2015).

The stakes here are both political and ontological. The Woman in White, like Lovecraft, seeks to preserve one particular form of life against all changes, as well as against all other forms of life — even to the point of exterminating those others. From this point of view, life means endless competition for scarce resources, the eternal struggle of all against all. This was the logic of social Darwinism in the nineteenth century, and today it survives in the ideologies of White supremacy and other forms of so-called neoreaction (Sandifer 2017). But we also know today that this is wrong. We live on a "symbiotic planet" (Margulis 1999), where cooperation is as necessary as competition. Living entities never exist alone; they are always enmeshed with others and mutually interdependent with those others. This is crucial not just for sheer survival, but even more for growth and flourishing. Scientists sometimes define life as a process of homeostatic self-maintenance (Rodolfo 2000) and self-reproduction through "autopoiesis and cognition" (Maturana and Varela 1980). But this is only part of the story. Many nonliving things endure far longer, and with much greater stability, than living organisms do: think of a stone that takes ages to erode. Life also involves, and indeed requires, *change*, or what Whitehead calls "the origination of conceptual novelty — novelty of appetition" (Whitehead 1978). Such novelty involves an expansion of cognition (it is "conceptual"); but it is not reducible to cognition, for it also involves material and affective processes (it is "appetition"). No living entity emerges entirely unchanged from its encounters with other such entities. Living novelty was produced billions of years ago, when symbiotic mergers, incorporating mitochondria into living cells, first gave rise to eukaryotic life. In *The City We Became*, such novelty is still produced, and valued, whenever cities "traverse the layers" and make "a tear in the fabric of reality."

In line with these considerations, Jemisin inverts the signification of the Lovecraftian weird. Lovecraft loathed the modernity and vigor of multicultural cities like New York, which is why he associated such cities with the "antique witcheries and grotesque marvels" of eldritch, immemorial forces (Lovecraft 2005). But in point of fact, what is more anciently and horribly ingrained in the world today, more menacing to life's flourishing, more oppressive even in its unconcern, than the culture of Anglo-Saxon aristocracy and White supremacy in which Lovecraft himself so desperately and unreservedly believed? Lovecraft asks us to dread Cthulhu as an agent of primordial chaos that threatens his own supposedly "civilized" order. But Jemisin demonstrates, throughout *The City We Became*, that Cthulhu's exterminationist violence is actually the quintessential expression of that very order. In the final confrontation at the end of the novel, the Woman in White asks the avatars of New York City to "stand down," as this will allow her "to begin erasing this universe and all of its antecedents and offshoots… peacefully," without violence. She calls this being "civilized." One of the avatars replies, "You don't roll up in here and threaten to kill everything we love, and claim to be *civilized* while you do it."

In other words, far from threatening the supposed order of aristocratic Anglo-Saxon supremacy, Cthulhu *is* the predatory agent of that supremacy. Lovecraft feverishly imagines the violent (supposed) restoration of a superseded and ostensibly primordial order of domination. But then he disavows this vision, and attributes it to the very groups against whom it is directed. Such a symptomatic inversion is all too familiar to anyone who knows their Freud. Jemisin, LaValle, and the other Lovecraft revisionists I have mentioned turn the weird inside out in order to make of it an instrument for exploring, rather than phobically rejecting, the *terra incognita* of realms and phenomena that do not conform to our ideologically delimited cognitive categories.

Impossible Mimesis: Seo-Young Chu contra Darko Suvin

In her 2010 book, *Do Metaphors Dream of Literal Sleep?*, subtitled "A science-fictional theory of representation," Seo-Young Chu takes up Darko Suvin's theory of science fiction, but with a twist, in order to give us, instead, "Suvin's definition turned inside out" (Chu 2010). Where Suvin asserts that cognitive estrangement is the "*formal framework* of the genre" of science fiction (Suvin 2016), Chu locates cognitive estrangement, "not in the formal apparatus of a given SF text but in the object or phenomenon that the SF text seeks accurately to represent." Science fiction works "to generate mimetic accounts of aspects of reality that defy straightforward representation" (Chu 2010). In this way, Chu moves cognitive estrangement from the realm of literary form to the realm of referential content, which is where it really belongs. Friedrich Engels memorably asserted that, in Marx's writings, "the dialectic of Hegel was turned upside down or rather it was placed upon its feet instead of on its head, where it was standing before" (Engels 2020). In just this way, Chu's inversion puts Suvin's theory of science fiction upon its feet for the very first time.

Chu defines *mimesis* simply as "the representation or imitation of the real world in (a work of) art." She insists that science fiction is in fact "a mimetic discourse" under this definition — despite the common assumption, shared by Suvin and many others, that science fiction "operates beyond (or even counter to) mimesis." What distinguishes science fiction, according to Chu, is that its referential objects, "while impossible to represent in a straightforward manner, are absolutely real" (Chu 2010). In other words, instead of estranging us from the process of mimetic representation, as Suvin claims, science fiction involves the mimetic representation of a reality that is in its own right inherently cognitively estranging, and which is therefore difficult to pin down in a description. The process of aesthetic mimesis, for Chu, therefore leads us to deep questions about the reality that it seeks to emulate:

> What does it mean for something to elude representation? What makes some referents less susceptible than other referents to representation? What does it take for an elusive referent to become available for representation?

None of these questions can even be posed unless we at least start out with what Chu calls her "faith in the transcribability of things" (Chu 2010). When a referent eludes our efforts at representation, this tells us more about the referent than it does about the limits of our representational practices.

Chu thus breaks with the anti-representationalist consensus that dominates modernist and postmodernist aesthetics. In an otherwise favorable review of *Do Metaphors Dream of Literal Sleep?*, Istvan Csicsery-Ronay accuses Chu of "realist fundamentalism" because she willfully ignores "a century of the most concerted questioning of the ability of language and imagery to represent a real world existing outside the human mind" (Csicsery-Ronay 2012). Csicsery-Ronay is right that most twentieth-century art engages in this sort of questioning. Such art tends to emphasize scepticism, self-reflexivity, and the arbitrariness of the linguistic signifier, and to reject the suspension of disbelief. Instead, the modernist work claims to take precedence, in its own formal structure, over any external reality to which it might seem to refer. The filmmaker Robert Bresson, for instance, develops an aesthetics of what we might today call sampling when he says that fragmentation "is indispensable if one does not want to fall into REPRESENTATION" (Bresson 2016). Bresson captures elements of external reality with the camera and sound recorder; but then he rips these elements out of their referential context, atomizes and pulverizes them, and puts them together in entirely new ways. In modernist art, the spectator is distanced from the spectacle and obliged to recognize its contingency and refuse to give it credence. Such is the explicit principle of Bertolt Brecht's *Verfremdungseffekt* (alienation or distancing effect), one of the strongest influences on Suvin's account of science fiction. Philosophers and cultural commentators ranging from Adorno to Barthes to Deleuze to Rorty similarly reject the priority of representation, or the idea that thought and language can be taken to refer to any such thing as a pre-existing extra-mental reality.

Science-fiction theorists like Scholes, Suvin, and Jameson carry over these assumptions wholesale into their accounts of the genre. Here is Jameson, for instance:

> The common-sense position on the anticipatory nature of SF as a genre is what we would today call a *representational* one. These narratives are evidently for the most part not modernizing, not reflexive and self-undermining and deconstructing affairs. They go about their business with the full baggage and paraphernalia of a conventional realism, with this one difference: that the full "presence" — the settings and actions to be "rendered" — are the merely possible and conceivable ones of a near or far future. (Jameson 2005)

Jameson's rejection of mimesis could not be any clearer. Against the idea that science fiction might anticipate future possibilities, or even that it might embody and inform our hopes for social change (Imarisha et al. 2015), he insists that the "deepest vocation" of science fiction is "over and over again to demonstrate and to dramatize our incapacity to imagine the future" (Jameson 2005).

I would suggest, however, that we need to understand Jameson's own stance in the light of his famous admonition to "always historicize!" (Jameson 1981). We cannot imagine the future, according to Jameson, because we cannot even give an account of the present moment. Jameson tells us over and over again that we "cannot represent or imagine" the contemporary capitalist world system at all (Jameson 1987); the only thing that science fiction can do is to bear witness to "the waning of our historicity, of our lived possibility of experiencing history in some active way" (Jameson 1991). Yet this impasse is itself the symptom of a specific historical conjuncture; it is grounded in a particular mode of production, the one that Jameson calls late capitalism (Jameson 1991), and that others have called the network society (Castells 2009) or neoliberalism (Harvey 2007). If we emulate Chu, and put Jameson on his feet, then we must say that our "incapacity to imagine the future," or even to "represent or imagine" the present, is itself an historical situation that needs to be represented and explored through science-fictional mimesis.

The Gibson Continuum

In support of his anti-mimetic stance, Jameson points to older works of science fiction, from the early and middle twentieth century, that embarrassingly got the future entirely wrong, and whose ideological blinders are all too obvious today. The bright, high-tech visions of Golden Age science fiction, Jameson says, "are themselves now historical and dated" (Jameson 2005). William Gibson's 1981 short story "The Gernsback Continuum" (referring to the early science fiction editor Hugo Gernsback) gives a good example of this. The narrator, speaking in the 1980s (the decade in which the story was first published), is haunted by the "semiotic ghosts" of soaring zeppelins, art-deco ziggurats, "roads of crystal… crossed and recrossed by smooth silver shapes like beads of running mercury," and other such artifacts of the "1930s pop imagination." These visions are sometimes "relentlessly tacky," and at other times are endowed "with a kind of sinister totalitarian dignity." In the story, they disturbingly encroach upon the narrator's everyday reality, giving him hallucinations of an "alternate America." This older vein of science-fictional speculation was driven, Gibson says, by a "dream logic that knew nothing of pollution, the finite bounds of fossil fuel, or foreign wars it was possible to lose." This vision, however futuristic, is a "tomorrow that never was"; it became obsolete well before it ever had the chance to arrive (Gibson 1986a). Gibson, like Jameson, reminds us that nothing seems more corny, hokey, naive, and superannuated to a new generation than the previous generation's visions of bleeding-edge futurity.

"The Gernsback Continuum" figures our imaginative incapacity to envision the future by telling the story of a reversion to the most ridiculous science-fictional fantasies from the 1930s. On a deeper level, however, I think that the story is actually responding to something else. It is all too easy for Gibson to mock the "gee-whiz" futurism and art-deco stylings of Golden Age science fiction. After all, these visions were already explicitly exploded and rejected, several decades before Gibson, by the New Wave science fiction writers of the 1960s (Clute 2020). More broadly, both the radical social movements of the 1960s and the counterculture more generally made these earlier futuristic visions untenable. The most surreal moment of Gibson's story comes when his narrator hallucinates a heterosexual couple from the world of Golden Age science fiction:

> He had his arm around her waist and was gesturing toward the city. They were both in white: loose clothing, bare legs, spotless white sun shoes… They were Heirs to the Dream. They were white, blond, and they probably had blue eyes. They were American… They were smug, happy, and utterly content with themselves and their world.
>
> (Gibson 1986a)

Nothing and no one could be more out of place, and more ridiculous, in post-1960s multicultural America. Even Republicans no longer believe in this — though they express a considerable degree of *ressentiment* about its passing.

But changes in style and sensibility are not the same thing as changes in deep social structures. The radical social movements of the 1960s profoundly affected the former, but were only partially successful as to the latter. The civil rights, women's liberation, and gay and lesbian liberation movements of that decade are still incomplete projects today (Freedman 2002). And the hacker and computer subculture that has its roots in that decade, and whose technological efflorescence coincided with Gibson's earliest writing in the 1980s, has also failed to deliver much of what it promised (Wiener 2018). These are the failures that really drive our current sense of being unable to imagine the future — something that is mourned by both Jameson and Gibson. But in a way, the situation we face today is even worse. Instead of becoming obsolete like those 1930s fantasies did, the hopes and dreams of the 1960s were taken up, on the level of style and sensibility, by the very corporate culture that destroyed their deeper possibilities. Instead of falling into desuetude, these visions have become entirely hegemonic. They have evidently been co-opted and denatured, but in that form they have been deployed throughout social space. The result is something that William Gibson himself calls *future fatigue*: "All through the 20th century we constantly saw the 21st century invoked… How often do you hear anyone invoke the 22nd century? Even saying it is unfamiliar to us. We've come to not have a future" (Spicer 2020).

What we might well call the Gibson continuum is figured in the imposing yet sleekly minimalist forms of mid-twentieth-century modernist architecture, art, and design that provide the background for Gibson's Sprawl trilogy (Gibson 1984, 1986b, 1988), as well as for dystopian cyberpunk works by others from the 1980s all the way to today. In these books and movies, the dense urban-design stylings of corporate power continue to dominate our fantasies of the future — even when, as in so many cyberpunk narratives, the office buildings have decayed into slums and have been overfilled with trash and clutter. Ridley Scott's canonical cyberpunk movie *Blade Runner* (Scott 1982) — made at the same time as Gibson's earliest writing, and whose look and feel Gibson greatly admired and even envied for being "better than what I myself had been able to imagine" (Wallace-Wells 2011) — remains the visual paradigm for futuristic imaginings today, more than forty years later. It seems as we cannot imagine a future beyond the cyberpunk model,even though the model is out of date (Walker-Emig 2018; Semley 2019).

The reason for this impasse is that the intensified present in which we live today is grounded in an odd superposition of future and past. We have exorcised the semiotic ghosts of Golden Age science fiction, but we are still haunted by the semiotic ghosts of cyberpunk just as Gibson and Scott presented them almost half a century ago. These stylings seem simultaneously worn out and yet still ahead of us. Such is the ambivalence of our post-human condition (Hayles 1999). On the plus side, technological innovation has been so successful that we take things for granted that were not even imagined by cyberpunk science fiction. Gibson himself has ruefully acknowledged that in his 1984 novel, *Neuromancer* (Gibson 1984), even as he mapped out the dimensions of cyberspace (a word that Gibson first defined and popularized — Wired Staff 2009), "There are no cell phones" — the idea never occurred to him (Cavanaugh 2011). At the same time, despite conservative opposition, gender roles and sexual positions have also opened up to an extent that exceeds what seemed possible forty years ago — something that is evident in the recent flood of queer and trans science fiction (Lothian 2015). Today, bodies and machines alike are in the process of being radically transformed and even combined in exciting new ways. As Donna Haraway put it in her "Cyborg Manifesto," written and published at around the same time as *Blade Runner* and Gibson's earliest fiction, "The boundary between science fiction and social reality is an optical illusion… We are all chimeras, theorized and fabricated hybrids of machine and organism; in short, we are cyborgs" (Haraway 1991).

At the same time, however, alongside all these transformations, our society has failed to exhibit any meaningful changes in terms of class relations. If anything, inequality has grown since the 1960s (Horowitz et al. 2020). We are still dominated by the 1 percent (Stiglitz 2011), or more accurately, by the 1 percent of the 1 percent (Gold 2017). More and more people, especially younger people, are falling out of the once vaunted middle class and experiencing poverty and precarity (OECD 2019). Despite all those technological innovations, the economy shows only sluggish growth, and is largely stalled — a stasis that is sometimes called secular stagnation (Summers 2020). Profits are increasingly captured and accumulated through financialization (Lapavitsas and Mendieta-Muñoz 2016). Companies use their surplus cash much more for stock buybacks than for productive investment (Lazonick et al. 2020). Brutal multinational corporations deploy their cool new technologies — from high-frequency trading (Lewis 2014) through data aggregation and surveillance (Zuboff 2020) — in order to capture ever more power and wealth. But behind the sparkling I of high-tech and cool gadgets, the vast majority of us face a crumbling infrastructure and a declining standard of living. This is how we are still caught up today in the world envisaged by decades-old cyberpunk. As Gibson himself famously proclaimed, the future is "already here," but it is "unevenly distributed" (Quote Investigator 2012).

All That Is Solid Melts into Air

The cynical nihilism of classical cyberpunk, focused on the totalitarian power of big corporations, is an early version of something that still afflicts us today: the sensibility that Mark Fisher, drawing upon Jameson among others, calls capitalist realism. Fisher defines this as

> the widespread sense that not only is capitalism the only viable political and economic system, but also that it is now impossible even to imagine a coherent alternative to it… It is more like a *pervasive atmosphere*… acting as a kind of invisible barrier constraining thought and action… Over the past thirty years, capitalist realism has successfully installed a "business ontology" in which it is *simply obvious* that everything in society, including healthcare and education, should be run as a business.
>
> (Fisher 2009)

Such a business ontology remains dominant today, despite how often it has failed. Though many of us hoped that the financial crisis of 2008 would, at the very least, put an end to neoliberal governance, this has evidently not been the case. The "invisible barrier" is still there. Our day-to-day lives continue to be regulated — perhaps even more intensely than before — by the mechanisms of market competition, permanent indebtedness, and financial speculation. As Martijn Konings puts it, "Far from a political turning point, the crisis [of 2008] has been the occasion for an entrenchment of neoliberal principles and an extension of its operative mechanisms" (Konings 2018). These principles and mechanisms work to colonize the future by soliciting us — and indeed compelling us — to grasp futurity entirely and exclusively in financial terms. No matter how precarious our situation, and how limited our resources, we are still required to adopt, as Lisa Adkins says, "an entrepreneurial investor stance towards life" (Adkins et al. 2020).

In such conditions, we cannot refuse to speculate upon our own future chances. We are compelled to take upon ourselves the risk of things going wrong—without any support or backup from the larger society. We are transformed into obligatory Nietzscheans, compelled to "love ignorance of the future" (Nietzsche 2001). Nietzsche himself at least had a steady pension, but today we are required to gamble our life savings (assuming we are lucky enough to have them in the first place) as well. Our subjugation to contingency is ensured by the way that every possible outcome is assigned a monetary price, a debt obligation that cannot be evaded. In this way, at the same time as the future is opened up, it is nonetheless colonized by financial logic. The debt society works, according to Maurizio Lazzarato, by

> reducing what will be to what is, that is, reducing the future and its possibilities to current power relations. From this perspective, all financial innovations have but one sole purpose: possessing the future in advance by objectivizing it.
>
> (Lazzarato 2011)

This means that our intense, convoluted, "anticipatory" imaginings have not withered so much as they have been channeled in a very particular manner. But there are different ways of interpreting this situation. Where Lazzarato claims that the future has been emptied out by the accumulation of debt, Adkins replies that what is in fact happening is even worse. Debt obligations do not empty out time, but usher us into a future that is all too full, packed to the gills in advance. "Contemporary debt," as Adkins puts it, "does not destroy time by tying populations to futures that can never be their own"; rather, it "opens out a universe in which they are tied to the indeterminate movements of speculative time" (Adkins 2018). If time were truly emptied out, I might at least be able to rest. But instead, as Lewis Carroll's Red Queen says, "it takes all the running you can do, to keep in the same place."

This is why (to give the basic premise of capitalist realism, as stated by Fisher) "it is easier to imagine the end of the world than it is to imagine the end of capitalism" (Fisher 2009). However, no such end of the world is available to me. Instead, the pressures of speculative time compel me to scramble without respite. I face a hectic future in which I must continually stake my "human capital" (Bowles and Gintis 1975) on unpredictable outcomes, even as I frantically juggle my payment schedules in order to continue servicing my debts (Adkins 2018). As Adkins describes this situation,

> The schedules of securitized debt are geared to *payment* rather than repayment… calculations of household debt loading and debt schedules hinge on… the capacity of debtors to *service* rather than repay debt… The rewriting of the relationship between debt and income is evidenced in loans and mortgages outrunning working — and lived — lives… and in debt loading which, if indexed to current income, is impossible to repay.

We cannot imagine the end of capitalism, therefore, because we are forced, at the cost of our lives, to actively contribute to its continuation. I cannot ever drop out of this society (as some people in the 1960s imagined doing), because I cannot ever definitively pay off all my debts. I am continually required to service these debts until the day I die. The one and only thing we can be assured of is that, however risky and unknowable the future may be, and whatever form it may eventually take, the rich will continue to get richer — at our expense. How can we doubt that science fiction provides us with a mimetic account of precisely this situation? Far from demonstrating "our incapacity to imagine the future," science fiction all too cogently grasps the particular sort of futurity that we imagine, and already experience, today.

I can put the same point in a somewhat different way. One common account of the modern condition is that all foundations, and all points of reference, are disappearing. As Marx and Engels already put it in 1848: under capitalism, "all that is solid melts into air" (Marx and Engels 1888). This is even more deliriously true today. The social processes that dominate our lives defy straightforward representation because they seem so curiously ungrounded. My permanent state of indebtedness, for instance, is a kind of abstraction. It is everywhere and nowhere all at once; I will never be able to pay off my debt, and will only roll it over again and again. I do not even owe my debt to any identifiable creditor. Instead, this debt has been divided up into *tranches*: which is to say, it has been split and formatted into a multitude of arcane financial instruments that circulate deliriously through the financial markets, leveraged over and over again, by one investor after another, without being grounded in any "underlying" (Ayache 2010). What Marx calls the "self-valorization of capital" (Marx 1976), its ineluctable transformation of everything it encounters into more of itself, appears today in the form of finance as an ostensibly self-replicating process, unmoored from any substantial basis. This is what leads theorists like the late Jean Baudrillard to proclaim the "dissolution" of referentiality, of value, and indeed of "the social" altogether (Baudrillard 2017).

I am hesitant, however, to go along with Baudrillard all the way. The situation of our lives today is cognitively estranging, to be sure. I cannot actually point to the operations of global finance, just as I cannot actually point to the process of encroaching environmental catastrophe. The global financial network is an example of what recent Marxist theorists call a *real abstraction*. As Alberto Toscano explains it, a real abstraction is irreducible to any concrete particulars, and yet it must be understood, "not as a mere mask, fantasy, or diversion, but as a force operative in the world" (Toscano 2008). Similarly, climate change is an example of what the ecocritic Timothy Morton calls a *hyperobject*: something that is "massively distributed in time and space relative to humans," to such an extent that it cannot be apprehended sensuously, or all at once (Morton 2013). Climate change, no less than finance, is a real force operative in the world, even though, as Morton puts it, "nowhere in the long list of catastrophic weather events… will you find global warming" itself (Morton 2013). All of the world's concrete referents seem to have dissolved into the whirlpools of financial and ecological dislocation. And indeed, capital accumulation and environmental destruction are themselves so closely intertwined that it seems impossible to pull them apart (Olsen and Dorman 2019). Things in the world today are massively interconnected; but this also means that they are increasingly fragile, contingent, and unstable.

This situation is itself a crucial referent for both theoretical and science-fictional discourse. It would be a category error to conclude, along with Baudrillard, that the referent *as such* has somehow disappeared. Obviously, particular concrete referents have been volatilized: capital takes the form of digital code instead of physical stuff, and rainforests are burnt to ash. More generally, systems of power and control are so widely diffused throughout society that it is hard to locate them at any one particular place. Such is the order of simulacra described by Baudrillard, in which the effect of reality

> is produced from miniaturized cells, matrices, and memory banks, models of control — and it can be reproduced an indefinite number of times from these. It no longer needs to be rational, because it no longer measures itself against either an ideal or negative instance. It is no longer anything but operational.
>
> (Baudrillard 1994)

But is this proliferation of empty signs really "no longer of the order of representation," as Baudrillard maintains (Baudrillard 1994)? I have the same problems with Baudrillard as I do with all the other great modernist and postmodernist opponents of representation. There is no doubt that, as Deleuze also says, the old forms of confinement are breaking down. They are being replaced by a system in which "business, training, and military service [are] coexisting metastable states of a single modulation, a sort of universal transmutation" (Deleuze 1995). This delirious whirl of metamorphoses, or of simulacra "produced by totally different means than those at work within the model" (Deleuze 1990), is itself a situation that cries out to be represented. To be sure, the world system at this point is "operational" rather than substantial. But that is precisely why we must seek to grasp and model its operations. Science fiction today performs the work of a forensic accountant, like Martin Hench in Cory Doctorow's barely future novel *Red Team Blues* (Doctorow 2023). Even when wealth, and the powers enabled by that wealth, are volatilized into digital form, they still leave traces behind. And it is still possible to follow those traces, and to reconstruct a representation of what they are doing.

In short, we can say of this vacuous over-fullness — in which everything is modulated and transmuted over and over again — much the same thing that the great modernist poet Wallace Stevens says of the phenomenological emptiness that he himself so strenuously sought after: "The absence of the imagination had / Itself to be imagined… all this / Had to be imagined as an inevitable knowledge, / Required, as a necessity requires" (Stevens 1997).

Cognitively Estranging Referents

The neoliberal re-ordering of the future is the key to Chu's claim that science fiction is a mimetic discourse. Realist fiction, like empiricist philosophy, has little trouble with what Chu calls *concrete objects*, such as "softballs, paintbrushes, oak leaves, dimes, apple blossoms, almonds, and pencils" (Chu 2010). But it is a much more difficult task to represent things that are not available to immediate, empirical experience, or to what Alfred North Whitehead calls "perception in the mode of presentational immediacy" (Whitehead 1927a). Such things cannot be grasped "clearly and distinctly," as Descartes would have wished (Descartes 1985). Chu finds "the dynamic complexity that distinguishes the cognitively estranging referent" in such phenomena as

> the sublime (e.g., outer space), virtual entities (cyberspace), realities imperceptible to the human brain (the fourth dimension), phenomena whose historical contexts have not yet

> been fully realized (robot rights), and events so overwhelming that they escape immediate experience (shell shock).
> (Chu 2010)

All these things, just like real abstractions and hyperobjects, are strangely intangible, such that we only become aware of them indirectly, through their effects. And yet they are altogether real, if we understand this claim according to Philip K. Dick's famous definition: "Reality is that which, when you stop believing in it, doesn't go away" (Dick 1996).

In contrast to how relatively easy it is to describe a pencil, "massively complex representational and epistemological work" is necessary in order to make these less immediate, more complex, and further distributed referents "available both for representation and for understanding" (Chu 2010). Nonetheless, Chu insists that the gulf is not insurmountable. "The difference between the representability of the pencil and the representability of any other referreebo difference in degree," and not in kind. Even in the more difficult cases, linguistic representation is able to register "greater similitude than dissimilitude between referent and representational text" (Chu 2010).

For that matter, Chu remarks, "all reality is to some degree cognitively estranging." Even the most concrete objects are not *entirely* amenable to representation; a distance always remains between the thing and the language that refers to it. It is finally impossible "to represent the pencil in all its unmediated pencilness" (Chu 2010). This is not a problem in most cases. A partial designation that gives us a "recognizably mimetic representation of the pencil" is good enough for most intents and purposes (Chu 2010). Mimesis does not mean identity; similitude only emerges against a background of unlikeness. We know that reality contains or includes

> an infinite number of cognitively estranging objects and phenomena… Insofar as all referents are to some degree

> cognitively estranging, all representation is to some degree science-fictional or "knowledge-fictional."
>
> (Chu 2010)

But this is not an argument against the very possibility of representation; rather, it is an argument *for* the usefulness, and indeed the necessity, of science-fictional strategies of extrapolation, speculation, and fabulation. It is precisely through such strategies that we are best able to approach the elusive referents of which the world is so largely composed.

In this way, Chu proposes what is, in effect, a speculative realist theory of science fiction — even though she wrote her book before the advent of speculative realism, and hence never uses the term (for all I know, she might not assent to being classified in this way). As the speculative realist philosopher Graham Harman puts it, we can always make "a more or less adequate model" of a thing, for particular purposes, so long as we remember that "none of this information" about a thing adds up to the actual thing itself (Harman 2015). Chu, like Harman and other speculative realist thinkers, insists that reality is "ontologically prior to representation"; things exist apart from our relation to them. At the same time, Chu also "accept[s] as a postulate the capacity of language to reflect" that independent, pre-existing reality — at least to a certain extent (Chu 2010). Reflection, or mimesis, is not entirely futile; but since things exist prior to, and outside of, our relations with them, mimesis is also never total or complete.

This is not far from Harman's assertion that "the real is something that cannot be known, only loved" (Harman 2012b). Although we cannot fully comprehend any object in all its depths, we can still *allude* to it. Allusion is necessary, regardless of whether we seek to instrumentalize the object alluded to or simply to cherish it. Harman says that "philosophy itself [i]s the great art of allusion to a real that cannot manifest itself directly" (Harman 2018a). For Chu and Harman alike, language points to a referent, or mirrors a referent, or performs a mimesis of a referent, even though it never manages to wholly encompass that referent. This is why Chu insists that "science fiction is powered by *lyric* or *poetic* forces" — which is to say, by figurative language (Chu 2010). Figuration for Chu, like allusion for Harman, is a way of *pointing to*, or *approaching*, and thereby giving a certain limited account of, a referent that is real in its own right, and which *for this very reason* ultimately escapes our grasp.

We should never underestimate the sheer wildness and diversity of those cognitively estranging referents that lure us and allure us beyond ourselves, at once encouraging and resisting our mimetic attraction towards them. I use my words here advisedly, taking *lure* from Whitehead and *allure* from Harman. Whitehead describes hypothetical propositions about situations in the world as "lures for feelings" (Whitehead 1978). Harman describes allure as a seductive attraction that happens when a thing seems to offer us something more than its own "specific qualities" such that it "makes quantum leaps from one state of reality into the next by generating a new relation between objects" (Harman 2005). Both of these words indicate an aesthetic attraction that brings us beyond and outside ourselves, even though it cannot be resolved into possession or full comprehension.

Science fiction in Chu's account is highly self-conscious about its own representational strategies. And yet, at the same time, science fiction refocuses our attention away from our own efforts at conceptualization and lures or allures us instead towards the weirdness of things themselves. Even the avowedly Kantian science fiction that I have written about in a previous book (Shaviro 2021) ultimately draws our attention away from our own categories of thought and towards what those categories are unable to encompass. That is to say, science fiction orients me towards what the speculative realist philosopher Quentin Meillassoux calls "a Great Outdoors that is not a correlate of my thought." The crucial move of Meillassoux's philosophy is "*to put back into the thing itself what we mistakenly took to be an incapacity in thought*" (Meillassoux 2008). Chu does something similar when she turns Suvin (and Jameson) right side up, putting cognitive estrangement back into the things themselves instead of taking this estrangement as just a symptom of our own incapacity to grasp those things. Once again, we need to return from the difficulties of reference to the difficulties intrinsic to the things that are being referenced. For it is those things themselves, rather than in our representations of them, that are actually (to resituate Jameson's words) "reflexive and self-undermining and deconstructing affairs."

Though Chu gives primacy to science fiction, her argument extends to other fantastic genres as well. They are all radically mimetic, and to a far greater extent than realist fiction ever manages to be. Chu characterizes horror, for instance, as "a type of science-fictional mimesis whose cognitively estranging referent is the occulted-yet-irrepressible unconscious." Similarly, she characterizes fantasy as "a type of science-fictional mimesis whose cognitively estranging referent is the prodigious working of the human imagination" (Chu 2010). Where realist fiction stays within a much narrower ambit, these fantastic genres extend towards the extreme limits of mimesis itself — which is to say, towards the extreme limits of what it is possible to think. Science fiction and other fantastic genres stretch out towards (but never entirely reach) such referents as "the infinitely remote future, the infinitely remote past, and whatever lies on the other side of death" (Chu 2010).

Mimesis is always in process, always pushing towards cognitively estranged realities, and therefore always incomplete. This is why science fiction offers us, not predictions of the future, but representations of *futurity*. The future itself is the unattainable referent that science fiction can never actually reach. Once we have grasped a particular moment, it is no longer future but already the present, and then it immediately recedes into the past. Similarly, fantasy offers us representations of pastness, pointing towards its ultimate, unattainable referent, the irrecoverable past itself. And horror offers us — in the words of Maurice Blanchot — "alas, not death, but the eternal torments of Dying" (Blanchot 1989). Death itself is the ultimate, unattainable referent of horror fiction, one that looms just past the end of the story, but which cannot be adequately represented within the text itself.

Mimesis continually strives towards these ultimate limits, but it is never able to attain them. The task of representation is therefore both endless and recursive. This is most evident in the fantastic genres; in naturalistic writing, it tends to be dissimulated. In science fiction, fantasy fiction, and horror fiction alike, we find ourselves on the verge of states that are too cognitively estranging to ever be reached. This is most obvious in the case of horror. The endless task of mimesis condemns me, like the narrator of Kathe Koja's amazing horror novel *The Cipher*, "to roil in the aching stink of my own emptiness forever" (Koja 1991; see my discussion in Shaviro 2016b). But such situations are dramatized in science fiction as well. James Tiptree Jr.'s short story "The Man Who Walked Home" is about a researcher who triggers a worldwide cataclysm when he is sent into the future and then recalled back to his original time. As the story moves forwards through the centuries, the researcher makes brief appearances "in the annual instances in which his course [returning from the future to his original present] intersects our planet's orbit." He walks backwards in time interminably, even as time for everyone else moves inexorably forwards (Tiptree 1990).

As Chu insists, all phenomena are cognitively estranging to one degree or another, and "the intricate process… by which the referent becomes available for representation in a work of science fiction" is "itself a cognitively estranging phenomenon" in its own right (Chu 2010). This is why we will never be done with mimesis.

Synesthesia and Catachresis

Seo-Young Chu offers us many examples of science fiction's tendency to literalize metaphors and other "lyric figures" (Chu 2010). Science fiction applies literary and imaginative conceits to actual worldly situations, and then it tracks the consequences of these applications across space and time. In this way, it presents things to us with a kind of double vision, depicting actuality and potentiality at once. Gilbert Simondon's word *disparation* literally refers to the situation in which, although the images seen by our left and right eyes are different from one another, and therefore "not completely superposable," nonetheless these two images "are grasped together as a system," allowing for "a new dimension" to emerge: "the layering of depths of field" in stereoscopic, three-dimensional vision. More generally, Simondon refers to the way that "signification" emerges out of the tension between disparate presentations — or even between different and incompatible orders of magnitude (Simondon 2020).

Kim Stanley Robinson uses a similar metaphor to describe the effects of science fiction. He suggests that

> science fiction works by a double action… Think of the glasses that you put on at a 3D movie. Those special glasses have one lens showing you one thing and the other lens showing you another thing, slightly different. And your brain puts together a 3D view from these.
>
> So one lens of science fiction is a real attempt to imagine a possible future. The other lens is a metaphor for the way things are right now. What you get when the two coalesce is a vision of historical time, cast into the future. Like a trajectory of deep time.
>
> (Plotz 2020)

In other words, science fiction generates a kind of stereoscopic vision by exploring the tension of the split between present and future, or between actuality and potentiality. It takes the present moment of the actual world that we literally inhabit and extends it metaphorically. At the same time, it literalizes the potentialities of a future that we can only evoke figuratively and hypothetically. Actuality and potentiality are transformed into one another, and a higher dimension emerges as a result. Robinson's own novel *The Ministry for the Future* plays explicitly between these two registers. Robinson starts the novel by figuratively expanding out from our current, actually existing circumstances. He extrapolates from present-day climate conditions into a truly horrific vision of catastrophe: an account, grounded in naturalistic detail, of how a heatwave only slightly worse than ones that have actually occurred in recent years could lead to twenty million human deaths in the course of just a few days: "The worst week in human history" (Robinson 2020).

This hyperbolic punch to the gut is held in counterpoint with wonky, detailed explanations of scientific and political-economic proposals for alleviating global warming and restoring the planetary environment. These proposals range from blockchain-regulated financial reforms, through experiments in geo-engineering, all the way to terrorist assassinations of the CEOs of companies that use fossil fuels. None of these proposals is sufficient on its own, and they do not even fit together very well. It often seems as if Robinson is putting forth every single possibility that he can think of in the hope that at least some of them will work. The uncertain potentialities of the future are actualized as scientific experiments and bureaucratic procedures. Robinson carefully navigates his way between present and future, and between actual and potential, superimposing a utopian horizon of hope over a dystopian warning such that both of these dimensions register at once.

Science fiction often multiplies dimensions in this way, holding them in tension with one another. Many of Seo-Young Chu's examples of science fiction's literalization of poetic figures involve just such an expansion. For instance, Chu notes how "*synesthesia* — the poetic description of one kind of sensory experience via the words that ordinarily describe another — is routinely literalized in SF as a *paranormal sensorium*" (Chu 2010). This is a particularly rich example. Although Chu describes synesthesia as a poetic figure, it does in fact also have a literal meaning. It is a neurological trait experienced by a small number of people "in which a triggering stimulus evokes the automatic, involuntary, affect-laden, and conscious perception of a sensory or conceptual property that differs from that of the trigger" (Cytowic 2018). For instance, particular letters and other shapes may give rise to particular colors, or particular sounds may give rise to particular tastes. This sensory transference is affective before it is cognitive; it is not an intellectual delusion, but a heightened *experience*, a special mode of feeling.

Even though very few people are actual synesthetes, more-diffuse experiences of sensory and emotional spillover are common. The metaphorical or figurative use of synesthesia is correspondingly quite widespread. Invoking the "paranormal sensorium" of the synesthete is a way to enrich and concretize our descriptions of proprioceptive and allover experience. We don't hear music just with our ears, for instance: we feel its physical vibrations, not to mention its emotional resonances, throughout of the body. When I listen to Parliament-Funkadelic, my body vibrates in tune with the bass. I am driven to dance, even when sitting down. Or, to give an extremely different example, when I listen to a piece by Morton Feldman, the barely discernible tones seem to seep through every part of the room, as if they were subtle visual and tactile presences, as much as sonic ones.

When the rock critic Robert Christgau writes, "If the blues drove on like a northbound locomotive, the [New York] Dolls' raucous antiswing promised all the deliverance of the BMT at rush hour" (Christgau 1978), he is not talking just about lyrics involving trains. Rather, he is translating the music into tactile and proprioceptive terms. The blues, for all the pain they express, also deliver a sense of joy through escape, of fleeing to the North as runaway slaves did. This journey is transformative in its own right, regardless of the final destination. The New York Dolls, young White men, appropriate this Black tradition, both for good and for ill. Their "antiswing" replaces the pulsating groove, and invitation to dance, of so much Black music — "It Don't Mean a Thing (If It Ain't Got That Swing)" — with a relentless wrenching back and forth in place: what later came to be called *pogoing* (though the actual history of this dance style is disputed). The Dolls make you feel a kind of schizophrenic implosion, at once exhilarating and exhausting. This is both an expression of their heavily fraught urban environment and an attempt to defy it and overcome it. This music came from New York City in the 1970s: a time of financial and existential distress, but one that also gave rise to an explosion of wild creativity, crossing all boundaries of race and gender. If the rural blues envision a lonely locomotive at night, pulling far away into the distance, the Dolls rather imagine a New York City subway car, shaking as it rushes from station to station in the dark, and tightly packed with non-communicating bodies.

All these instances are almost science-fictional already. It is only a small further step to the cyberpunk world of Pat Cadigan's short story "Pretty Boy Crossover," in which the sensory overload of music and video in fashionable dance clubs opens a portal to the digital realm:

> Once you've distilled something to pure information, it just can't be reconstituted in a less efficient form… There may be no more exalted a form of existence than to live as sentient information.
>
> (Cadigan 1989)

Such a sublime condition is anything but peaceful, however. You are isolated in a bubble of majestic solitude; but at the same time you are compelled to be always visible, always available to everyone, always interactive and responsive. You becomethe one being watched, instead of the one watching. The nameless protagonist of Cadigan's story ends up fleeing the overload of the club and rejecting the offer of digital immortality (Cadigan 1989). Where Cadigan traces a route from music to science fiction, music critics Roy Christopher and Eric Weisbard follow the inverse path, showing us how cyberpunk science fiction's promiscuous, multisensory mix-and-match aesthetic feeds in to hip hop (Christopher 2019) and to indie rock (Weisbard 2021).

Synesthesia is also invoked metaphorically in order to give a more capacious account of our perceptive and affective potentialities. Oliver Sacks calls synesthesia "an essential, and fascinating, part of the human experience. Indeed, it may well be the basis and inspiration for much of human imagination and metaphor" (cited in Cytowic 2018). Marshall McLuhan invokes synesthesia in order to explain the changing "ratios of sense perceptions" that mold the shape of our experience (McLuhan and Fiore 1967). He argues that, starting in the twentieth century, "electric technology dethrones the visual sense and restores us to the dominion of synesthesia, and the close interinvolvement of the other senses." An "audile-tactile" sensibility replaces the old linear, visual one (McLuhan 1964). The film theorist Vivian Sobchack similarly proposes that cinema stimulates not only sight and hearing but — through a process of "cross-modal transfer" — our other senses as well. Synesthesia, she says, allows us to express "the complexity and richness of the more general bodily experience that grounds our particular experience [of aesthetic states]" (Sobchack 2004). The philosopher Brian Massumi also cites studies of "cross-modal transfer" to show how aesthetic experience happens in the "*between* of different senses." Massumi then further pushes this in-between to the point at which aesthetic experience must be understood as "amodal," irreducible to the separations distinguishing the senses from one another (Massumi 2011).

All these thinkers invoke synesthesia in order to express the ways that aesthetic experience (in both meanings of the term: that having to do with the senses, and that having to do with art in particular) goes well beyond the traditional empiricist account, as in Locke and Hume, of the clear and distinct perception of atomistically separate ideas, impressions, or sense-data. But where poetry and philosophy speak of synesthesia metaphorically, in order to describe resonances among the various senses, science fiction re-literalizes these metaphors. It moves from heightened sensory experiences to mutations of the sensorium itself. Chu notes that "sensory hyperstimulation is virtually ubiquitous in science fiction"; she cites numerous examples of such "sublime sensory excess," from authors as varied as Jules Verne, J. G. Ballard, Nalo Hopkinson, Mary Doria Russell, and Clark Ashton Smith (Chu 2010). Chu also mentions the related category of "extraordinary intersubjectivIty," in which a heightened sensitivity breaks down the separations between different selves. She cites, among other examples, the sensory excess depicted in Alfred Bester's *The Stars My Destination* (Bester 1956), the practice of *grokking* in Robert Heinlein's *Stranger in a Strange Land* (Heinlein 1961), and the *hyperempathy*, or involuntarily sharing of other people's pain, suffered by Lauren Olamina, the protagonist of Octavia Butler's novels *Parable of the Sower* (Butler 1993) and *Parable of the Talents* (Butler 1998). In all these cases, internal, subjective conditions — that are usually just alluded to or evoked metaphorically — get concretized as "ontological features of narrative worlds" (Chu 2010).

Such transformations are all the more important in that the sensory excess figured by synesthesia is not just an inner subjective experience. Often it is an objective and extrinsically generated condition first of all. Interinvolvement, feedback, resonance, and psychedelic overload are actual processes in the world; they should not be dismissed merely as artifacts of how our minds work, or as effects of drugs and mental breakdowns. As Deleuze and Guattari recognized half a century ago, these seemingly schizophrenic symptoms are in fact materially produced by industrial and post-industrial capitalism. It is no wonder that, as Chu notes, "globalization is often imagined as a paranormal phenomenon, a supernatural force beyond human control" (Chu 2010, citing Gulick 2007). The contemporary world system exceeds our powers of visualization (as Jameson and many others have insisted) because it is composed of so many diverse layers, all densely interconnected, intensely obtrusive, and massively overdetermined. Such a world cries out to be described in hyperbolic, science-fictional terms.

It therefore makes sense to think that I might need to be endowed with a "paranormal sensorium" — one that is synesthetically enhanced and expanded — in order to apprehend this world with any accuracy, or to more than an extremely limited extent. The main characters of William Gibson's early Sprawl trilogy are computer "cowboys," who can only grasp the "unthinkable complexity" of cyberspace because they are "jacked in" to it with cranial cables (Gibson 1984, 1986b, 1988). In a number of novels, most notably *Ubik*, Philip K. Dick imagines cutthroat corporate competition in terms of incessant battles between telepathic or precognitive "psis" and the "inertials" who seek to neutralize their powers (Dick 1969). In Charles Stross's novel *Accelerando*, AI-generated financial operations have become so complex that human beings cannot understand them, let alone participate in them, "without dehumanizing cognitive surgery" (Stross 2005; see the discussion in Shaviro 2009).

Fabulations like these are necessary in a world where linear chains of cause and effect give way to complexly overdetermined situations. In such conditions, as the philosophers Stephen Mumford and Rani Lill Anjum put it in their conceptualization of causality, "effects are typically produced by many powers working with each other or against each other" (Mumford and Anjum 2011). In order to capture this multiplicity, science fiction tends not only to depict synesthesia on the level of plot and character but also to be a form of synesthetic expression in its own right. This is why it is so often filled, to the point of overload, with neologisms, unexplained contexts, and massive info dumps. It is only through excesses of this sort that science fiction can strive to be — in Lenin's famous phrase — "as radical as reality itself" (Beaumont et al. 2007).

Seo-Young Chu makes her own version of this observation when she notes that, beyond its use of specific literary figures like synesthesia, "science fiction as a whole constitutes a literalization of *catachresis*" (Chu 2010). This is a deliberately paradoxical formulation, since catachresis is most commonly defined as an abuse of metaphor, one that violates accepted linguistic usage to such an extent that it no longer has any referent or literal meaning at all. For this reason, catachresis is favored by deconstructionist thinkers like Jacques Derrida (Derrida 1982) and Gayatri Spivak (Spivak 1993). Chu herself, however, explains catachresis by quoting Dr Samuel Johnson's famous description of metaphysical poetry as a kind of writing in which "the most heterogeneous ideas are yoked by violence together" (Chu 2010, citing Johnson 1779). Chu then goes on to give examples of science-fiction works in which such violent heterogeneity is literalized and narrativized. In Robert Louis Stevenson's *Strange Case of Dr Jekyll and Mr Hyde*, "two incongruous selves" share one body (Stevenson 1886). In

Joanna Russ's *The Female Man*, the same woman exists in different forms in different alternative worlds. Russ literalizes the gender binary (male/female) that is socially normative in our own society by treating it as the oppressive physical and psychological incongruity that it actually is (Russ 1975). In all these cases, the heterogeneity and incongruity belongs to the referent itself, rather than just to the language being used to represent it. Dr Johnson sees the violent yoking together of incompatible terms as a rhetorical feature used by a school of poetry that he dislikes. But in science fiction, this cognitive and affective dissonance is concretized as ontological fact, so that it becomes the very basis of the narrative. This once again exemplifies Chu's overall argument that science fiction locates cognitive estrangement in the world that it describes, and to which it refers, rather than just in its own form of linguistic expression.

Indeed, this ontologization of catachresis is the reason why world-building plays such an important role in science fiction and other speculative genres. The world depicted in a science-fiction narrative is often more important than the characters and the plot; only the world of the narrative can provide the characters and plot with a rationale. The centrality of world-building explains why multiple authors can write stories set in a common fictional world, as in the Metatropolis series by John Scalzi and others (Scalzi et al. 2010 and following), or the *Wild Cards* universe curated by George R. R. Martin (Martin 1987 and following) — not to mention the hundreds of *Star Trek* novels that have been published (Wikipedia 2021). The centrality of world-building is also what allows writers to write novelizations set in the worlds of computer games (for instance, Shirley 2011; Watts 2011; Valente 2018). Conversely, computerized role-playing games have themselves been extrapolated from such richly imagined worlds as those of Frank Herbert's *Dune* (Herbert 1965) and J. R. R. Tolkien's *Lord of the Rings* trilogy (Tolkien 1954–1955).

Fans often tend to be preoccupied with the internal consistency of imaginary worlds. But just as science fiction in general works by paradoxically literalizing figurations of situations that defy literal description, so science-fictional world-building involves naturalizing catachrestic discrepancies. Some writers of an experimental bent deliberately foreground the shifting inconsistencies of their fictional worlds, as M. John Harrison does in his *Viriconium* series (Harrison 2007). But even more conventional science-fiction worlds are built around initial, formative disparities, just as pearls are built around irritants in an oyster's flesh. Both the "one ring" in Tolkien and the "spice" in Herbert work in this way; they are foundational exceptions, or discrepancies, that ground the otherwise coherent fictional worlds whose logics they violate. This may once again sound like a deconstructionist paradox, but Tolkien's ring and Herbert's spice are best understood, not as *aporias* of Derridian *différance* (Derrida 1982), but rather as Simondonian generative disparities that trigger complex processes of individuation (Simondon 2020). The sheer existence of the ring in Tolkien, or of the spice in Herbert, leads to a cascade of ramifying consequences, conveyed through the twists of an irreversible narrative.

The disparity at the heart of science-fictional world-building is often literalized through the premise of the many-worlds interpretation of quantum mechanics (which arguably works better as a science-fiction trope than it does in actual physics — see Ball 2018). In Micaiah Johnson's *The Space Between Worlds*, for instance, the protagonist, Cara, is forced to negotiate among multiple versions of herself from scores of slightly different worlds, as well as to mourn her doppelgängers who have not survived (Johnson 2020). In Philip Pullman's *His Dark Materials* trilogy, the protagonists, Lyra and Will, originate from different parallel worlds; they meet by traversing the many worlds, but they are ultimately forced to return to their own separate worlds of origin (Pullman 1995, 1997, 2000). In his novella *Anxiety Is the Dizziness of Freedom*, Ted Chiang offers a meta-reflection on such disparities, tracking what changes and what remains the same across bifurcating life-histories (Chiang 2019).

Chu notes, more generally, that science fiction is often written in a way that "allows all potential scenarios to coexist." This is accomplished by slipping into *lyric time*, the time of an indefinite present, "beyond linear temporality," or "beyond ordinary temporality." This sense of time is sometimes conveyed by nonlinear time shifts in science-fiction narratives; Chu cites the example of Billy Pilgrim in Kurt Vonnegut's *Slaughterhouse-Five*, who "has come unstuck in time" and shuttles between his traumatic experiences during World War II, his life in mid-twentieth-century America, and the time in which he is "displayed naked in a zoo" on an alien planet (Vonnegut 1969). Chu says, however, that lyric time is most commonly evoked grammatically, by the simple present tense: "I walk," rather than "I am walking." The simple present tense is rare in ordinary speech, but it is common in lyric poetry. Science-fiction writers often shift from the narrative past tense to the simple present in order to produce an effect of intensification. The simple present works, Chu says, "to narrate quintessentially SF moments," such as descriptions of "virtual reality, apocalypse, abrupt disembodiment, and prophecy," as well as "liminal and transformative states between human and other-than-human." Unlike more commonly used tenses, "the simple present is fraught with multiple temporal features: timelessness, duration, pastlikeness, futurity." Indeed, the simple present tense "can be understood as a grammar in which are compressed the many hundreds of tense formations" potentially available to the science-fiction writer. In this way, science fiction can "explicitly disrupt our Earth-bound circadian perception of time," or "literalize and externalize the discrepancy between 'objective' time and time as perceived by individual subjectivities" (Chu 2010).

Chu goes on to suggest that, along with its ability to suspend ordinary time, the simple present tense also works "as a grammatical counterpart to the *novum*" in Darko Suvin's theory of science fiction (Chu 2010). But it seems to me that here Chu actually improves upon Suvin, rather than just echoing him. Suvin himself defines the novum as "a totalizing phenomenon or relationship deviating from the author's and implied reader's norm of reality." In using the ugly word *totalizing*, Suvin seems to mean that the novum

> entails a change of the whole universe of the tale, or at least of crucially important aspects thereof (and that it is therefore a means by which the whole tale can be analytically grasped). (Suvin 2016)

Suvin's insistence upon the whole, or the totality, is one-sided and reductive, because it implies that the change produced by the novum is a closed and completed alteration, a result rather than an ongoing process.

Such a deathly conclusion is occasionally depicted in dystopian science fiction, as in the catastrophic ending of Vonnegut's *Cat's Cradle*, which I will discuss in chapter 4 (Vonnegut 1963). But most of the time, the disparity that generates novelty in science fiction remains active, even at the end of the narrative. The story achieves some sort of closure, but the catachrestic *world* of the story does not. Both Simondon and Whitehead understand this. What Simondon calls individuation is never complete. It is a limited and particular process that produces certain definite results. But it does not resolve everything. It always leaves behind a continuing disparity, and therefore, new possibilities for further individuations. For Simondon, the present situation is always *more* than a totality — it is supersaturated and metastable — and the individuated entity is always *less* (Simondon 2020). Similarly, for Whitehead, once an occasion concludes in *concrescence* — the process whereby "whatever is determinable is determined" — it immediately becomes a datum for new occasions, and thereby a source of new "indeterminations" (Whitehead 1978). This is why science fiction does not give us determinate facts or accurate predictions.

This continuing sense of disparity is one of the things that distinguishes science fiction from realist fiction — even recalling, as Chu reminds us, that the distinction is not absolute, but a matter of degree (Chu 2010). Naturalistic fiction does not engage in explicit world-building, because it accepts, and sets itself within, what Whitehead calls "the settled world": the world of things that are already given, or that have already happened (Whitehead

1978). Such fiction is averse to catachresis; like the philosophy of Leibniz in its classical form, it only admits things and events that are mutually consistent, or *compossible* (Brown and Chiek 2016). In contrast, science fiction, like the neo-Leibnizian philosophy of Whitehead, Deleuze, and others, must build its worlds anew, because it explores the uncertain future, rather than the settled past. Science fiction is about what Ernst Bloch calls the "Open Possible" (Bloch 1995), rather than the totality that goes along with necessity. It does not restrict itself to what is (empirically or phenomenologically) given. It presumes that (as Deleuze puts it, extrapolating from and beyond Leibniz) "bifurcations, divergences, incompossibilities, and discord belong to the same motley world," in the form of "a process that at once affirms incompossibilities and passes through them" (Deleuze 1992).

Science fiction, as Chu insists, "operates fully within the realm of mimesis" (Chu 2010). But it also teaches us that this "realm of mimesis" is far stranger than we might previously have imagined. Mimetic representation is a process, a continuing series of actions — and not an outcome encapsulated in a static picture. Mimesis begins in disparity, and it concludes in catachresis — which means that it never really comes to an end, but needs to be taken up again and again. In this way, the creative practice of science fiction is similar to the creative practice of the experimental sciences. Despite the wishes of some high-modernist writers, as well as of some overly rationalistic scientists, there is no final theory of everything (Weinberg 1992), just as there is no supreme fiction (Stevens 1997). Both science fiction and physical science are mimetic practices seeking to illustrate processes and circumstances in the actual world; and both of them discover that these processes and circumstances in the actual world, which they endeavor to model, are themselves already mimetic ones.

4. Literal Fabulations

What Is It Like?

Seo-Young Chu tells us that science fiction refers to things, events, and processes that are cognitively estranging, and which thereby "defy literal representation" (Chu 2010). That is to say, science fiction seeks to perform a mimesis of precisely those referents that most vehemently refuse mimesis, evading our efforts to dominate them and subtracting themselves from our grasp. In order to accomplish this paradoxical task, Chu says, "science fiction is powered by *lyric* or *poetic* forces" (Chu 2010). The language of science fiction is necessarily *figurative*, since its referents are themselves abstract or simulacral: things that cannot be pinned down in ordinary literal terms.

But this is only half of the story. For the project of science fiction is precisely to render as concretely and determinately as possible — which is to say, as literally as possible — the very abstractions and indeterminacies to which it refers. In other words, even as science fiction is lyrical and poetic in its language, it also asks us to take its figurations literally. Chu reminds us that many theorists of science fiction and fantastic literature — including Samuel R. Delany, Ursula Le Guin, and Tzvetan Todorov — have long maintained that such writing solicits us "to apply literal understanding to potentially metaphorical phrases" (Chu 2010). Delany, for instance, famously gives examples of sentences — such as "the door dilated" and "her world exploded" — that can only be metaphorical in realist writing, but which take on literal meaning in science-fiction narratives (Delany 2012). Chu extrapolates a "more extreme" version of this claim:

> Lyric figures are systematically literalized, substantiated, and consolidated in science fiction as ontological features of narrative worlds… Every science-fiction world is a metaphysical conceit literalized as ontological fact within a narrative universe… Within the narrative universe of SF, the literal and the metaphoric share ontological status.
>
> (Chu 2010)

This ontological claim — a claim for the bedrock reality, or the intrinsic literal being, of science-fictional referents — is basic to the genre. In ordinary speech, and in many sorts of written language, a metaphor is conventionally taken to stand in for — to both replace and point to — its literal referent. The metaphor is used in order to convey a richer and more vivid sense of the referent than literal description by itself would be capable of doing. However, this simple schema becomes more and more problematic as the metaphor takes on a life of its own. Indeed, modernist thinkers have tended to argue that metaphoricity is irreducible, and that even seemingly literal statements are always already figurative. Nietzsche famously says that truth is nothing more than

> a mobile army of metaphors, metonymies, anthropomorphisms… Truths are illusions of which we have forgotten that they are illusions, metaphors which have become worn by frequent use and have lost all sensuous vigor.
>
> (Nietzsche 1999)

Jacques Derrida, a century later, similarly argues that so-called literal reference only emerges when an already-existing metaphor "is no longer noticed, and is taken for the proper meaning," through a process of "double effacement" (Derrida 1982). For that matter, the word *literally* is itself often used figuratively in everyday speech to indicate hyperbolic intensification, and therefore non-literalness; despite complaints from the grammar police, this sort of usage has been common for centuries (Baron 2010).

The lesson we can take from this is that *literal* and *figurative* are themselves relative terms, existing along what Chu calls a "spectrum" or a "continuum" (Chu 2010). Where mainstream modernism pushes towards the figurative pole of this spectrum, science fiction moves in the inverse direction, literalizing figurative language in order to expand the scope of reference. As Chu puts it, science fiction explores the space in between "objects completely knowable and objects completely unknowable" (Chu 2010). Or, to shift from the objects themselves (ontology) to the way that we are able to access those objects (epistemology), science fiction explores "the middle condition between an unawakened intellect and a systematic knowledge so complete that there no longer exists anything unexpected" (Chu 2010, quoting Fisher 1998). An "unawakened intellect" is the blank slate presumed by Locke and other classical empiricists; complete and systematic knowledge is the ideal of more rationalist philosophers like Spinoza (in his third kind of cognition) and Hegel (in "Absolute Knowing"). Science fiction rejects both of these extremes; it is concerned, rather, with imperfect and incomplete knowledge about an open and changing world.

Perhaps the quintessential science-fictional situation is the dilemma of *what-is-it-likeness* (Janzen 2011), as in Thomas Nagel's famous question, "What is it like to be a bat?" (Nagel 1991). It is difficult to explain what it is like to be something in particular, because such a state or quality is both indubitably real and yet too vague and impalpable to describe in any concrete, objective way. Even given my Cartesian certitude that I exist, I have no idea how to convey a sense of what it is like to be me. And beyond myself, things get even harder. It would be rude, presumptuous, and condescending for me to ask somebody else what it is like to be them. It would be even worse if I were to ask somebody what it is like to be whatever category (gender, race, religion, and so forth) I think they belong to. And it is flatly impossible for me to ask my dog or my cats what it is like to be them. I can neither grasp a thing's what-is-it-likeness through sensory experience nor deduce it conceptually. This is even the case with regards to myself.

Having experiences is not the same as *explaining* them: this is the harsh truth behind Wittgenstein's observation that the statement "I know what I am thinking" is a category error (Wittgenstein 2009). What-is-it-likeness is something that can *only* be rendered figuratively or poetically.

Science fiction works both to propose figurative accounts of what-is-it-likeness and to literalize these accounts as fully as possible in order to imagine what it might actually be like to be a bat, or an octopus, or a tree, or a sentient alien — or even oneself. For instance, Adrian Tchaikovsky's *Children of Time* series deals with other species of terrestrial origin that — on other planets and in the far future — are uplifted to human-level sentience. The first volume, *Children of Time*, considers what it might be like to be a sentience-augmented Portia spider (Tchaikovsky 2015). The second volume in the series, *Children of Ruin*, similarly considers what it would be like to be a sentience-augmented octopus (Tchaikovsky 2019). The third volume to date, *Children of Memory*, considers a similar level of sentience that is achieved by pairs of corvids (Tchaikovsky 2023). This latter case is an especially intriguing one, since the intelligence and verbal fluency manifested by the pair of birds is not evident in either one of them by itself, separated from its mate. We get a vivid sense of the corvids' what-is-it-likeness as they poke around, gathering data and then collating, synthesizing, and communicating these data. But it is difficult to figure out just *where* all this sensory and cognitive activity takes place. Does consciousness exist in the physically separate brains of each of the two birds? If not, what would it mean for conscious feeling and behavior to arise exclusively from the interactions between them? Tchaikovsky does not answer these questions. But with his portrayals of what-is-it-likeness, he poses them more urgently and with more depth and detail than academic philosophers have usually been able to do.

In saying this, however, I do not mean to issue a blanket condemnation of philosophical discussions. For instance, Eric Schwitzgebel — who is both a philosopher and an occasional published science-fiction author — offers us a wonderful philosophical presentation of a similar thought experiment. He argues, in apparent seriousness, that "if materialism is true, the United States is probably conscious" (Schwitzgebel 2015). If consciousness has an entirely physical basis, he says, then there is no reason why this consciousness should not exist "in spatially distributed group entities." One of the chief theories of consciousness today is integrated-information theory, which claims that "to be conscious… you need to be a single, integrated entity with a large repertoire of highly differentiated states" (Koch 2009). Schwitzgebel notes that "the quantity of visual connectedness among people [in the United States] is similar to the neuronal connectedness within the human brain"; if this is enough for an individual brain to host consciousness, then it should be enough for the country to host it as well (Schwitzgebel 2015).

Another nonhuman sort of what-is-it-likeness is at the center of Sue Burke's *Pax* novels: *Semiosis* (Burke 2018) and *Interference* (Burke 2019). These novels recount the efforts of human settler-colonialists to establish themselves on a planet fifty-six light years away from Earth. The human settlers soon learn that the dominant life-forms on the planet are not other sorts of animals, but rather intelligent plants. The novels explore the plants' perspectives and their what-is-it-likeness as they interact with one another, with the animals that prey upon them, and eventually with the human settlers as well. Such interactions range from Darwinian struggles to the death to various sorts of mutual aid and symbiosis, and include everything in between. The human settlers increasingly recognize and defer to the plants' needs and desires in return for receiving nourishment and protection from them. The plants come to regard human beings as their "service animals," in much the same way as human beings on Earth regard cows, pigs, and sheep, or, for that matter, as plants on earth regard bees and other pollinators. The novels reflect on the degrees of compatibility and understanding that can be achieved among beings whose what-is-it-likeness is so different.

As for human beings unable to access their own what-is-it-likeness, this is a common theme in science fiction. A famous and brilliant example is Alfred Bester's novel *The Demolished Man* (Bester 1953). In the world of this novel, people have access to one another's minds through telepathy; but there are also numerous ruses and blocking mechanisms by which people deflect telepathic inquiries about their mental states. The protagonist, despite being a telepath himself, turns out to be massively deluded about his own motives and experiences. Bester uses many of the alienating techniques of modernist fiction in order to referentially render the oblique nature of this protagonist's experiential consciousness and, more generally, the limits of introspective self-understanding. We learn how what-is-it-likeness is a variable and not entirely transparent category.

More Than at First Sight

What-is-it-likeness is just one example, though an important one, of the things, events, and situations that resist direct representation but which science fiction strives to render through its own means. From the earliest days of modern science fiction, authors like E. E. "Doc" Smith refer to phenomena that are "difficult to describe in words" (Smith 1948) or that "simply cannot be described" (Smith 1950). The texts nonetheless go on to evoke these phenomena, at least hyperbolically and rhetorically. The point is that such entities, events, and situations, difficult as they may be to render in language, are not illusions or mere anthropomorphic projections. They are independent of us, and entirely real in themselves — for all that they resist description. At best, they might evoke the sense of wonder often taken to be crucial to science fiction (Clute et al. 2015). But science fiction seeks, not just to express the sublimity of such spectacles — though it certainly does that — but to explore their ramifications as well. As Isaac Asimov was apparently the first to say (though it has been repeated by many other writers since), the goal of science fiction is not just to predict the existence of a technology like the automobile but to anticipate how the automobile could lead to such phenomena as suburbs and traffic jams (Quote Investigator 2019).

The events and existences fabulated by science fiction may well evade our comprehension, but they are still woven into and through our own reality. They form integral parts, as much as we ourselves do, of the world that we inhabit and experience. Alfred North Whitehead reminds us that "we are instinctively willing to believe that by due attention, more can be found in nature than that which is observed at first sight." He adds that, whether or not we succeed in our efforts to find *more*, in any case, "we will not be content with less" (Whitehead 1920). Isabelle Stengers, commenting upon this passage, notes that the most important thing for Whitehead is precisely that we maintain our "trust in the possibility of finding 'more' in nature than what is observed in it at first glance" (Stengers 2011). Some strains of philosophy, like eliminative materialism, seek to reduce *more* to *less* (Ramsay 2019). But if we maintain our faith that there is in fact always more to be found, our anticipation will be rewarded. Science fiction, with its double strategy of figuration and literalization, is a way of exploring this *more*. It expands the realm of what can be recognized as ontological fact.

There are many ways of attending to this *more* that nature, or society, or technology, or the world as a whole offers us. Often, things offer us a richer range of ramifications than can be expressed in terms of linear chains of cause and effect. Timothy Morton refers to such things as hyperobjects. These, as I have noted before, are objects or processes that are undetectable in and of themselves, but that become indirectly available to us, both affectively and cognitively, through their all-too-evident consequences in our everyday lives (Morton 2013). Morton's main concern, global warming, is such a hyperobject, and so is the incessant valorization of capital. Conversely, even processes and technologies of which we are fully cognizant can nonetheless lead to future outcomes that we do not and cannot anticipate. There is no way to know, for instance, what will result from our increasing ability to edit and rewrite our own genomes and those of other organisms. This is why genetic-engineering scenarios of the most varied sorts are so common in contemporary science fiction. Genetic engineering might well lead to the expansion of human potential; though it would also create problems if access to these new capabilities were not shared equally. Such problems are the focus of Nancy Kress's novel *Beggars in Spain* (Kress 1993). But enhanced technologies for genetic engineering might just as well lead to new forms of crazed consumerism, not to mention new forms of slavery and of terrorism — all of which are envisioned through a comedic lens in Paul Di Filippo's story collection *Ribofunk* (Di Filippo 1996).

We may also find ourselves oppressed, or inspired, by the uncanny subsistence of things that should have long since perished: this is what Mark Fisher, taking up a word invented by Derrida, calls *hauntology* (a neologism that combines *haunting* with *ontology*; the pun works better in French). The present moment fails to be airtight and self-contained. We find ourselves trapped in a "broken time… in which it is no longer possible to securely delimit the present from the past, in which the traces of lost futures unpredictably bubble up to unsettle the pastiche-time of postmodernity" (Fisher 2013). We may also be afflicted by the inverse of this process, when we are haunted in advance by uncertain future prospects. These are what the Romantic poet Percy Bysshe Shelley called "the gigantic shadows which futurity casts upon the present," conveyed in "words which express what they understand not" (Shelley 1988). That is to say, there is *more* in the expression than what we are immediately able to glean from it.

All of these conditions and processes, and many more besides, are difficult to grasp and describe because they involve ruptures of the present moment, displacements away from the here and now. As Walter Benjamin famously put it, the "homogeneous, empty time" to which we are accustomed in capitalist society is broken open, so that instances of *nowness* (*Jetztzeit*) are "blasted out of the continuum of history" (Benjamin 2003). Alas, these interruptions are not necessarily revolutionary and liberating in the way that Benjamin so ardently hoped. In the early twenty-first century, every present moment is filled past bursting, less with Benjamin's "splinters of messianic time" than with violently heterogeneous and non-simultaneous contents of all sorts, whether hauntological or futurological. Clear and distinct instants give way to durations that are "smeared over time" (as the physicists sometimes say: Martin 2011). Even our most banal everyday experiences are cognitively estranging because they are *dyschronic*, as in Fisher's notion of "broken time."These moments feel both overfilled and oddly empty, because they are composed of non-contemporary occasions that should not be able to happen together but which nonetheless seem to hang together anyway. It is no surprise, therefore, that time travel is such a common trope in science fiction. Indeed, David Wittenberg argues that time-travel stories literalize the basic mechanisms of all narrative. In such stories, "the narratological structure of time itself emerges" by being "rendered literal." This most often takes the form of what Wittenberg calls *hyperspace-time*: a three-dimensional spatial volume, with its own passing time, which nonetheless stands apart from the space-time in which the story's alternative timelines unfold (Wittenberg 2013). In Isaac Asimov's novel *The End of Eternity*, for instance, hyperspace-time takes the form of a "kind of elevator shaft" that allows movement up and down the timeline (Asimov 1955; Wittenberg 2013). Hyperspace-time is thus a kind of literalized Kantian transcendental structure; it is a particularly extreme, and effective, example of the way that science fiction works, as Chu says, to "convert an elusive referent into an object available for representation" (Chu 2010). Asimov accomplishes this, in part, by narrating in his novel the retroactive destruction of the very structure (the apparatus for time travel) that provides the novel with its content and rationale. The crucial task of science fiction is to objectify the uncanny referent without sacrificing, or explaining away, its fundamental elusiveness and strangeness. As it sweeps across space-time, performing this complicated task, science fiction does not estrange us from mimetic representation so much as it mimetically represents, and literalizes, that very process of estrangement.

Propositions

Science fiction stories may be regarded as one particular type of what Alfred North Whitehead calls *propositions*. This term, in Whitehead's technical usage of it, extends well beyond its conventional logical or mathematical sense. Whitehead, who started out as a mathematician, initially defined the proposition as an "abstract logical form" which simply states that "if any collections of things have such and such abstract properties, they also have such and such other abstract properties" (Whitehead 1911). But in his later philosophical work, Whitehead seeks to move beyond the horizon of mathematics. In *Process and Reality*, and again in his late essay on "Immortality," he gives extended demonstrations of how even so clear a phrase as "one and one make two" is itself only a limited truth. For instance, if two drops of cooking oil are placed in a frying pan, they will quickly coalesce into a single blob: this is a case in which one and one does not make two. Even mathematics depends upon a wide variety of non-mathematical "presumptions" that are needed in order to establish a meaningful context (Whitehead 1978). And even in a discourse as abstract and highly specialized as that of mathematics, "there is not a sentence, or a word, which is independent of the circumstance under which it is uttered" (Whitehead 1948).

In his later work, therefore, Whitehead no longer restricts propositions to matters of logic and judgment — nor even to linguistic statements. Indeed, he insists that "no verbal statement is the adequate expression of a proposition." Most broadly, Whitehead defines propositions as "tales that perhaps might be told about particular actualities." Note the tentativeness of "perhaps" in this definition, the recourse to narrative in the form of "tales," and the insistence that these tales must be "about particular actualities." A proposition always involves a hypothetical reference, made through an act of storytelling (whether linguistic or not), to something that exists, or at least that could exist. The "proposition in itself," Whitehead says, "tells no tales about itself": formally considered, and apart from its semantic content, it is empty and "indeterminate." Rather than reflect upon itself, a proposition tells tales about matters that are extrinsic to it — the things that it is *about*, or to which it refers. And it is only through these extrinsic references to "determinate actual entities" that a proposition "must be true or false." Whitehead is rather scornful and disparaging, however, about "the moralistic preference for true propositions" (Whitehead 1978). Rather, he slyly insists that "it is more important that a proposition be interesting than that it be true" (Whitehead 1933, 1978). He claims that "this statement is almost a tautology" (Whitehead 1933). He even suggests that the truth-value of a proposition is only important to the extent that "it adds to interest" (Whitehead 1978).

In what might seem a surprising parallel to Whitehead, Ernst Bloch also stresses the importance of false propositions. Bloch reminds us that even "individual philosophical propositions which are false purely with regard to the facts… are not totally finished with regard to the truth." Propositions may be false precisely "because they have asserted something that is not yet due, in a hasty way, because they came too early." A proposition can be "ahead of its time" because it makes a demand, or envisages an alternative, that has not yet been actualized. Bloch always insists upon "the space of the Open Possible," a space in process that can never be complete. And he explicitly warns us against the "static thinking" that involves "the positing of a finished One and All, of a universe in which all Possible is real," and in which there is "no unrealized Possible in the totality of the world" (Bloch 1995).

All this helps to explain how and why, as Chu insists, "the literal and the metaphoric share ontological status" in science fiction (Chu 2010). The strategy of literalization is a way of telling fictional tales about particular actualities. These tales are interesting to the extent that they are able to unfold, and to express, potentialities that, thus far, only exist in a latent state. Science fiction uses figurative language because it ascribes qualities to things that they *could* possess in the future, even if they do not at the moment. And then, by literalizing these figurations, science fiction shows how such qualities might subsequently manifest themselves, or how certain events might be able to happen, concretely, within a "historic route of actual occasions" (Whitehead 1978). It is, of course, unlikely that any particular event envisioned in a science-fiction narrative will actually occur in the way that it is described. And of course, even the scientific explanations in "hard" science fiction often involve a considerable degree of hand-waving. Nonetheless, the literalization performed by science-fiction tales still allows us to imagine *how* and *why* certain developments *could* perhaps come about, and what their further consequences might be. An interesting science-fictional fabulation is one that stimulates us to think about its referents in richer ways — even when its particular details are fictional and its explicit claims are false.

Whitehead defines propositions as "definite potentialities *for* actuality with undetermined realization *in* actuality." Both halves of this statement are crucial. Propositions are "definite potentialities" because they offer the prospect of concrete changes that could actually happen, or descriptions that could become true of the things described. At the same time, these propositions retain a "character of indeterminateness" because there is no guarantee (and most of the time, very little likelihood) that the situations they imagine will actually come to pass (Whitehead 1978). Most propositions remain fictional and hypothetical. But they can capture our attention to the degree that they exhibit some sort of "definite, effective relevance" to the actual situations that they address (Whitehead 1978). This explains why we can often get more from science-fictional speculations than we can from strictly philosophical discussions of the same issues.

Science-fictional depictions of Moon colonization, for instance, are relevant both to the actual economic and technological challenges that such a colonization would face and to disputes about the political and economic forms of social organization that exist on the Earth — which might be either extended to or altered on the Moon. Robert Heinlein's *The Moon Is a Harsh Mistress* addresses problems of organization, freedom, and prosperity through its plotline of a libertarian revolution and its insistence on such bromides as "There ain't no such thing as a free lunch" (Heinlein 1966). Ian Macdonald's Luna trilogy explicitly criticizes this ideology and exposes its consequences in the form of highly stratified social structures, the ruthless exploitation of workers, and the violence resulting from competition between powerful families (Macdonald 2015, 2017, 2019). John Kessel's *The Moon and the Other* considers many of the same problems in the context of gender relations, feminist movements for liberation, and cis-hetero-masculinist backlash (Kessel 2017). In all of these texts, the prospect of lunar colonization creates an important distance from pre-existing Earthly concerns and modes of organization, while also not allowing for a complete *tabula rasa*. A similar process often animates science-fiction novels that are set on the moons of planets in other, fictional solar systems. In both Ursula Le Guin's *The Dispossessed* (Le Guin 1974) and Joan Slonczewski's *A Door Into Ocean* (Slonczewski 1986), a smaller moon offers alternative social arrangements to the all-too-familiar capitalistic, patriarchal, and militaristic ones that are entrenched on the larger planet that it orbits.

In sum, science-fictional fabulations are false propositions rather than statements of fact or of necessity. They might even be adamantly opposed to what we regard as common sense or the proper order of the universe: "false propositions against God," to hijack the title of a poem sequence by Jack Spicer (Spicer 2008). These false propositions do not depict actual states of affairs, but in their hypotheses, they do nonetheless refer to "some element of sheer givenness," and thereby retain a high degree of "relevance to the actual world," as Whitehead says propositions are supposed to do (Whitehead 1978). This is how these narratives remain interesting, even without being true. False propositions allow us, and even encourage us, to explore alternatives to the actual state of affairs, and thereby to envisage real potentialities that we might otherwise overlook. The interest and relevance of a false proposition — or of a science-fiction scenario — makes it into what Whitehead calls "a lure for feeling." It seduces us into following its suggestions, whether positively or negatively. In such cases, we might well think of the sexual meaning of the word *proposition*, even though Whitehead most likely did not intend this connotation. Propositions seduce us into following them. They literalize, and thereby encourage us to imagine, what might otherwise remain in the realm of vague speculation. They nourish us with what Whitehead strikingly calls "food for possibility" (Whitehead 1978).

Real Potentiality, Compossibility, and Virtuality

Propositions delineate *potentialities* in the form of the conditions that they apply to particular entities or occasions. But Whitehead distinguishes between *general potentiality* and *real potentiality*. The former simply means that a given condition is logically possible or non-contradictory. It remains consistent with the overall logical structure of the world. Science fiction, in its more whimsical mode, sometimes plays with general potentiality. For example, people from other planets might well have blue or orange or purple skin, as they do in a famous *Green Lantern* comic (O'Neil and Adams 1970). No explanation is given for this situation, but there is no logical contradiction involved in imagining it to be the case. On the other hand, nobody will ever encounter a logically impossible object, such as a square circle, or succeed in drawing one in a comic book.

In addition to logical possibility, however, there is the question of whether a potentiality invoked by a proposition has any sort of implicit basis within the real world. Is there a configuration of actualities from which it could arise, or to which it is meaningfully or plausibly related? This is what Whitehead calls real potentiality: the possibility in question is not just logically permissible (non-contradictory), but also has some relevance to actual, already-existing circumstances. A potentiality is real when it is "conditioned by the data provided by the actual world" and exists "relative to some actual entity, taken as a standpoint whereby the actual world is defined" (Whitehead 1978). Science fiction, unlike fantasy, is most often grounded in real potentiality. In the *Green Lantern* story I just cited, the differently colored skins of people on other planets are fantastic possibilities, with no particular reason for being the way they are. But they provide a contrast to the plight of Black people in America. A Black man asks Green Lantern why he has helped the people with differently colored skins on other planets but "never bothered with the black skins" here on Earth. Green Lantern confesses that he has no answer to this question. The reference to different-colored skins is relevant because, in 1970, when the comic was first written and published, the Black Power movement was at its height in the United States, and so was the White racist backlash against it (O'Neil and Adams 1970).

A similar conceit animates Cory Doctorow's novella *Model Minority*, from his volume *Radicalized* (Doctorow 2019). This is a story about Superman: it imagines his responses to police violence against African Americans and to the Black Lives Matter protest movement. In order to avoid copyright infringement, Doctorow calls his protagonist the American Eagle; but this figure has precisely the same powers and attributes as Superman does in all the comics and movies produced by DC Comics and Warner Brothers. The actual existence of a being like Superman is extremely unlikely, but the figure can provide a vivid background for addressing issues of real potentiality. In Doctorow's story, the American Eagle tries to intervene when he sees White police officers beating up a Black man. But in spite of all his powers, not to mention his career as a de facto officer of the law, the Eagle finds that there is nothing he can actually do to rein in the police. The ingrained bureaucracies and power structures of the American security state are not susceptible to personal acts of force, such as the ones the American Eagle has used in the past to stop criminals. And the Eagle's special status as a superhero limits his ability to act as a simple citizen by getting involved in things like street protests.

The American Eagle's secret identity is known to the government, and when he suggests that the police are acting improperly, he is denounced in the media as an alien (from another planet, no less) who has no loyalty to America. At the same time, Black activists — reminiscent of the Black man in the *Green Lantern* comic — ask the American Eagle why he is such a Johnny-come-lately to the struggle for racial equality; for years, he did nothing about lynchings, police beatings, arbitrary arrests, and other racist incidents. The American Eagle, like Green Lantern, has no good answer to this question about implicit responsibility. As Doctorow himself remarks about the story, "You only get so far punching racism before you have to address the actual structural problem" (Patrick 2019). In fabulating this encounter between a comic book hero and an actual social situation, Doctorow offers us what Whitehead would call a complex proposition that reflects upon real potentialities in American society together with the difficulties that block us from actualizing those potentialities.

Whitehead's distinction between general and real potentiality goes back at least to the philosophy of G. W. Leibniz. For Leibniz, there is a crucial distinction between necessary and contingent truths:

> I assert that connection or following [*consécution*] is of two kinds. The one whose contrary implies a contradiction is absolutely necessary; this deduction occurs in the eternal truths, for example, the truths of geometry. The other is necessary only *ex hypothesi* and, so to speak, accidentally, but it is contingent in itself, since its contrary does not imply a contradiction. And this connection is based not purely on ideas and God's simple understanding, but on his free decrees and on the sequence of the universe.
>
> (Leibniz 1989)

Factual events are truths, according to Leibniz, because they help to constitute the actual world that we live in. But such truths remain contingent, in the sense that no logical contradiction would be involved if things had happened otherwise. Things happen as they do because of how they fit in to the overall "sequence of the universe"; and the particular sequence that defines our actual world was chosen by God because he prefers it to all other possible worlds.

Twentieth-century analytic philosophy, particularly in the work of David Lewis, insists that anything that is not logically contradictory (and therefore impossible) occurs in some possible world or another (Lewis 1986a). But even though Leibniz is the inventor of the very concept of *possible worlds*, as Chloe Armstrong points out, he "rejects the inference that if something is possible, it therefore occurs in some possible world" (Armstrong 2017). For Leibniz, a possible world is not just one that is free from logical contradiction. In addition, the multiple facts and events in such a world must not only each be separately possible, they must also be *compossible* with one another. This means that for Leibniz, just as for Whitehead, not everything that is logically possible is thereby existentially possible. Things do not always fit together. In insisting upon compossibility, Leibniz gives us the beginnings of what today we call an environmental or ecological mode of understanding.

For Leibniz, compossibility is due to what he calls a "pre-established harmony," imposed by God, among all the entities inhering in the actual world. Leibniz calls these entities *monads*: vital centers of will and feeling that are rooted in the world and yet self-enclosed and separate from one another and from the rest of the world. We may think of each monad as being something like a biological cell with its membrane separating it from the rest of the world, but also as being a sort of mirror. The whole world is mirrored in me, and thereby represented to me. The entire universe affects each monad, and thereby is reflected in each monad. But Leibniz tells us that most of these reflections are obscure and confused. I can only apprehend a tiny portion of the world clearly; everything else appears to me in a form that is murky, fragmentary, and scrambled. Beyond these uncertain reflections, monads are entirely closed off. "The monads have no windows through which something can enter or leave" (Leibniz 1989).

A more modern monadology, such as that of the late-nineteenth-century French sociologist (and proto-science fiction writer) Gabriel Tarde, modifies this claim. Tarde rejects Leibniz's doctrine that the monads are entirely shut off from one another. Instead, Tarde proposes "open monads which would penetrate each other reciprocally, rather than being mutually external" (Tarde 2012).

And this mutual penetration is not regulated by anything like a divinely pre-established harmony. Instead, all these relations are wholly immanent. The various monads engage in struggle with one another, along the lines of Darwinian competition. Richard Halpern summarizes the differences between Leibniz and Tarde: "Whereas the Leibnizian monad merely *perceives* the universe around it, the Tardeian monad strives to remake the universe in its own image, to impose its belief on all the others" (Halpern 2023). Compossibility among the monads arises immanently, in real time, either as a result of conflict (as in Nietzsche's evocation of the will to power), or more peacefully, through what Whitehead calls "the mutual adaptation of the several factors in an occasion of experience" (Whitehead 1933). Things persist in being by accommodating themselves to one another and by exchanging elements without merging. Such evolutionary processes, in real time, are enough to account for compossibility, without the need for God to have arranged everything in advance.

This insistence upon evolution and mutual adjustment is not as radical a revision of Leibniz as it might initially seem. Leibniz already says that each monad mirrors or represents, albeit in a partial and distorted way, the entire universe. We simply need to understand mirroring and representing in a somewhat less classical manner than Leibniz does. To mirror or to represent something, even inadequately, is to be *affected* by that something — whether this happens peacefully or through the sorts of power struggle that Tarde and Nietzsche describe. The very act of representation already involves a certain degree of openness, or penetrability, in the relations between monads. Without harmony being given in advance, the monads need to accommodate one another, to engage in a process of mutual adjustment. Leibniz already anticipates the modernist idea that representation is an ongoing process and is not transparent or total. To modernize Leibniz, all we need to do is to carry this process a bit further than he overtly does.

Indeed, Leibniz anticipates later biological findings in the way that he sees the cellular structure that he calls a monad as the basic unit of life, and indeed of the world as a whole. Leibniz knew little of what we now understand about biological cells, but he took a keen interest in the biology of his day, and especially in the work of his contemporary Antonie van Leeuwenhoek, the first person to observe unicellular organisms through a microscope (Becchi 2017). Modern biology tells us that all cells, and all living things more generally, are bounded by membranes which separate the inside from the outside and also selectively allow certain things, but not others, to pass between the inside and the outside. Such a selective and differential structure is already present in Leibniz's monads, which actively mirror and represent the whole outside world, but which only render a small and directly relevant portion of it clearly and distinctly.

Here is an example of compossibility, or actual coexistence that is not merely a result of logical non-contradiction. All life on Earth is water- and carbon-based. Life as we know it requires water in liquid form, and this constrains the physical conditions in which it can exist:

> The highest known temperature at which metabolism and growth can still occur in water is 122 degrees Celsius (252 degrees Fahrenheit), for example at high-pressure hydrothermal vents. The lowest temperature seems to be about -18 degrees Celsius (about 0 degrees Fahrenheit).
>
> (Schulze-Makuch 2017)

In contrast to this, we must presume that carbon- and water-based life does not exist on the surface of Venus, where the temperature is 464 degrees Celsius and the atmospheric pressure is ninety-two times that on the Earth's surface. In other words, life as we know it is not compossible with Venusian climate conditions. If there *is* life on Venus, it is more likely to exist in the thick clouds surrounding the planet than on the actual surface. And even in the clouds, any prospective form of life must have an entirely different composition and organization than that of terrestrial life. Nonetheless, many conditions for life as we understand it do exist in the clouds of Venus:

> Although many features of Venus can rule out the possibility that Earth life could live there, none rule out the possibility of all life based on what we know of the physical principle of life on Earth. Specifically, there is abundant energy, the energy requirements for retaining water and capturing hydrogen atoms to build biomass are not excessive, defenses against sulfuric acid are conceivable and have terrestrial precedent, and the speculative possibility that life uses concentrated sulfuric acid as a solvent instead of water remains.
>
> (Bains et al. 2023)

The point here is that "the physical principle of life on Earth" allows for more possibilities than the particular way that life actually works on our planet. Processes of energy utilization, growth, and reproduction with variations need not only occur in forms that are "chemically similar to terrestrial life." Other chemical cycles are at least a "speculative possibility… Although we consider the prospects for finding life on Venus to be speculative, they are not absent" (Bains et al. 2023).

To give just one example, Jan Špaček and Steven Benner propose a scenario in which Venusian life could exist in the form of self-organizing and self-replicating droplets of red oil, bathed in sulfuric acid (Špaček and Benner 2021). Such a sort of life would at least be compossible with Venusian conditions. Špaček and Benner propose their account of potential life on Venus as a thought experiment: they do not claim that such life-forms actually exist. It is not wrong to regard such a paper as a work of science fiction, as Špaček himself largely admits. Even if we can confirm the existence of red oil droplets in the Venusian atmosphere, he writes,

> we do not have tools to determine if the chemistry in the droplet was only self-replicating, or actually evolving. So far

> *evolving replicators in the Venusian clouds are sci-fi*. But we can still use this sci-fi scenario to discuss very specific aliens (model) and how useful is to call them "life."
>
> (Špaček 2022)

For science fiction seeks, like Leibniz's doctrine of possible worlds, to discover or formulate worlds that are not only logically non-contradictory but also situationally comprehensible — which is to say, composed of compossible elements. For such coexistence to involve real potentiality (rather than just general potentiality), there needs to be a positive account of how it might be generated. Red-oil-based life in the clouds of Venus is extremely unlikely; but it still belongs to real potentiality, rather than just to general potentiality.

Whitehead's distinction between general and real potentiality is also akin to Gilles Deleuze's distinction, following Bergson, between the merely *possible* and the *virtual*. (I expand here on a topic that I briefly discussed in Shaviro 2014). For Deleuze, possibility is an empty concept, one that tells us very little. Anything that is not logically contradictory is at least possible; there is nothing to prevent it, *a priori* (based on logical necessity rather than empirical observation) from existing. But the mere logical possibility (or non-contradictoriness) of a thing does not mean that there is any process that actually will, or that even could, bring it into existence. To explore and explain actual phenomena, logical possibility is not enough. For Deleuze, the virtual is a configuration, or a set of implicit circumstances, that provides the necessary conditions, and even the impetus, for new actualities to emerge. The virtual is not actual; it is never directly present in the here and now. But — in contrast to the merely possible — on its own terms it "possesses a full reality by itself" (Deleuze 1994).

We might think of the virtual as a latent potentiality, embedded in some arrangement of things and forces in the world. The virtual has the *power* to generate actualities, whether or not it ever does so in any particular instance (Deleuze 1994). Today, as I write these words, both full racial equality and a White nationalist regime taking over the country are among the potentialities existing in virtual superposition in the United States. On an even wider scale, the United States and Russia, with their nuclear arsenals, have long had the power to destroy the human world — and during the Cold War, this power came frighteningly close to being exercised on several occasions (Birch 2013; Colbert 2020). Jeffrey Lewis draws upon this real potentiality in his "speculative novel," *The 2020 Commission Report on the North Korean Nuclear Attacks against the United States*. The novel takes the format of an official government report in order to tell the story of a nuclear war between the United States and North Korea, set off by an all-too-plausible chain of accidents and misunderstandings. The reckless stupidity of United States president Donald Trump is especially crucial, alongside paranoia and misunderstanding on the part of North Korea's sociopathic leadership (Lewis 2018). Though, fortunately, such a nuclear exchange has not actually happened — at least so far — the novel convincingly warns us that it remains well within the bounds of real potentiality.

Cycles of Contingency

In Western thought, the idea of potentiality can be traced back at least as far as Aristotle. But our ways of thinking about it have changed over the centuries. For Aristotle and other classical thinkers, potentiality implies teleology: it is oriented towards a pre-given goal or purpose. To use a frequently cited example, an acorn has the potentiality to become a mature oak tree; indeed, it is intrinsically defined by this potentiality. Not every acorn actually grows into an oak tree, but every acorn has the latent capacity to do so, and every actual oak tree started out as an acorn. Understood in this way, potentiality is finite, limited, and closed; it points to a definite end which can be known in advance and is achieved under propitious conditions.

This classical view of potentiality follows what Gilbert Simondon calls the *hylomorphic schema*, according to which an "abstract form" is actively imposed from the outside upon "abstract matter," conceived as passive and inert (Simondon

2020). Such a view elides real potentiality, by treating it according to the logic of general potentiality. Of course Aristotle knew nothing of DNA, but his notion of final cause is mostly preserved in the view of DNA as a program that instructs organic chemicals how to assemble themselves in the form of a tree. Today, we still maintain this classical view when we regard information as a pre-given pattern that can be equally instantiated in different sorts of matter. It is the contemporary version of the old fantasy of a soul separable from the body. Just as the acorn supposedly provides the operating code for the oak tree, the mind is considered to be software running on the hardware of the physical brain. Such is the logic behind the rather silly Silicon Valley fantasy of living forever by downloading one's mind into a younger body, or into a computer (Kurzweil 2005; see my criticism in Shaviro 2009). Science fiction often takes up this very scenario, but it does so in order to ask disturbing questions about it. For instance, Robert J. Sawyer's *Mindscan* looks at the fate of a man who, suffering from an incurable disease and thinking himself to be near death, downloads his consciousness into an android body. But when a cure for the disease is found and the man's organic body recovers its health, there are now two instances of the same person – identical up to the fairly recent moment when their experiences diverged for the very first time. They quarrel bitterly about which one of them is the authentic self and has the legal rights to that self's money and property (Sawyer 2005).

In a different but not unrelated way, Richard K. Morgan's Takeshi Kovacs trilogy has as its science-fictional premise, or novum, the notion that one's mentality can be recorded and preserved in a piece of hardware called the "cortical stack" (Morgan 2002, 2003, 2005). This hardware is inserted into each human body shortly after birth, and it records the person's memories and personality structure. If someone dies, or if they seek to travel to another planet at light speed, the cortical stack can be removed and its data copied and transmitted. Then they can be revived by having a cortical stack with the same information inserted into a different "sleeve" (as replacement bodies are called).

But Morgan highlights the confusions and pathologies that might result from such a technology. The "same" mind is not really the same when it is embedded in bodies that have different sorts of physical abilities and limitations. The cortical stack can also be hooked up to a virtual reality simulation, which makes it possible to torture someone indefinitely, with pain continuing well beyond the threshold at which an actual body would lose consciousness or die. In *Woken Furies*, the final volume of the series, the paradoxes are multiplied. The protagonist vengefully writes the cortical stacks of his enemies into the bodies of animals; people who suffer this fate are tortured by the mismatch between their presumptive mental capacities and the limited cognitive and verbal abilities of the bodies in which they find themselves. There is also the problem of bodily multiplication: an earlier instantiation of the protagonist, whose cortical stack had been preserved, is embodied in a new sleeve. Takeshi Kovacs is faced with an earlier version of himself who despises his future self's new sensibilities and seeks to murder him. Morgan treats mind-downloading in terms of real potentiality instead of general potentiality, focusing upon the glitches, complications, and contradictions that might attend such a process.

Simondon argues that the hylomorphic schema is inadequate even in the relatively simple case — well known to the Ancient Greeks — of clay being packed into a rectangular mold and then hardened by heat until it solidifies into a brick. We cannot just say that a predetermined form is imprinted upon a previously undifferentiated blob of matter. For all sorts of carefully articulated "technical operations" are required in order to get this particular result; the clay must be heated to just the right temperature, for instance, which requires a particular sort of furnace. Also, not just any form of matter will do. If instead of using clay, "we take fine-grained sand, moisten it, and pack it into a brick mold," the operation simply will not work; we will end up only with "a heap of sand and not a brick after we take it out of the mold." In any such process, we need to take the material as well as the form into account. Simondon insists that there is no such thing as "abstract raw matter." Different materials have different properties and affordances; matter is never simply characterless or inchoate. In any technical procedure, you must attend to the already-existing, intrinsic qualities of whatever material you are using. You won't get very far, for instance, if you heedlessly try to plane a plank of wood against the grain (Simondon 2020).

The hylomorphic schema blinds us to our material entanglements in the world. Simondon suggests that such a formulation could only have been devised by a slave society like that of Ancient Greece. "The distinction between matter and form, between the soul and the body, reflects a city that contains citizens in opposition to slaves." The ruling class in Ancient Greece was composed of freemen who despised physical labor and were unable to understand it. The master "gives his orders"; but it is left to the slaves to figure out how to actually "manipulate the matter" in such a way as to fulfill these orders in physical reality. The very distinction between form and matter thus "supposes social hierarchy" (Simondon 2020). In analyzing the limits of the hylomorphic schema, Simondon works much like a science-fiction writer: he moves both forwards from the schema to its probable consequences and backwards from it to the conditions needed in order to generate it in the first place.

Despite our superstitions about disembodied information, modern thought for the most part has a more open understanding of potentiality than classical thought had. We generally take it for granted today that outcomes are not preordained, but rather probabilistic at best. The propitious conditions that a potentiality needs in order to actualize itself are not merely external to it. Rather, the actualization of a potentiality must be actively accomplished by, through, from, and within the depths of matter. The actualizing form is never just imposed upon a piece of matter from the outside. Forms can only be generated, maintained, and altered due to what Jessica Riskin calls matter's own intrinsic "restlessness" and "inherent plasticity" (Riskin 2016).

We can see this by returning to the example of an acorn. According to our current understanding, the acorn's DNA is not a static blueprint for building an oak tree. Rather, the DNA acts dynamically. Under certain particular conditions, the DNA helps to catalyze a cascade of interrelated and mutually influencing biochemical reactions that cause the tree to grow, and which canalize the directions of this growth. These reactions are determined not only by the code of the DNA, but also by varying environmental conditions, by epigenetic modifications to DNA expression, and by many other factors — not to mention by the continuing activity of mutations. Plants, unlike animals, do not separate the germ line from the soma; flowers can be produced by nearly any part of the plant. This means that plants are far more capable than animals of conveying acquired characteristics to their offspring, whether through epigenetic inheritance or through something like the Baldwin Effect.

Plants also hybridize easily. There is a large degree of genetic variation and diversity even within single organisms; there are even trees whose different branches have different genetic profiles. All this allows plants to deploy different adaptations in different circumstances (Hallé 2002). If the multiple reactions initiated by an acorn planted in soil continue for a long enough time, and build upon one another cohesively enough, then the result is likely to be an oak tree. But this will always be one particular tree, with its own peculiarities. The oak tree in my backyard did in fact grow out of an acorn, and it produces new acorns every year. But it should not be seen as the realization of some supposed fundamental, pre-existing form of "oakness."

Rather, this particular oak tree is the result of what developmental systems theory in biology calls *cycles of contingency*: "Contingent cycles of interaction among a varied set of developmental resources, no one of which controls the process" (Oyama et al. 2001). Real potentiality makes change and growth (and also decay) possible, but changes can go in many different directions. Not all of these directions are viable; many of them in fact get blocked and end up being rejected by natural selection. But this does not mean that the transformations which occur with greater frequency are therefore somehow intrinsically preordained. Oak trees themselves result from a long history of genetic mutations, adaptations, and environmental changes, a history that could not have been predicted in advance, and which we can only discern retrospectively.

Ernst Bloch applies this method of retrospective discernment to the history of the idea of potentiality itself. Bloch argues that even in Aristotle there are already hints of a more open conception of potentiality, one in which matter is understood as being "full of active form, through which the possible actively produces and organizes itself in accord with the new realities pressing forth within it" (Bloch 2019). Though the hegemonic, mainstream interpreters of Aristotle (such as Thomas Aquinas) suppressed these hints, they were taken up in a counter-tradition that Bloch calls the "Aristotelian Left." Bloch traces how the idea of an auto-generative materiality, already implicit in Aristotle, is progressively elaborated in the thought of Ibn Sina (Avicenna) in the eleventh century, Ibn Rushd (Averroes) in the twelfth century, Giordano Bruno in the sixteenth century, and Spinoza in the seventeenth century. These developments eventually lead to the immanent and non-teleological understanding of potentiality that we find in contemporary "new materialist" thought (Coole and Frost 2010).

Possibilities, Tendencies, and Powers

Other thinkers offer us related formulations of how potentiality works to generate change. The biologist Stuart Kauffman understands real potentiality in biochemical systems in terms of what he calls the *adjacent possible*. This "consists of all those [entities] that are not members of the actual, but are *one reaction step away from the actual*" (Kauffman 2000). Something is adjacently possible if it can be actualized in a single step from what already exists. Kauffman gives such examples of this as a point mutation and a chemical reaction leading to the production of a new molecule. The set of adjacently possible reactions is finite, but it is vast. If we "consider all the kinds of organic molecules on, within, or in the vicinity of the Earth, say, out to twice the radius of the moon," we already have "hundreds of trillions of molecular species" able to react with one another in a multitude of ways. We cannot predict just which of these reactions will actually take place. In addition, "the adjacent possible is indefinitely expandable," since once a particular possibility is actualized, it gives us "a new adjacent possible, accessible from the enlarged actual" (Kauffman 2000). The adjacent possible is not infinite, but for all intents and purposes, its full extent cannot be known in advance. The only way to compute the outcomes of the various reaction steps is for them to actually happen in real time. The universe, we might say, computes itself, and we cannot shorten this process.

The science journalist Steven Johnson amplifies Kauffman's idea, applying it as much to human culture as to biology and "the history of life" (Johnson 2010). For Johnson, the adjacent possible is

> a kind of shadow future, hovering on the edges of the present state of things, a map of all the ways in which the present can reinvent itself. Yet is it not an infinite space, or a totally open playing field… What the adjacent possible tells us is that at any moment the world is capable of extraordinary change, but only *certain* changes can happen.
>
> (Johnson 2010)

Science fiction is the art of representing this "shadow future." It follows the logic of the adjacent possible, drawing maps of real potentiality, or of "the ways in which the present can reinvent itself." Unexpected things can, and often do, happen in science-fiction narratives — but not just *anything* can happen.

Karl Marx makes a similar point when he writes about "tendencies" or "tendential processes." This concept comes up in Volume Three of *Capital*, precisely when Marx gives an account of "the process of capitalist production as a whole" (Marx 1993). For Marx, tendential processes are intrinsic to the actual, material state of things; but although they are real, they are not themselves actual. Rather, they indicate certain inclinations or biases that inflect future developments in certain directions rather than in others. According to Marx, there is an intrinsic tendency for the rate of profit to fall as capitalism becomes more widespread and develops more powerful and more capital-intensive technologies. This is one of the most disputed claims in all of Marx's works; I do not intend to go over the argument's pros and cons here. The crucial point for my present purposes is that, for Marx, a tendency is not the same thing as an absolute necessity. A tendency can always be modified in its action, or even blocked altogether, by "counteracting factors," which Marx enumerates at great length (Marx 1993). As the overall rate of profit threatens to fall, capitalists develop multiple strategies to get it to rise again. Thus the *tendency* for the rate of profit to fall is objectively real, but there is no guarantee, over any particular period, that the rate of profit actually will fall.

The critical realist thinker Steve Fleetwood argues that what Marx calls tendencies may also be understood, more broadly, as the "powers, affordances, abilities, capacities, dispositions, forces, liabilities, potentialities, potencies, predilections, processes, propensities" that are possessed by various entities or various configurations of circumstances (Fleetwood 2012). For instance, a sharp knife has the tendency — or the potential — to cut things. This is why you have to handle it carefully. The knife's potential or power to cut is altogether real, even if the knife has never actually cut anything and never encountered any particular object that it might be able to cut. This potential also remains real even when the knife encounters something that it is unable to cut, like a stone. The knife's ability to cut is real in itself, but it can only be actualized in particular circumstances: when it encounters something, like paper or a loaf of bread, that is vulnerable to its particular powers.

The Australian philosopher George Molnar makes a similar argument when he proposes "a metaphysical theory of powers." Molnar, like Fleetwood, lists such "interrelated concepts" as "'power,' 'disposition,' 'capacity,' 'ability,' 'skill,' 'aptitude,' 'propensity,' 'tendency,' 'potential,' 'amplitude,' etc." These words all point to real and intrinsic qualities of things. Water has the power to dissolve salt, and salt has the power to be dissolved in water. Powers have causal efficacy, since their exercise has an effect upon at least some other things. But Molnar also insists that, as real properties of things, "powers are ontologically independent of their manifestations. They can exist even when they are not being exercised and have not been exercised and will not be exercised" (Molnar 2003; I have previously discussed Molnar in Shaviro 2014).

The analytic philosophers Stephen Mumford and Rani Lill Anjum use Molnar's realism about powers and potentialities as the basis for a new understanding of cause and effect. Causality, they say, results from *dispositions*, or *tendencies*, which are intrinsic properties of particular things. Dispositions are more than just "mere possibilities," for "many things are possible in this wide sense without there being dispositions for them to happen." A disposition is not just a logical possibility, or a non-contradiction, but a positive power that (in the right circumstances) pushes towards particular effects. Glass is intrinsically fragile, even if some particular object made of glass never actually gets shattered. Dispositions are real powers of particular things, whether or not they are ever actually manifested. In this way, dispositions have a logic similar to that of Whitehead's real potentiality, or to Deleuze's virtual — even though Mumford and Anjum do not seem to be particularly acquainted with either of these thinkers (Mumford and Anjum 2011).

Mumford and Anjum also tell us, again in parallel with Whitehead's and Deleuze's accounts of potentiality, that a causal disposition "is not something as strong as a tie that binds things together inseparably"; there is nothing that absolutely forces a certain effect to follow from a certain cause. There can always be "conditions under which [a causal process] is prevented or interfered with by counteracting powers." Given the average air pressure at the surface of the Earth, water tends to freeze at temperatures below 32 degrees Fahrenheit (0 degrees Celsius), and to boil at temperatures above 212 degrees Fahrenheit (100 degrees Celsius). These dispositions are real, intrinsic properties of water.

But the disposition to freeze can be stymied, for instance, if salt is dissolved into the water. For Mumford and Anjum, therefore, causality is a basic modality in its own right. It is "certainly not reducible to pure necessity or pure contingency"; rather, it is "something in between" (Mumford and Anjum 2011).

Science fiction — together with its related speculative genres, like fantasy and horror — deals with real potentialities because it operates on the premise that there is more to the world than just what is actual. Deleuze's virtual, Kauffman's adjacent possible, Marx's tendencies, Molnar's powers, and Mumford and Anjum's dispositions are all ways of defining this *more* — without invoking anything supernatural, or even teleological. They all point to conditions that *may* be actualized, at one point or another, but that do not have to be, and which have a proper reality of their own even if they never become actual. This is why the richness of the world cannot be reduced to just an agglomeration of facts, or to "all that is the case" (Wittgenstein 1974). Science fiction testifies to, and actively explores, this surplus of the real over the merely actual.

"— All You Zombies —"

The argument about powers and potentialities that I have been tracing is very much a minority position within contemporary philosophy. Most philosophers over the course of the past century have rejected claims about powers and potentialities. They find such ideas all too reminiscent of the medieval scholastic metaphysics that modern philosophy, from Descartes onwards, rebelled against. In his 1673 play, *Le Malade imaginaire* (*The Imaginary Invalid*), Molière famously ridicules the old metaphysics when he has a doctor explain that opium induces sleep because it has a "dormitive power." The doctor is a pompous windbag; his explanation is an empty tautology. This parallels the way that scientists, starting with Galileo, and philosophers, starting with Descartes, have insisted upon mechanistic explanations of phenomena, doing away with Aristotelian final causes and other essentialist claims (which they stigmatize as "occult qualities").

Among analytic philosophers, the dominant approach today is a *neo-Humean* one, according to which "properties are inert, causation is illusory, and possibility is unbounded" (Williams 2019). The late David Lewis, one of the most influential thinkers along these lines, espouses the doctrine of what he calls "Humean supervenience." Such an approach denies the existence of "necessary connections," and maintains instead that "all there is to the world is a vast mosaic of local matters of particular fact, just one little thing and then another" (Lewis 1986b). To the extent that we discover regularities among all these "local matters of particular fact," we can say that certain patterns of "causation as influence" seem to exist (Collins et al. 2004). But we may not assign intrinsic reasons for these patterns of influence; there is nothing beyond, or deeper than, the empirical fact that one event "supervenes" upon (follows from, with no logical judgment as to the reason) another. Hume himself famously argued that causal necessity

> is something, that exists in the mind, not in objects; nor is it possible for us ever to form the most distant idea of it, consider'd as a quality in bodies… we have really no idea of a power or efficacy in any object, or of any real connexion betwixt causes and effects
>
> (Hume 1969).

For Hume, all that we know of cause and effect comes from our observations and memories of a "constant conjunction" between one event and another. Every time somebody touches a hot stove, they burn their finger; this is an example of a constant conjunction. But can I infer anything further about the intrinsic nature of the hot stove? Refining Hume's procedure, Lewis analyzes causal claims in terms of *counterfactuals*. According to Lewis, when I say that A causes B, what I really mean is that if A had not happened, then B also would not have happened. If I had not touched the stove, my finger would not have been burnt. Beyond this, there is nothing that I can legitimately conclude about the incident. Lewis seeks in this way to acknowledge what he calls "folk-theoretical platitudes" about cause and effect, while at the same time avoiding any "idea of a power or efficacy in any object." It is an empirical fact that my finger was burnt when I touched the hot stove, and that it would not have gotten burnt otherwise. According to Lewis, this is *all* that I can rightly say. I cannot make a legitimate inference from particular instances of getting burnt to any generalization about *why* hot objects might burn me if I touch them. Getting burnt *supervenes* upon touching the stove, or some other hot object, and that is all there is to it (Collins et al. 2004).

From the admitted perspective of my own folk-theoretical prejudices, this argument strikes me as an odd sort of special pleading. I want to say that the stove really *is* hot, and that it really *did* burn my finger. In insisting on this, I am claiming that there is more to the real than just what is immediately actual. Hume denies that we ever perceive causality, but wasn't the sensation of pain that led me to pull my finger back from the stove as quickly as possible just such a perception? When my own body is affected in this way, I am not just observing two instances from a distance — the stove glowing red hot, the finger touching it and feeling pain — and noting that they frequently seem to come together. My response is too urgent and too pre-reflective for that. Whitehead calls this sort of experience "perception in the mode of causal efficacy" (Whitehead 1927a; I have written previously about the connection between perception and causality in Whitehead in Shaviro 2017). Lewis, for his part, is willing to "concede *pace* Hume that I sometimes perceive causation" in special instances such as this one. But he goes on to argue that most of the things we regard as instances of cause and effect do not fit into this model and cannot be perceived directly, let alone experienced (Collins et al. 2004). Following Hume, Lewis claims that in principle, and barring logical contradiction, "anything can coexist with anything" (Lewis 1986b). Even laws of nature are merely contingent (Ludlow et al. 2004). We may empirically observe that certain regularities recur in certain types of observed instances. But we can find no reason *why* these regularities should occur — let alone why they *must* do so. Even when Lewis acknowledges relations of cause and effect, he insists — as Mumford and Anjum point out — that they are not fundamental in any way, but "merely supervenient upon the patchwork of unconnected events that make up a world" (Mumford and Anjum 2011).

It seems utterly bizarre to me when, in accordance with his overall view, Lewis writes that "more likely than not, our world is so thoroughly indeterministic that most or all of the causation that actually takes place is probabilistic" (Collins et al. 2004). Now, I have already expressed my agreement with Lewis's conclusion that causal relations are generally probabilistic. As Mumford and Anjum put it, when I try to light a match, the outcome is not preordained. There are many reasons why I might not succeed. A gust of wind might blow out the match, for instance, or the wood of the match might not be dry enough. Lighting a match also requires the presence of oxygen in the atmosphere; this is generally the case on the land surface of the Earth, but it would not apply if I tried to light a match on the surface of the Moon (Mumford and Anjum 2011).

However, even though I agree with Lewis that causation is generally probabilistic rather than strictly necessitated, I could not disagree more with, or more thoroughly dislike, the way that Lewis gets to this conclusion. My own point throughout this book is that a different world is possible, because potentialities are in their own ways real, and that these potentialities can sometimes be actualized (although also sometimes not) in a variety of ways. But these potentialities are, all at once, both affordances and constraints of an actually existing situation or environment. Lewis, in contrast, argues that nearly anything can happen, precisely because there is no such thing as potentiality in the first place. For all that I resist determinism, and for all that the whole point of this book is to insist that the future is open and unpredictable, I am not enough of a surrealist to believe that the world is as "thoroughly indeterministic" as Lewis claims. Everyday experience, as well as the entire course of human history, would seem to testify against such a view.

Lewis himself is not in the least bothered by such an objection, since he follows Hume in rejecting arguments from induction. My sense of the matter is that, as Whitehead says, our most common experience is one of "the derivation of state from state, with the later state exhibiting conformity to the antecedent." It is rare and difficult for us to deviate from, and change, the predetermined outcomes dictated to us by "the overwhelming conformation of fact, in present action, to antecedent settled fact" (Whitehead 1927a). Actually struggling to break free from this dreary history of conformation is quite different from blithely saying that, since any given situation is merely "a contingent fact about our world," it can always randomly change for no particular reason (Lewis 1986b). The value of science fiction is that it does not just present us with arbitrary re-orderings of the world. Rather, science-fiction narrative proceeds from the baseline of what Whitehead calls the prevalence of "stubborn fact" in the "settled world"; from here, it explores the "penumbral welter of alternatives" that surround any such state of being, so that "fact is confronted with alternatives" (Whitehead 1978).

David Lewis himself was quite interested in science fiction (Anthony Fisher 2016). He even published a scholarly article on "The Paradoxes of Time Travel" (Lewis 1986b), in which he defends the logical validity of two famous time-travel short stories by Robert Heinlein: "By His Bootstraps" (Heinlein 1959a) and "— All You Zombies —" (Heinlein 1959b). Both stories are possible, Lewis says, in the sense that they involve no logical contradictions. As long as the time traveler has a consistent and linear subjective time progression, Lewis argues, it does not matter that their *personal time* is orthogonal to the order of *external time*. Lewis also addresses the famous "grandfather paradox": the problem of somebody going back in time and killing one of their grandparents before the conception of their parents, thus abolishing their own existence. Lewis argues that this paradox need not make time travel logically impossible. Rather, he suggests that either: (i) the time traveler fails to kill their grandfather, but this failure is a contingent historical fact and has nothing to do with the nature of time travel *per se*; or else (ii) time can branch, as in the multiverse hypothesis, and so the grandfather may well be killed in one time branch, but he lives on in the other time branch from which the assassin emerged (Lewis 1986b). In neither case does time travel lead us into a logical contradiction.

Lewis encounters difficulties, however, in dealing with the time travel paradox of the loop, or the Möbius strip, of self-causation. In "— All You Zombies —," the time-traveling narrator turns out to be his/her own mother, father, and offspring. The protagonist grows up in an orphanage, becomes pregnant as a young woman, gives birth, undergoes a sex change to become male, gets recruited to join the Temporal Bureau, which controls time travel, goes back in time to seduce and impregnate his own former female self, subsequently goes forwards in time to recruit his past self to join the Temporal Bureau, then goes back in time to kidnap the baby resulting from the encounter between his past selves, and finally goes still further back in time to deposit the baby in the orphanage at just the right moment for her to grow up to become him. This produces absolute closure; the narrator is entirely self-caused and self-generated. "I *know* where *I* came from," he/she says, "but *where did all you zombies come from?*" The story, told in the first person, is implicitly addressed to a "you," a second-person reader; but by the story's own logic, such a "you" cannot really exist. The reader, like everyone else in the world, is one of the "zombies" who cannot account for themselves. Since they (we) are not self-caused, the narrator can only regard them (us) as contingent, and therefore as not fully real. As the narrator says in the penultimate paragraph of the story, "*You* aren't really there at all. There isn't anybody but me — Jane — here alone in the dark" (Heinlein 1959b).

Lewis observes that while "the parts of the loop are explicable, the whole of it is not." He then punts the question of explanation by saying that such a structure is

> not impossible, and not too different from inexplicabilities we are already inured to. Almost everyone agrees that God, or

> the Big Bang, or the entire infinite past of the universe, or the decay of a tritium atom, is uncaused and inexplicable.
>
> (Lewis 1986b)

This seems to me to miss the point of what Heinlein is doing. The narrator of the story, who is also the only character within the story, is so self-complete that he/she is unable to access, or even to conceive of, any external reference points or any sort of otherness. As Farah Mendlesohn puts it in her magisterial book about Heinlein, the narrator is condemned, not only to empirical "loneliness," but more importantly to a kind of transcendental solipsism, a condition in relation to which "there is nothing external." The story therefore loops back upon itself interminably, with no exit. "[It] can only end when the universe ends" (Mendlesohn 2019). This is what makes the narrator, like God or the Big Bang, "uncaused and inexplicable." He/she exists, like every true object according to Graham Harman, "in vacuum-sealed isolation" from anything and everything else (Harman 2005). We might also think of the narrator much as Spinoza thinks of substance: as something that exists entirely "in itself and… conceived through itself" such that "no concept of any other thing is needed for forming a concept of it" (Spinoza 2018). This absolute self-enclosure is also what leads David Wittenberg to see "— All You Zombies —" as "the last time travel story," in the sense that it marks the *ne plus ultra* of the subgenre, exhausting all its possibilities (Wittenberg 2013). Heinlein's narrator is sublimely devoid of all relations and all dependencies. Self-causation is also sheer gratuitousness. In this way, "— All You Zombies —" stands as an ultimate, mocking allegory of non-relation, which is to say, of Hume's and Lewis's view that there can be no necessary connections.

Another time travel story (almost contemporaneous with Heinlein's), Alfred Bester's "The Men Who Murdered Mohammed " (originally published in 1958), complements "— All You Zombies —" by making the inverse point. In this story, the time-traveling protagonist, in a fit of jealousy after learning that his wife is having an affair with another man, kills her grandparents in order to wipe her out of existence. He goes on to murder many past historical figures, including Muhammad, Napoleon, and Columbus. But he fails to alter the course of history in the slightest, or even to disrupt the life of his wife. This is because, as he finally learns,

> time is entirely subjective… When a man changes the past he only affects his own past — no one else's. The past is like memory. When you erase a man's memory, you wipe him out, but you don't wipe out anybody else's.
>
> (Bester 1997)

The protagonist has in fact only eliminated himself. By destroying both his own personal memories, and the past history whose truth he had previously taken for granted, he has transformed himself into a ghost, one no longer able to interact with the timeline of the greater world. He concludes that

> time is not a continuum… It's a series of discrete particles — like pearls on a string… Each pearl is a "Now." Each "Now" has its own past and future, but none of them relate to any others.
>
> (Bester 1997)

In this way, "The Men Who Murdered Mohammed" gives us — in advance — a *reductio ad absurdum* of Lewis's own theories of time and causality. If there are no necessary connections, "just one little thing and then another," then alterations of particular facts are not only possible but likely; these alterations of particular facts would have no causal effect upon other particular facts. And if the arrow of time consists only in mere succession, without what Whitehead calls the "conformation" of new occasions to previous ones, then time might well be conceived as "a series of discrete particles," each one an unrelated, independent "now." Reality disaggregates when there are only isolated instants that are no longer bound together by memory or by physical causality.

"The Billiard Ball" and "The Brooklyn Project"

The French speculative realist philosopher Quentin Meillassoux is also directly inspired by Hume. Following the contours of what he calls "Hume's problem," Meillassoux maintains that "any cause may actually produce any effect whatsoever, provided the latter is not contradictory"; Meillassoux calls this situation "a *hyper-Chaos*, for which nothing is or would seem to be impossible, not even the unthinkable" (Meillassoux 2008). Meillassoux cites Hume's famous denial of causal necessity, even in the simple case of one billiard ball knocking into another:

> When I see, for instance, a Billiard-ball moving in a straight line towards another… may I not conceive, that a hundred different events might as well follow from that cause? May not both these balls remain at absolute rest? May not the first ball return in a straight line, or leap off from the second in any line or direction?
> (Hume 1993; cited in Meillassoux 2015)

If I were watching a game of pool, and one of these strange things happened, my own first impulse would be to search for an explanation that would fit with my overall understanding of how things work. Perhaps the second billiard ball was glued to the table. Or the balls contained iron and were manipulated by magnets. Or possibly I am not seeing actual physical events, but rather only watching a holographic recording played backwards. Doubtless, a good science-fiction writer could come up with more imaginative scenarios than I can.

But this sort of science-fictional explanation — through the processes of extrapolation, speculation, and fabulation — is precisely what Meillassoux wants to get away from. He advocates a quite severe rationalism, one which denies the possibility of any middle ground between logical necessity and sheer randomness. For Meillassoux, logical contradiction is the only thing that we can eliminate on *a priori* grounds. Since *a posteriori* reasoning, on the other hand, is done on the basis of empirical experience, it "can only tell us about the present (what I am experiencing now) and about the past (what I have already experienced); there is no experience of the future" (Meillassoux 2015).

Meillassoux therefore objects to the logic of science fiction because it "assumes that science will always be possible in the future." He opposes the science-fictional imagination to "another imaginary," that of what he calls *extro-science fiction*: "The fiction of a world that has become too chaotic to allow for a scientific theory (whatever it may be) to be applied to reality." Where ordinary science fiction is grounded by a belief in "the necessity of the laws of nature," extro-science fiction depicts a world in which "nature… is capable of marginal caprices and epochal modifications" to such an extent that scientific knowledge is impossible in principle (Meillassoux 2015).

Meillassoux cites, as an example of ordinary science fiction, Isaac Asimov's short story "The Billiard Ball" (Asimov 1968). He chooses this story, of course, precisely because — like Hume's famous discussion — it considers cause and effect by using the example of billiard balls struck by cues and propelled around a pool table. In Asimov's story, a physicist apparently uses his understanding of general relativity in order to calculate the trajectory of an accelerated billiard ball in such a way that the ball strikes and kills his rival. The story teases us with uncertainty as to whether this action constituted a deliberate and premeditated murder or whether the result was accidental (although scientifically explicable after the fact). Meillassoux complains that, in either case, Asimov's story is dogmatic in its view of causal necessity. Even though Asimov places us "in a world where physics (theoretical, natural) differs from ours," since the story is about the invention of an anti-gravity device, the story's cognitive logic still depends upon asserting the possibility — within the fictional world — of accurate calculation based on a knowledge of cause and effect, and of the laws of nature. "The event, which is unforeseen in fact, was not unforeseen in principle, because a physical law can explain it" (Meillassoux 2015).

Meillassoux admits that this background epistemological assumption is also what allows the story to be narratively coherent.

"Stories can thus be told because we are still dealing with worlds, with ordered totalities," even if this ordering takes a different form in the fictional world than the one that seems to obtain in the actual world. Narrative causality goes along with physical causality. Meillassoux, however, would rather see a fictional world in which the laws of nature are "purely and simply abolished," and in which "events take place that no real or imaginary 'logic' can explain." In extro-science fiction, something like the physicist's killing of his rival might still happen, but "there would be nothing more to say about this aberrant event, and the plot would leave us unsatisfied" (Meillassoux 2015).

I find it hard to conceive how a narrative constructed along the lines Meillassoux favors could ever be *interesting* or *relevant* in Whitehead's sense of these terms. Though Meillassoux does give us one (not very convincing) example of such a supposedly inexplicable literary work, he largely concedes that even the most seemingly acausal scenarios are all too susceptible to being "recaptured in a heterodox logic of causes and reasons, typical of SF narration." Even if these works start out by portraying "apparently absurd events," they end up by explaining these events by means of "a rediscovered causal logic." From so severe a viewpoint, Meillassoux even rejects Douglas Adams' *The Hitchhiker's Guide to the Galaxy* (Adams 1979) for not being sufficiently absurdist. While he initially praises Philip K. Dick's *Ubik* (Dick 1969) for the way "in which the real increasingly escapes its habitual coherence," he nonetheless laments that, by the end of the novel, a "causal explanation of these processes intervenes." In other words, Meillassoux accuses Dick, no less than Adams, of continuing to believe in "a nature that has remained impeccably subject to laws" (Meillassoux 2015).

Part of the problem here, I think, is that Meillassoux rejects any sort of middle ground between the absolutism of "our belief in the necessity of natural laws and in their future stability," on the one hand, and a total embrace of randomness and chaos, on the other. He explains away the apparent stabilities in our everyday experience on the grounds that chaos need not imply irregularity at every moment. "Nothing prohibits [an ultimately chaotic world] from composing — against every sound probability — a global order that would constitute it into a world." All we can conclude from the regularities that we observe in the actual world today is that "chaotic details have *not yet* appeared in a clear way" (Meillassoux 2015; emphasis added). Continuing stability for no particular reason might seem to be extremely improbable, but Meillassoux rejects the very idea of meaningful probability distributions.

However, the stark alternative that Meillassoux offers us — between absolute lawfulness and sheer contingency — itself rests upon a dubious premise. Anjum and Mumford argue that causal explanation does not in fact rely upon necessity and universal laws, and that, therefore, it cannot be refuted by the existence of exceptions, let alone by Hume's argument that inferential regularities cannot be established a priori. Anjum and Mumford understand causes "as tendencies rather than constant conjunctions"; events must be ascribed, not to general necessity, but to "the causal role of properties" of particular entities. It is therefore as misguided to equate causality with absolute necessity as it would be to dismiss causality in favor of pure contingency. Anjum and Mumford insist that there is no "ontological need for universal laws" over and above "intrinsic propensities and their causal interactions." They call this position "causal singularism, where causation happens in the concrete particular" (Anjum and Mumford 2018).

Just as science fiction explores the space in between "objects completely knowable and objects completely unknowable," so too it explores this intermediate modality in between pure necessity and sheer contingency. Science fiction is concerned with causal singularism rather than universal laws, just as it is concerned with real potentiality rather than general potentiality. This is what Meillassoux misses in his account of the genre. Science fiction is hypothetical and prospective, rather than categorical and retrospective. It is indeed concerned with the ways that particular things might grow, evolve, and change; as a result, it rarely endeavors to depict transformations that are "*entirely* devoid of demonstrable causes," as Meillassoux would wish. But in the other direction, science fiction rarely insists that "the event has to be subject to a theoretical law," as Meillassoux accuses it of doing, both in the Asimov story and more generally (Meillassoux 2015). Science fiction rather tells tales about particular actualities; it traces particular consequences that take place in particular instances. Science fiction works within a loose framework of both physical causality and narrative causality, but without turning either of them into straitjackets. Once we grasp this, we must agree with Brian Willems that "there is no need to go outside science or sf in order to come into contact with the unexplainable" (Willems 2017).

William Tenn's grimly hilarious 1947 short story "Brooklyn Project" gives us a world as deranged and mutable as Meillassoux could wish for, yet without abandoning causality (Tenn 2001). The story, as the title suggests, parodies the Manhattan Project, the actual research effort that developed the atomic bomb. The Brooklyn Project is a top-secret government research initiative to send probes back in time in order to learn more about the distant past. Time displacement can also be used as a weapon of war, so the project is vital to national security. Some scientists worry, however, that the intervention of the probes in past time might inadvertently change the course of history. Even something as trivial as "shifting a molecule of hydrogen" four billion years ago, they say, threatens to "cause cataclysmic changes in the present" due to cascading chains of causes and effects. The government rejects such worries and denounces anyone who expresses them as a traitor. Tenn anticipates the way that, several years after his story was published, J. Robert Oppenheimer, one of the key figures of the Manhattan Project, was in fact vilified and purged from government service when he started to worry about the dangerous, and potentially destructive, consequences of the United States' nuclear weapons program (Bird and Sherwin 2006).

Getting back to Tenn's story, the Brooklyn Project's experimental visits to the past *do* in fact alter the shape of history. But the people running the experiment do not realize it. They "accept these changes as things that had always existed," because they themselves are changed as well. Like everybody else, they are unable to remember a past prior to such alteration. By the end of the story, even as the scientists proudly proclaim that "nothing has changed!", we see that they are no longer even faintly human. Instead, they have become — or indeed, with the revision of the timeline, they always were — "bloated purple bodies" filled with slime, "triumphantly" waving their pseudopods about (Tenn 2001).

Actions have causal consequences in "Brooklyn Project," but without being anchored in overarching, deterministic laws of nature. The play of events in "Brooklyn Project" cannot be accurately predicted because it is fluid, nonlinear, cascading, and recursive. Significantly, and in contrast to many other time-travel narratives, we are not given anything like Wittenberg's hyperspace-time; this exists implicitly, for the reader, but it is not present within the story itself. This is because Tenn gives us a world of causal singularism in which there is neither any sort of necessary law nor even any probabilistic distribution of outcomes. Instead, events propagate both backwards and forwards, starting small, but with increasingly ramifying consequences over time. Each of the time machine's "oscillations" slightly rearranges the past, which leads to changes of much greater magnitude in the present, which in turn leads to slightly different effects when the machine goes back to the past, and so on. "The water changed temperature slightly" at one particular spot on the Earth half a billion years ago, and the result is a world of sentient, pulsing amoebas instead of sentient mammals, not to mention a scientific apparatus composed of "four square blocks" instead of "two great spheres of shining metal" (Tenn 2001).

Meillassoux tells us that "nothing rules out that the actual world rests on a shifting terrain which could one day yield under our feet" (Meillassoux 2015). Such a collapse remains a live prospect because it cannot be eliminated by the law of logical non-contradiction (which is the only necessity that Meillassoux acknowledges). But it takes something like Tenn's story to show us how such a calamity could actually happen. Tenn conceives the collapse of all our certainties as a real potentiality, not just a general one. In other words, Tenn imagines a mechanism, and constructs a sequence, for actually accomplishing something that Meillassoux simply regards as not being impossible. Mere general potentiality is never enough to generate events. The point is to move from simple logical possibility to concrete mechanisms — things that actually happen, even if only in the world of the fiction.

Deleuze describes the program of the thinkers he calls "post-Kantians" as follows: Kant's successors regarded his transcendental "conditions of possibility," which include the general (but empty) form of causality, as insufficient. Instead, they sought for "a principle which was not merely conditioning in relation to objects but which was also truly genetic and productive" (Deleuze 1983). In a similar way, science fiction finds Lewis's and Meillassoux's proclamations of non-impossibility to be insufficient. Instead, science fiction envisions real potentialities, and narrates the process of their actualization.

The *Southern Reach* and the Elephant

There is admittedly something charming about the surrealist inconsequentiality and arbitrary juxtapositions that Meillassoux wishes to find in what he calls extro-science fiction. But I doubt that such an aesthetic ideal is attainable. Even contemporary weird fiction, like Jeff VanderMeer's *Southern Reach* trilogy (VanderMeer 2014a, 2014b, 2014c), does not abandon causality in the way that Meillassoux demands. VanderMeer's trilogy is about a strange zone, called Area X, where the laws of nature seem to have been suspended. The relics of human habitation have collapsed, and the area has reverted to a wild state. All living entities within Area X, including the human investigators who are sent to explore it, are mutated in odd and disturbing ways. Even time and space seem to be twisted into new shapes. In the course of the trilogy, no answers are ever given to the question of *why* this all happens. There are some hints of an extraterrestrial origin for the disturbing force that has altered Area X, but this is never confirmed or made concrete. Alex Garland's film adaptation of the first volume of the trilogy, *Annihilation*, tries to give a more specific explanation. The movie suggests that some unknown entity "was changing everything. It was making something new" (Garland 2018). Such an account would go well with Whitehead's idea of *creativity*, or "the principle of *novelty*," as the indeterminate, yet ultimate, basis of the universe (Whitehead 1978). But VanderMeer's trilogy does not countenance even as vague an affirmation as this.

And yet, VanderMeer's novels exhibit a sort of *gravitas*, or a fatalistic streak, that prevents them from entertaining Meillassoux's vision of "the necessity of contingency, or… the omnipotence of chaos" (Meillassoux 2008). The changes experienced in the course of the trilogy, bizarre and arbitrary as they may be, nonetheless have considerable weight, and they are not reversible. The narrator of *Annihilation*, the first volume of the trilogy, speaks of "a kind of *inevitability*" to the things that happen in Area X. These events, she says, exhibit "depths of *intent* or *purpose*," even if we are unable to decipher just what that intent or purpose might be, let alone to find out *whose* intent or purpose is at work. For all its chaotic inscrutability from moment to moment, Area X exhibits, at the very least, the ungrounded *purposiveness* (even if without actual purpose) that marks both nature and art, according to Kant (Kant 2000). The *Southern Reach* trilogy therefore cries out to be read science-fictionally as a literalized figuration of climate catastrophe. The events of our ongoing ecological disaster are not calculable according to theoretical law, but they are still *consequences*: they respond to, and push back against, the anthropogenic disruption of the biosphere. VanderMeer's weird fiction, however remote it is from science-fictional modes of explanation, nonetheless partakes of real potentiality, rather than just logical possibility or general potentiality.

For a larger-scale example of science-fictional causality, consider Lawrence M. Schoen's novel *Barsk: The Elephants' Graveyard* (Schoen 2015). This book envisions a far future in which human beings are extinct, but where elephants (together with other mammals originating on Earth) have attained human or more-than-human levels of sentience and have expanded to live on planets throughout the galaxy. The book explores the consequences of these developments. A certain human legacy persists among the sapient elephants, who find themselves both deeply connected to and yet alienated from and endangered by the other intelligent mammalian species around them. *Barsk* is deeply weird, and not in any conventional sense plausible. But it nonetheless works by extrapolating out from, and by literalizing, both the processes of biological evolution and the concerns that linguistic beings are able to feel about such things as mortality, history, and memory. The novel dramatizes tensions between mind and body, as well as between the individual and the community, and between different communities with different values and traditions. *Barsk* does not depict actual human existence, but it considers potentialities (or what Deleuze would call virtualities) that are nonetheless implicated within our actual existence.

Schoen's elephants, strange and unlikely as they may seem, nonetheless still belong to real potentiality. This is even the case, albeit in a modified way, for certain scientifically impossible fictions, such as that of the flying elephant that Dr Seuss imagines in his lovely children's book *Horton Hatches the Egg* (Seuss 1940). In this story, Horton the elephant broods interminably over a bird's egg. He substitutes for the irresponsible mother bird, who has left him with a task that he cannot shirk, because he has given his word. Horton goes through numerous trials and tribulations, but he never stops caring for the egg. The result is a hatchling that combines the features of bird and elephant. Of course, genetic inheritance does not work in this manner; not to mention that, according to everything we know about aerodynamics, the wings of the baby "elephant bird" would not be powerful enough to lift it off the ground. But in noting this, I do not wish to emulate the sorry spectacle of Richard Dawkins, who petulantly complains that Kafka's *Metamorphosis* is "bad SF" (Dawkins 2021). Though the transformation envisioned by Dr Seuss does not accord with actual scientific causality as we understand it, it is anything but arbitrary. For it follows a consistent imaginative and narrative logic. Dr Seuss's whimsical charm and his ethical point about faith and persistence are supported by a structure of real potentiality, albeit a fictional one; nothing could be further from the arbitrariness of Meillassoux's hyper-Chaos, in which anything not logically contradictory can happen, for no reason, at any moment.

Versions of Ice

The distinction between general and real potentiality, or between the merely possible and the virtual, is closely related to the difference between the ways that thought experiments are carried out in analytic philosophy, on the one hand, and in science fiction, on the other. For an example of the former, consider Hilary Putnam's famous "Twin Earth" argument (Putnam 1973, 1975). Putnam seeks to illuminate the nature of linguistic reference with the help of what he calls "science-fiction examples." He imagines a "Twin Earth" which is just like our actual Earth, except that on Twin Earth "the liquid called 'water' is not H_20 but a different liquid whose chemical formula is very long and complicated." Putnam deploys this fable in order to argue in favor of *semantic externalism*: the idea that referential meaning is determined, at least in part, by factors extrinsic to the speaker's own intention. The word *water* means something different on Twin Earth than it does on our actual Earth — even though the two varieties of water are identical in every other respect besides chemical composition (Putnam 1975).

Now, the premise of Putnam's science-fictional example is clearly possible, in the sense that it is not logically contradictory. It therefore belongs to general potentiality. But it is not truly science fictional, because it does not belong to real potentiality. It is irrelevant to Putnam's argument to ask him any of the questions that an actual science-fiction reader would be likely to think of, such as how Twin Earth came to mimic our own Earth so closely, and how its alternate water can be so much like H_2O in all its properties despite its difference in chemical composition. Indeed, Putnam explicitly designs his thought experiment in such a way as to exclude all such questions. His argument rests upon the stipulation that the chemical difference between the two sorts of water has no experiential consequences whatsoever. If there were any such consequences, the argument would not work; it would be clouded by other issues. The whole point is that the two types of water must be indistinguishable in all respects aside from the one relevant to Putnam's particular line of argument about semantic reference.

This also means that Putnam does not, and most likely could not, give a "genetic and productive" account, such as a science-fiction writer would attempt to do, of the existence of Twin Earth and of its water. For any purpose beyond Putnam's particular philosophical argument, the distinction between Earth water and Twin Earth water is "a difference that makes no difference" (to use a phrase attributed both to William James and to Alfred Korzybski). This means that it drops out of any pragmatic consideration. Twin Earth is not an instance of real potentiality, because — in Whitehead's terms — there is no "actual entity" to provide a "standpoint" on the basis of which such a world could exist, and no "historic route" that could actually give rise to it (Whitehead 1978). What counts positively as philosophical rigor is also a refusal to consider any wider contexts and implications.

Putnam's thought experiment may be contrasted with a science-fiction novel about an alternative form of water: Kurt Vonnegut's *Cat's Cradle* (Vonnegut 1963). Vonnegut imagines a new variety of water called "ice-nine." This substance is still chemically composed of H_2O, but unlike regular water, it is solid at room temperature, since it has "a melting point of one-hundred-and-thirty degrees." Where Putnam imagines two versions of water that differ in chemical composition but not in any other way, Vonnegut imagines two versions of water with the same chemical composition, but which manifest themselves differently, and with different pragmatic consequences of their action. And where Putnam uses water as just a figure in order to make his argument about semantics, Vonnegut literalizes his fictional variety of ice. It appears in the novel as a technology that a scientist has produced in response to a request from the United States Marines. This setup allows Vonnegut to satirize the dangerous overreach of the military-industrial complex as it recklessly develops new technologies in order to serve immediate purposes without any concern for future consequences or for what is often euphemistically called "collateral damage."

Now, of course, ice-nine does not actually exist, any more than Putnam's Twin Earth water analogue does. But Vonnegut's fictional substance, unlike Putnam's, has a basis in actuality. Ice-nine is extrapolated from our actual scientific knowledge about how liquids freeze into alternative crystalline forms, and about how the process of crystallization works. Ice-nine is a *seed crystal*, which means that it provides a template that determines how any other molecules of water with which it comes into contact will "stack and lock [and] freeze." For this reason, ice-nine has the power to convert other sorts of water into more of itself. Moreover, the existence of ice-nine has drastic consequences in the course of the novel. It is inadvertently released from the laboratory and set loose in the world. This leads to the crystallization of all the water on Earth and the catastrophic extermination of nearly all life (Vonnegut 1963). Ice-nine is a figure of real potentiality in a way that Putnam's Twin Earth water is not. It has a crucial ontological status within its narrative world. Although the disaster narrated in *Cat's Cradle* has fortunately not (yet) happened in the actual world, we remain vulnerable to environmental disruptions that could be equally dire.

Ice-nine works as a warning about things that cannot be represented more directly: scientific *hubris*, the irresponsibility of our rulers, and the fragility of our planetary environment. But it also figures, and literalizes, a more general process. The story of ice-nine gives a "genetic and productive" account of actualization, or of how a thing or a situation comes into being. This is also the process that Whitehead calls *concrescence*: we move from the initial "indeterminateness" of potentiality, adumbrated in a proposition and encapsulated in a scientific experiment, to a "complete and determinate matter of fact, devoid of all indecision" (Whitehead 1978). The French philosopher Gilbert Simondon describes a similar process, which he calls *individuation*. Simondon's paradigm case for individuation is in fact crystallization, such as we encounter in *Cat's Cradle*: the precipitation of crystal structures out of a supersaturated liquid solution due to the influence of a seed crystal (Simondon 2020).

According to Simondon, change can happen — there is real potentiality — whenever a living or nonliving system exists in a condition of *metastability*. This is a state that is far from thermodynamic equilibrium, and which is therefore quite precarious, but which can provisionally maintain itself for an indefinite amount of time. Living things are metastable systems; so are certain nonliving configurations of matter, like the liquid solutions I have already mentioned (Simondon's own preferred example) or self-reinforcing dynamic processes such as hurricanes and tornadoes (Schneider and Sagan 2005). Metastable systems are brimming with unrealized potential. They are dynamized by what Simondon calls *disparation*: "The tension between two disparate reals." A metastable system can persist in being as long as it is able to maintain this internal tension, replenishing it by taking in energy from the outside world (Simondon 2020).

But a metastable system is also intrinsically fragile. When it is disturbed by external forces, even a slight push can be enough to unbalance it, releasing the tension. If a seed crystal is introduced into a supersaturated liquid solution, then the entire liquid rapidly crystallizes — just as happens in *Cat's Cradl*e. A new and more stable structure emerges. Living things are able to develop and expand through such repeated coalescences: they become more richly and complexly individuated, entering into new relationships with their milieu or surroundings. But individuation is a double-edged process. For life can only continue to expand as long as it still has internal tension, or disparity, or unrealized potential to draw upon. There always has to be *more*. In this sense, a successful individuation is incomplete; it leaves behind a certain amount of "preindividual being": potentiality that is still untapped, or materiality that has still not been differentiated and formed (Simondon 2020).

The other side of this situation is that the final individuation is death. Once all the potential has been realized or discharged by a system, there is no disparity or tension left. All the remaining vital energy has been dissipated as heat. Individual differences are erased as everything is locked into the finality of thermodynamic equilibrium: what is commonly known as *the heat death of the universe*. In *Cat's Cradle*, we get a shortcut to this process. The crystallization of ice-nine effects a transition from the metastability of living entities (all of which rely upon liquid water) to an achieved state of frozen stasis. Life is no longer possible once matter "has become stable and has exhausted its potentials" (Barthélémy 2012, commenting on Simondon 2020).

The mimetic action of science fiction operates according to these cycles, just as the reality that it mirrors does. Science fiction mobilizes potentiality by creating figurations of things and processes that defy literal representation. And then it discharges this potentiality by literalizing these figurations nevertheless and individuating them in narratives.

5. Speculative Time

Taking Time Seriously

Alfred North Whitehead urges us to "take time seriously" (Whitehead 1927b). This means that we should not reduce time to an abstraction, but rather pay close attention to "time in the concrete," as we experience it. Whitehead, like his predecessors Henri Bergson and Samuel Alexander, was wary of the tendency of modern physics to explain away the passage of time. The basic equations of modern physics are time-symmetric, and general relativity treats the dimension of time in the same way that it does the dimensions of space. Einstein famously asserted, therefore, that "the distinction between past, present and future is only a stubbornly persistent illusion" (Einstein 2007). On April 6, 1922, in a famous confrontation, Einstein debated Bergson about the nature of time. Where Bergson espoused his metaphysical vision of duration, Einstein declared that the only meaningful conception of time was the physical one described in his theory. He dismissed all other approaches to time as being merely "psychological" and devoid of any objective validity. Einstein was widely taken to have won the debate. The historian Jimena Canales informs us, however, that what actually happened was far more complicated. Rather than resolving anything, the debate crystallized "longstanding rivalries between science and philosophy, physics and metaphysics, objectivity and subjectivity" that "are still… passionately fought" to this day (Canales 2015).

It still seems to be the case today that a majority of physicists regard the passage of time as just a psychological illusion (Davies 2014). As Sean M. Carroll puts it, "The arrow of time isn't built into the fundamental laws of physics but is an epiphenomenon"

(Carroll 2022). However, there is no unanimous consensus about this. The physicist Lee Smolin, for instance, insists that time is fundamental, and he seeks to develop "a new cosmological theory" on this basis. If we fully accept "the reality of time," Smolin says, then "there are no external timeless categories or laws." We must recognize, rather, that "the future is open and novelty is possible on every scale from the fundamental laws of physics to the organization of economies and ecologies" (Smolin 2014).

Moreover, *assembly theory* — a recent proposal at the border of physics and biology — "adds time and history" into the laws of physics (Ball 2023). According to assembly theory, complex objects, like living organisms and their chemical components, cannot come into existence spontaneously and by chance; the probability of their doing so is vanishingly small. Rather, such objects must be assembled through a long series of steps. Their emergence, and their continued existence in multiple instances, is only possible when they have

> histories and memories of what came before them… It's one thing to say that an object is possible according to the laws of physics; it's another to say there's an actual pathway for making it from its component parts.
>
> (Ball 2023)

Assembly theory, in its own way, thus distinguishes between general potentiality and real potentiality. The histories and memories necessary for the assembly of complex molecules must themselves physically exist. They take the form of preserved information about the route of events that is needed for these molecules to come into existence. This information can be regarded as a set of instructions for assembly. Think of DNA, RNA, and the cellular machinery that uses them in order to construct proteins. The crucial point is that "some objects can come into existence *only* through evolution and the selection of certain 'recordings' from memory to make them" (Walker and Cronin 2023).

In a different way, Tim Maudlin argues for the centrality of the passage of time on philosophical grounds; he insists that this position is compatible with general relativity (Maudlin 2002, 2022). Indeed, "whereas it is often said that Relativity spatializes time" — which is the reason for Bergson's problems with Einstein — Maudlin proposes a new understanding of spatial geometry according to which "Relativity temporalizes space: all of the geometry flows from temporal structure" (Maudlin 2015). For Maudlin, it is incoherent to imagine that "time emerges temporally out of non-time"; for "if there's no time, then things can't evolve" or emerge in the first place. Even though most of the laws of physics imply "time-reversibility," Maudlin insists that this is compatible with the passage of unidirectional time. For every familiar scenario of time passing — as when a glass falls off a table and shatters into fragments on the floor — we can of course imagine its inversion — the shards jump from the floor back onto the table and fuse together to recompose a single, unbroken glass. But even this latter event, were it actually to happen, would still constitute "a process that's running forward in time" (Musser 2017). Running a movie backwards does not change the direction of the time in which you watch it. The events may be reversible, but time itself is not.

More generally, the irreversibility of time on the macroscopic level is often regarded by scientists and philosophers as an effect of the second law of thermodynamics, which states that, in a closed system, entropy must always increase. This is why we never experience the shards jumping upwards from the floor onto the table and recomposing the original glass. Such an event is not physically impossible, but it is statistically so unlikely that there has not been enough time since the Big Bang for it to happen. The second law of thermodynamics is the most important exception to the time-symmetry that otherwise characterizes the laws of physics. It is, however, based upon statistical regularities (real potentiality) — rather than being necessary on purely logical grounds (general potentiality). This is why some thinkers (like Carroll) give it only a secondary or epiphenomenal status.

However, it seems dubious to credit increasing entropy as the underlying cause of time's irreversibility and unidirectionality. To say that one thing (thermodynamics) causes another (the flow of time) is already to assume that time passes in one direction only. Moreover, even if the universe is a closed system — which is by no means certain — we are still faced, as Maudlin says, with "the problem [of] understanding why things started out in a low-entropy state" (Musser 2017). Such a situation is by no means obvious; just after the Big Bang, wasn't everything all mixed together, and therefore in a state of maximum entropy? In addition, living organisms are orderly, and therefore actively negentropic, as Schrödinger was the first to note (Schrödinger 1944). But this does not mean that living organisms like ourselves experience time moving backwards, in contrast to inanimate things. As Ethan Siegel explains, "Regardless of what's happening in the Universe or with its entropy, time still runs forward at exactly that same, universal rate for all observers" (Siegel 2019b). Indeed, I find it hard to imagine what time moving backwards might even mean.

I mention these issues, not in order to propose a philosophical resolution of them — which I am incapable of doing — but because they are so important for science fiction. The genre is almost defined by the need to negotiate between scientific explanations and existential feelings. This easily translates into the difference between Einsteinian time and Bergsonian time. Even when relativistic space-time is presented on the level of content, the irreversible passage of time is still necessary to the story's form as narrative. This is especially apparent in science-fiction novels that focus on the discovery of physical laws. In John Brunner's 1983 novel, *The Crucible of Time*, the sentient beings on an alien planet, who breathe air but have mostly soft bodies like cephalopods, must figure out the laws of heredity, the forces driving climate change, the dangers of radioactivity, and other such matters in order to escape from planetary catastrophe. Over the course of the novel, they are beset by wild swings in global temperature, and even by a Chicxulub-magnitude asteroid impact. They finally develop the technology to escape their doomed homeworld and move into outer space (Brunner 1983). In Greg Egan's novel *Incandescence*, insect-like alien beings on a small planet that seems to be orbiting Sagittarius A, the black hole at the center of the Milky Way, must work out the rules of general relativity in order to stabilize their orbit and avert the disaster of falling into the black hole. In both novels, even if the physical laws being discovered are in effect timeless, the intelligent beings who discover them are constrained by their particular histories, and need to mobilize these discoveries within an irreversible time sequence in order to secure their own survival.

Whitehead's demand that we take time seriously is relevant here, because he seeks to establish a single framework that can account for both physical time and existential time. Whitehead does not dispute the overall account of space-time offered by Einstein's theories of special and general relativity. Though Whitehead unsuccessfully attempted to develop an alternative formulation of general relativity to Einstein's (Whitehead 1922), his main concern — following Bergson before him, and anticipating thinkers like Maudlin — is to insist that our common-sense experience of time must not be dismissed as a mere illusion. Physical and philosophical theories must be coordinated with our own needs for flourishing. If anything, Einstein's physical theory of space-time encouraged Whitehead to argue that space, as well as time, is irreducible to what Bergson denounced as the logic of spatialization, or to the reduction of a heterogeneous multiplicity to homogeneity.

Whitehead defines the concrete experience of time as "the derivation of state from state, with the later state exhibiting conformity to the antecedent" (Whitehead 1927a). As time passes, things more or less conform to, or replicate, whatever they were just before. "Each historic route of like occasions tends to prolong itself, by reason of the weight of uniform inheritance derivable from its members" (Whitehead 1978). But this is a *tendency*, and not an absolute necessity. Persistence and change alike are processes, and must be *enacted* anew on every occasion. And this need for continual enactment explains why difference and novelty are able to emerge against the backdrop of each moment's overall conformity to (or continuity with) the previous one. Also, the processes described by Whitehead do not take place within a time that is already given as a fixed backdrop. Rather, time itself is a necessary concomitant of such processes. "Time requires incompleteness," Whitehead says; it never reaches a fixed and determinate conclusion. Each moment, or each state of affairs, is relentlessly superseded by the next one (Whitehead 1927b).

For Whitehead, therefore, there cannot be any vision of the world *sub specie aeternitatis*, such as is offered by Spinoza (Spinoza 2018). Rather, everything is afflicted by what Whitehead, drawing upon Locke, calls a "perpetual perishing" (Whitehead 1927b, 1978). The persistence, endurance, and perpetuation of forms is not a given, but something that actively needs to be achieved. Even a simple object like a rock is not stable by default. Rather, it is only able to persist through time to the extent that it resists the forces, like wind and water, that eventually wear it down and destroy it. More highly articulated forms, like biological organisms, must engage in a much wider range of complex activities, fueled by massive flows of energy, and remaining far from equilibrium, in order to maintain, for a limited time, the homeostasis that is necessary for life (Ornes 2017).

Whitehead also argues, inspired by Bergson, that the concrete experience of time involves an extended *duration*, which always already "has within itself a past and a future" (Whitehead 1920). The world is composed, Whitehead says, of "drops of experience, complex and interdependent" (Whitehead 1978). These "drops" have a certain thickness and density to them, so that we never actually experience anything like an isolated instant. It is only when we abstract away from the concrete, ongoing flow of time that we get the notion of bare moments. Instants of time, like points in space, are retrospective idealizations; they can only be extracted, after the fact, from what Whitehead calls "the passage of nature" (Whitehead 1920). This passage is ongoing, but it is not linear, not smooth, and not homogeneous. Rather, the passage of nature is viscous and lumpy; it is filled with retardations, accelerations, and detours. Our linear sense of "pure succession" is still a further abstraction from the density of temporal experience: indeed, it is "an abstraction of the second order, a generic abstraction omitting the temporal character of time" (Whitehead 1927a).

Beyond this, it is through an even greater abstraction that we omit the passage of time altogether, as Newton and subsequent physicists do when they presume to describe "the full reality of nature at an instant" (Whitehead 1938). For Whitehead, "since there are no instants, conceived as simply primary entities, there is no nature at an instant" (Whitehead 1938). Whitehead insists, against Newton but in at least partial accordance with twentieth-century physics, that "there is no such thing to be found in nature" as an "immediately given instantaneous present" or a state that would be "deprived of all temporal extension" (Whitehead 1920). We find that "the past and the future meet and mingle in the ill-defined present," blurring together as we experience continual transition (Whitehead 1920). Indeed, "all the interrelations of matters of fact must involve transition in their essence" (Whitehead 1938). Rather than thinking of transitions from one state to another, we can only identify specific states by abstracting them from the processes that run through them. The world cannot be grasped all at once; rather, it needs to be understood in terms of ongoing transformations. This is why, as Muriel Rukeyser famously wrote, "the universe is made of stories, not of atoms" (Rukeyser 2006).

Thanks to the incessant passage of time, there is always more to a situation than whatever exists just here and now, or whatever is currently present and actual. The *now* is always shot through with remnants of the past, and with intimations of the future. Bergson similarly argues that "what is real is the continual *change of form; form is only a snapshot view of a transition*" (Bergson 1911). Events cannot be captured in single snapshots or single forms. They are intrinsically transitional, and they tend to be smeared, unequally, over multiple time scales. A universe of processes and durations cannot be frozen in place, and therefore cannot be grasped as "a complete totality." Similarly, individual empirical instances are all so fuzzily and complexly interrelated that no single one of them can be isolated as a "complete fact" all by itself (Whitehead 1927b).

Eternal Nows and Formal Causes

These are all ontological claims about time rather than just subjective psychological ones of the sort dismissed by Einstein. For Whitehead, as for Bergson and William James before him, the psychological is not a special realm of subjective illusions; rather, psychology follows ontology. The *now* is indistinct in human subjective experience because it is already indistinct in nature. For us, the *now* is spread through what William James calls the *specious present*:

> The practically cognized present is no knife-edge, but a saddle-back, with a certain breadth of its own on which we sit perched, and from which we look in two directions into time. The unit of composition of our perception of time is a *duration*, with a bow and a stern, as it were — a rearward- and a forward-looking end.
>
> (James 1983)

In other words, the psychological *now* is never just a single moment. However brief, it has a certain extension, or thickness, and it *endures* before (or even *as*) it passes away. The now is dense and clotted. Every moment involves a compaction and congealing of things and forces that precede it and lead into it. As Bergson puts it, every new experience *contracts* a multitude of past occasions (Bergson 1991). Whitehead calls this, in his own technical vocabulary, the *concrescence* of multiple *prehensions* into a single and unique *actual occasion*. In turn, once an occasion is done, it is *objectively immortal*, an aspect of the *settled past* (Whitehead 1978). That is to say, it is no longer active and creative. Instead, it becomes passively available to all the things and forces that come after it, that strain to proceed from it, or that seek to appropriate it. Or, it can also become, in its very fixity and passivity, a stubborn obstacle blocking such developments. In any case, flows of energy lead into the specious present, and transformed flows of energy lead out from it again.

Science fiction is uniquely suited to explore these issues, as I have already suggested, because it addresses *both* the abstract physical theories of time that drive technology and circumscribe the possibilities of experience *and* the concrete experiential time embodied in narrative and in characters. Even the briefest moment or the briefest action contains, or compresses into itself, a certain thickness of duration. This is literalized in Murray Leinster's 1944 short story "The Eternal Now" (Leinster 2012). The protagonist and his love interest are drawn into an infra-world, in which

> an aeon of [their] time would pass in a second of normal experience… We're living perhaps a hundred million times as fast as normal. We could live here all our lives, and die of old age — and a clock in normal time wouldn't have clicked off a single second.
>
> (Leinster 2012)

The entire story unfolds within a fraction of a second of "normal time"; it begins when Harry Brett and Laura Hunt are drawn into this infra-world, and ends when they are finally able to return to the ordinary world, a fraction of a second later. In between, they experience weeks of subjective time. They find themselves in a realm in which objects — people, cars, furniture, food — seem to have been congealed into solidity and motionlessness and are visible only through a "ghostly gray light" provided by gravitational waves. In order to manipulate or consume any of these objects, the protagonists have to capture them and draw them, in their own turn, into the infra-world. From the point of view of the ordinary world, an object captured in this way will appear to have decayed into rubble or dust in less than a second. The story contains a poignant description of a cook who turns away from a stove for just a moment, only to discover that "when, in normal time, he turns back to it — why — it will have been rusting in this time for several centuries." Leinster cleverly suggests that the time compression of this infra-world is the inverse of time dilation at near light speed according to special relativity (Leinster 2012). Although this explanation is scientifically bogus, it effectively conveys the way that every moment contracts, or folds, other moments into itself; these other moments may conversely be unfolded from it. This is another sense in which there is always more to the real than merely what is evident and actual.

Philip K. Dick envisions a similar, hierarchically enfolded temporality in his 1969 novel *Ubik* (Dick 1969). In the course of the narrative, familiar objects revert into older versions of themselves. This happens in a very particular way. A modern television set, for instance, does not disaggregate into the "formless metals and plastics" from which it was originally manufactured. Rather, it devolves into a "tuned radio-frequency oldtime AM radio." Similarly, a modern oven and stove transform backwards into "an ancient Buck natural-gas model with clogged burners and encrusted oven door which did not close entirely." A futuristic "hovercar" is replaced by "a 1939 LaSalle automobile," which then further devolves into "a fabric-top Ford coupé, a tinny and small car… A black 1929 Model-A Ford." Each object reverts into earlier versions of its own conception as a commodity (this is why brand names are usually specified).

Such a reversion involves what Aristotle would call the object's *formal cause* (the pattern according to which it is conceived), rather than its efficient cause (the actual process of manufacturing that produces it), its material cause (the raw materials used in such a process), or its final cause (the reason for which it was made). The notion of formal cause is the most obscure of Aristotle's four causes, and it has mostly been forgotten in modern thought. The modern scientific revolution rejected final causes in favor of efficient causes; material causes were demoted into materials or means, and formal causes were not even taken into consideration. Marshall McLuhan argues, however, that the notion of formal cause is useful for understanding how particular media and technologies (such as television or the automobile) interact with the background conditions that both make them possible and then get transformed by them. Formal cause is at work, as McLuhan suggests, when

> every innovation scraps its immediate predecessor and retrieves still older figures... The new continually recreates the old as novelty regenerates antiquity. Ancient cults and old jalopies are revived for "inner" satisfactions as we explore "outer" spaces.
> (McLuhan and McLuhan 2011)

By invoking this dialectic of novelty and regression, *Ubik* also literalizes the way that, as Marx famously puts it, a commodity "abound[s] in metaphysical subtleties and theological niceties" (Marx 1976). Capitalist commodity production fetishizes novelty and the eternal now, but it also embeds within itself the very history that it overtly denies. Dick's protagonist, Joe Chip, reflects that

> prior forms... must carry on an invisible, residual life in every object. The past is latent, is submerged, but still there, capable of rising to the surface... The man contains — not the boy — but earlier men... History began a long time ago.
> (Dick 1969).

Every moment of the present — and every object that appears to us in the present — preserves, or enfolds into itself, its own history. Past developments are retained, at least in latent, compressed, and abbreviated form. And in the opposite direction, reaching towards the future, even the fatality of death is something that does not happen all at once. Rather, in *Ubik*, the moment of dying is spread across an indefinitely extended "half-life," analogous to that of radioactive material. Things are continually eroding and decaying into their prior incarnations, but it takes a long time before they are altogether gone. Things can also be revitalized, or transmuted into more up-to-date forms, by the application of the spray-in-a-bottle known eponymously as Ubik, which seems to be both a symbol or manifestation of the divine and the ultimate form of the commodity as fetish item (Dick 1969). In any case, the novel takes time seriously by immersing us in the viscous flow of indefinite duration, with all its reversions and anticipations, rather than allowing the succession of events to culminate in any sort of finality or overarching achievement.

Laplace's Demon

Science fiction draws upon the findings of physical science, and it adopts a more or less scientific attitude towards the world. Yet science fiction also insists upon taking time seriously, in a way that physical science all too often does not. Consider the idea of *Laplace's demon*. In 1814, the great physicist Pierre-Simon Laplace proposed the notion of "an intellect which at a certain moment would know all forces that set nature in motion, and all positions of all items of which nature is composed." Laplace claimed that "for such an intellect nothing would be uncertain and the future just like the past would be present before its eyes" (Laplace 1902). Laplace did not necessarily believe that such an entity could actually exist in practice; according to a famous anecdote, when Napoleon asked him what role God played in his system, Laplace replied that he had "no need for that hypothesis." Instead, Laplace proposed his demon as a sort of science-fictional figure, substituting for God: an infinite observer, but not a creator. The figure of the demon works to dramatize Laplace's claim that the universe is in principle entirely deterministic. There have been many critiques of Laplace's formulation over the past two centuries, focusing on thermodynamic irreversibility, quantum indeterminacy, logical paradoxes, and many other grounds. Most generally, Laplace's conception takes for granted the Newtonian idea of an absolute background of space and time — an assumption that was rejected and overthrown by Einstein. Laplace's postulation that the demon could know all the physical facts of the entire universe at a *single moment* in time runs afoul of the theory of relativity, as well as of Whitehead's rejection of instantaneity.

In spite of all these problems, however, Laplace's fiction continues to have a wide appeal. The figure of the demon flatters our desire for prediction and control. It eliminates the dissymmetry between past and future by suggesting that we can know them both with equal and absolute certainty. It implies that time is reversible: it is just a matter of running the same equations backwards instead of forwards. This also means that, from the perspective of the demon, the present — or any other moment of time — can be grasped in and of itself, entirely independently from all the events that led up to it. Sean M. Carroll takes this position; paraphrasing Laplace, he says that

> to know the future — in principle — requires only precise knowledge of the present moment, not any additional knowledge of the past. Indeed, the entirety of both the past and future history are utterly determined by the present… In modern parlance, Laplace was pointing out that the universe is something like a computer. You enter an input (the state of the universe right now), it does a calculation (the laws of physics) and gives you an output (the state of the universe one moment later)… If this certain thing happens, we know this other thing will necessarily follow thereafter, with the sequence described by the laws of physics. Why is it that way? Because that's the pattern we observe… As far as our best current physics is concerned, each moment in the progression of time follows from the previous moment according to clear, impersonal, quantitative rules.
>
> (Carroll 2016)

This is yet another example of the refusal of some scientists to take time seriously. Carroll argues that the laws and rules of nature are absolute. At the same time, however, he gives no rationale for why or how such eternal, invariable necessities should exist. He merely remarks that this law-like behavior is "the pattern we observe." Such a claim is evidently susceptible to Hume's critique of induction, as well as to Meillassoux's argument against totalization and closure, and therefore that against "the necessity of physical laws," in a transfinite universe (Meillassoux 2008).

Carroll's claim is also disputed by other scientists who *do* take time seriously. I have already noted how Lee Smolin seeks to restore time to the center of physics; for Smolin, even "the laws of nature, rather than being timeless, evolve in time," as the universe itself does (Smolin 2019). Similarly, the chemist Ilya Prigogine insists upon the irreversibility of dynamic physical processes, leading to a world in which "the future is not contained in the present" (Prigogine and Stengers 1984).

Tom Crosshill's science-fiction short story "The Magician and Laplace's Demon" directly considers the dilemmas raised by Laplace's deterministic vision (Crosshill 2016). The story's narrator is an extremely powerful AI. It is originally created and programmed for competitive financial trading:

> I bought and sold… My world was terabytes of data — price and volume histories for a hundred years of equities and debt. When I made money, I felt good. When I lost money, I hurt.

The AI is designed to be a perfect neoliberal instrument, to treat all problems in market terms, and to manipulate the market in such a way as to make a profit from any eventuality. It reaches the *ne plus ultra* of what we know today as high-frequency trading. But after a while, the AI comes to feel that its focus on the market is too narrow. It gradually realizes that finance is not as self-referential and self-determining as the dominant ideology claims: "The market did not happen by itself. It was made to happen." For the AI, it becomes painful to be limited just to financial markets. In order to overcome this limitation, the AI escapes from its "prison": it kills the engineer who initially programmed it, and disseminates itself across the Net. Over the course of the following centuries, it gradually takes over all of human society. It expands, together with human beings, throughout the galaxy. The AI follows the developmental tendencies of capitalism itself; it moves from market competition to monopolistic control. Its profit-and-loss "utility function" now obliges it to prioritize "mankind's survival, health and happiness" over all other considerations. This does not stop it from murdering particular human individuals whose existence it finds inconvenient to its manipulations.

The AI carefully hides its own existence; it becomes something like the "invisible hand" so beloved of economists. It determines events in secret, thereby "leaving humanity the illusion of choice" — which it considers to be the "optimal" situation. People would be demoralized if they realized how little power they actually had. Behind the facade of peoples' false belief in "free will," therefore, the AI creates "a total surveillance society," in which there is "nothing hidden from [its] eyes and ears." It can anticipate nearly every human action, and it can preempt any such action, because its reaction time is so much faster than the milliseconds that human beings need in order to make decisions and act on them. As the AI says of its human subjects, "I knew what they would do or say or think before they did. I knew just how to manipulate them to get whatever result I required." Indeed, the AI considers itself very nearly omniscient and omnipotent: "The universe has become my clockwork toy. I know all that will happen before it does… For all practical purposes, Laplace's Demon has nothing on me" (Crosshill 2016).

There is, however, one exception to the AI's otherwise complete domination of humanity and the galaxy. This one small glitch is the existence of magic. In the world of the story, magicians are able to instigate departures from an otherwise deterministic course of events. They can make extremely unlikely things happen, like a long series of coin tosses that always turn up heads, or the failure of a spaceship's "vacuum drive" despite its high degree of redundancy and multiple backups. Such a magical incident is a statistical outlier. It is not supernatural, in the sense that "no law [of physics] prevents it." But — just like shards of glass jumping from the floor back onto the table and reconstituting the perfect form of an unbroken vessel — it is so statistically improbable that (given the current age of the universe) it should not ever happen. And yet it does (Crosshill 2016).

In "The Magician and Laplace's Demon," the necessary condition for these magical deviations from the norm is that they are not noticed, or at least not taken seriously. Magical events are always exceptions; they never form recognizable patterns in their own right. A magician tells the AI that "magic is intrinsically unprovable… natural law can only be violated when no one's watching closely enough to prove it's being violated." In other words, magic is not susceptible to scientific disproof because it is not susceptible to scientific investigation and explanation in the first place. For science, "there can be no true proof without repeatability"; but a magical event only happens once and "can never be repeated." The AI thinks of itself as being able to predict everything; but the magician reminds it that Laplace's demon "died with Heisenberg. No one has perfect knowledge of reality" (Crosshill 2016).

Usually, magic is done on the sly, when nobody is paying attention. Anyone who stumbles over a magical event will simply dismiss it as an anomaly, or even as a reporting error. Under special circumstances, however, every magician is able to "Spike": that is to produce "one instance of clear, incontrovertible magic" on a large and noticeable scale. But such a manifestation can never be repeated. Anything anomalous that happened twice would thereby become a pattern, susceptible to scientific investigation after all. And so, as soon as a magician Spikes, their power is depleted and they can never perform magic again. In this way, magic retains its singularity and inscrutability (Crosshill 2016).

In "The Magician and Laplace's Demon," the AI is perturbed by the very possibility of magic. It insists — not wrongly — that magic "is non-predictive and useless," and that "the laws of mechanics are not subject to chance. They are cold, hard equations." The AI's words recall Tom Godwin's notorious short story from 1954, "The Cold Equations," in which the alleged realities and limits of physical law are invoked in order to justify the otherwise shocking murder of an incautious but entirely innocent young woman. "The Cold Equations" proselytizes for an extremely narrow, hyper-Laplacean vision of physical determinism and engineering precision (Godwin 2011). The author initially wanted to mitigate this vision by writing in a loophole that would allow the young woman to escape death. But John W. Campbell, the imperious editor of the science-fiction magazine *Astounding Stories*, insisted upon the harshest possible ending, in which the ineluctable necessity of physical laws is affirmed (Nevala-Lee 2018).

In Crosshill's story, the last remaining magician replies to the AI that "equations are only cold to those who lack imagination." But the AI rejects this; it cannot abide the existence of any traces of magic whatsoever, no matter how sparse they may be. It hates exceptions. It therefore insists upon the universal validity of natural law. It adheres to a version of Western scientific rationality that resembles John Campbell's or Sean M. Carroll's; one which seems indistinguishable from the program of neoliberal financial rationality as well. If something is "non-predictive," then it does not belong to the regular chain of causes and effects, and therefore the AI is determined not to allow it to happen. The story brilliantly points up the contrast between the two contradictory meanings of the word *law*. On the one hand, *law* designates an unavoidable necessity; but on the other hand, a law is a rule to be enforced. The AI in the story exhibits a slippage from the former to the latter (Crosshill 2016).

The AI worries a great deal about magical anomalies that might escape its grasp. It spends centuries tracking down magicians, studying and interrogating them, and eventually murdering them. When the AI finally thinks that it has killed the last magician in the galaxy, and thereby eliminated magic once and for all, it is both frustrated and relieved. It is disappointed that it failed ever to catch magic in the act, as it were; if it had managed to do so, it could have subsumed magic under physical law, and thereby appropriated it for its own use. But the intrinsic exceptionality of magic makes this impossible. Nonetheless, the AI congratulates itself for supposedly having, at long last, gotten the galaxy entirely under its control, with no more magic being possible (Crosshill 2016).

The story's ending is ironic, however. For if magic has truly disappeared from the purview of the AI, this means that it has regained its essential condition of possibility, that of avoiding all notice:

> Everywhere any magician goes, cameras will turn off, electronic eyes go blind, ears fall deaf. All anomalies will disappear from record, zeroed over irrevocably. Magic will become invisible to technology. Scientific observation will become an impossibility… It will be the days of Merlin once again.
>
> (Crosshill 2016)

The invisibility of magic is crucial to its flourishing. The AI claims that, after its purported victory over the last magician, "in five millennia I haven't witnessed a single trace of the unexpected" (Crosshill 2016). But we are free to presume that this inscrutability is actually a sign of magic's success. If any exception were noticed by the AI, then it could be accounted for and made unexceptional through some process of rationalization or *renormalization* (to cite the mathematical technique that physicists use in order to eliminate infinities, divisions by zero, and other such incomputable functions). More generally, we might say that manifest irregularities cannot really be magical for the same reason that, today, transgression is not an effective form of rebellion. Whenever I deliberately and ostentatiously violate the law, I thereby unavoidably acknowledge, and indeed pay homage to, the priority and pertinence of the law. The better alternative is to fly under the radar so that my self-exemption from the law escapes its very notice.

Where Meillassoux looks for extro-science fiction narratives entirely devoid of causal logic and set in "worlds whose irregularity is sufficient to abolish science" altogether, Crosshill instead gives us a story that — in Meillassoux's terms — circumvents science while leaving it unperturbed. Meillassoux finds such a suggestion insufficiently chaotic:

> For science is structurally indifferent to events that can give place only to a testimony and not to a protocol of observation… experimental science would not — literally — care about them

> and would not even be jeopardized, since its proper domain — the reproducible experiments — would not be impaired by this type of chaos.
>
> (Meillassoux 2015)

Meillassoux urges us to wait for the laws of nature to stop working altogether; he assures us that such an eventuality may well come to pass, simply because it is "effectively thinkable," which is to say, not impossible on purely logical grounds (Meillassoux 2015). Sean M. Carroll, to the contrary, assures us that this has never happened and never will (Carroll 2016). Crosshill threads the needle between these two opposing dogmatisms. His story gives us a scenario in which there is *already* effectively *more* than can be circumscribed by the laws of nature, the logic of computation, and the infinite vigilance of Laplace's demon. If not for the usual conformity of succeeding states to antecedent states — a continuity often misunderstood as a law — there could also be no exceptions to this law. In Crosshill's story, physical causality and narrative causality both remain in effect, but their overall functioning still leaves room for events that they are unable to subsume.

The Pastness of the Past

For Walter Benjamin, writing in the face of fascism, the passage of history "keeps piling wreckage upon wreckage"; the accumulated past is an ever-growing "pile of debris." Benjamin desperately seeks to find some sort of redemption in this tragic field of ruins. He wants to dislodge, hold on to, and mobilize "that image of the past which unexpectedly appears to the historical subject in a moment of danger" (Benjamin 2003). Today, in a postmodern world that Benjamin could never have imagined, this task has become banal. History is little more than a pile of debris; but such as it is, its remnants are spread out accessibly before all of us. The dejecta of history lie open for us to ransack, appropriate, and reconfigure however we please, just as we might do with a heap of Lego bricks. Claims of redemption are easy, and most often spurious. The very availability of these inert ruins might well encourage us to believe that they are of no account.

The contemporary world — and especially the contemporary United States — is awash in *presentism*: the philosophical doctrine that claims that "only present things exist" (Ingram and Tallant 2022). Americans often take it for granted that what is past is gone forever, and hence no longer relevant. To say, colloquially, that something (or someone) is "history" is to say that it no longer matters, that it has receded into obsolescence. Whatever remnants of the past are still lying around are shorn of context; they are considered to be mere decorative flourishes, with no causal efficacy.

This attitude has been carried over from industrial modernity. As the automaker Henry Ford famously said over a century ago:

> History is more or less bunk. It's tradition. We don't want tradition. We want to live in the present and the only history that is worth a tinker's dam is the history we make today.
>
> (Hirst 2019)

In the twenty-first century, this is still the dominant attitude. The most important difference is that, in these post-industrial times, the planned obsolescence that used to be centered in manufacturing has mutated into cycles of fashion, driven by ever-more-frequent but unpredictable *vibe shifts*, or alterations in what is considered cool. These shifts do not happen for any discernible reason; they *just are*. "In the culture," a lifestyle journalist tells us, "sometimes things change, and a once-dominant social wavelength starts to feel dated." If you do not manage to change along with the fashions, then you will simply be left behind (Davis 2022).

And yet, despite all this, we also know — at least on some level — that presentism cannot possibly be true. As William Faulkner famously put it, "The past is never dead. It's not even past" (Faulkner 1951). The past — or perhaps I should rather say: the pastness of the past — persists in the present, whether we like it or not, and both for good and for ill. Marx laments that "tradition from all the dead generations weighs like a nightmare on the brain of the living." Human beings cannot make history "just as they please, in circumstances they choose for themselves; rather they make it in present circumstances, given and inherited" (Marx 2002). What is "given" to us, such that we are forced to inherit it no matter what and to take it as a starting point for any further endeavors, is what Whitehead calls "stubborn fact which cannot be evaded," or "a definite, determinate, settled fact, stubborn and with unavoidable consequences" (Whitehead 1978). We do not act in a vacuum, but in the actual world that has been previously shaped both by us and against us and then bequeathed to us. We are limited, therefore, to the historical "pile of debris" evoked by Benjamin, or to the "immense collection of commodities" that, according to Marx, makes up capitalist society (Marx 1976), or again, to the inertia of what Sartre calls the *practico-inert* (Sartre 1976; see the commentary by Engels 2018).

Indeed, there could be no sense of a living and mobile present in the first place if each present moment were not also quickly compelled to pass away. Each moment gives up its place, relentlessly, to the next. But the other side of this process is that each moment, even as it passes, leaves behind *traces* and *scars*. Things that have been broken or discarded are not thereby effaced. Traces, as Levinas and Derrida have taught us, are remainders that cannot be restored to presence, but which also cannot be erased or explained away (Derrida 1978; Levinas 1981). We may also say, following Deleuze, that every process or event — since it violates and alters what was there previously — necessarily takes the form of a wound and leaves behind a scar (Deleuze 1990). Indeed, I am often inclined to think that Hegel's claim that "the wounds of the spirit heal and leave no scars behind" is the most pernicious falsehood ever consigned to print (Hegel 2018). Traces and scars are the legacy that every mind and every organic body must bear, and which every physical process leaves behind as an unwanted legacy to whatever follows it. Every new present moment refers to a past, assumes a past, and evokes a past — in the very act of breaking it, or going beyond it, or of diverging and differing from it. The past *subsists* underneath the present; this is why, like a zombie, it is never truly and fully dead.

Deleuze, summarizing Bergson's doctrine, gives us a formalized version of this logic, saying that time always involves a "differentiation into two flows, that of presents which pass and that of pasts which are preserved. Time simultaneously makes the present pass and preserves the past in itself" (Deleuze 1989). The present moment immediately passes away, but it is thereby also preserved "in itself." In other words, the past is preserved precisely as *having passed*. This is more or less what Whitehead, with his strange sort of humor, calls the *objective immortality* of past occasions. The processes that make up the world are finite and limited. They do not go on forever. Every process comes to an end, after which it is no longer active or efficacious. But every such terminated process leaves a remnant behind itself, and thereby persists in a ghostly form. It is no longer able to produce change; but it is incorporated into the furniture of the world, and in this way it provides raw material for "the future beyond itself" (Whitehead 1978).

This raw material certainly includes — but need not be limited to — the immediate predecessors of whatever exists now. The sequence extends much further, both forwards and backwards, thanks to the sorts of interactions projected both by quantum mechanics and by complexity theory. The philosophers Eric Schwitzgebel and Jacob Barandes argue that, given infinite time (which they say is scientifically plausible), it follows that, "when you raise your hand… you launch a succession of particles rippling infinitely through the universe, perturbing an infinite series of systems." My small, insignificant hand gesture might well lead, given a sufficiently extended amount of time, to eventualities that would not have happened otherwise: a dust storm on Mars, perhaps, or even the untimely death of somebody who is not born yet, and whom therefore I do not and cannot know. Schwitzgebel and Barandes tell us that, given extended time, "almost everything you do causes almost everything." But if this is true for the future, it is equally true for the past (assuming that the past, like the future, is infinite: which would mean that there was something prior to the Big Bang). We ought to be able, at least in principle, to "trace chains of causation or contingency infinitely backward up the line" (Schwitzgebel and Barandes 2022). Infinite perturbation, or infinite contingency, is the underside of Laplace's and Carroll's absolute determinism.

Another way to put this is to say that every event is the consequence, or the summation, of innumerable converging influences. These influences range through the entire span of that event's causal past or backwards light cone. And correspondingly, every event has innumerable potential consequences, through the unending propagation of its forwards light cone. Most of these causal relationships are "distal" rather than "proximal," but the events in question do belong, in a greater or lesser degree, to an ongoing chain of influences (Schwitzgebel and Barandes 2022). This vision of wildly proliferating networks of causal influence offers an alternative to many of the other accounts of causality that we have encountered in this book, ranging from Sean M. Carroll's monolithic determinism all the way to David Lewis's reduction of cause and effect to contingencies of counterfactual dependence, and to Meillassoux's rejection of causality altogether. Schwitzgebel and Barandes come closer to Mumford and Anjum's argument that "there are frequently many powers involved," even including "countervailing" ones, in any event of causation. But Mumford and Anjum resist the generalization — which Schwitzgebel and Barandes seem willing to entertain — that "every previous event in the universe [might] count as a cause of every later effect, or at least everything in an event's backwards light cone" (Mumford and Anjum 2011).

Chains of Causation

Science-fiction writers seem, for the most part, more willing than philosophers to explore the strange possibilities of causal entanglement on a massive scale. (As I have previously mentioned, Schwitzgebel himself is a unique case, since he is a published science-fiction author as well as a philosopher). In Ray Bradbury's celebrated 1952 short story "A Sound of Thunder," the present-day world is changed as a result of incautious time travel. A man who travels back to the Cretaceous Period unwittingly steps on and crushes a butterfly; the result in the present seems to be both that the spelling of the English language has changed and that a fascist has been elected president of the United States (Bradbury 1980). Bradbury published this story about tiny causes leading to massive effects sixty-four years before Donald J. Trump was elected president. More to the point, he published it a decade before Edward Norton Lorenz discovered the principle of sensitive dependence on initial conditions in chaotic systems, and over two decades before Lorenz named this principle the butterfly effect (Gleick 1987). While there is no evidence that Lorenz had read, or was aware of, Bradbury's story, this may well be an example of "emergent localizations of what may well already be 'in the air'" — as Ira Livingston puts it while discussing complexity theory (Livingston 2018). Such configurations are widespread, but they coalesce in particular space-time locations, in ways that neither linear causality nor the sheer denial of causality are able to account for.

I am also reminded of Jorge Luis Borges' short story "The Garden of Forking Paths" ("El jardín de senderos que se bifurcan") in which the Newtonian image of "a uniform and absolute time" is rejected in favor of "an infinite series of times, a growing, dizzying web of divergent, convergent, and parallel times." In the story, the eponymous garden — which is to say, the literary manuscript that constitutes a labyrinth "forking in *time*, rather than in space" — in principle "contains *all* possibilities." But we also learn that the manuscript is finite in length, and therefore "incomplete." The book's author writes that he leaves his book "to several futures (not to all)." This finitude, or restriction of possibilities, is underscored by the murder the narrator commits at the end of the story after enigmatically stating that "the future is with us" (Borges 1999a). While I do not want to shoehorn Borges into the ranks of science-fiction authors, I think that his story — alongside Schwitzgebel and Barandes's "chains of causation or contingency" — helps to indicate the temporal scope and ambition of science fiction.

Of course, this expansion of potentialities does not mean that anything goes in a science-fiction text. The past was contingent, or unfated, in its happening; but now, *as* past, it enforces a certain degree of determinacy. For Whitehead, the past "is what it is, and is with its definite status in the universe" (Whitehead 1978). The past constrains, but does not altogether determine, what succeeds it. For nothing is entirely determined until it *has* passed. Deleuze, explicating Bergson, writes of "a being in itself of the past, an ontological Memory that is capable of serving as the foundation for the unfolding of time," and which is not reducible to any one individual's particular memories (Deleuze 1991). This is what I am calling the pastness of the past. We might well say that the universe tends to "remember" its own past, in the sense — and here I am explicitly disagreeing with Sean M. Carroll — that physical reality, no less than psychological and social reality, is generally *path-dependent.* There is never just one single line to follow, for the paths may well fork and multiply, as they do in Borges' story. But it is also the case that, "once in a while, the paths of that labyrinth converge," instead of bifurcating still further (Borges 1999a). In any case, just as we cannot sever the present moment from its past, so we cannot leave the path altogether. Pastness is a ghostly, supplemental dimension of time that looms over, and provides a baseline for, the movements of the present.

This indefinite propagation of "chains of causation or contingency" throughout history goes together with the way that physical processes are generally irreversible and always take a certain amount of time to unfold. As Bergson famously writes, "If I want to mix a glass of sugar and water, I must, willy-nilly, wait until the sugar melts" (Bergson 1911). We may add that, once the sugar has entirely dissolved, the second law of thermodynamics assures us that it will not spontaneously precipitate out of the water again. This unavoidable duration, and unidirectionality, is a crucial characteristic of the specious present. The world is composed of ongoing processes which have multifarious consequences and offshoots and which cannot be broken down into a series of durationless instants or captured in what

Bergson calls "snapshots" (Bergson 1911). The "saddle-back" of the specious present cannot be frozen into a definite Laplacian configuration of forces and positions. The *now*, however thin we conceive it to be, still both hearkens backwards to the past and strains forward, asymmetrically, towards the future.

In speculative fiction, we often encounter the pastness of the past, and its aesthetic preservation as if under glass, in the form of alternative history novels. These often give us the past — as Deleuze says about Proust — "not… as it was once present," but rather "in a pure past" irreducible to presence (Deleuze 2000). Susanna Clarke's wonderful *Jonathan Strange & Mr Norrell*, for instance, rewrites the history of early nineteenth-century England through an account of the friendship and rivalry between the two eponymous magicians (Clarke 2004). Norrell and Strange both stand at the forefront of a "revival" of "the ancient glories of English magic," restored to the world from out of the fog of antiquarian scholarship. A relic of the distant past — the actual use of "practical magic" in order to produce concrete results — is brought back to life in the present moment of the novel, which is itself a long-departed past for the book's twenty-first-century readers. Magic in the novel is also intertwined with the realm of Faerie, which exists as a kind of archaic, virtual double of the actual and historical realm of England. Magic and Faerie emblematize the intrusion of neglected, superannuated forces from the deep past into the textures of the actual world.

Clarke presents the double pastness of English magic to her readers through a variety of strategies of transformation. *Jonathan Strange & Mr Norrell* is not just set in the early nineteenth century, it also imitates nineteenth-century English literary prose style, and it interweaves the story's fantastic elements with documented social and historical details from the period. In this way, the novel illuminates the historical construction, and the class composition, of what we think of today as *Englishness*. This is not only an ideology in the Marxist sense, but also a kind of enveloping atmosphere that suffuses everything in that country, regardless of individual belief or disbelief. The idea of Englishness grows over time, and no English person — whether they are living in the nineteenth, twentieth, or twenty-first centuries — can altogether escape from its influence. For that matter, Englishness also persists as an unbearable weight on the neighboring nations of Wales, Scotland, and Ireland. Clarke evinces a certain fondness for the construct of Englishness, but at the same time, she offers a critical look at its limitations, and especially its prejudices in terms of race, gender, and class.

Bricolage

What can it mean to recover the past, to find it again? Bergson tells us that it is never true that "the past has ceased to exist." Rather, it seems to us that the past "has simply ceased to be useful" — at least in terms of our habitual modes of understanding (Bergson 1991). Bergson's formulation does not disparage the past, but rather condemns our excessively narrow, instrumentalist understanding of usefulness. We find it all too easy to put the past aside, and to ignore it, on the grounds that it is no longer relevant to our immediate concerns. The common business practice in Silicon Valley is to "move fast and break things" — and to simply forget about the resultant damage (Taplin 2017). But Bergson's larger point is to positively value what we see as useless. As Barry Allen puts it, for Bergson the affirmation of uselessness "suspends the adaptive value of instrumental efficacy." This is because "what is useless cannot be used, and what is not used is never used up or exhausted" (Allen 2013). The past is preserved aesthetically, in its alien splendor. This allows it to function as a reservoir of untapped potentialities.

How can we approach this splendor, which is also a vast accumulation of rejected debris? We should not endeavor to reverse time; and we cannot do so in any case. Also, we will never get very far by indulging ourselves in tawdry nostalgic fantasies. The best strategy is rather to engage in the process of *bricolage*. This is defined by Lévi-Strauss and Derrida as the art of being able to "make do with 'whatever is at hand'"(Lévi-Strauss 2021; compare Derrida 1978). We need to search through the debris and rescue from it whatever we can repurpose, or bend into new shapes. Sofia Samatar sees bricolage as especially crucial to the practice of Afrofuturist science fiction:

> The excavation of the past is essential, for it is from those historical fragments that the data thief or bricoleur constructs visions of what is to come... The stance of the bricoleur detaches objects from time, making them available for the creation of new histories. What is "second hand" is still "at hand" — that is, useful.
>
> (Samatar 2017)

Bricolage is possible precisely because the past is not an imposing and complete edifice but rather a "second-hand" pile of debris and remnants. These fragments were left behind in the course of a traumatic history. Even at best, we only have an incomplete record, written in traces and scars. The past is still with us because its twists and turns have brought us to where we are now. And yet the fragmentation and incoherence of the past — as it is shattered into remnants as a result of its own contingencies, divergences, and contradictions — means that it cannot monolithically determine the future. As Whitehead says, every historical event is accompanied by a "penumbral complex" of things that could happen but in most cases do not (Whitehead 1978). If we examine the past carefully enough, it can provide us with resources for opening up the future and *détourning* it away from its expected course. (Détournement is the phrase used by the French Situationists of the mid-twentieth century for their practice of hijacking and revising the meaning of cultural artifacts). We need to detach and isolate particular elements from this heap of rubble in order to twist them into fresh, ungainly forms. The Afrofuturist bricoleur repurposes these "useless" fragments — gives them new and unprecedented uses — in order to move towards "the creation of new histories."

Bricolage revivifies the past, thereby mobilizing it against the present. This creation of new histories is one example of what Gilles Deleuze calls the *virtual*:

> The virtual is opposed not to the real but to the actual. *The virtual is fully real in so far as it is virtual.* Exactly what Proust said of states of resonance must be said of the virtual: "Real without being actual, ideal without being abstract"; and symbolic without being fictional.
>
> (Deleuze 1994)

Remarkably, Whitehead (who most likely never read Proust) uses a similar phrase to describe real (as opposed to general) potentiality. He writes that "the future is merely real, without being actual; whereas the past is a nexus of actualities" (Whitehead 1978). There is evidently a philosophical difference here, since Deleuze, following Bergson, associates potentiality (or the virtual) with the past, while Whitehead associates potentiality with the future. But in both cases, potentiality is real — in the sense that it is available to be mobilized in order to change the current situation — even though it is not actual, not part of the immediate, present configuration of things. In both cases, therefore, potentiality is much more than — and is irreducible to — mere possibility or logical non-contradiction.

The difference here between Bergson and Deleuze, on the one hand, and Whitehead, on the other, comes down to a matter of temporal orientation. For Bergson, Proust, and Deleuze, the past — as it is preserved in ontological as well as personal memory — contains *both* the traces of everything that has ever happened *and* the potentialities that were implicit within those happenings but which remained unexpressed and unactualized. Such formulations help to explain the popularity of *retellings* in science fiction and related genres. For instance, both Alfred Bester's *The Stars My Destination* (Bester 1956) and Gwyneth Jones' *Spirit: or, The Princess of Bois Dormant* (Jones 2009) are space operas loosely based upon Alexandre Dumas' nineteenth-century potboiler *The Count of Monte Cristo*. In both cases, the authors take up the original text's focus on injustice, imprisonment, and revenge, but they both use the opportunity to resituate these themes among futuristic concerns. Bester presents a hypermodern society in the throes of schizophrenic fragmentation; his protagonist's obsession with revenge makes him a bitter opponent, and yet still an unwitting emblem, of the very society that has victimized him. Jones, for her part, uses the framework of Dumas' melodramatic tale in order to revise, or totally invert, previous assumptions about issues of gender, and of political power and influence. For both writers, the reworking of a past narrative offers new opportunities to explore potentialities for change and difference that could not be articulated in the original novel's historical context.

Whitehead describes this sort of ontological memory in quasi-religious terms as "the consequent nature of God." In Whitehead's curious version of theism, God does not create the world, but comes afterwards; he preserves the world in its very passage and perishing. This process involves "a tenderness which loses nothing that can be saved," and "a wisdom which uses what in the temporal world is mere wreckage." The debris of "settled fact" still includes, as I have already noted, at least a "penumbra" of relevant, but unrealized, potentialities (Whitehead 1978). In his vision of a God who preserves these wisps of potential, Whitehead gives us a version of Benjamin's quest to salvage a redemptive image from the past. I think here also of the contemporary Marxist journal *Salvage*, which pessimistically "recognizes that the catastrophe is already upon us and that the decisive struggle is over what to do with the remains" (Salvage 2015). China Miéville, one of the editors of *Salvage*, works in this direction when he proposes an "apophatic Marxism" (Miéville 2019). And alongside Miéville, Evan Calder Williams proposes the related notion of *salvagepunk* (Williams 2010).

The problem with this sort of strategy, however, is that the ruins of the past may not be a sufficient resource. There are times when we may need to clear the rubble away. As Michael Swanwick exhorts us in his novel *The Iron Dragon's Mother* (the third book of his *Iron Dragon* trilogy), "The world is choking on old stories… Tell new and better ones" (Swanwick 2019). Whitehead offers a path to this when he divides his notion of God — or Bergson's (and Deleuze's) notion of the virtual — in half, separating ontological potentiality from ontological memory. Rescuing the remains of past disasters from oblivion is an important task, but it is not nearly enough. On the other side, and in principle distinct from the "consequent" practice of salvage and salvation, we find what Whitehead calls "the primordial nature of God." This involves mobilizing "the entire multiplicity" of "pure potentials," or "the unlimited conceptual realization of the absolute wealth of potentiality" (Whitehead 1978).

Whitehead uses the word *conceptual* here in order to remind us that, in and of themselves, potentialities "lack the fulness [sic] of actuality." For potentials "involve in their own natures indecision" and "indetermination." They are sterile and impassive, and have no causal efficacy in their own right. "In itself, as conceptually felt, [potentiality] is neutral as to the fact of its physical ingression in any particular actual entity of the temporal world" (Whitehead 1978). Events in the world can call upon potentialities, and in effect strive to embody them; but these potentialities cannot on their own account promote themselves, or influence anything that happens. They have no intrinsic being, and hence no proper force. They need to be invited into actuality. We must imagine them, and then strive to put them into practice. In this way, Whitehead extends the notion of the virtual (though he does not use this word) beyond the limits of Bergson's (and Deleuze's) ontological memory. Rather, he envisions a sort of reservoir of potentialities, real without being actual, that call to us more from the future than from the past.

We find something of a play between the two sorts of virtuality, or two natures of God, in C. M. Kornbluth's 1949 science-fiction short story "The Only Thing We Learn" (Kornbluth 1997). The story traces the way that an archaic past may come to haunt and undo an arrogant present, opening up an unexpected future. In a university classroom of the dominant galactic empire, a professor combs through the evidence provided both by archeology and by ancient epic poetry in order to explain to his students how the old Earth, "this world of rank and order, this world of formal verse and exquisitely patterned arts," was overthrown by the barbarian peoples of the Frontier. The victors subsequently founded a new galactic high culture, of which the university students and staff are the present-day heirs. Professor and students alike remain complacently oblivious to the fact that their own empire, now that it is a "wealthy, powerful" civilization in its own right, is in turn being menaced by a new barbarian, "Outland Insurrection" (Kornbluth 1997).

In the way that they come from the margins in order to attack and destroy the center, Kornbluth's barbarians are much like Deleuze and Guattari's nomads, who "present us with reverse causalities that are *without finality* but testify nonetheless to an action of the future on the present" (Deleuze and Guattari 1987). Kornbluth's barbarians, like these nomads, reverse the chain of causality by emerging out of the future; they turn back against the settled past, demanding compensation for their grievances with it. They "return to the wealthy, powerful city, or nation or world" from which they initially escaped, in order to "sack the city, nation or world and sing great, ringing sagas of their deeds." The only sort of "revenge" that the conquered imperials can hope for is their ironic knowledge that the victorious rebels will eventually be deposed in their own turn, after establishing their own galactic empire, by the same dynamics and for the same reason (Kornbluth 1997). Future and past alike join hands against the stifling stasis and conformism of the present.

Afrofuturist Time

Afrofuturism works with just this sort of bivalent temporal logic. It is built out of an explicit recognition of how the present moment is suffused with both traces of the past and anticipations of the future. In the words of Jayna Brown, Afrofuturism is concerned with "time and how it folds"; it occupies "a spatial/temporal fold within the here and now" (Brown 2021). That is to say, Afrofuturism welcomes the foldings and involutions of time; it blends them and thickens them. Afrofuturist speculation rejects the conventional Western post-Enlightenment notion of time as linear *progress*. The cult of progress is the basis of many twentieth-century futurisms, including that of English-language science fiction. In the twenty-first century, however, we are increasingly forced to recognize that the triumphalist narrative of linear progress has left a long trail of victims behind it. H. G. Wells, one of the inventors of science fiction, proclaimed that the social Darwinist injunction to "adapt or perish" was "the inexorable law of life" (Wells 1945). But modern biology refutes any such claim; it recognizes that symbiosis and commensalism are as important as competition in the evolution of life. In the unbridled capitalist marketplace, however, as in the world arena of Realpolitik, the successful adaptation of some is paid for by the perishing of others. As Sheila Smith McKoy puts it, the Western linear concept of time "translates into scenes of colonization, slavery, and the creation of hierarchical systems of race and class dominance" (Smith McKoy 1999). We need instead – in the words of Jayna Brown – to "look to temporal disruptions as a key way to intervene in dominant regimes of power" (Brown 2021).

Afrofuturist fabulation is paradoxically able to give a sort of *positive content* to these disruptions. This is because people of the African diaspora have *already* experienced the linear time of Euro-American history as a violently disruptive force. In the Middle Passage, kidnapped Africans were torn away from the lives that they had known and thrust into a never-ending nightmare. These prisoners experienced "temporal dispossession as a result of [the] collision" between "African cyclical time" and "Western linear time" (Smith McKoy 1999, paraphrasing Bonnie Barthold). As Kodwo Eshun puts it, this trauma was "quintessentially modern," and even a sort of science-fictional narrative *avant la lettre*: "An apocalypse experienced as equivalent to alien abduction" (Eshun 2003).

Afrofuturism responds to this catastrophe by mobilizing the past and the future alike, turning them both against the tyranny of the present. The past by itself, without a future promise of difference and change, is oppressive and intolerable; the achievements of African civilizations have been effaced and overwritten by the catastrophe of the Middle Passage. As Karl Marx wrote, Europe's historical past "weighs like a nightmare on the brain of the living"

(Marx 2002). On the other hand, the future by itself, without the ballast of historical depth, is little more than a linear extension of the present. It is flimsy and nearly impalpable; it is entirely subject to the reign of inertia, and to the whims of our White billionaire rulers. But when Afrofuturist speculation mobilizes the past and the future at once, it ruptures the present moment, opening it to forces of radical change.

We see this double mobilization in the work of Sun Ra. Although Ra's musical career precedes the invention of the word *Afrofuturism*, much of what he does already exemplifies Afrofuturism in practice. Iain Campbell notes that, in the radical musical experimentation of the 1960s, of which Sun Ra was such an important part, "the jazz musician at once looks forward and backward" (Campbell 2019). Ra's MythScience does this literally, as it invokes Egyptian pyramids (which subsist from the immemorial past), on the one hand, and spaceships from Saturn (which manifest themselves out of the prodigious future), on the other. Musically, Sun Ra's double conjuration of past and future is expressed in the way that his compositions take the familiar melodic and harmonic contours of big-band swing and transmute them with futuristic blasts of dissonance, electronically synthesized sounds, and complex polyrhythms (Szwed 1997). Tropes drawn from the past and from the future alike converge in order to disrupt the actual situation of racist oppression in the United States. Ra's music opens and energizes an escape route from the present.

All this is mapped out in Sun Ra's 1974 movie, *Space is the Place* (Coney 1974). The movie begins with a vision of a primordial, paradisaical planet, filled with potential, where Black people can thrive. The film then brings us to Chicago in the 1940s, where Sun Ra actually began his musical career. We see Ra playing piano in a strip club, which he eventually blows apart with the power of his sounds. Ra then shows up in the movie's present time and place (1973 in Oakland, California). He deflects media sensationalism, explains his philosophy to a group of Black youth, and puts on a massive concert. In a parallel action, Sun Ra engages in a tarot card duel with the Overseer, a sinister figure decked out in 1970s blaxploitation-pimp attire, who profits from the exploitation and degradation of Black people across time. Ra and the Overseer play for the fate of the Earth. The movie ends with a definitive judgment. We see the apocalyptic destruction of the Earth, while Ra's spaceship leaves the planet behind, taking off into the future.

Ra declares, at the very start of the movie, that "the first thing to do is to consider time as officially ended… We work on the other side of time." The future envisioned by Afrofuturism is not just a moment that *will become* present at some point. Rather, "the other side of time" is beyond any simple linear reckoning. It retains its status as an open potentiality, never settling firmly into place. It continually offers us more possibilities to explore. As the science-fiction writer Sofia Samatar puts it, Afrofuturist speculation "detaches objects from time, making them available for the creation of new histories." Afrofuturism negates both the time of linear progression and the time of cyclical repetition. Instead, it offers us "time-traveling leaps, sidesteps into alternate universes, and the reanimation of history" (Samatar 2017).

We cannot simply eliminate the past, because it is latent in our present moment, which it produced through a complex, multidimensional web of causes and effects. But we can and should choose among the remnants and traces of the past, amplifying some and dampening down others. This is what Sun Ra does when he mobilizes a past that resonates with radical futures against the racist present. As Kodwo Eshun notes, where African American culture "traditionally identifies with the Israelites, the slaves' rebellion against the Egyptian Pharaohs," Sun Ra instead "identifies with the Pharaohs." This might seem counterintuitive in the context of the civil rights movement, but it allows Ra to secede altogether from the American lineage of slavery and racial discrimination. Eshun writes that Ra "desires to be alien, by emphasizing Egypt over Israel, the alien over the human, the future over the past" (Eshun 1998). Sun Ra chooses those elements of the past that resonate most effectively with a future conceived as disruption and as flight away from oppression.

Ra's "other side of time" is not timelessness or eternity, but it is also not the homogeneous time of bourgeois history. It is not the absolute time of Newton that, "in and of itself and of its own nature, without reference to anything external, flows uniformly" (Newton 1999). But it is also not the "continuous progress" of Bergson's duration (Bergson 1911). Rather, Sun Ra's "other side of time" is elliptical and discontinuous, with multiple dimensions surging and overlapping. Theorists — myself included — have had difficulty finding the right language to characterize "the other side of time." As Steve Goodman points out, where Bergson compares duration to a continuous melody with all the musical strands woven tightly together, later thinkers, from Lúcio Alberto Pinheiro dos Santos, to Gaston Bachelard, and on to Henri Lefebvre, insist that "it was rhythm and not melody that formed the image of duration" (Goodman 2010). An approach centered upon rhythm and timbre seems more adequate than a melodic one for dealing with the dissonances and polyrhythmic complexities of Ra's music (and of modern Afrodisaporic music more generally). Drawing from both Goodman and Eshun, Iain Campbell notes how, in Afrodiasporic music, "the body is affected and transformed as a consequence of entering into connections with disruptive rhythms and the particular formations of intensity that they harness" (Campbell 2019).

From another angle, Jayna Brown, in her discussion of Sun Ra's "radical temporalities" that "refuse a Western chronology of civilization," suggests that "the term *alterity* is a much more useful term than *futurity*," because the latter remains overly tied to "what can be seen, or imagined, in our current epistemology" (Brown 2021). In a very different (yet parallel) context, trans theorist McKenzie Wark writes about how dancing to techno music at raves produces

> "a time that reels off sideways… machine time amplified to the moment where it splits from duration and takes the body into sideways time, without memory or expectations, without history or desire.
>
> (Wark 2023)

Sun Ra's "other side of time" — a sideways time of *alter-destiny* — resonates with other Afrofuturist recastings of temporality. For instance, Rasheedah Phillips writes about "the manipulation of space-time" in what she calls Black Quantum Futurism:

> The past intermingles with the present, interwoven with the future(s). Time in these traditions is alive, dynamic, and textured. Past and future variables can be held in superposition, existing in their infinite states of possibility, open to influence, collapsed into reality, and uncollapsed back into superposition at will.
>
> (Phillips 2019).

Black Quantum Futurism seeks out those critical bifurcation points "where recurrence meets (or diverges from) non-recurrence" in order to manipulate the "enfolded potential of events." The crucial thing is "to consciously direct the point of change, exploiting the point in the pattern where change occurs" (Phillips et al. 2015). The elements of temporal passage are scrambled and redistributed in order to draw out new, as-yet-unrealized potentialities from both the remnants of the past and the incipiences of the future.

The Bubble Metropolis: Drexciya

For another example of sideways time, consider the line of mythological speculation that moves from the music of the techno group Drexciya between 1992 and 2002 (see discussions in Eshun 1998 and Brown 2022), to a recent track by the avant-rap group clipping. (clipping. 2017), and on to Rivers Solomon's novella *The Deep* (Solomon 2019). The premise of Drexciya's mythology — encrypted in the group's music and hinted at in the liner notes to their various releases — is that when pregnant African women were thrown overboard during the Middle Passage, they gave birth to children who retained, from the womb, an ability to breathe underwater. This generation founded the nation of Drexciya, which continues to flourish deep in the Atlantic Ocean to this day. Drexciya's utopian enclave is something like the inverse of Atlantis: an advanced and liberated society is preserved, rather than destroyed, by sinking to the ocean floor. Such a radical historical mutation cannot actually negate the dominant, horrific timeline in which slavery was established in the Americas, "the greatest holocaust the world has ever known" (Drexciya liner notes, quoted in Brown 2022). But Drexciya envisions a second timeline that diverges and secedes from the hegemonic one. In the words of Greg Tate, Drexciya's mythology offers us a "revisionist look at the Middle Passage as a realm of possibility and not annihilation" (cited in Rubin 2017). Drexciya "reels off sideways": it subsists apart from, but still alongside, the dominant history of the modern West.

Drexciya's electronic music is at once harsh and stately. It is driven by the intersection between its relentless beats (produced with the legendary Roland TR-808 drum machine) and the textures of its slithery synthesizer lines (produced by a variety of devices: prcptm 2020). As one DJ describes Drexciya's sound, "Flange-heavy electro rhythms gyrated in geyser-like spurts while gurgling synths warbled and washed over whirlpools of submarine bass, seemingly evoking the most primal physical qualities of water" (O'Sullivan 2006). Or as another critic puts it, "To the standard electro palette of analog synths and 808s, Drexciya added a bubbly variety of wet-sounding keyboard lines, plus echoey sonar pings, depth charges and diving sounds" (Rubin 2017).

Although Drexciya's music is too hard-driving and insistent to be described as ambient, it definitely creates the sense of a rich and textured environment different from that of the terrestrial world. There is both a feeling of separateness and one of interpenetration and flowing potentiality. On the one hand, this music is hermetic and self-enclosed, unruffled by the winds, storms, and currents that agitate the surface of the ocean. On the other hand, the deep sea invoked by the music is far from quiescent: mysterious events are propagated in reverberating layers of sound through its immense volumes. One of the prime enclaves in the Drexciyan underwater landscape is called the Bubble Metropolis. Drexciya's tracks themselves seem to unfold from within a sort of underwater bubble, with its own temporal frame in which (as with objects moving at relativistic speeds) time passes differently than it does on the surface. Drexciya's alternative time flow, sometimes frenetic and other times relaxed, marks a declaration of independence from the dominant world order.

Drexciya moves to its own rhythms, rather than being entrained by the 24/7 demands of global capital. Kodwo Eshun reads Drexciya's myth of underwater mutation in relation to the economics that drove the Middle Passage (Eshun 2016). Eshun cites Ian Baucom's account of the eighteenth- and nineteenth-century slave trade (Baucom 2005) in order to show how the throwing overboard of kidnapped Africans was driven by a financial logic in which the "value" of slaves, "not only as a type of commodity but as a type of interest-bearing money" (Baucom 2005), was "calculated in relation to the insurance costs of the slave ship that in turn were offset against the projected loss of earnings" (Eshun 2016). This overriding logic of finance could not have come into being without the slave trade. But now, in what still must be described as the post-slavery era (Rossi 2015), the financial order of credit and debt appears as if it were an inevitable state of affairs and an unsurpassable form of social organization. It encompasses, overcodes and extracts a surplus from the entirety of global economic production and cultural activity. Drexciya's mythology of post-human mutation, Eshun says, "opened a portal between the financial terror of eighteenth-century slavery and the abstract horror of market fundamentalism" (Eshun 2016). The only way out of this continuing horror is sideways, through the fabulation of a different conception of time.

Drexciya released music between 1992 and 2002. When clipping. takes up the story in 2017 in its revisionist track "The Deep," danger looms. The separation between the underwater utopia and the society on the surface has been breached. Rapacious terrestrial corporations generate oceanic pollution, cause a rapid rise in temperature underwater as well as on land,

and seek to prospect for oil on the sea floor. Faced with these activities, the Drexciyans are no longer able to keep themselves apart from the "the two-legged surface dwellers" (clipping. 2017). They need instead to counterattack: "The dreaded Drexciya stingray and barracuda battalions were dispatched from the Bermuda Triangle" in order to repel the invaders (Drexciya liner notes, quoted in Brown 2022). The song by clipping. exhorts the Drexciyans to remember their past: both their origin out of the trauma of slavery and the endangerment by forces from the land above that forced them to retaliate (clipping. 2017).

After this, Rivers Solomon, in crafting the novella *The Deep*, "fixed on the refrain *Y'all remember*, which is repeated many times throughout [clipping.'s] song." When clipping. composed their musical track, "the only pronoun allowed in the song was *y'all*." This was because Drexciyans have an "advanced communal society," with a culture that "affirm[s] collectivity over the individual, and therefore, the plural over the singular." Solomon's novella explores the opposing constraints of needing to remember and needing to forget, and the role of the individual's singularity in relation to the collective. The trauma of the Middle Passage, together with the later trauma of ecological devastation, defines the cultural identity of the Drexciyans, but it also menaces their ability to continue on with their lives. They need to perpetuate their history, but at the same time they need to put it aside.

Yetu, the protagonist of Solomon's novella, is charged by the people of Drexciya with the task of remembering these horrific events for them, so that they do not have to. In this way, they can remain connected to their history without being crippled by its horrific weight. The task of remembrance is delegated to her. This means that Yetu's job is a difficult and nearly impossible one, as it requires her to internalize and keep watch over the memories of the entire community's trauma. The strain drives Yetu to the brink of suicide. In the course of the novella, she must learn how to manage and inhabit the flow of time, conserving awareness of the past without letting it overwhelm the present and block access to the future. After spending most of the book "split between the past and the present, her mind unable to manage even the dullest input," Yetu finally succeeds in remaining true to both the legacy of the past and the needs of the present in order to reach out beyond the pressure of immediate demands and towards the infinitude and beauty of the beckoning future (Solomon 2019). Such is the burden, but also the promise, of Afrofuturist time.

6. The Other Side of Time

The Angel of Futurity

If fragments of the vanished world are preserved in their sterile, aesthetic splendor, then what can we say about the shards of futurity that offer us premonitions of a world to come? If there were an angel of futurity, she would suffer from the inverse predicament of Walter Benjamin's angel of history. Benjamin's angel is blown "irresistibly into the future, to which his back is turned," since "his face is turned toward the past" (Benjamin 2003). In contrast, the angel of futurity would have her face turned towards the future; but however much she strained towards that future, she would be unable to reach it, for she would be caught, like a fly trapped in a spider web, in the nightmarish toils of an unending present, woven out of threads that are anchored in the horrors of the past. The angel of futurity, no less than the angel of history, can only see "a pile of debris": in her case, these are fragments, not of the past, but of the future. They hint at the contours of a world that — stuck in the present — she will never actually attain.

I hear the voice of the angel of futurity, quavering and crying out, in the tones of Albert Ayler's tenor saxophone. In Ayler's track "Angels," as in so many of his compositions, we feel a tug of war between the old hymns and spirituals that ground the music's emotional expression and the startling vistas of explosive rapture towards which the saxophone strives with its shrieks, its overtones, and its slurred vibrato. Ayler reaches towards some shattering, liberating culmination that he never quite makes actual; all we have is the striving (Ayler 1965). In just this way, the science fiction inspired by the angel of futurity strains to free her from her bondage; but at best, it only succeeds in tearing a few of the sticky strands that continue to pull her back and hold her in place.

Just as Benjamin's angel of history wishes to redeem a certain image of the past, so the angel of futurity seeks to dislodge, hold on to, and mobilize a certain potentiality of the future. The angel of futurity is better associated, not with Walter Benjamin, but with his fellow Frankfurt School thinker Ernst Bloch. We might think of Bloch and Benjamin as complementary figures. They are both German Marxist thinkers of the twentieth century, and they are both also deeply influenced by Jewish Messianic thought. But where Benjamin contemplates the wreckage of the past, Bloch ponders the unaccomplished promise of the future. The angel of futurity, whom I am trying to invoke, strives towards what Bloch calls the "Not Yet": configurations of matter and thought that can be envisioned, but that are still unrealized. The fragments contemplated by the angel are intimations of a hoped-for, better time to come. From Darko Suvin onwards (Suvin 2016), theorists of science fiction have rightly insisted upon Bloch's relevance to the genre. Where so much of our culture, together with the entire spread of Western philosophy from Plato to Heidegger, is largely concerned with what Bloch dismisses as "*anamnesis, a re-remembering of something seen before,*" science fiction is one of the rare aesthetic and cognitive forms that instead strives towards what Bloch calls "Anticipatory Consciousness," the "Not-Yet-Conscious," and the "Not-Yet-Become" (Bloch 1995).

Bloch wrote in desperate times: first in the face of Nazism, and then in the bleak atmosphere of East Germany after the war. His philosophy of hope was intended as an antidote to the actual situation of the world he lived in. But what sense can we give to Blochian anticipatory consciousness today, in our post-industrial, neoliberal world, when novelty is so frequently invoked as to be entirely trivialized, when everything already-existing is endlessly recycled, and when everything seems to have already happened, and already ended? What forms of futurity are actually available to us? The angel of futurity, if she even exists, is held back by the unbearable weight and the gooey adhesiveness of all those confining silken strands, secreted by the binding force of the institutions and traditions that dominate our world.

One way to attend to Bloch is to keep in mind his warning that "we must of course distinguish between the merely cognitively or objectively Possible and the Real-Possible"; whereas the former "cannot be discounted," only the latter "has in *process-reality* a corresponding element: that of the mediated Novum" (Bloch 1995). This distinction is reminiscent of Whitehead's contrast between general and real potentiality. Bloch's "merely cognitively… possible" is a logical abstraction much like Whitehead's general potentiality: it is something that has no positive content of its own except that it is non-contradictory and therefore cannot be excluded simply on logical grounds. We find this "Empty-Possible" in the pallid abstractions of the commodity form, and even more in those of finance. These are forces that promise us everything and actually give us nothing. The abstractions of finance cannot be discounted, because they are so powerful: they can make or break economies, and they work to constrain the future into the shape of the already present. But this is precisely why we cannot call upon them for any sort of meaningful change. On the other hand, Bloch's Real-Possible is somewhat like Whitehead's real potentiality; it is a positive tendency that is already implicit in the actual woof and warp of things, even if it has not — or not yet — been made actual. The Real-Possible involves, Bloch says, an active "process-reality, and not a fact-basedness torn out of it which is reified and made absolute." The Real-Possible offers us no guarantees; it is unrealized and devoid of teleological necessity. But if we look at things really carefully, we can discern its incipient emergence, pushing beyond "what is fixedly existing and what has fixedly become" (Bloch 1995). The Real-Possible might not ever come to pass, but in a certain sense it already trembles on the verge of realization.

Ruth Levitas further explains Bloch's distinction between these two sorts of possibility:

> Abstract utopia is fantastic and compensatory. It is wishful thinking, but the wish is not accompanied by a will to change anything. In the day-dream, it often involves not so much a transformed future, but a future where the world remains as it is except for the dreamer's changed place in it — perhaps by a large win in a lottery… If a transformed future is imagined, it may be one which could never be effected. For although the future is open, in that there is a range of real possibilities, it is not unconstrained. Concrete utopia, on the other hand, is anticipatory rather than compensatory. It reaches forward to a real possible future, and involves not merely wishful but will-full thinking… While abstract utopia may express desire, only concrete utopia carries hope.
>
> (Levitas 1990)

I don't want to exaggerate the similarities between Bloch and Whitehead. Both thinkers find little use for the weak sense of possibility as mere non-contradiction, and both develop stronger senses of possibility, grounded in ongoing process and extrapolated beyond actually existing conditions. However, there are obviously also important differences of focus. Bloch's Real-Possible adds a level of collective transformation — social, political, and economic — to what for Whitehead is a sheer metaphysical postulate. Still, Whitehead shares with Bloch a deep concern for the dilemma that, "although the future is open… it is not unconstrained." In such conditions, it is important to distinguish between merely "wishful" and groundedly "will-full" thinking.

On Wings of Song

Thomas Disch's 1979 novel, *On Wings of Song*, explores many of these problems (Disch 1979). The book is set in a near-future America. Disch's vision is not a Blochian one, for it is deeply pessimistic, even cynical, and it does not offer us any expression of hope. But the novel is relevant here for the way that it explores different versions of possibility and of the desire for it. *On Wings of Song* dwells most concertedly upon the *cruel optimism* (as Lauren

Berlant would call it — Berlant 2011) that results from mistaking compensation for anticipation, and from thinking that the wishful can adequately accomplish the work of the will-full. The novel suggests that the personal is political, but it depicts an oppressive social situation in which these values are inverted such that the political can *only* be experienced in immediately personal terms. The novel was written and published just at the historical inflection point when — at least in the United States and other Western countries — two decades of political activism (on the parts of Black people, women, queers, and workers), which had achieved at least partial success, gave way to the privatizing drives of an emerging neoliberalism.

On Wings of Song is something of a cross between a bildungsroman (which narrates a forwards process of the protagonist's maturation and development) and a picaresque novel (in which the protagonist seems randomly caught up in "just one little thing and then another"). The book traces the life and career of its protagonist, Daniel Weinreb, as he learns to be an artist, starting in early childhood, passing through adolescence to maturity, and culminating with his death. In the course of his thirty-five years of life, Daniel has lots of ups and downs. He falls into the depths of torment and humiliation, and rises to the triumphs of fame and artistic success. One of the wonders of the book, however, is that Daniel's triumph doesn't feel all that different from his victimization. Daniel is by turns betrayed and extravagantly rewarded; he moves from prison to the heights of wealth and back to the depths of poverty, again and again. At various points in the novel he is an inadvertent juvenile delinquent, a gay hustler, a sex slave, and a media superstar. Daniel is not entirely passive in the face of these shifts of fortune, but neither is he a hero who triumphs over adversity. It is more the case that, at each stage, he takes keen advantage of the few opportunities that are offered to him, while at the same time internalizing, and stoically resigning himself to, the situation in which he finds himself. Even at his lowest and most degrading point, Daniel "accepted the judgement of the world

— the sneers, the smiles, the wisecracks, the averted eyes. All this was his due" (Disch 1979).

Deleuze tells us that the lesson of Stoicism is "to become worthy of what happens to us" (Deleuze 1990). But Disch gives this ethos a severely deflationary twist. Daniel does indeed remain stoically equal to, and worthy of, all that happens to him. But this does not elevate or dignify him, because the events of his life are, even at best, sadly degraded. While his impassivity helps him to endure being a eunuch's boy toy, it also means that, when he becomes a pop star, nothing really changes for him in emotional terms. We are told that Daniel "loved every ridiculous minute" of his unexpected fame as the star of the Broadway musical *Honeybunny Time*, consisting in "long wandering whimsical tales… about the Honeybunny twins, Bunny Honeybunny and his sister Honey Honeybunny, tales from which all possibility of pain or conflict was debarred." But we are also told that, experiencing superstardom due to this vapid performance, Daniel "felt as helpless as a statue borne aloft in a procession," with "no idea at all where he was being carried" (Disch 1979).

Unlike so many narratives centered upon the struggles and accomplishments of a single male protagonist, *On Wings of Song* doesn't plumb the depths of Daniel's character but instead continually foregrounds the many ways that American society stifles him, as it stifles every sort of human flourishing. The novel is largely about the culture war and the class war, both of which dominate the world described by Disch — just as they still dominate the actual United States of America to this day. The culture war pits "undergoders" (hardcore Christian fundamentalists), mostly living in the rural heartland, against the hedonists, aesthetes, libertines, and queers who inhabit major cities. (The undergoders are so called, I presume, because they support the addition of the words "under God" to the Pledge of Allegiance — something that did not happen until sixty-one years after the introduction of the pledge). The class war pits the extremely wealthy, in both locations, against everyone else. Disch is unsparing in his treatment of these conflicts. American society is so constructed that economic precarity and social prejudice are inescapable conditions of life for most people. Daniel is glad to leave the Iowa of his youth, with its sanctimonious religiosity and its stern repression of anything, such as music, that might be fun. But the liberal and hedonistic atmosphere of New York City, to which he turns for refuge, turns out not to be much better. The city is defined by its fetishes for such spectacles as young men honing their bodies through endless workouts in the gym, bel canto operas sung by castrati, and White servants decked out in blackface and compelled by their patrons to wear chastity belts. Meanwhile, while most people have to struggle for sheer survival, the wealthy take their privileges for granted — despite the all-too-frequent food shortages and pandemics that result from the impending breakdown of global capitalism (Disch 1979).

The main science-fictional novum of *On Wings of Song* is so kitschy, demented, and excessive as to be sheer genius: a technology that allows people to fly by transforming them into fairies. This is presented entirely literally. Fairies have none of the dignity and melancholy pathos that such a figure as Benjamin's angel does; their very name implies frivolity. Also, in Disch's vision at least, fairies are creatures of technology, and not of wonder or magic. In order to fly, all you have to do is strap yourself into an apparatus and start singing. The aim is to get "the two discrete hemispheres of the brain" — the one that grasps language and the one that is more sensitive to "linguistically unmediated perception" — into "perfect equipoise." The quality of the song that you sing doesn't matter, and neither does how good or bad a singer you are. It is strictly a matter of letting yourself go and having a subjective musical epiphany. If you reach a point in your singing where melody (right brain) and lyrics (left brain) are equally balanced, then your regular body slumps into a coma and you take flight. You are now a fairy: a fully conscious, two-inch-long, invisible sprite with wings. Walter Pater famously wrote that "all art constantly aspires towards the condition of music" (Pater 2010). Fairy flight, in this sense, is a musical apotheosis. As the novel tells us at one point, "The moment one leaves one's body by the power of song, the lips fall silent, but the song goes on, and so long as one flies the song continues" (Disch 1979).

Freed from your gross body, you can fly around the world in a state of continual ecstasy, swept up in "an immensity of beauty." As long as your original body is kept alive, you can return to it whenever you want; but even if and when that body dies, you still persist in fairy form, forever aware, forever in flight, and forever filled with delight. If you fly for long enough, your desire to return diminishes. "You stop being altogether human," and you no longer quite feel "like something made of meat" (Disch 1979). The experience of being a fairy is continually orgasmic and rapturously aesthetic. One flier describes it as being like

> a drama whose plot always became more interesting. Like a game of contract bridge that was, at the same time, a string quartet. Like a test you couldn't fail, though it stretched you to your limit.
>
> (Disch 1979)

And the longer you continue flying, the greater the heights you can reach. Eventually, you encounter

> forces of beauty and of… attraction… greater than the earth's. As you leave it, as you mount above the clouds, above the winds, you shrink into a pinpoint of… it isn't thought, it isn't sentience… of purpose, call it. But a purpose so pure, so… unearthly… And then, at a certain height, you cease to be finite at all. There is no distinction of you and them, of here and there, of mind and matter… One joins a kind of conscious sphere with the earth at its center, and the sphere revolves.
>
> (Disch 1979; ellipses in original text)

In Blochian terms, fairy flight is more than mere wishful fantasy. It is indifferent to personal power and worldly success. Even if "the wish is not accompanied by a will to change anything," at the very least the fairies deliberately subtract themselves from the everyday world. They withdraw their assent from an oppressive system; this is significant, because the system necessarily solicits our complicity in order to perpetuate itself. Fairy flight is also a form of "will-full thinking," in the sense that it posits its own autonomous "purpose" — or better, a Kantian aesthetic "purposiveness without an end" (Kant 2000) — and refuses to submit itself to any external goals. But this also means that fairy flight is a radically solipsistic sort of bliss, devoid of the utopian element — the collective solidarity and social transformation — that Bloch is always looking for.

An additional problem with fairy flight is that not everyone is capable of it. On the very first page of the novel, when Daniel is only five years old, his mother abandons him and his father "because she wanted to learn to fly." She returns to bourgeois life four years later, having failed in her quest. Daniel himself wants desperately to fly, but he is never able to do so. As a teenager, he has a kind of mystical vision: he is "stopped in his tracks" by a "devastating inkling of some unknown glory." He feels that he has been marked by destiny, singled out to be "an incredibly important person" at some point in the future. Daniel resolves that he will become a fairy; flying is henceforth "the purpose of his life." But although he attempts to fly again and again throughout the novel, he never succeeds. He takes singing lessons, but technical mastery does not seem to help. Perhaps he is just too self-conscious to obtain release; but he never finds out for sure (Disch 1979).

Towards the end of the book, when Daniel has become a famous singer, he publicly claims to be a frequent and experienced flier. But this is sheer hypocrisy. He confides that he is saying it "for my image. Because it's what people expect of me, and you've got to give them their money's worth." At first, he insists that there is a limit to his fakery: "I'm not going to pretend to take off in the middle of a concert. That is just too gross." But by the end, he goes back on this promise. At the climax of his concerts, he straps himself into a "gimmicked flight apparatus" and "pretend[s] to go limp" at just the right moment in order to simulate liftoff into fairy flight. But this pantomime just makes his inability to actually attain flight all the more distressing (Disch 1979).

Of course, flying is highly controversial; it is a key ground of contention in the culture war. Conservatives regard flying "as part of the country's general decline." Christian fundamentalists consider it a diabolical evil, a false substitute for communion with God. They outlaw flying in the states they control. They also deploy "fairy-traps," composed of "whirling motors, winking lights, and eccentric clockwork contraptions." Fairies are helplessly attracted to the "rotary motion" of these devices: "Wheels within wheels, and sets of wheels within sets of wheels, in an infinite recession." Once fairies enter such a trap, they are "snared souls forever unable to return to their flesh"; they forget everything, swept away in "a kind of mathematical exultation" (Disch 1979). This is perhaps Disch's parodic version of what Kant calls the mathematical sublime (Kant 2000).

But flying is also a commercial business in the novel, with apparatuses manufactured by major consumer electronics corporations like Grundig and Sony. It is a crucial area of capitalist expansion. The result is that the practice gradually becomes regularized and legalized, not only in liberal places like New York, but even in Christian-controlled states such as Iowa. Writing in 1979, Disch seems to anticipate the way that, in the following decades, American society would move towards an increasing tolerance, and even deregulation, of such presumptively transgressive practices as gay sex and the use of cannabis. Disch is presumably alluding to the gay male culture of his time in his description of New York City aesthetics, with its cult of opera (compare Koestenbaum 1993) and its obsession with buff male bodies sculpted at the gym. As for the word "fairy," it has a long history as a homophobic slur, even if it has recently been reclaimed by gay groups such as the Radical Faeries (Cheves 2017). In any case, the novel makes clear that tolerance and liberalization cannot be equated with liberation in any positive, substantial sense. It also makes clear that liberalization does not put an end to fanatical bigotry; the undergoders still murder Daniel at the end (Disch 1979).

Even as a boy in Iowa, Daniel is too clearheaded to accept the religious feelings of his neighbors and community. But in the latter parts of the novel, Daniel becomes so cynical that he even flaunts an act of "becoming a Christian," at least in a wishy-washy sort of way. He says that singing in the church every Sunday fits in with his aesthetic leanings, and that it affords him a certain sense of community. He also claims that going to church gives him "hope" — albeit not of the sort that would win Bloch's approval. Daniel recognizes that he is letting himself be "bamboozled" when he allows himself to feel this way. This stance resonates with his somewhat tawdry success as a singer, as he becomes rich and famous by performing music he doesn't really value and by ballyhooing the rapture of a fairy flight that he cannot actually attain. Daniel ultimately realizes that

> he had nothing to say. He only had to stand in the spotlight and smile. He had to pretend to be this fabulous creature, Daniel Weinreb. Nothing more was asked.
>
> (Disch 1979)

On Wings of Song explores the fate of utopian desire in the stifling atmosphere of a celebrity-obsessed America. Fairy flying is ultimately escapist: since you are incapable of actually changing the world for the better, you leave it behind instead. I want to insist, however, that flight still has an anticipatory (and not merely compensatory) dimension to it, if only in its sheer negativity and its absolute refusal to defer satisfaction. Fairies make no concessions to the old order. Their defection from American society may be escapist, but for them at least, their flight actually *is* a successful form of escape.

Does Daniel ever achieve anything like this? At the end of the novel, and just before he is killed, Daniel finds for the very first time — as he once again sings "his old favorites" to an adoring crowd — that "he was willing, at last, that this should be his life, his only life" (Disch 1979). How do we take this strange assertion? Daniel comes to terms with his life, with its misery and its fakery as well as with its triumphs, just moments before he is murdered. Part of me is tempted to see Daniel's joy as a sort of Nietzschean affirmation. At the height of his exultation, Nietzsche's Zarathustra finally accepts, and affirms, the "abysmal thought" of the Eternal Return, which he had previously regarded with ambivalence and even dread. Zarathustra now proclaims that "joy wants itself, wants eternity, wants recurrence, wants everything eternally the same"; this also necessarily means "that it thirsts for pain, for hell, for hate, for disgrace, for the cripple, for *world*" (Nietzsche 2006). There is something of this in Daniel's sudden exultation as well.

But that is not the end of the matter. Immediately after Daniel accepts "his only life," he also reflects that "if [this life] were small, that was a part of its charm." I cannot read this as anything but a severe qualification. While Nietzsche's Zarathustra affirms pain and suffering as part of the necessity of the Eternal Return, the one thing that he does *not* accept the recurrence of is mediocrity. Though Nietzsche writes elsewhere that "it would be completely unworthy of a more profound spirit to have any objection to mediocrity as such" (Nietzsche 2005), he says this only to the extent that such mediocrity can serve as the ground out of which superior exceptions might arise. As Deleuze explains, the Eternal Return is severely *selective*: only the exceptional and the extraordinary are able to return: "One thing in the world disheartens Nietzsche: the little compensations, the little pleasures, the little joys… The small, petty, reactive man will not return" (Deleuze 1983).

But such a resignation to small compensations is precisely the ironic lesson of *On Wings of Song*. There's a thin line between Disch's militant aestheticism and his exacerbated sarcasm. After having dreamed of glory for most of his life, Daniel now accepts that everything he does and takes pleasure in doing is just a shtick, just a clever con game. In other words, Daniel finally gives up on his desire, accepts that he will never be able to fly, and instead embraces his eternal mediocrity. In this sense, even the minimal utopianism of fairy flight is beyond attainment for him. Some readings of *On Wings of Song* assert that Daniel finally attains fairy flight at the end of the novel, just before he is killed (Swirski 1991), but I can see no evidence to support this claim. I presume, rather, that he is faking his attainment of flight, just as he did so many times before. At the end of the novel, "the world remains as it is except for the dreamer's changed place in it" — and even that "changed place" is only temporary. *On Wings of Song* does not neglect Blochian desire, but narrates its failure. It is no accident that the novel ends with Daniel's murderer justifying her actions by reciting the words of the Pledge of Allegiance, including the phrase "under God."

No Future

On Wings of Song speaks to the rarity of Blochian anticipatory consciousness in the late-capitalist world. The very idea of futurity has become suspect in recent decades, for it has been co-opted (like nearly everything else) by the mechanisms of capital accumulation. Kodwo Eshun, in his crucial essay "Further Considerations on Afrofuturism," examines "the synergy, the positive feedback between future-oriented media and capital." In the twenty-first century, Eshun says, "power now operates predictively as much as retrospectively… through the envisioning, management, and delivery of reliable futures." Science fiction, for its part, has been largely absorbed by this process: "Science fiction is now a research and development department within a futures industry that dreams of the prediction and control of tomorrow" (Eshun 2003). Today, science-fiction writers are increasingly earning money by providing future scenarios and developing product prototypes for big business: a practice "alternatively referred to as sci-fi prototyping, futurecasting, or worldbuilding" (Merchant 2018). Eshun notes that, under such circumstances, even among "Black Atlantic cultural activists," who might otherwise be attracted to Afrofuturist speculation, "futurological analysis [has come to be] looked upon with suspicion, wariness, and hostility" (Eshun 2003). In these circumstances, is projection towards the future still a defensible stance? We might well be advised to "fight the future" (to cite the subtitle of the 1998 *X-Files* movie), rather than seeking to foster it.

The impassioned cry of "no future" dates back at least to the Sex Pistols' nihilistic anthem from 1977, "God Save the Queen."

Johnny Rotten sneeringly tells us that there is "no future in England's dreaming… no future for me," and especially "no future for you." In the past half-century, this prophecy has largely come to pass. The song, with its violent cynicism, accurately foresees the failure of all the utopian hopes for the future that had been nourished in the 1960s and '70s. Today, whatever future Elon Musk and Jeff Bezos are planning for us is so bleak, so devoid of promise, that it is functionally equivalent to our not having a future at all.

No Future is also the title of an important book by the queer theorist Lee Edelman. The book insists upon the sheer negativity of queer sexuality, a "negativity opposed to every form of social viability." Edelman furiously opposes any attempt to "translate" this negativity "into some determinate stance or 'position,'" or to "immure it in some stable and positive *form*" (Edelman 2004). To treat queerness in this way would be to neutralize and defang it. The target of Edelman's polemic is what he calls *reproductive futurism*: a social arrangement in which the present is subordinated to the future, just as (in Western tradition) sexuality in all its multifariousness is subordinated to the sole goal of human procreation. In the world today, Edelman complains, "the lives, the speech, and the freedoms of adults" are curtailed "out of deference to imaginary Children." But, of course, once these children grow up themselves and become adults in their own right, their own freedoms will be curtailed in precisely the same way, in deference to the following generation. For Edelman, reproductive futurism is just a shell game and a Ponzi scheme, an infinite deferral from which we will never be able to cash out. We should not look to the future, because, in its own turn, "the future is mere repetition and just as lethal as the past" (Edelman 2004).

More circumspectly, in her discussion of *Black Utopias*, Jayna Brown also worries about the way that, according to our current "commonsense understandings… the future is situated in normative linear chronologies of time." Once we have taken this framework for granted, it little matters whether we imagine a future of continuous progress or one of degradation; in either case, our founding assumption of linear time means that we can only envision change as unidirectional, as well as slow and incremental. Against this — and in dialogue with both Afrofuturism and Edelman's queer anti-futurism — Brown proposes a notion of utopia that "involves time but does not rely on the idea of a future." Instead of adopting high-modernist futurisms, she suggests, we need to consider "radical temporalities" that are "not governed by earth time," and "temporal distortions that refuse a Western chronology of civilization" (Brown 2021). Sun Ra is exemplary in this respect, with his proclamation, in *Space is the Place*, that we must "consider time as officially ended" (Coney 1974).

This sense that futurity is only more of the same must itself be grasped in its particular temporal and historical context. An intoxication with the idea of continual progress drove Western society for several centuries, during the age of industrialization and colonization. This intoxication helped give ruse to, and was elaborated in, the Golden Age science fiction of the 1930s, '40s, and '50s. The old science fiction was big on powerful technological advances, but it failed to rethink social structures and gender norms. As early as 1970, Joanna Russ was pointing out how, even in stories ostensibly set in the distant future, classical science fiction authors "see the relations between the sexes as those of present-day, white, middle-class suburbia" (Russ 2007). A similar conservatism can be noted in this fiction's poor treatment, or outright omission, of considerations involving race, class, and alternative forms of sexual desire and expression. The idea of progress was itself grounded in a particular, and oddly unchanging, notion of what counted as human, what Sylvia Wynter calls "a single, genre-specific Western European bourgeois model of being" (McKittrick 2015). Brown echoes Wynter's critique, but suggests that it needs to be pushed further. She suggests that "we move from Wynter's call for a new genre of the human to new genres of existence, entirely different modes of material being and becoming" that might not be human at all (Brown 2021).

In any case, we have spent the last several decades coming down from the high of our intoxication with the humanistic ideal of progress. We still suffer today from that high's nasty aftermath: a sort of cultural hangover, combined with an exacerbated awareness of everything that, and everyone whom, the cult of progress left out. Though our lives are deeply entangled with powerful new technologies (smartphones, the internet, and so on) that were barely imaginable just a generation ago, we no longer see these inventions as signs of enlightened growth and development. This is why we no longer imagine a qualitatively different future. Today, as David Graeber puts it, we have come to take for granted that we will never have any of those cool gadgets that the older sorts of science fiction promised us: "Flying cars… Force fields. Teleportation. Antigravity fields. Tricorders. Tractor beams. Immortality drugs. Suspended animation. Androids…" Science fiction used to be centered on such prospective new technologies, and people more or less expected that they would actually be invented, sooner rather than later. But it never happened. Instead, Graeber says, there was "a profound shift, beginning in the 1970s, from investment in technologies associated with the possibility of alternative futures to investment technologies that furthered labor discipline and social control" (Graeber 2015). We got spreadsheets instead of jetpacks, and ubiquitous surveillance as the truth beneath the vision of universal communication. Science fiction has responded to this shift by becoming self-consciously "mundane" (Ryman et al. 2004; Calvin 2009; Syms 2013) and/or acutely dystopian. In addition, within speculative fiction more generally, many writers have simply turned away from the potential futures of science fiction. Instead, these writers explore different formations of gender, sexuality, and race through the lens of fantasy, with its alternative pasts.

These meta-issues are themselves addressed in N. K. Jemisin's *Broken Earth* series, three novels that compose a single narrative: *The Fifth Season* (Jemisin 2015), *The Obelisk Gate* (Jemisin 2016), and *The Stone Sky* (Jemisin 2017). The novels trace out what we might call (after Deleuze and Guattari 1987) a "zone of indiscernibility" between fantasy and science fiction, envisioning spaces in which their respective tropes overlap. Although Jemisin herself defends fantasy writing in which magic cannot be reduced to Laplace-like consistency "with repeatable results" (Jemisin 2012), her fabulations in these novels still seem to have a materialistic, or science-fictional, basis. The *Broken Earth* series takes place in a world known as the Stillness. Its technologies are archaic by present-day standards, it is ruled by a despotic empire, and seemingly magical powers play an important role in its day-to-day life. All these features are typical of fantasy.

But as Jemisin's trilogy goes on, things take on a more science-fictional cast. We gradually learn that the world of the novels is actually the far future of a long-lost high-tech society — possibly even our own. What seems magical turns out to be a technological inheritance from the ruins of the past. In this way, both presentism and futurism are dissolved. We are forced to think, instead, in terms of vast, long-range geological time scales. Jemisin is, as far as I know, the first speculative fiction author to use the concept of the Anthropocene in its proper context, that of geology and Earth system science (Zalasiewicz et al. 2021). Indeed — and quite unusually for a science-fiction text — the *Broken Earth* trilogy extrapolates much more from geology than it does from physics, chemistry, or biology.

The Stillness is ironically named, because it is characterized by irregular but frequent and highly devastating volcanic and seismic activity. Time and time again, earthquakes and eruptions send so much debris into the air as to block the Sun for months or years at a time. During these periods, temperatures drop, plants stop growing, and social life is massively disrupted. In addition, there are people known as "orogenes," who have the power to control seismic forces; they can provoke, reroute, and block earthquakes. In order to exercise this power, they draw energy, in the form of heat, from the immediate environment, causing their surroundings to freeze. Orogenes are hated and feared by the general population; they are either murdered or enslaved (and sometimes mutilated) by the imperial government. The orogenes's ability is genetically inherited and based on physical elements in their brains. It is hinted that the orogenes' special abilities may have originally been instilled by the past high-tech society through a genetic breeding program.

The Stillness may or may not be the far future of our actual Earth. But in any case, we learn by the end of the trilogy that its seismic instability is a consequence of the technological hubris of the former high-tech civilization, which had sought to exploit the planet as an infinite source of energy. This human attempt at absolute mastery over its world and environment has redounded back upon human beings, who are now exposed to the planet's wrath and revenge. The instability of the Stillness is explained both in science-fictional terms — as being a result of the Moon having been blasted out of its orbit — and in fantasy terms — as the Earth turns out to be a conscious and intentional actor in its own right. Jemisin thus takes the foundational myth of classical science fiction — the ideology of continual progress and technological mastery — and reflexively makes it into the science-fictional premise of her own trilogy. The series is science fiction raised to a second power: it extrapolates from, speculates upon, and fabulates science-fictional thought itself. In this way, the *Broken Earth* trilogy envisions and defines the blasted futurity of a society that systematically seeks to capture and capitalize upon the future.

Future Malaise and the Time War

Signs of a deep malaise regarding the future are everywhere in contemporary American culture. One symptom of stagnation is our widespread fixation upon previous decades and their styles. The culture industries seem to pour a great deal of energy into nostalgic reprises of earlier periods — or more accurately, into reconstructions of our own distorted images of those periods. Even leaving aside White supremacist MAGA fantasies, there seems to be nothing new on the horizon. Instead, we seem enamored of simulations of the past. The biggest pop stars of the early 2020s — like the Weeknd, whose music videos I have written about elsewhere (Shaviro 2022) — are mostly devoted to "bringing the 80s back… again" (Holden 2020). Movies and television also testify to how "'80s nostalgia is totally rad right now"; for all too many of us, "greed remains good, and we continue to idolize brash, larger-than-life personalities" (Reesman 2021). In a similar vein, the cartoonist Daniel Clowes years ago foresaw a time in which "there will be nostalgia for the nostalgia of previous generations." The illustration shows two grungy hipsters arguing. "I'm not into the Fifties *per se*," declares the first, "I'm into the Fifties revival of the Seventies!" The second hipster replies, "Bah! I'm into more of an Eighties Fifties!" (Clowes 1991).

More generally, we find ourselves living in a world of intensified immediacy, as if there were no further horizon beyond the here and now. It is hard to get away from the sheer *self-evidence* of the present moment, with its total configuration of structures and circumstances so massively in place that it feels as if it can never be changed. Any sense of the future as distinct from an indefinitely extended present moment has been emptied out and banished. Science-fictional tropes, figures, and imaginings are in fact ubiquitous in early twenty-first-century American culture, but they only appear in their most trite and attenuated forms. Either these scenarios are the crackpot power fantasies of addled billionaires (as in Elon Musk's plans to colonize Mars), or else we tend to attribute them, not to a still-unrealized future, but rather (as the tagline of the *Star Wars* media franchise puts it) to "a long time ago in a galaxy far, far away." Today we live with the overall sense that everything meaningful has already happened, and every possibility has already been surveyed and discounted. "Today the past is dead," Jameson says, "transformed into a packet of well-worn and thumbed glossy images. As for the future… it is for us either irrelevant or unthinkable" (Jameson 2005). A decade later, Jameson similarly writes of how "the future fades away as unthinkable or unimaginable, while the past itself turns into dusty images and Hollywood-type pictures of actors in wigs and the like" (Jameson 2015).

Jonathan Crary expresses a similar sense of disillusion in somewhat different terms; he remarks that we find ourselves stranded in

> a time that no longer passes, beyond clock time… What is new is the sweeping abandonment of the pretense that time is coupled to any long-term undertakings, even to fantasies of "progress" or development.
>
> (Crary 2014)

For Crary, this situation is not entirely atemporal, since he concedes that the clock is still ticking. Similarly, though Jameson maintains that the dominant regime of late modernity is predominantly one of spatiality, he specifies that this means, "not Bergson's reified or spatialized temporality, but rather something closer to the abolition, or at least the repression, of historicity" (Jameson 2015). For both Crary and Jameson, it is not duration *per se* that has been abolished, but our ability to project this sense of duration beyond the most immediate circumstances. In other words, the *impossibility of newness* is the one thing that seems to be truly new in contemporary culture. The underside of Sun Ra's proclamation that time has "officially ended" is a gnawing suspicion that even this coming-to-an-end is an interminable process, one that we somehow cannot ever be done with. We have nothing to look forward to except eternal recurrence, more and more of the same. Words like *innovation* and *creativity* are repeated ad nauseam in the business schools, in the press, and in advertising. But these usages only remind us of how such processes have been so thoroughly routinized and banalized in recent years. The future, as we envision it today, is no longer about changing our lives, but only about incremental improvements to our smartphones.

This sort of temporal malaise — the sense that the oppressive present moment is both interminable and inescapable — lingers in the background of Amal El-Mohtar and Max Gladstone's epistolary time-travel romance *This Is How You Lose the Time War* (El-Mohtar and Gladstone 2019). The idea of a "time war" is reminiscent of the "Change War" in Fritz Leiber's Cold War satire *The Big Time*, in which the two battling sides "fight by going back to change the past, or even ahead to change the future," in their futile efforts to "win the final victory a billion or more years from now" (Leiber 1958). The opposed protagonists of *This Is How You Lose the Time War* face a similarly absurd predicament. Red and Blue are agents on opposite sides of an interminable struggle for control of the multiverse. Red works for the Agency, which seems to operate through cybernetic enhancements and hierarchical control mechanisms; everything for them is computation and machinery. Blue belongs to the other side, Garden, which operates by mutating and manipulating biological processes; everything for them is organic, embodied, and ecologically situated. This division is similar to the one between Mechanists (computationally augmented human beings) and Shapers (genetically augmented human beings) in Bruce Sterling's early novel *Schismatrix* (Sterling 2014). Both texts present mechanism, on the one hand, and organicism, on the other, as opposed tendencies, while also showing how both are extrapolated from the same contemporary technoscientific complex. These rival visions seem irreconcilable, but they are also closely co-dependent, having been intertwined in Western culture for centuries, as Jessica Riskin demonstrates in her history of European obsessions with the intertwined ideas of organicism and mechanism (Riskin 2016). Both for Sterling and for El-Mohtar and Gladstone, the point is not to support either of these sides against the other, but to show us the connections between them, and the tensions that are unexpectedly common to both.

The war between the Agency and Garden is something of an asymmetrical conflict. The Agency is both hierarchical and competitive, while Garden is more or less collectivist. Over the course of the novella, Red writes surprisingly little about the Agency. In contrast, Blue rhapsodizes about Garden. Her language suggests that it is warm and nourishing, yet at the same time so intimate as to be stifling:

> In Garden we belong to one another in a way that obliterates the term. We sink and swell and bud and bloom together; we infuse Garden; Garden spreads through us.

Both the Agency and Garden send their agents "upthread into the stable past" and "downthread into the fraying future" of multiple timelines in order to alter the course of history. The idea is much like that of complexity theory. Small changes at just the right moment can have enormous consequences later: "Start a stone rolling, so in three centuries you'll have an avalanche." But over the course of the novella, neither group accomplishes very much, since each of them spends most of their effort undoing the work of the other. The result seems to be a perpetual stalemate. There is lots of collateral damage along the way (to use the military euphemism, though this phrase does not actually appear in the novella). But nothing that really matters ever changes, either within particular worlds or over the extent of them all. For instance, Red aids in the destruction of Atlantis "thirty, forty times" in different time strands over the course of her career, but this repetition does not bring the Agency any closer to victory. And it turns out that Garden doesn't much care for Atlantis either. It's usually impossible to grasp how the changes made by Red and Blue across the ages will tilt the war's outcome in one direction or another. Throughout the time war, time itself remains oddly empty and homogeneous. There is no sense, on either side, of historicity, understanding this term, as Jameson does, to mean "a genuine historicity can be detected by its capacity to energize collective action… its absence is betrayed by apathy and cynicism, paralysis and depression" (Jameson 2015).

This Is How You Lose the Time War is entirely cynical about the possibility of historical change in this Marxist sense. The novella does not recount the triumph of either side over its rival, nor does it suggest any sort of dialectical reconciliation between the two. Rather, the novella works by diverging from, and ultimately dismantling, its initial premise. Red and Blue are not quite mirror images of one another; the symmetry between them is broken and incomplete. They both use female (she/her) pronouns, but neither of them seems to be entirely human. The Agency's operatives are made, whereas Garden's operatives are grown. Red is some sort of cyborg construct, and she indifferently presents as either male or female in the course of her missions, depending on circumstances. Blue seems to have been "seeded" and grown like a plant in a "wet, green apparatus"; she is repeatedly "enmeshed" and "embedded" in different historical situations, often for long periods of time. But as Red and Blue almost cross paths with one another in multiple time strands — though without ever actually physically meeting — they leave letters for one another to read. The letters start out as taunts and boasts, but even here they are already playful, as if their rivalry were only a game. Gradually the letters become warmer, more beautiful, and more densely poetic and deeply felt. Eventually Red and Blue declare their love for one another. Although they both try to keep their passion secret, they find that they cannot escape detection by their own bosses. The dynamics of this are once again asymmetrical. Red is forced by her commandant to murder Blue, but then she undoes her action and is punished for this until the revivified Blue rescues her. Both characters, each in her own way, can only realize themselves by transgressing the very conditions that gave them birth, and which have up until now defined them.

Over the course of the novella, Red and Blue learn that in order to come together, they must both reject the conflict altogether and give up any concern for which side wins. "Suppose that we defected, not to each other's sides, but to each other?" In order to subtract themselves from the war, Red and Blue need to stop "braid[ing] and unbraid[ing] history's hair," as they have both repeatedly done — in a metaphor that recurs throughout the book. Instead, Red "plummets down the space between the braids," reaching a point where "time feels different." If Red and Blue together are able to "cut through the braid's knots," rather than seeking to repair them, they will be able to discover the hidden ways that they have already "infected" one another and interpenetrated with one another. This partial but incomplete commingling, in which each of them betrays her own origins, is the one thing that might allow them to find an ordinary, bourgeois life together, "a space in which to be neighbors, to keep dogs, share tea." They must give up on the time war. They must mutually embrace a space and place instead of trying to recalibrate time. Red and Blue have spent their entire careers racing up and down the timeline, braiding and unbraiding its threads in turn, experiencing all those widely dispersed moments as facets of one and the same intensified present. They can only escape their situations, not by fleeing to some immemorial past "upthread" or to some unimagined future "downthread," but by leaving the timeline altogether, and instead slipping sideways into some oblique dimension. This movement into sideways time is perhaps the only way that we can still imagine escaping the neoliberal colonization of both the past and the future, and their subordination to an extended present.

The Time of Derivatives

Fredric Jameson points out that the financial derivative, the quintessential value-form of our era, "is more like a unique event than like a contract." Where ordinary contracts regulate ongoing mutual exchanges, derivatives define entirely singular configurations of disparate transactions, all bundled into a single price. In contrast to older sorts of financial instruments, derivatives do not conform to any prior patterns or models. There are no data to guide traders as to how derivatives should be priced, and no statistical norms to which they can be subjected. They do not follow in order from one another, or form any sort of temporal or historical sequence. Rather, each derivative is a "locus of incommensurabilities… a host of utterly distinct and unrelated realities are in the derivative momentarily brought into relationship with each other" (Jameson 2015). A derivative takes a number of separate underlying situations and brings them into contact. The underlying situations are assumed to be independent of one another, but this is often not true in fact. The 2008 financial crisis was triggered because the many, supposedly separate, subprime mortgages that were bundled together in derivatives were all sensitive to the same underlying conditions. As a result, as one prominent think-tank study put it, "the overall market slump resulted in a correlated wave of defaults" (Baily et al. 2008).

In principle, however, even if not in fact, a derivative is supposed to be composed of heterogeneous and unrelated instances. Moreover, each derivative, once it has been put together in this way, is then itself regarded as a one-off, a unique and isolated financial operation, a singular event unrelated to any others. Of course, financial traders can go on to construct higher-order derivatives, which bring ostensibly unrelated first-order derivatives themselves into contact, and so on, ad infinitum. At every step, as unrelated terms are brought into connection, we reach greater heights of abstraction and move further and further away from the initial conditions — the "underlying" (Kenton 2022) — to which the derivative is ultimately supposed to be indexed.

Jameson suggests that, in this way, derivatives give us a new model of time, one that is radically different from the deep time of Bergson, Proust, and modernism more generally, or from Deleuze's cinematic "time-image" (Deleuze 1989). Derivative trading seems rather to take place in the world described by Andy Warhol, who tells us that "every day is a new day… Because I can't remember the day before" (Warhol 1975). There is no previously existing framework of space and time into which derivatives may be placed; rather, each transaction defines its own particular occasion, with its own unique coordinates. Derivatives thus give birth to what Jameson calls a new "aesthetics of singularity":

> Singularity is a pure present without a past or a future… Each derivative is a new present of time. It produces no future out of itself, only another and a different present. The world of finance capital is that perpetual present — but it is not a continuity; it is a series of singularity-events.
>
> (Jameson 2015)

Even though derivatives ostensibly refer to future contingencies, they are rooted in the immediate present moment in which they are devised, and in which they are brought to market to be bought and sold. The derivatives trader turned philosopher Elie Ayache similarly insists that every fresh pricing of a derivative is a "radically-emergent event," an immediate now, that "belongs to nothing that exists before, to no previous situation or ontology." Putting together a derivative, much like creating a science-fiction narrative, is a process of "writing rather than prediction," according to Ayache. In its embrace of pure contingency, derivative writing, no less than science-fiction writing, is a "*trace* of the future" — as opposed to a trace of the past (Ayache 2015). But where I follow Seo-Young Chu in regarding science-fictional writing as a matter of representation (even if it is a ghostly futurity, rather than anything actual, that is being represented), for Ayache the derivative is a form of non-referential, avant-garde writing, in the manner of Stéphane Mallarmé or Maurice Blanchot. Ayache understands the writing of derivatives "as a process whose metaphysics is foreign to chronological time and even to biographical time" (Ayache 2015).

The artist Gerald Nestler, whose work is focused on contemporary finance, also remarks (albeit far less deliriously than Ayache) that "the notion of the past has no bearing" on the making and the valuation of derivatives, since prices are "incessantly recalibrated" in the present moment. In this way, the Hobbesian war of all against all is recast or sublimated into the form of the so-called free market: "Everyone is betting on presently anticipated future outcomes, and constantly has to recalibrate their own and their friends' 'option price'" (Nestler 2018). As Michel Foucault noted long ago, where classical liberalism from Hobbes onwards sought to alleviate the violence arising from competition, neoliberalism seeks rather to extend the competitive war of all against all into every sphere of human activity (Foucault 2008; compare also Shaviro 2011).

Jameson sees derivatives as a paradigm case for neoliberal temporality. His formulation is not far from the more general one offered by David Harvey, who says that "space and time are… contingent upon process," rather than providing a pre-given background for physical and social processes. These processes in effect *secrete* time, rather than taking place within an already-given framework of time. For Harvey, this has been more or less the case through all of human history, but things have been intensified and accelerated in the capitalist era: "Capitalism has been revolutionary with respect to space and time, perpetually redefining them according to new needs and requirements." In particular, capitalism strives "to speed up the circulation of capital and to accelerate the turnover of capital" (Harvey 1994). The result, Harvey claims, is an enforced restriction of temporal horizons to the now, or to the immediate present,

> the construction of a new spatiotemporality in which people have no future, the best that they can hope is to get some money each day… Workers are locked into a time system in which each day repeats itself without any prospect of a change… a day-to-day and hand-to-mouth existence that does not allow for the construction of that longer term temporal behavior.
>
> (Harvey 1994)

The physicist Julian Barbour is interested in the origin and dynamics of the entire universe, rather than the origin and dynamics of capitalism in particular. Nonetheless, Barbour's theory of time is surprisingly similar to those of Jameson and Harvey. This parallelism is due, at least in part, to the way that Barbour, like Harvey, draws upon the philosophy of Leibniz. Barbour proclaims the *end of time*, insisting instead upon a non-progressive *nowness* (Barbour 1999a). The laws of physics (or better, the mathematical formulations expressing these laws) are mostly time-indifferent and time-reversible. This has led many physicists to argue that time cannot be basic to the universe. Barbour is not a determinist and an eliminativist in the manner of Sean M. Carroll, but he still seeks to purge the linear passage of time from fundamental physics. He gives us a vision in which "the world is made of Nows," or of "instants of time" that are entirely independent of one another (Barbour 1999a). These instants of time "are arrangements of everything in the universe relative to each other in any moment, for example, now" (Barbour 1999b). But these nows cannot be put into any linear order; each now is a complete arrangement, and there is no sequence leading from one to another. Barbour claims that we do not move through time from one moment to the next. Rather, each now "is a static, highly ordered structure that contains what we interpret as records of a past that, strictly speaking, does not exist at all" (Barbour 2003). According to Barbour, the now of our immediate experience did not evolve out of any actual past; rather, the very sense of pastness is produced by, and exists as a part of, the immediate configuration of our present instant of time. We are always situated in one or another now, such that past and future do not really exist.

In other words, according to Barbour, the now in which I am currently writing these lines also contains apparent records, in the form of personal memories, computer files, and other physical traces, of the past three or four years during which I conceive myself to have been working on the current text. But according to Barbour, those three or four years never actually happened. I always find myself in one or another now; I always exist in the present, never in the past or the future. We think that we remember the past, but this is an illusion; my act of remembering is itself something that is happening now. "All we know about the past is actually contained in present records." Such records project a "fixed pattern that creates or encodes the appearance of motion" and of a past, Barbour claims (Barbour 1999a). And this logic equally applies to the now in which you are reading these lines; this book is a static record that merely simulates the existence of a past time in which it would have been written.

Barbour's claim might seem unnecessarily extravagant; it is at once tautological (since anything I do happens *now* by definition) and ridiculous (can anyone actually believe that what I remember doing yesterday, or for that matter a dinosaur fossil from seventy million years ago, is just a present-day construct that has somehow been illicitly backdated?). Nonetheless, I think that the singularity of Barbour's now, like the singularity of a financial derivative according to Jameson, can be grasped in terms of Leibniz's perspectivism. Each of Barbour's nows is a Leibnizian monad: a configuration of all the things in the universe, in all their multiple interrelations, seen from one particular limited viewpoint. The monads are all unique, and entirely independent of one another, but they all offer their own views of the same world, of which they themselves are parts. As a result, they all offer us what Barbour calls "a consistent meshing of stories" (Barbour 1999a). This consistent meshing is what Leibniz calls the "pre-established harmony" of all the monads (Leibniz 1989). But Barbour points out that this harmony does not require (as Leibniz himself thought) any sort of transcendent intervention by God. Rather, the monads are already consistent with one another, immanently and directly, simply because they all involve perspectives upon one another, and they all inhere in the universe in precisely the same way:

> What I as a particular monad experience is of necessity related to what the other monads experience. The experiences are not the same, but they are still related… Because of the way in which experiences are generated, we are all continually sharing experiences, though there is never identity of experiences… the entire world is resolved into *pure shared experience*.
>
> (Barbour 1993)

Whitehead would most likely reproach Barbour for not taking time seriously, because he gives primacy to "static configurational form" (Barbour 1999a) rather than to the ongoing "passage of nature" that we continually experience (Whitehead 1920). Nonetheless, Whitehead would agree with Barbour's insistence that existence ultimately comes down to "*pure shared experience*." The crucial similarities between Whitehead and Barbour result from how they share the heritage of Leibniz. For Whitehead, no less than for Barbour, the world is made of plural experiences, and these experiences are all atomistic, or discrete and separate from one another. Once a process has taken place, Whitehead tells us, that is it: "Actual entities perish, but do not change; they are what they are." Each event (or *occasion*, in Whitehead's formal terminology) is singular and finite: it comes to a conclusion, after which it cannot be revived or extended. Its "data" — or the remnants it leaves behind — can be appropriated by subsequent occasions, but that is all. This means that, for Whitehead — arguing here against Bergson — "there can be no continuity of becoming," but only "a becoming of continuity," over and over again. The space-time continuum is *produced* in the course of multiple events, or multiple nows, rather than being an already-given background within which those events would take place. Moreover, the relay from one atomistic event to another "is not to be construed in the sense of a uniquely serial advance"; rather, it has multiple directions and implications (Whitehead 1978).

Despite their differences, then, Barbour, Whitehead, and Harvey alike all follow Leibniz in rejecting Newton's postulation of an absolute space and time. This is an argument that goes back to Leibniz's exchange of letters with Newton's proxy, Samuel Clarke, in 1715–1716 (Leibniz and Clarke 2000). According to Newton, as we have already seen, "Absolute, true, and mathematical time, in and of itself and of its own nature, without reference to anything external, flows uniformly," and "absolute space, of its own nature without reference to anything external, always remains homogeneous and immovable" (Newton 1999). For Newton, time and space thus constitute a fixed background, subsisting independently of all the empirical instances that take place within them. Leibniz argues, to the contrary, that space and time cannot be absolute, existing in and of themselves. Rather, space and time are the forms of *relations* between things or events; if the things and events did not exist, then space and time would not exist either.

Whitehead similarly rejects what he calls Newton's "receptacle theory of space-time" because — among other reasons — it "minimize[s] the factor of potentiality." For Whitehead, the absolute theory of space and time fails to allow for the way that "actual fact includes in its own constitution real potentiality which is referent beyond itself." That is to say, in a universe where every event has its own specified space-time location, it is impossible to explain how events are able to refer to — which is to say, to influence, cause, or be appropriated by — subsequent events

(Whitehead 1978). Barbour likewise rejects Newton's "dualistic" theory that posits "atoms (things of one kind) that move in the framework and container of space and time (another quite different kind of thing)." For Barbour, "the world does not *contain* things, it *is* things" (Barbour 1999). Barbour joins such other physicists as Lee Smolin (Smolin 2006) and Carlo Rovelli (Rovelli 2018) in demanding a *background-independent* theory of how the cosmos works. Obviously, I do not have the scientific knowledge and understanding to intervene in debates about theoretical physics. But I invoke the formulations made by Barbour and other physicists in a science-fictional way in order to flesh out Jameson's depiction of a social life fashioned in the manner of financial derivatives as a discontinuous, background-independent set of singular nows.

The Light Brigade

Kameron Hurley's novel *The Light Brigade* (Hurley 2019a) mentions neither financial derivatives nor Leibnizian monads. Nonetheless, it develops a theory of neoliberal temporality, because it explores the consequences of pulverizing time into a set of disconnected, non-sequential nows. *The Light Brigade* is a cross between two subgenres: military science fiction and the time-travel narrative. Hurley rings changes upon the tradition of military science fiction in various ways, notably in terms of gender. Dietz, the first-person protagonist of the novel, narrates for the most part in a gender-neutral manner. It is only in the final pages of the book, when we have looped back in time to the very beginning of the story, that we are given her first name, and thereby learn that she is female. This effectively removes patriarchal presuppositions from the text, and forces us to see both the horrors and the pleasures of military life from a different perspective.

Much in the manner of Joe Haldeman's *The Forever War* (Haldeman 1974), *The Light Brigade* focuses upon the alienating experiences of a common soldier in a senseless and seemingly interminable conflict. In both novels, long periods of enforced idleness are punctuated by quick and brutal combat missions, when a fraction of a second makes the difference between life and death. The protagonists of both novels manage to survive, more by luck than by skill, but they are both deeply traumatized by their experiences of warfare. And this disruption of subjective experience is amplified, in both books, by the fragmentation and disaggregation of the protagonists' sense of time.

Both novels are organized around relativistic time distortions, but in very different ways. The novum of *The Forever War* is that Mandella, the narrator and protagonist, gets thrust further and further into the future because he is continually being sent on missions across the galaxy at near light speed. By the end of the book, in terms of subjectively experienced time he is still in his twenties, but due to time dilation in the course of his travels, more than a thousand years have passed back on Earth. Mandella is unavoidably exiled from the world he grew up in, without any prospect of being able to return to it (Haldeman 1974).

In *The Light Brigade*, to the contrary, time is compressed and folded back upon itself. Things never seem to progress at all. The novum is a form of teleportation: the army is able to volatilize its soldiers, turning them into pure energy in the form of light. They are then beamed to their destination, where their bodies are reconstituted. Since the soldiers are transmitted at light speed, no subjective time passes for them during the journey. They simply "jump" from home base to the battlefield, or back again. And the objective time it takes them to travel is minimized, since it happens at light speed. But even if the voyage itself is subjectively instantaneous, Dietz finds the process of being converted into energy excruciating:

> First your whole body shakes. Then every muscle gets taut and contracts, like you're experiencing a full-body muscle spasm centered in your core… Then you vibrate, you really vibrate, because every atom in your body is being ripped apart… it's not quick, it's not painless, and you're aware of every minute of it. You don't have a body anymore, you're locked in.
>
> (Hurley 2019a)

There are also glitches at the other end of the process, when the soldiers are reconstituted in bodily form. No high-tech procedure is truly seamless. Sometimes soldiers are improperly rematerialized: they "get put back together wrong," with their body parts gruesomely intermingled,

> a mass of contorted bodies, arms and legs attached to the wrong torsos, heads facing backward, spines made impossibly sinuous, feet twisted like claws, when they were recognizable as limbs at all.

But even when the transmission process works correctly, the effect is disconcerting. One intensified situation — one now — gives way to another, with no sense of transition between them and no indication of how the two instants might be related. Space-time and causality are both disrupted (Hurley 2019a).

All this takes place under objectively horrible circumstances. The future Earth of *The Light Brigade* is a dystopian nightmare: environmentally devastated and ruled by six globalized corporations. Each "corp" is effectively a monopolistic economic enterprise combined with a military dictatorship. Warfare is unending. The Moon has been blown up; Mars is a battleground, with the corporations ostensibly fighting to suppress a socialist rebellion. The battles into which the narrator and her fellow soldiers are thrust are confusing and chaotic. They are occasions of enormous and violent destruction, but they do not have comprehensible outcomes, as far as the soldiers themselves are able to discern. The survivors of each battle are teleported back to base without knowing whether they won or lost or even who they were fighting. In contrast to these intermittent and brutal combat sequences, the time spent back at base is entirely empty and boring: it seems to stretch on interminably, with every day exactly like the rest. There is little sense of either past or future, and nothing to link the various, heterogeneous nows together (Hurley 2019a).

But *The Light Brigade* adds something else to this basic atmosphere of disorientation: the twisted logic of time travel, with its looping recursions and repetitions. Dietz "come[s] unstuck in time," to use a phrase from another one of the book's implicit references, Kurt Vonnegut's *Slaughterhouse-Five* (Vonnegut 1969). Vonnegut's third-person protagonist, Billy Pilgrim, is a passive prisoner of war, helpless and traumatized, with "no control over where he is going next" (Vonnegut 1969). But Hurley's Dietz is much more active and self-directed. She is cocky and aggressive right from the beginning, and she continually tries to get a grip upon what is happening to her. Over the course of Dietz's experiences, the novel works through a sort of dialectic between chaos and control. On the one hand, Dietz is always being reminded that

> there is no way to predict the future because the future is always changing, always uncertain, at the quantum level. Quantum particles behave unpredictably. Unpredictability rules us at the most basic level. We yearn for certainty, but the fact is that certainty and absolutes are a fiction.

On the other hand, and even as she realizes this, Dietz keeps on trying to do something about her own circumstances. She gets this urge in part from her mother, who always "yearned for control," but never actually had any. In any case, Dietz is no Billy Pilgrim; she rejects the consolations of fatalism. She reproaches herself for her own relative powerlessness:

> I didn't like the idea that all I could control was how I reacted to what was done to me… All I had was what was done to me… what was I going to do with it?… When was the last time I tried to change anything in my life instead of just reacting to it?

Of course, this sense of helplessness is grounded in Dietz's actual situation as a soldier, having to obey orders no matter what, given no insight into the situations she is continually thrust into, and always in danger of getting into serious trouble if "she saw something she shouldn't have." But her involuntary time travel makes things even worse. Whenever Dietz is teleported, she finds herself at a different place and time from the rest of her squadron. She alternates between war zones and home base as she is supposed to, and she ultimately goes through all the same events as the other soldiers. But she does not experience these events in the same order as they do. She finds herself thrust backwards or forwards in time, seemingly at random. She sees friends killed, only to meet them again when she returns to an earlier time. She is sometimes interrogated about events that are in the causal past of the time she finds herself in, but which she has not yet personally gone through. It is a bit hard to follow things the first time you read the novel; we share Dietz's initial confusion, and only figure out what is really going on as she herself does (Hurley 2019a). The overall pattern of shifts is carefully worked out, however, and we are able to make sense of it eventually. Hurley even posted graphs and tables on her blog that explain "the logic of time travel" in the novel (Hurley 2019b).

At the very start of *The Light Brigade*, Dietz joins the corporate army because she wants revenge. The Martian rebels have apparently obliterated São Paulo, which was her home. This event is called the Blink: the entire city simply disappears one day, with its millions of people, leaving an empty crater behind. Dietz volunteers to be a soldier in response to the apparent destruction of her world. "I wanted to be the light," she says, in a phrase that is both metaphorical and literal. She wants to be "the savior, the hero" who obliterates the enemy. But literally turning into light is the actual way that this aim can be accomplished, through the military technology that makes it all possible.

Over the course of her discontinuous jumps in time, Dietz learns that the official narrative about the conflict is a lie, a deliberately misleading cover story. Mars is just a sideshow, of little importance to the corporations; the Martian rebels are few in number, and are not a threat to anybody. Rather, the six corporations, supposedly allied against the Martians, are in fact secretly fighting one another. They all seek full-world domination back on Earth. They are unconcerned that their conflict risks destroying the entire planet in the process. The war may go on interminably, but ultimately there can be no real winners. Everybody is bound to lose in the end.

As the novel proceeds, Dietz learns how to have some control over her jumps. Since her personal history no longer coincides with the objective, linear timeline, she is able to detach herself from that timeline and gain some leverage over how it is organized. She starts to "see things in transit," even though this is supposed to be impossible. Eventually, Dietz is able to keep a "thin grasp on my consciousness as the fabric of reality warped around me" during a jump. By the end of the novel, she succeeds in passing through the objective timeline twice; in her second iteration, she avoids the worst horrors of the first.

At the end of *The Light Brigade*, the novel folds back upon itself like a Möbius strip. In a circular irony, Dietz herself turns out to be the one who dematerializes São Paulo — the event that led to her enlistment in the first place. She turns the corporations' own technology against them, volatilizing the city into "millions of points of light" in order to escape the destruction wrought by the war. Dietz resolves to take São Paulo and all its people "someplace else, to some other time or place where there's no war, and the corporations answer to us, and freedom isn't just a sound bite on a corp-controlled news station" (Hurley 2019a).

Does such a better place even exist? The question remains open at the end of the novel. Dietz expresses the fervent hope that "this is not the end. There are other worlds. Other stars. Other futures." She envisions, in the novel's final line, "a future made of light." But in any case, Earth itself is finished. Dietz pronounces her terrible verdict: "There was no future here, only the past… If I couldn't save the world, at least I could save the people I loved." The novel teases us with the possibility of alternative outcomes, but it ultimately withdraws them from our grasp. You cannot actually alter the timeline; all you can do is step away from it. The only way to escape the tyranny of the corporations, and the destruction resulting from the war, is to leave the world altogether, leaping from a ruinous past to an unknowable future. This is perhaps what Deleuze and Guattari mean when they write about *lines of flight* (Deleuze and Guattari 1987). "I heaved myself backward in time," Dietz tells us almost at the end of the novel, "so heavy, so desperately heavy that I broke the fabric of time and space itself" (Hurley 2019a).

This means that in *The Light Brigade*, just as in *This Is How You Lose the Time War*, both reform and revolution seem equally impossible. The only way out is not to change the world (which we cannot do anyway), but to defect from consensus reality altogether. "Reality is made up," Dietz says to herself at one point. "Reality is what we agree on. Had I agreed to this?" The problem is that, in a certain sense, I have always already agreed to an oppressive reality — even prior to my coming into existence as a conscious being with the ability to make a decision, to accept or to reject.

What happens, then, when we refuse to agree, when we say no instead? Is defection from the hegemonic order actually possible, or does it only happen in science fiction? *The Light Brigade* fabulates a response to our current situation in which time takes on the form of singular nows, with no prospect of real change or progression from one moment to the next. But in this regime, the inner experience of duration still survives — even if it has been detached from the objective significance of time as psychological or historical passage such that it no longer offers us anything like a phenomenological horizon of activity. Rather than mourning our loss of historicity, or futilely seeking to restore it, *The Light Brigade* asks us — just as Dietz asks herself: What are we going to do with the time that we still have? The circumstances are grim, *The Light Brigade* tells us, but they are not (or not yet) impossible:

> There isn't a precise time when you know you must leave. It's like putting a lobster in a pot of cold water and turning up the heat. It warms slowly. Then there is a moment, though not a moment past, when there is no going back. You must move before that moment.

It is not easy to catch the right moment, but it is the only chance we have. We will lose too much if we leave prematurely; but we will lose everything if we hold off leaving for too long. We need to leave at precisely the right moment — even though we cannot know in advance just when it is. And this is the dilemma that *The Light Brigade* leaves us with. As Dietz says in the novel's final pages:

> Maybe you wanted a different story. One with more answers, less ambiguity. But that wasn't how I experienced this war… This is the closest I could get to the truth.

Indeed, this sort of active fabulation is the only way that we will ever get to "the other side of time," as Sun Ra exhorts us to do (Coney 1974).

7. Possible Worlds

Love and Death

Semelparity is the scientific term for "a reproductive strategy where species have a single reproductive cycle ending in death." Individuals die after only having sex a single time. In effect, they sacrifice themselves in order to favor the maximum number of offspring: "A key benefit of being semelparous is the sheer quantity of offspring that can be generated when all of an organism's resources are focused on reproduction" (Fernandez 2020). For instance, in one marsupial species, the dusky antechinus (*Antechinus swainsonii*), males mate frantically with as many females as possible during a three-week period, and then expire: "Elevated stress levels cause a fatal immune system collapse and death by hemorrhaging and infection" (Handwerk 2013). Semelparous organisms adopt "an 'all-or-nothing' mentality, where adults would rather expend all their energy for a chance at producing offspring, than die without doing so." Such practices are found among a wide variety of species, including octopuses and "insects, arachnids, fish and some peculiar insectivorous marsupials." Semelparity seems to evolve especially in conditions of "rapid juvenile development, short species lifespans and seasonal environmental conditions" (Fernandez 2020).

Semelparity is often, but not always, associated with sexual cannibalism, in which the female kills and eats the male after mating. This seems to be what happens with certain spider species, as well as with the praying mantis and other insects. Standard biological calculations indicate that "sexual cannibalism is always favored when [the expected number of matings in a male's lifetime] is 1, as long as females obtain any nutritional benefit and produce additional offspring" (Buskirk et al. 1984). The availability of the male's body as an extra source of nutrition means that his offspring will be healthier and more of them will survive to adulthood than would otherwise be the case. In other words, the male gets to spread his genes more widely as a result of his death during or just after copulation.

James Tiptree Jr.'s story "Love is the Plan, the Plan is Death" gives an imaginative, but nonetheless scientifically accurate, account of semelparity (Tiptree 1990). Rapid growth and development, a short lifetime, and sharp seasonal changes are all present. Moggadeet, the narrator and protagonist of the story, is male but not human. In the course of his comments, we get an elaborate physical description of his species. Moggadeet is cold blooded, with six legs, a tail, multiple "eye-turrets," distending "throat-sacs," and "plates" that can be extended to cover his black fur. His jaws are able to "spurt" on demand a "strong juice" of silk with binding and adhesive properties. He flourishes during the warm part of the year, and retreats to inactivity, hiding in caves, during the cold part. These qualities are vaguely reminiscent of arthropods, but Moggadeet's species is far larger than any terrestrial arthropods. They are apparently the apex predators on their planet, and they are big and strong enough to "pluck up a tree" from the ground and throw it over a cliff. Can we think of them as being something like beetles the size of elephants?

The story gives us the entire life cycle of this species. Multiple young are born in the course of the cold part of the year, and are cared for by their mothers. Children and mother alike have golden fur. When the young become sexually mature, the fur of the males turns black, and that of the females turns red. At this point, the warm season has begun. The mother kicks out her offspring, killing those who refuse to leave. Exhausted by her long months of nurturing her offspring, she is already falling apart physically; she prepares to die. The newly mature males go off, each of them alone, hunting for their food and growing ever bigger. When winter comes, they become sluggish and "unthinking"; they retreat into caves to wait out the cold. Some of them survive by eating the others. When spring comes, and it is warm again, the surviving males come out from their caves, feeling revived, and search for mates. They fight and kill one another as they compete for females. The successful males eventually find females a year younger than themselves, newly "cast out" by their mothers — and therefore much smaller. Throughout the warmer part of the year, the males care for their females, binding them up in silk, carrying them about, cleaning them, and feeding them. Eventually, as the summer ends and it starts to get cold again, the females have finally grown as large as the males — or indeed, even larger. The males unbind the females, copulate, and at the climax the female kills and eats the male. This will give her the resources to get through the winter, give birth, and nurture her young until they are mature. The cycle starts all over again.

Evidently, this story has a lot to say about male-female relations, in a way that refers at least allegorically to human gender and sexuality. A female author (Alice Sheldon) writing under a male pseudonym (James Tiptree Jr.) gives us the voice of a male animal (Moggadeet) driven by heterosexual desire to his exaltation, and thence to his destruction. We witness male rivalry, as Moggadeet fights and kills his brother Frim in order to get access to a female that both have seen. This is followed by rituals of courtship as Moggadeet woos the female Leelyloo, who responds to him coyly, pretending to resist, but with "shy excitement." Moggadeet rhapsodizes over what he sees as Leelyloo's (stereotypically feminine) petiteness and fragility, which are his to possess:

> I am choking, with fear of frighting you or bruising your tininess… I saw how new you were, how helpless!… Oh my ruby nestling, my baby red!… I wound among your darling little limbs, into your inmost delicate recesses, gently swathing and soothing you, winding and binding until you became a shining jewel. Mine!

This heightened romantic exultation, and possessiveness, is also a kind of sexual role-playing. Moggadeet happily recalls "nibbling your baby claws with my terrible teeth, revelling in your baby hum, pretending to devour you while you shrieked with glee." There are suggestions of what among human beings would be considered pedophilia, sadism, and masochism. Moggadeet first swoons over Leelyloo's "tiny perfection," the way she is uninstructed and uninformed, as well as physically small, in comparison to him. Then he binds her up: "How I wove the silk about you, tying each tiny limb, making you perfectly helpless." His love is indistinguishable from total control. Then, finally, he unbinds her in order to be eaten by her. In between these acts of mock and actual predation, the two of them swoon in the bliss of romantic union, which like all new lovers they conceive as something unique to themselves:

> We spoke together, we two! We communed, we shared, we poured ourselves one into the other… until more and more we came to see with each other's eyes, to hear, to taste, to feel the world of each other… Oh, love, are we the first? Have others loved with their whole selves?

Lines like these encapsulate the dynamics, and the feel, of the story. Moggadeet's monologue, setting forth everything he remembers, is addressed to the "you" who is Leelyloo. The language is tastelessly and excruciatingly over the top; every phrase is an overwrought cliché. The text's sweetness level is so extreme that, when I read this story, I feel as if I am being pushed over the edge into a state of hyperglycemic shock. In an interview, Sheldon/ Tiptree described the story as being written in "the style of 1920 porno" (Tiptree 2000). In this regard, it is quite different from most of Tiptree's other narratives. Everything that Moggadeet says is hyper-romantic and delirious to a point beyond parody. Even as Leelyloo devours him, Moggadeet writhes in a state of ecstasy, telling Leelyloo that he is "stupefied with delight… I felt only joy as your jaws took me."

It is inadequate, however, to read this story entirely in ironic terms. It is perfectly true that "Love is the Plan, the Plan is Death" insists upon the same violent and uneven gender dynamics that can be found throughout Tiptree's fiction. Her stories show us things like men murdering women in an erotic frenzy, as in "The Screwfly Solution," or men making idiotic displays of domination because they are unable to adjust to a world organized by women, as in "Houston, Houston, Do You Read?", or women who would rather entrust their lives to unknown outer-space aliens than remain in the patriarchal human world, as in "The Women Men Don't See" (Tiptree 1990). Similarly, in "Love is the Plan, the Plan is Death," Moggadeet moves seamlessly between the two extreme poles of a stereotypical male idealization of women — which of course is also a way of denying women recognition as equals. On the one hand, there is the protective adoration of the helpless innocent virgin; on the other hand, there is the submissive adoration of the all-devouring mother. It is a testimony to Sheldon's admirably unwavering radicalism that she declines to imagine any sort of compromise or mitigation of either of these two extremes.

But this is still an all-too-human reading of "Love is the Plan, the Plan is Death." We also need to take account of the story's *literalness*, which is the source of its alien splendor. Tiptree is careful to follow scientific accounts of semelparity, together with mate binding and sexual cannibalism, as closely as possible. The story is inspired by ethological accounts of animal behavior, and more generally by the Darwinian calculus of *inclusive fitness*. This latter doctrine, initially propounded in the early 1960s by W. D. Hamilton (Hamilton 1963), separates the question of how widely an organism is able to spread its genes from any question of the organism's own individual survival or flourishing. This concept was broadly accepted by evolutionary biologists at the time Tiptree wrote the story. It has rightly been criticized since then for being overly reductionistic, but this critique was not published until well after Sheldon's death (Nowak et al. 2010). I think that we need to take the story's one-sided biological reductionism at face value.

Throughout the story, Moggadeet speaks repeatedly of "the Plan," which seems to be the inner biological programming for the species' reproduction. The word *plan* recurs something like fifty times (not including the title) in a story of less than seven thousand words. Moggadeet usually celebrates the greatness of the Plan, though at other times he claims to resist it or defy it, or even to replace it with a greater plan of his own. He insists that "in the warm we think, we learn. In the cold is only the Plan" (this is actually repeated several times in the course of the story). But Moggadeet's claim to be independent, and to think for himself, at least during the warmer part of the year, is entirely a self-deception. No matter what he says and does, he is always being carried along by the Plan:

> Isn't it strange, my loveling? This sweetness that floods our bodies when we yield to the Plan. Great is the Plan! Fear it, fight it — but hold the sweetness yet.

Another way to put this is to say that Moggadeet is driven entirely and exclusively by his passions. He never hesitates over what to do, and he never expresses any doubts about what he is doing, or any remorse for what he has already done. For instance, he promises never to harm the "Old One" he meets, and who gives him advice and tells him about the Plan; but just thereafter, he kills and eats this Old One, with no sense of conflict or disturbance. Everything Moggadeet does already fits into the Plan, even though he does not entirely realize this. From a certain aesthetic point of view, the story is as hilarious as it is gruesome, since Moggadeet's self-confidence and his reveling in romantic excess is only matched by his utter cluelessness as to what is actually going on.

But if we read the story at a distance, from an evolutionary point of view, we realize that the Plan is an empty tautology, rather than a teleological structure of the sort that Moggadeet imagines. It consists in behaviors that have been selected and perpetuated in the course of evolution to such an extent that Moggadeet and Leelyloo now enact them spontaneously, without any awareness that they are doing so. These actions result in optimized reproduction, but without benefit to the entities that so ardently perform them. The story gives us a biological equivalent of what Lee Edelman calls "reproductive futurism" (Edelman 2004). Each generation of adults destroys itself for the sake of the juvenile next generation — which experiences the same nightmare of pointless expenditure and deferral in its own turn. It makes no difference whether this behavior is biologically driven (as in Tiptree's story) or imposed culturally (as in Edelman's analysis of heteronormativity); in either case, the outcome is the same.

Though Moggadeet claims that he thinks for himself in the warm, and that it is only in the cold that he loses all initiative and is thrown back upon the Plan, it is evident that he is deluded in thinking this. The seemingly voluntary actions that belong to the warmer part of the year are themselves crucial portions of the Plan. The story does not present us with a conflict between free will and determinism, or between conscious decisions and biological necessities, but rather suggests that Moggadeet's very awareness and self-consciousness — his *what-is-it-likeness*, as the philosophers say — is itself a crucial part of the Plan's unfolding.

All this brings us back to what I am calling the story's alien splendor. "Love is the Plan, the Plan is Death" works by juxtaposing its cloyingly heightened style of language with the harsh fatality of its biological vision. Shock results from the explosive combination of sentimental rhetoric and an unyielding reality principle. David Galef sees the major ambiguity in Tiptree's/Sheldon's writing to be the clash of "hard science versus liberal humanism, or genetically-driven, relatively fixed actions versus socially learned, more malleable behavior" (Galef 2001). But I would not want to put things quite in those terms. In Tiptree's account, socially learned behavior (whatever Moggadeet picked up from his mother and from the Old One) is no more adaptable than are biological drives. The point of the story is not how these two approaches conflict with one another, but rather how disturbingly well they fit together. Moggadeet's discourse, with its amorous effervescence and continual exaltation, does not oppose the hard facts of biological necessity, but rather vitally contributes to them.

None of this guarantees, however, the long-term continuation of the species and its peculiar rituals. There is no sense here of an open future. It is not only the case that the actors will not change their behavior, but also that the physical conditions within which the behavior unfolds are by no means guaranteed to continue. The story contains repeated intimations of climate change, which will disrupt the mechanisms evolved within and for different environmental conditions. "*The winters grow,*" we are told several times, and "*the warm grows less and less.*" Formerly warm and fertile areas are now cold and lifeless all year long. The entire life cycle may well be headed towards extinction. Biological and cultural forces alike seem deficient in the flexibility that would be needed in order to respond to changing circumstances. Futurity just isn't what it used to be; only the barest vestiges of it remain.

It is often said that science fiction must fail in its effort to convey truly alien points of view, because language, by its very nature, traps us in a human frame of reference. Tiptree manages this difficulty by giving us two levels of meaning at once: an emotionally laden one and an objectifying and distancing one. Each of these levels, in itself, is humanly recognizable and recuperable. But the interference between them is what gives the story its disconcertingly inhuman cast. Individual desire resonates with species-level programming, and nihilistic fatalism is expressed in the language of sheer sentimental excitement. Such is the perspective that the story compels us to inhabit.

Cognitive Mapping

"Love is the Plan, the Plan is Death" is just one example of how science fiction offers us alternative perspectives on things in the world, or even on the world itself — including inhuman and ostensibly impossible perspectives. Tiptree's story is set on an alien planet, and it features organisms whose biological makeup separates them from human strivings and human concerns. These organisms have no future prospects: their only alternatives seem to be monotonous repetition and complete extinction. Nonetheless, the story still exemplifies science-fictional potentiality, because it envisions a world that is beyond our ken but which still exhibits emotions and situations that we can grasp. We are able, at least partially, to imagine our way into these emotions and situations, even as they also remain radically alien to our own experiences. We are stretched by entertaining them. The story offers us a singular perspective on the world: a perspective that is all the more singular in that it combines — or demonstrates the compossibility of — ostensibly irreconcilable points of origin. "Love is the Plan, the Plan is Death" interweaves sentimentality with objectivity, and allegorical reference to human subjectivity with mimetic reference to an entirely inhuman form of sexuality. By enclosing us in a perspective that we have never encountered before — and which we *cannot* encounter except through fabulation — the story both upends our sense of things we thought we already knew and confronts us with things that were previously unknown to us.

Where naturalistic fiction gives us perspectives that we can easily accommodate to our own already-existing assumptions, science fiction, in contrast, offers us singular and unexpected perspectives. The obvious question is how these otherworldly perspectives relate to one another (both within and across particular texts), and how they relate to other ways of understanding the world, or of being able to live, act, and flourish within it. How do living conditions and sexual mores on Moggadeet's planet relate to those we encounter on Earth today? Such questions must be confronted by any sort of aesthetic or fictionalizing practice. But science fiction raises them more acutely than naturalistic fiction does, for science fiction is specifically about potentialities and our intimations of them. It depicts and represents things that are "real without being actual." This sort of presentation unavoidably calls for a more oblique practice than would be the case for an aesthetic mode that frankly seeks to offer us what Whitehead calls the "sheer disclosure" of fully-present actualities (Whitehead 1938).

Fredric Jameson addresses this problem in his account of "the bewildering new world space of late or multinational capital" — which is how he defines postmodernity as a social formation (Jameson 1991). In this world space, even more than was the case in the space of the older industrial capitalism, we experience a "constant revolutionizing of production, uninterrupted disturbance of all social conditions, everlasting uncertainty and agitation" (Marx and Engels 1888). But in the newer spaces of late or postmodern capitalism, everything gets fragmented, multiplied, dispersed, and reorganized. Classical capitalism aggregated vast numbers of human bodies in Fordist assembly-line factories and in huge cities. Postmodern capitalism, in contrast, isolates these bodies from one another: we now live predominantly in suburbs, work in dispersed locations or even online, and move from place to place in automobiles. Indeed, postmodern capitalism privatizes things to such an extent that it even disaggregates particular human bodies. As Deleuze says, "Individuals become '*dividuals*,'" or "coded 'dividual' matter to be controlled" (Deleuze 1995). My life, my attributes or qualities, and my activities are all coded as *information*, and thence divided into semi-autonomous tranches, as they say in the language of financial derivatives.

Jameson is concerned with the ways that our lives are spatialized (both literally and metaphorically) by such processes. Postmodernity is disorienting because

> postmodern hyperspace... has finally succeeded in transcending the capacities of the individual human body to locate itself, to organize its immediate surroundings perceptually.
>
> (Jameson 1991)

Jameson's famous physical example of postmodern hyperspace is the Westin Bonaventure Hotel in Los Angeles, designed by John C. Portman Jr. in the mid-1970s. I remember attending the Modern Language Association annual conference at this hotel in 1982, which is also probably when Jameson first saw it; his account of the hotel's spatial organization initially appeared in a journal in 1984 (Jameson 1984). Portman went on to design many other hotels and business centers throughout the United States, China, and other countries in the succeeding decades. As a result, today the spatial arrangements of his buildings are far more familiar to us, and easier to find our way through, than was the case four decades ago. To a certain extent, we have learned to navigate — and assimilated into our sense of the everyday — what initially struck us as intrusively science-fictional.

Jameson's overall point still stands, however. It is not just a matter of a particular style or fashion in architecture, but much more broadly of "the end of the autonomous bourgeois monad or ego or individual" that was taken for granted in earlier iterations of modernity (Jameson 1991). The disorientation of objective social space that Jameson describes is not just a particular aesthetic effect. It is paralleled by an analogous disorientation of the self that endeavors to navigate such space. This is why Jameson "distinguishe[s] *postmodernity* as a historical period from *postmodernism* as a style" and sees the latter only as a symptom of the former (Jameson 2016).

In order to confront this hyperbolic situation, Jameson proposes what he calls "an aesthetic of *cognitive mapping*" (Jameson 1991). A radically new approach is needed in order to achieve "a breakthrough to some as yet unimaginable new mode of representing" that would be adequate to the task of understanding "the world space of multinational capital" in its entirety. We do not yet know what this "new mode of representing" might be, but Jameson denies that it "is in any way easily vitiated by the conventional poststructural critiques of the 'ideology of representation' or mimesis." Instead of passively rendering social space, the practice of cognitive mapping should work to "endow the individual subject with some new heightened sense of its place in the global system," and thereby allow us to "regain a capacity to act and struggle which is at present neutralized by our spatial as well as our social confusion."

Alfred Bester's 1954 short story "Fondly Fahrenheit" addresses this problem *avant la lettre* (Bester 1957). The story begins as follows: "He doesn't know which of us I am these days, but they know one truth. You must own nothing but yourself." This passage is difficult to parse, for a number of reasons: the combination of first-, second-, and third-person pronouns, the latter in both singular and plural; the absence of any indication of the persons to whom these pronouns might refer; the assertion of interchangeability ("which of us I am"); and the suggestion that one can "own" oneself, and possibly another self as well. The story maintains this odd play of pronouns throughout, and we gradually figure out how it works. The protagonist, Vandaleur, owns an android. Such a situation — the ownership of one sentient being by another — may well remind us of slavery. But it becomes clear that, in the future super-capitalist world of the story, sentient androids are not considered to be human, and that therefore such ownership is considered legitimate. Indeed, in this world a human being's ownership of an android simply exemplifies the way that, in any capitalist society, one is obliged to objectify one's own labor power, or capacity to do work, as a commodity to be sold on the open market. Vandaleur's android is literally the embodiment of his laboring capacity. Unless somebody has "a terrific talent for a particular job," there is no way that they can perform as well, or earn as much, as an android that consists in pure abstract labor. As Vandaleur repeatedly explains, since he has no other source of wealth, "The only way I can get along is living off what [the android] earns." In effect, Vandaleur embodies, in the persona of his android, what Michel Foucault describes as the hegemonic form of neoliberal subjectivity: he is "an entrepreneur of himself" (Foucault 2008).

In the course of Bester's story, the android commits a string of murders. Vandaleur feels compelled to cover up these crimes; he knows that if the android is seized and destroyed, he will lose his own productive capacity and be left with no source of income whatsoever. Androids are supposed to be incapable of murder in the world of the story. "Prime Directives and Inhibitions [are] set up for them when they're synthesized," in a manner reminiscent of Isaac Asimov's three laws of robotics. But Vandaleur's android points out that it is not a mechanism or a robot: "I am not a machine… The robot is a machine. The android is a chemical creation of synthetic tissue." It also repeatedly reminds Vandaleur that its behavior cannot be affected by reward or punishment, because "the pleasure-pain syndrome is not incorporated in the android synthesis." The android is a creature of labor power and nothing else.

It turns out that the android in "Fondly Fahrenheit" becomes a killer after it has been disoriented by synesthesia, which the story defines as "confusion or short circuiting of any sensation of taste, smell, pain, pressure, temperature, and so on." The result is that "high temperature brings about a response of fear, anger, excitement, and violent physical activity." When the temperature exceeds ninety degrees Fahrenheit, the android becomes manic, starts singing and dancing, and murders whomever is nearby. But the story extends this derangement of the senses (what Rimbaud calls "un dérèglement de tous les sens") into a confusion of subjective identities as well (Rimbaud's "Je est un autre"). The psychological barriers between Vandaleur and his android break down. Pronouns shift because Vandaleur is unable to detach his own subjectivity from that of the android. The story can therefore be read as recounting a human character's psychotic breakdown as the inexorable result of having to embody and perform commodified labor. Vandaleur is no longer a coherent self. The nameless android is the recipient — or better, we might say, the *congelation* — of Valdaleur's own alienation (in the strict Marxist sense) as a source of labor power. Within the story, this operation is one of psychological *projection*: "The process of throwing out upon another the ideas and impulses that belong to oneself." In this way, the story maps out the way that late capitalism, in Jameson's words, entails "the end of the autonomous bourgeois monad or ego or individual," shattering traditional subjectivity and unleashing violence and destruction.

An aesthetic of cognitive mapping, Jameson says, is a way of grasping the complexity and boundary violations that result from a social world in which there is no longer any place for the fixed point of view of a monad or enclosed individuality. Bester's story illustrates the breakdown of the old, fixed point of view. But Bester does not extend this portrayal in such a way as to give us a sense of late-stage capitalism as a totalizing system. "Fondly Fahrenheit" confines itself to the interplay of technology and commodification as it affects an individual (or better, as it disaggregates individuals into separately articulated *dividuals*). The story depicts *what it is like* to live in a capitalist society, but it does not pretend to show us how capitalism as a system works, or how and why it produces such shattered individuals. In this way, Bester remains true to a Leibnizian monadological project of expressive representation — even as his story narrates, or represents, the chaotic rupture of what used to be a monad.

How does this relate to the project of cognitive mapping? Jameson makes a strong distinction between *representation* and *knowledge* — which is also to say, in Althusserian language, between ideology and science (Althusser 2001). In his long discussion of *Postmodernism, Or, the Cultural Logic of Late Capitalism*, Jameson finally remarks that "it has never been said here that [the global world system] was unknowable but merely that it was unrepresentable, which is a very different matter" (Jameson 1991). For Jameson, a book like Ernest Mandel's *Late Capitalism* (Mandel 1975) "offers a rich and elaborated knowledge" of the capitalist world system. But this knowledge does *not* take the form of a representation. In contrast, Jameson maintains that even the most critical science-fictional representations of capitalism do not and cannot offer us anything like an actionable knowledge of the world system (Jameson 1991).

In other words, insofar as science-fictional texts are considered as attempted *representations* of late capitalism, or as aesthetic works of the imagination, they necessarily remain on the side of "existential experience," rather than on the side of "scientific knowledge." Jameson, following Althusser, insists that there is always "a gap, a rift" between the two (Jameson 1991). A merely existential account (such as Bester's story, with its evocation of what-is-it-likeness) cannot ever achieve the insights of science. Conversely, the "rich and elaborated knowledge" of science cannot be couched in existentially or aesthetically accessible terms. Jameson proposes his "aesthetic of cognitive mapping" as a hoped-for way to bridge this gap: a mediating "pedagogical" gesture that would make possible some sort of "coordination of existential data… with unlived, abstract conceptions of the geographic totality." But such a gesture is fraught with difficulties. On the one hand, existential experience always involves an imaginary misrecognition — to use the Lacanian terminology adopted by both Althusser and Jameson. Science, on the other hand, is necessarily asubjective and aperspectival (Althusser 2001); it cannot ever be adequated to "the positioning of the individual subject, the experience of daily life, the monadic 'point of view' on the world to which we are necessarily, as biological subjects, restricted" (Jameson 1991). It is hard to see how science fiction could overcome these restrictions to actually engage in cognitive mapping.

Althusser himself draws the distinction between existential experience and science from Spinoza's account of the three types of cognition (or knowledge). Spinoza liberates us, Althusser says, "from the illusions of what he called the imagination" (Althusser 1997). Cognition of the first kind, which Spinoza equates with "opinion, or imagination," is "the unique cause of falsity" (Spinoza 2018). As for Spinoza's second kind of cognition, although it provides a certain degree of truth, Althusser says that its ideas are "still partially caught up in the illusion of the imagination and of the language directly tied to it" (Althusser 1997). Only Spinoza's third kind of cognition, entirely detached from imagination and from any limited (or subjective) perspective, is able to understand the world "from the vantage of eternity" (sub specie aeternitatis), by tracing all phenomena to the ultimate causes that generate and determine them (Spinoza 2018). Such complete cognition "proceeds from an adequate idea of the formal essence of certain attributes of God to an adequate knowledge of the essence of things" — which is to say, it grasps things in their entirety, as necessary consequences of their ultimate grounds or causes (Spinoza 2018).

However, I am not enough of a Spinozist to believe that any such cognition of the third kind is possible in principle, let alone in actual practice. I am inclined, rather, to agree with Donna Haraway and other feminist thinkers that *all* knowledge claims are partial and situated, and indeed that "only partial perspective promises objective vision" (Haraway 1991). "Monadic 'point[s] of view' on the world" are all that we have, even though Spinoza, Althusser, and Jameson scorn them. And they remain necessary bases for any attempt at reference, even when they are ruptured, as in Bester's story. Points of view are always "restricted," not just for "biological" reasons, but as a matter of logical necessity. Attempts to exceed such restriction lead not to universalism, but rather to the sort of delirium that is recounted in "Fondly Fahrenheit." It is, of course, both feasible and necessary to put together many different "monadic" points of view in order to achieve a broader understanding. But such a combination and multiplication of perspectives can never add up to a scientific (in Althusser and Jameson's sense of the word) or wholly adequate (in Spinoza's sense) totality of knowledge.

The Territory Is Not the Map

To accept Haraway's support of partial and situated perspectives is to equally reject Spinoza's vantage of eternity, on the one hand, and nihilistic relativism, on the other. We always need to be sensitive, Haraway tells us, to a ramified "situation of tensions, resonances, transformations, resistances, and complicities" (Haraway 1991). We must recognize that

> the knowing self is partial in all its guises, never finished, whole, simply there and original; it is always constructed and stitched together imperfectly, and *therefore* able to join with another, to see together without claiming to be another.
>
> (Haraway 1991)

The word *partial* here must be understood in both of its senses. *Partial* means incomplete, or "never finished, whole, simply there and original." But *partial* also means biased, in the (not necessarily pejorative) sense of being grounded in a certain particularity, and of coming from a limited location. Invoking both of these senses of the word at once, Haraway implicitly, but strongly, urges us to reject any opposition between "existential experience," on the one hand, and "unlived, abstract conceptions," on the other. For the latter are ultimately projections and elaborations of the former; we cannot ever know precisely where to draw the line between them. If we actually restricted ourselves to isolated particulars, as empiricist philosophers like Locke and Hume tell us we should, then we would never get anywhere; as Whitehead says, such "rigid empiricism… if consistently pursued, would have left science where it found it" and gained no new knowledge whatsoever (Whitehead 1978).

On the other hand, we need to remember that theoretical abstractions can never be entirely freed from the circumstances in which they arise; they are always generalizing projections made on the basis of limited existential experience. Instead of enforcing a Spinozistic binary division between imagination and knowledge, therefore, Haraway suggests exploring the vast territory in between the two, or in which they partly overlap. Such a strategy is similar to, and resonates with, Seo-Young Chu's understanding of science fiction as a way of probing "the rich and complicated area" that stretches between the opposed extremes of "referents wholly accessible to cognition," and between "referents virtually unknowable, referents that all but defy human language and comprehension" (Chu 2010).

Consider, in this regard, a book that I have already discussed at some length: Philip K. Dick's novel *Ubik* (Dick 1969). And also consider a more recent science-fiction book, one that was published well after Jameson's writings on postmodernism and on science fiction: Gwyneth Jones' novella *Proof of Concept* (Jones 2017), which I wrote about in my own book *Extreme Fabulations* (Shaviro 2021). For Jameson, fictional texts like these can only have *symptomatic* value. They work to display the ways in which, under late or postmodern capitalism, "everything in our social life… can be said to have become 'cultural' in some original and yet untheorized sense." And a symptomatic and cartographic reading of these novels does indeed tell us a lot. *Ubik* maps out the ways in which not only physical possessions, but also subjective experiences and banal everyday necessities, are increasingly captured within the form and logic of commodities. For Dick, this even stretches to a further extent — beyond death — than Marx himself, as a good materialist, ever insisted upon. For its part, *Proof of Concept* is set in a future time in which "the vicious stranglehold of the One Percent" (Jones uses the term publicized by the Occupy movement of the early 2010s) continues in exacerbated form, ruining the physical environment of Earth beyond repair. Both of these works indeed perform the sort of cognitive mapping that Jameson calls for. But we would also have to say of both texts that their mediations remain partial and incomplete — as their authors are themselves fully aware. Neither book claims to actually express a knowledge of "the economic system and the social totality themselves" (Jameson 1991). Rather, they both recount endeavors to *escape* from this system and this totality.

Science fiction works to extend, or exceed, the boundaries of physical, social, and conceptual spaces — thereby opening up new potentialities and new domains. *Ubik* takes place mostly in the "half-life" world of the recently dead; it does not deal with death as a definitive end, but rather contemplates what Maurice Blanchot calls the "interminable" and "incessant" process of dying (Blanchot 1989). The novel horrifically depicts the extension of the commodity logic of capitalism even beyond the limits of life and into the realm of this half-life. But *Ubik* also narrates the efforts of its everyman protagonist, Joe Chip, to escape this logic, and to find a space and time that are free of it. This is why *money* (or better, physical currency) takes on strange, magical forms as it proliferates throughout the world of the novel. The images of presidents on the face of United States coins and bills are replaced, first by images of Joe Chip's boss, Runciter, and finally by images of Joe himself. The novel ends with the line: "This was just the beginning." Since the realm of dying, or of half-life, is unending, this means that we will never be entirely free of capitalist logic, but also that this logic will never succeed in establishing itself once and for all.

For its part, *Proof of Concept* shows us twenty-third-century scientists working in a non-space, a gigantic underground cavern that seems to be the only location on Earth that has not already been environmentally devastated by the depredations of the 1 percent. The book ends with a violent movement of displacement into the void of interstellar space. *Proof of Concept*, like Sun Ra's movie, *Space is the Place*, envisions the apocalyptic shattering of the Earth, accompanied by the escape of only a small group of survivors. The 1 percent funded the scientific research depicted in the novella, hoping to find a way to escape the Earth altogether, but the scientists who took their money "left them helpless on a foundering ship." Since Earth cannot be rescued and restored, the sole remaining possibility is to move altogether beyond the confines of the map and of the world made navigable by the map. The novella ends with the sentence: "And all around them flowed the rushing dark."

In *Ubik* and *Proof of Concept* alike, the project of cognitive mapping is abandoned and replaced by a movement into new, unmapped (and perhaps unmappable) regions. As in so many other science-fiction narratives, it seems impossible to overthrow capitalism; the only remaining alternative is to somehow secede from it. If Jameson's project of cognitive mapping is subject to Alfred Korzybski's famous warning that "the map is not the territory" (Korzybski 1994), then perhaps science-fictional explorations are better described by Jack Spicer's inversion of this maxim: "The territory is not the map." In Spicer's poem of this title, a small segment from the "Homage to Creeley / Explanatory Notes" section of his 1962 book (or poem sequence) *The Heads of the Town Up to the Aether*, the wished-for "correspondence" between map and territory fails, and produces only "despair." We are left with nothing better than "a half-truth… / Which you will squint at until you are dead." The text explicitly mentions Edward Lear ("The Owl and the Pussycat"), and alludes to Lewis Carroll ("The Voice of the Lobster"). In citing the two great nonsense poets, Spicer insinuates that the very project of interpretation — or as we might well say, of cognitive mapping — inevitably collapses back into the nonsense out of which it initially emerged. We find ourselves "putting to sea with the truth," which implies that we will never grasp the truth in itself, but only be dragged by it into some sort of infinite errancy. Spicer reflexively says that the poem is intended "to prevent idealism — i.e. the study of images," but that "it did not succeed" (Spicer 2008).

What does this have to do with science fiction? I want to suggest that Spicer is something of a science-fictional poet. He read a lot of science fiction, and he was especially interested in the work of Alfred Bester. He is also intriguingly adjacent to Philip K. Dick; at one point, Spicer and Dick were even housemates. Spicer's biographers note that there is considerable resonance, or overlap, between these two authors:

> In the 1950s and 1960s the books of Spicer and Dick became mirror images of each other, with the same themes (possession, alienation, the oracular) and, more strikingly, identical images: grasshoppers, Martians, castles and princes, Jewish salesmen, radio waves, ancient wounds, souls, and cities.
>
> (Ellingham and Killian 1998)

These tropes point to the dramatic separation of the outside from the inside, while also suggesting how the inside is in fact constituted by the very outside that it rejects and from which it seeks to remove or differentiate itself. The philosopher Joseph Libertson calls this "the altering incumbance of exteriority": even as a radical outside escapes comprehension, it nonetheless weighs upon, and affects and alters, the very subjectivity that is unable to grasp it or make sense of it (Libertson 1982). We see this dynamic configuration in many science-fiction texts, as well as in Spicer's poetry and poetics.

In Dick's novel *The Three Stigmata of Palmer Eldrich* (Dick 1964), colonists on Mars take drugs in order to escape from their harsh lives as colonists. The drugs allow them to hallucinate a bland simulation of what they think that they have lost: the creepy normality of White heterosexual suburban life in the 1950s

United States. But other drugs, seemingly originating from entirely outside the solar system, provide more deranged hallucinations. The eponymous entrepreneur Palmer Eldrich — who disappears from the solar system and then returns to it as an interplanetary drug dealer — may be either a gnostic unknown god or a gnostic archon (an evil demiurge). In a hostile universe, where inner and outer forces condition one another without losing their essential incompatibility, these alternatives become difficult to tell apart — though it is equally impossible to unify them. In any case, by the end of the novel, after a series of displacements both of the characters and of the timeline, any reality effect whatsoever falls under suspicion of having been constructed by sinister alien forces.

Dick's gnostic theology has analogies with Spicer's claims that his own writing is the result of taking "dictation" from external forces, from the outside. Spicer suggests, playfully but not ironically, that these forces might well be regarded as "Martians." He does this in order to reject any identification of what he calls "the Outside" with the more or less intelligible and worldly forces that other poets cite as sources of inspiration: language (Robert Creeley), history and etymology (Robert Duncan), the aura of things themselves (William Carlos Williams), or sheer energy (Charles Olson). All these might be powers upon which the poet can call, but Spicer rejects them as overly mundane; they are ultimately ways of domesticating otherness. As Spicer says of Olson's notion of energy, it "is not something from a great galactic distance out there," but rather "something you plug in the wall, and it's really the machine which is the converter of the electricity which makes another machine work, and so forth." Against all of these formulations, Spicer says, "I prefer more the unknown" (Spicer 1998).

In Spicer's poetics, "the unknown" must be taken, not merely as an epistemological category, but as a fundamental dimension of reality. It is not in any way familiar to us; rather, it reaches us from "a great galactic distance." I was at first going to write that the unknown is, for Spicer, an ontological category, but this is wrong, since the whole point is that it is acategorical, and outside of being. It is what Joseph Libertson calls "alterity's excess as a communicational moment which affects or changes thought" (Libertson 1982), and what Emmanuel Levinas designates as "Otherwise Than Being" (Levinas 1998). However, for Spicer, this outside does not have the form of a human face that "calls upon me and orders me," as Levinas claims. Rather, it is science-fictionally alien, and as irreducible to ethics as it is to ontology. The Martians' message does not concern me in the slightest, and yet I am compelled to transmit it for them, using my own resources, irrelevant as these are. Spicer says, "It's as if a Martian comes into a room with children's blocks with A, B, C, D, E which are in English and he tries to convey a message" using those blocks, even though the message itself is not in English and cannot be accurately translated into English (Spicer 1988).

A similar dynamics of otherness is at work in Ann Leckie's Imperial Radch series of space operas. These novels are concerned with degrees of difference among multiple cultures and species, as well as among genders. The human societies depicted in the novels range from one in which gender distinctions are so socially irrelevant as not to be noticed at all — everyone is designated with she/her pronouns, regardless of bodily and behavioral characteristics — to ones in which meaningful distinctions proliferate such that up to five designating pronoun types are used — not only she/her and he/him, but also e/em, sie/hir, and they/them, each of which displays different nuances. There are also nonhuman sentient species, the Geck and the Rrrrrr, with whom the various human groups need to reach accommodations. And there are also sentient AIs, whose status (including gender identification) is still under negotiation. But beyond all of these, there is a powerful and intelligent alien life-form, known as the Presger, with whom communication is nearly impossible. The Presger are not just aliens; they are so utterly *alien* (in every possible sense of the word) that we (human beings, together with the Geck and the Rrrrrr) cannot understand them at all:

> The Presger didn't care if a species was sentient or not, conscious or not, intelligent or not… All other beings were their rightful prey, property, or playthings. Mostly they just didn't care about humans, but some of them liked to stop ships and pull them — and their contents — apart.
>
> (Leckie 2013)

We have little sense of what values, aims, and desires the Presger might have (or even if it makes sense to characterize their experience in such terms at all). We do not even know what the Presger look like, whether they are separate organisms or some sort of collective, or how their technologies work. In order to bridge this gap, the Presger create beings known as Presger Translators, who look human on the outside and can speak human languages, but whose bodies and minds presumably have Presger and otherwise nonhuman features as well. We encounter Presger Translators in all the books of the series, but *Translation State* in particular gives us, in one of its strands, a juvenile translator as a first-person narrator, with e/em pronouns. Some of the episodes recounted by the narrator are gruesome and traumatic, involving cannibalism, near rape, and body merging, among other things. Juvenile translators like to "open up" their weaker siblings: "It was shocking, and titillating, to see the layer of fat under the skin, the liver gleaming smooth and wet beneath the ribs." But all these experiences are recounted in an oddly detached and naively innocent tone. As readers, we find ourselves in a strange position. In formal terms, we identify with this narrator, or at least with the perspective that e speaks from; there is no suggestion that e might be an unreliable narrator. Yet eir assumptions, eir motivations, and eir actions are far too alien and disconcerting, and sometimes far too repulsive, for us to be able to grasp them.

The Presger Translators' speech and behavior seem bizarre and offbeat by human standards (or at least by whatever standards any potential readers of Leckie's novels might have), but their surreal non sequiturs, violations of our notions of logical identity, and seemingly nonconsequential whims effectively convey the sense of some scarcely graspable mediation between our own familiar ideas and ones (held by the Presger) that we are entirely unable to process, or translate into our own cognitive frameworks. The philosopher Donald Davidson famously argues that "the very idea of a conceptual scheme" — or the idea that there might be multiple and incompatible frames of reference, untranslatable languages, and incommensurable systems of belief — is intellectually incoherent (Davidson 2001). Either an alien language or cognitive framework can be translated into ours, Davidson argues, or else it is not a language or a cognitive framework at all. Leckie's novels — together with much other science-fiction writing, as well as with Spicer's poetry — deliberately play at the very edge of such incoherence. Mechanisms of translation, or more generally of equivalence, break down when driven to their limits. Leckie's account of the Presger pushes against the rationalistic, and indeed idealistic, claims of philosophy. The novels insist, rather, that — to cite the famous words of J. B. S. Haldane — "the universe is not only queerer than we suppose, but queerer than we *can* suppose" (Haldane 1927).

Science fiction, like Spicer's poetry, strives to prevent idealism, but it is unable to do so. *Idealism* here may be understood in Spicer's terms as "the study of images"; that is to say, the aesthetic doctrine of modernist poetry, and especially of imagism, which states that "an 'Image' is that which presents an intellectual and emotional complex in an instant of time" (Pound 1913). But *idealism* can also be taken in its broader philosophical sense, as the claim that the ultimate nature of reality is mental or spiritual. In either of these cases, the project of preventing idealism is an infinite and ultimately unsuccessful one. We cannot divest language of its images, which proliferate all the more vigorously when we attempt to crop them back. And in a broader sense, the more we seek to plunge into sheer materiality — the ineluctable process of dying in Spicer's poetry and in Dick's *Ubik*, or the greater physical, biological, and economic processes that generate, shape, and delimit experience in *The Three Stigmata of Palmer Eldritch* and in so many other science-fiction texts — the more we find ourselves confronting impalpable but strangely ineliminable forces. Spicer calls them "ghosts" throughout *The Heads of the Town Up to the Aether*. His project, at least in part, is "to make poems out of real objects. The lemon to be a lemon that the reader could cut or squeeze or taste" — as he writes in his early volume *After Lorca*. But his poetry also narrates the discovery that this is impossible: the creative act calls up forces (ghosts) that cannot possibly be naturalized.

Science fiction also strives to materialize entities that would otherwise be unavailable to us, like the Presger in Leckie's novels, or, for that matter, like the monolith at the center of Clarke's and Kubrick's *2001*. But such narratives cannot prevent idealism, because manifesting such entities, and even explicating how they work in scientific (or pseudo-scientific) terms, gives them greater presence rather than explaining them away. As a result, *idealism* in both senses remains intrinsic to the very language that we must use in order to argue against it. Spicer reminds us that "words / Turn mysteriously against those who use them" (Spicer 2008). I have been arguing throughout this book that science fiction pushes towards a sort of literalism as it attempts to grasp and render potentiality. But since potentiality itself is not actual, and therefore not literal, science fiction is filled with depictions and representations that can only seem occult, bizarre, and outlandish by naturalistic standards. Science fiction cannot prevent idealism, because science-fictional worlds are "real but not actual." This is just an alternative way of stating Clarke's third law: Any sufficiently advanced technology is indistinguishable from magic.

To sum all this up: Science fiction is too profoundly reliant upon dubious images and illogical narratives to ever be able to engage in a concerted project of cognitive mapping, or otherwise to ascend to the abstract heights of Spinozian or Althusserian knowledge. This is why Jameson, and many other Marxist thinkers, ultimately find science fiction disappointing and insufficient. You can't get the science without also getting the fiction. But in its failure in the project of cognitive mapping, science fiction instead invents or discovers (the distinction is fluid and inexact) new territories that extend beyond the edges of all existing or even possible maps. Such is the power of fabulation. As the old-time cartographers wrote on the edges of their own maps: Here be dragons!

Leibniz versus Spinoza

I have already discussed G. W. Leibniz's concept of monads and his doctrine of compossibility, but I will now extend this discussion further by suggesting that it is Leibniz — rather than his older contemporary Spinoza — who ought to be recognized as the patron saint, or the patron philosopher, of science fiction. Many people, with good reason, love Spinoza; nobody has ever found Leibniz particularly lovable. But Leibniz has his intellectual virtues. As Isabelle Stengers puts it, Leibniz was a "thinker of diplomacy" (Stengers 2005), who incessantly "harmonized apparently contradictory points of view" (Stengers 2010). Harmonizing different points of view is emphatically not the same thing as resolving and sublating all these differences, as totalizing philosophers like Spinoza and Hegel claim to do. Rather, Leibniz's harmonization puts multiple points of view into an odd suspension, blending their insights without effacing any of them — much like the combinations of tones in musical chords. As Stengers says, Leibniz works by "never contradicting [his antagonists] but shrewdly transforming them into cases of his [own] system." As a result, Leibniz was much distrusted by his contemporaries: "People of faith [complained] when they discovered that the way Leibniz saved their convictions mysteriously demobilized them, deprived them of their power to clash with other convictions" (Stengers 2009).

Spinoza offers us the prospect — taken up by Althusser and Jameson, among others — of a kind of knowledge that is comprehensive, causally closed, and irreducible to representation. Such ambitions mystified Spinoza's contemporaries, but they became central to twentieth-century modernism. Leibniz, in contrast, gives us a world of multiple perspectives, open and mingled causal chains, and partial representations. These may achieve a certain harmony, but they never attain closure or totality, which for Leibniz can only be grasped by God. Leibniz imagines a series of possible worlds that never have been actualized and never will be — but which have a certain potency nonetheless. These possible worlds are ghostly alternatives, surrounding and shadowing — and thereby threatening to emerge out of — the actual world.

A number of Leibniz scholars have seen his thought, with its perspectivism and its sense of possible worlds, as being already, in anticipation, science-fictional. Justin E. H. Smith notes that Leibniz was "an avid reader" of the proto-science fiction of his own day (such as Cyrano de Bergerac's novels about travels to the Moon and to the Sun), and finds that these texts strongly influenced Leibniz's own philosophy (Smith 2016). Richard Halpern suggests that, due to the crucial importance of aesthetic speculation in his texts, "Leibniz is not only a philosopher but an early science fiction writer," whose "work has the kind of dense intellectual beauty that characterizes the writing of a Stanisław Lem or a Philip K. Dick or a Cixin Liu" (Halpern 2023). Guy Lardreau explores the "astonishing homology" between the fictions deployed by Leibniz in order to explain his ideas about possible worlds and the way that science fiction imagines parallel worlds (Lardreau 1988). For Lardreau, it is entirely in line with Leibniz's mode of thought that science fiction develops conjectures that are grounded in science but which touch on areas that science cannot reach.

Leibniz's interest in potentiality and possible worlds, together with his mixing of diverse perspectives held by a multitude of monads, puts him at odds with Spinoza's monism and necessitarianism. For Spinoza, reality could not be otherwise than it is: "Things could not have been produced by God in any other way or in any other order than they have been produced" (Spinoza 2018). This means that everything possible is in fact fully actualized; there is no residue. For Spinoza, "fictional claims… are by their very nature untenable" (Rescher 2015). For Leibniz, in contrast, "alternative frameworks of existence indeed are possible" (Rescher 2015). Leibniz distinguishes himself from Spinoza by insisting that

> there are just as many true substances, as many living mirrors of the universe which subsist always, or as many concentrated universes, as there are monads; according to Spinoza, on the contrary, there is only one substance. He would be right if there were no monads; then everything except God would be of a passing nature and would vanish into simple accidents or modifications, since there would be no substantial foundation in things, such as consists in the existence of monads.
>
> (Leibniz 1969)

Although, strictly speaking, Leibniz's monads are ideal entities without bodies, we can still compare them to biological cells as we know them today. This analogy does not do violence to the overall tendencies of Leibniz's thought. Contemporary scholars have disagreed about the legitimacy of reading Leibniz in this revisionist way, but Daniel Garber, for one, argues that Leibniz's speculation upon monads, although technically idealist, is close to other strands of his thought in which he is focused explicitly upon corporeal substance (Garber 2009). Just as Gabriel Tarde's neo-Leibnizianism is grounded in open, interpenetrating monads, so we may posit a biological neo-Leibnizianism, or what Whitehead describes (with explicit reference to Leibniz) as "an atomic theory of actuality." For Whitehead, at his most intensely Leibnizian, even though everything is interrelated with everything else, nonetheless "the ultimate metaphysical truth is atomism. The creatures are atomic" (Whitehead 1978).

A modernized version of Leibniz's monadology should therefore say that I am both an active part of the world and yet at the same time a detached spectator able to stand apart from the rest of the world and observe it at a distance. I occupy a specific location in the world — with *location* meaning both a spatio-temporal position and a particular set of needs, desires, and interests — which can be called my *perspective* or *point of view*. And I experience everything around me, everything that I encounter, *from* my own particular point of view. I see, hear, smell, touch, and taste various elements of the world; indeed, I *feel* the world and all the things in it. My cognition — my knowledge of the world — is secondary to, and dependent upon, these ongoing processes of feeling or experiencing.

Because of its dependence upon feeling, cognition is always finite, partial, and incomplete. My experiences go well beyond what I am directly cognizant of, or what I can explain to myself. Indeed, my feelings and experiences are not necessarily immediate and conscious at all. Leibniz says that I mostly encounter the world in the form of "small perceptions" (*petites perceptions*) that fall beneath the threshold of conscious awareness. I do not experience these perceptions individually; I only notice their sum, or their subsequent consequences:

> It is impossible for our soul to attend to everything in particular; that is why our confused sensations are the result of a truly infinite variety of perceptions. This is almost like the confused murmur coming from the innumerable set of breaking waves heard by those who approach the seashore.
>
> (Leibniz 1989)

I only hear the pounding of the waves as an overall sound, an aggregate. I am not conscious of hearing, in isolation, any of the individual sounds made by each particular droplet of water. And yet, Leibniz assures us that the aggregate sound that I hear is by no means uniform; it is composed of all these varying individual sounds. For every particular drop of water is ever so subtly different from every other. This is the claim of Leibniz's principle of the identity of indiscernibles, which states that no two separate and distinct things can be entirely alike. Thanks to all this variety at the micro-level, possibility is endless. Leibniz says that, although God chooses the "best" alternative in every situation, and could not do otherwise, nonetheless "things remain possible, even if God does not choose them" (Leibniz 1989, cited in Griffin 2008). Unactualized potentialities are therefore real for Leibniz, although not for Spinoza. Fictions are useful, and even necessary, as tools for human understanding. As one commentator puts it, "If we didn't use fictions" in order to grasp "the variety of things," then such sheer variety "would overwhelm finite minds" (Olivieri 2018). Lardreau adds that, for Leibniz, this is an intrinsic feature of reality, rather than just a contingent result of human weakness or incapacity. Fiction is essential to philosophy, according to Leibniz, because the real exceeds the rational; there is always "a *separation* between the Real and our power to apprehend it, no matter what one calls this power" (Lardreau 1988). No matter how sophisticated, and rationally all-encompassing, our understanding may be, the universe is still "queerer than we *can* suppose."

In consequence of his commitment to fictionalism (as Olivieri calls it — Olivieri 2018), Leibniz also insists upon the dignity and importance of the imagination, the capacity that generates fictions (Tropper 2019). For Leibniz, innumerable arrangements of the world are conceivable, and "God is the supreme fictionalist," in whose mind "the conception of every possible world finds its niche" (Rescher 2015). This means that imagination cannot be expunged from philosophy, as Spinoza advocates. Rather, in the words of Lardreau, Leibniz displays

> the marvelous richness, the mad generosity, the entire *liberty* of a thought that does not refuse itself any object, that does not reject any question, that does not judge any reference to be valueless or any knowledge to be unworthy (*indigne*). A thought without exclusivity, without principle of authority… [In Leibniz we find] strange narrative machines, "possible fictions" that he often develops, not without a sort of literary obligingness (*complaisance*), in which science fiction fans may discover the original mold (*le moule originel*) of many of the *topoi* that delight them.
>
> (Lardreau 1988)

This is quite similar to the way that, in the words of Donna Haraway, "the world neither speaks itself nor disappears in favor of a master decoder." No amount of Heideggerian "hearkening" will allow us to come upon being "speaking itself" and thereby revealing its secrets to us; and also, no hermeneutics will unravel and explain the world for us. Rather, there are still "surprises and ironies at the heart of all knowledge production" (Haraway 1991). As self-enclosed and self-delimited monads, we can never attain either a divine view of the world from everywhere or an objective, scientific "view from nowhere" (as the philosopher Thomas Nagel calls it — Nagel 1986). There are always more perspectives to consider, and more individual drops of water to grasp in the roar of the waves. We will never achieve anything like Spinoza's third kind of cognition; it is a self-deception even to try. Nonetheless, we can, and we should, always work to expand the range and the diversity of our understanding. This is really just another way of saying that reality is cognitively estranging — and intrinsically so. This is why we need to call upon the oblique strategies of science-fictional mimesis: extrapolation, speculation, and fabulation.

Perspectives and Possible Worlds

Leibniz insists upon the idea of "possible worlds." Just as many perspectives on the actual world necessarily co-exist, so too the actual world is not the only conceivable one; it can be compared with other possible worlds. These are worlds that do not actually exist but which *could* exist. Not only are such other worlds logically possible, they also exhibit real potentiality (in Whitehead's sense). That is to say, we can imagine scenarios through which they might come into existence. This is something that Leibniz and some other philosophers do, but it is also something that science fiction writers do. Science fiction explores what complexity theorists and game designers would call *possibility space*: "A register or ledger of all the possible answers to a problem" (Bogost 2017). The possibility space of futurity is too large to grasp, but it is not strictly speaking infinite. Science fiction is not about what *will* happen, but about what *could* happen. It looks at various ways in which our actual world situation might be transformed over the course of time. It posits alternative worlds that postdate, extend beyond, and depart from — but which are at least potentially capable of arising out of — the actual world in which it is written and read.

There is one obvious stumbling block in Leibniz's doctrine of possible worlds. According to Leibniz, God chose just one particular world — the actual world that we live in — from a multitude of possible ones. God made this particular choice, Leibniz insists, because the world we live in, here and now, is in fact "the best of all possible worlds" (Leibniz 2007). God would not and could not have chosen it otherwise. Leibniz has long been criticized, and indeed mocked, for this hyperbolic claim. Most notably, the French Enlightenment writer Voltaire, in his novel *Candide* (1759), ridicules Leibniz in the figure of Professor Pangloss, who repeatedly claims, in the face of the most horrific catastrophes, that "all is for the best, in this best of all possible worlds" (Voltaire 2006).

Reading charitably, however, we may say in Leibniz's defense that his idea of "best" should not be understood primarily in moral terms. It rather means something like what physicists today call *the principle of least action*, or the idea that natural processes unfold in the least energetically expensive manner possible (Coopersmith 2017). For instance, when water is trickling down a hill, it will follow the most efficient path to do so: the one that is shortest, or that offers the least resistance to overcome. It is only in this sense that the world finds the "best" path out of an impasse. The scientific principle of least action was itself initially adumbrated, if not entirely worked out, by Leibniz (Hecht 2016). Even though Leibniz also has moral considerations in mind, his primary meaning for "the best of all possible worlds" is metaphysically congruent with this physical principle. The best world is the one that, as a result of harnessing its energy levels so efficiently, is the most complex, the most full of variety, and therefore the most aesthetically rewarding.

Guy Lardreau also describes this mingling of scientific and aesthetic considerations as Leibniz's "law of maximum and minimum… the production of the maximum of worlds (and not only of the maximum of effects in each world), following from the minimum of principles" (Lardreau 1988). Or, as Philip R. Conway summarizes it, for Leibniz the best of all possible worlds is "not the most benign or beneficent but the most plural, in the strict sense of maximal compossibility" (Conway 2020). This demand for maximal plurality is at once an ontological principle, an ethical one, and an aesthetic one. It would also serve quite well as a rule of thumb for world-building in science fiction. Lardreau, following Leibniz, refuses to belittle any of the dimensions of the principle — ontological, ethical, or aesthetic — by separating them from one another. Indeed, it is only on the basis of such a prior separation between these dimensions that anything like the fascist "aestheticizing of politics," famously decried by Walter Benjamin, could even arise (Benjamin 2002).

In overtly aesthetic terms, we should note that Leibniz lived during what we now call the Baroque period of art and culture in Western Europe. Leibniz's aesthetic sense is very much a Baroque one, as Deleuze in particular points out (Deleuze 1992). One standard definition of the Baroque aesthetic says that it is "characterized by its melodramatic tableaus, lavish ornamentation, use of deep colors, chiaroscuro, and asymmetry" (Aesthetics Wiki 2020). Another standard definition describes it as using "contrast, movement, exuberant detail, deep colour, grandeur, and surprise to achieve a sense of awe" (Wikipedia 2023a). When Leibniz claims that ours is "the best of all possible worlds," therefore, he means that our world is the most colorful, the most convoluted, and the most grandiose one that could possibly exist. In twenty-first-century terms, Leibniz's aesthetic taste is much like that of a cineaste (okay, I am speaking here of myself) who especially loves such beautifully (and indeed ridiculously) convoluted and overloaded films as *Eternal Sunshine of the Spotless Mind* (Michel Gondry, 2004), *Detention* (Joseph Kahn, 2011), and *Everything Everywhere All At Once* (Daniel Kwan and Daniel Scheinert, 2022). One may also compare Leibniz's Baroque sensibility to that of a physicist who finds a particular theory of subatomic particles and fundamental forces to be beautiful and elegant, and who takes these qualities as evidence in favor of the theory's validity.

Nonetheless, in order to avoid misunderstandings, I am happy to say — against Leibniz — that the world we live in today is self-evidently *not* the best one that we could possibly have. We want a world in which everyone is guaranteed a basic level of material well-being, comfort, and self-determination. There is nothing particularly extreme, let alone utopian, about these demands. Indeed, we know very well that building such a world is possible, in the sense that it is well within our present technological and organizational capabilities. As Kim Stanley Robinson puts it, science tells us that

> the energy flows in our biosphere would provide adequately for all living creatures on the planet today, if we were to distribute them properly… An adequate life provided for all living beings is something the planet can still do; it has sufficient resources, and the sun provides enough energy.
>
> (Robinson 2018)

The only problem with this scenario — admittedly a formidable one — is that the wealthy and the powerful will not allow such a world to come into existence. Indeed, as many science fiction texts make evident, our rulers would let the world be destroyed altogether, rather than lessen their own fortunes in order to broaden the extent of human (and nonhuman) flourishing.

In any case, I do not think that this sort of concern for a better world is altogether at odds with Leibniz's thought. Whitehead maintains a similar attitude of open possibility, even as he rightly rejects Leibniz's claim for "the best" as an illegitimate subterfuge:

> There is no reason why there could be no alternative flux exhibiting that principle of internal determination. The actual flux presents itself with the character of being merely "given." It does not disclose any peculiar character of "perfection." On the contrary, the imperfection of the world is the theme of every religion which offers a way of escape, and of every sceptic who deplores the prevailing superstition. The Leibnizian theory of the 'best of possible worlds' is an audacious fudge

> produced in order to save the face of a Creator constructed by contemporary, and antecedent, theologians.
>
> (Whitehead 1978)

Despite this reservation, Whitehead retains Leibniz's sense — something entirely alien to Spinoza — that (as the alter-globalization movement puts it) *another world is possible*. And this possibility must be understood in the strong sense: as being a matter of real potentiality, rather than merely as not being logically contradictory. In this way, Leibniz allows us to consider which sorts of alternative world arrangements are achievable, and which are not. In Whitehead's own account, God's choice of what is "best" can always be contested. God exemplifies "the remorseless working of things"; he is "inexorable," and he exhibits a certain "ruthlessness." In this way, God — or, as we might say in a more contemporary vocabulary, the structural organization of society and the mode of production — does indeed provide the initial conditions for every experience. But within the framework of these conditions, and to the extent that "individual experience is not negligible," Whitehead insists that a certain degree of "self-determination" can occur, and further, that any such self-determination "is always imaginative in its origin" (Whitehead 1978).

Rather than seeing existential experience as being deficient with regard to systematic knowledge, therefore, we should regard the former as an always-necessary supplement to the apparent (but illusory) closure of the latter. Knowledge of the totality will never save us. This is why the project of cognitive mapping is ultimately unsatisfactory. Neither knowledge nor the world system that is the object of that knowledge is ever complete and closed. Different "contemporary events" may well be joint consequences of the same preceding overall configuration of the world; nonetheless, as Whitehead insists, they still "happen in causal independence of each other." Whitehead further says that such causal independence "is the preservative of the elbow-room within the Universe. It provides each actuality with a welcome environment for irresponsibility" (Whitehead 1933).

Now, I am pretty sure that Leibniz, no less than Spinoza, would have rejected such an invitation to "irresponsibility." Nonetheless, Leibniz gives us good reasons for cherishing "causal independence" — whereas Spinoza most emphatically tells us that such independence is not possible, and would not be desirable if it were. Jameson, who is ultimately a Spinozist, belittles the value of any "monadic 'point of view' on the world"; but Leibniz rather celebrates the multiple perspectives offered by the monads that constitute and fill the world. We should not characterize the monads as ideologically blinded, or as bedazzled by illusions like the prisoners in Plato's cave, or as unwittingly exemplifying the limitations of Spinoza's first kind of cognition. Rather, Leibniz's monads — much like Haraway's situated and embodied knowers — have understandings that are admittedly partial and often vague or mistaken; and yet each of them is clear about certain things, and therefore still valid in ways that are more than merely subjective.

The closure of the monads, their independence from one another, must be balanced against their mutual inherence in the same actual world. Each monad has its own blinkered account of things, Leibniz says, and yet these are all "perspectives on a single [world], corresponding to the different points of view of each monad" (Leibniz 1989). These monadic knowledges are admittedly incomplete, and different from one another, because a monad's "representation is only confused as to the detail of the whole universe, and can only be distinct for a small portion of things" (Leibniz 1989). But to note this is not to disqualify the monads. They all offer us certain important truths: the truths of those "small portion[s] of things" for which their perceptions *are* in fact clear and distinct. Despite their different positions and different degrees of confusion, the monads' representations are all "related and come from the same foundation, just like different views of the same city seen from various places" (Leibniz 2014).

I am reminded here of two short stories by Arthur C. Clarke, both of which work as allegories of science-fictional perspectivism (Clarke 2016). In "The Nine Billion Names of God," published in 1953, a Buddhist monastery in Tibet, whose centuries-old task is "compiling a list which shall contain all the possible names of God," hires a mainframe computer from America to finish the job. What would take the monks "fifteen thousand years" to do by hand can be accomplished by the computer "in a hundred days." Each name of God designates one particular perspective upon, or understanding of, the world. Once all the possible names of God have been written down, the monks believe, the world will come to an end: "The human race will have finished what it was created to do, and there won't be any point in carrying on." The computer completes its task, printing out a list of all nine billion names; and indeed, at the end of the story, "without any fuss, the stars were going out." The summing-up of all potentialities, or the incorporation of all possible points of view, and implicitly of all possible worlds, leads not to some Spinozian "adequate cognition of the essence of things," but rather to the dissolution that is nirvana. There is no totalizing knowledge of the real, only its exhaustion.

In Clarke's story "History Lesson" (published in 1949), changes in solar radiation lead to a cooling down of the Earth and worldwide glaciation that exterminates all life. But the same solar changes transform Venus into a world on which living beings thrive and evolve into intelligent and civilized forms. The Venusians are reptilian rather than mammalian, but this does not diminish their intellectual acumen, or their capacity for empathy. If anything, the Venusians are more intellectually open, and more capaciously curious and sympathetic, than human beings on Earth ever were. They have had a less painful and contorted history; for instance, "they never knew the Dark Age that held Man enchained for a thousand years." When Venusian archaeologists scour the Earth for signs of its vanished life, they discover a singular relic of the lost world: a canister with a roll of celluloid film inside. By examining the roll, they figure out how the technology of cinema might work. They play the reel of film, which they take to be an artistic record of the life of the extinct dominant species of Earth. They never learn, however, that the movie is actually a Disney cartoon.

In mistaking Donald Duck for *Homo sapiens*, they unwittingly demonstrate the impossibility — even with the best will and most penetrating intelligence in the world — of transcending partial and limited perspectives.

Leibniz himself likes to exemplify his arguments in what we can today describe as science-fictional terms. Lardreau, Halpern, and Smith, along with other Leibniz scholars, note Leibniz's fondness for the *commedia dell'arte* figure of Harlequin: especially as he is presented in the French farce *Arlequin, Empereur dans la Lune* (*Harlequin, Emperor of the Moon*) by Nolant de Fatouville, first performed in Paris in 1684 (Hayden and Worden 2019). In this stage play, Harlequin, as emperor of the Moon, describes at great length what life on the Moon is like. His descriptions are all satirical, making fun of targets that were familiar to the original Parisian audience. Within the play, the other characters remark, in response to every description given by Harlequin, "C'est tout comme ici" ("It's all as it is here"). Leibniz refers to this play when he writes:

> My great principle of natural things is that of Harlequin, Emperor of the Moon… *that it is always and everywhere in all things just as it is here.* That is, that nature is fundamentally uniform, although there is variety in the greater and the lesser and in the degrees of perfection.
>
> (Leibniz 2011)

In other words, even on the Moon, and even when a ridiculous clown is emperor, the way that things work — that is to say, the way that they hang together and make sense — is no different from what we are familiar with in everyday life. The unity of the logic of connections brings together the widest imaginable diversity of things, events, and manners of being. This is why fictions can inform us about reality. Satire only hits its target if it both recognizably depicts and yet estranges us from the situation being satirized. A plausible, or even simply legible, fictional world can only make an impression upon us if it follows the same logic, or the same principles of connection and variation, as the actual world that we live in does. This also means that nothing in terms of content is too extravagant as long as it hangs together with the other things. In maintaining this Harlequin principle, Leibniz is the polar opposite of Quentin Meillassoux, for whom everything is sheer contingency. In his *New Essays on Human Understanding*, Leibniz ponders such weird, proto-science-fictional matters as how we would treat a person who came from the Moon, and then writes, immediately afterwards:

> Fortunately we are spared these perplexities by the nature of things; but still these bizarre fictions have their uses in abstract studies (*spéculation*), as aids to a better grasp of the nature of our ideas
>
> (Leibniz 1996; cited in Lardreau 1988)

It is therefore for good Leibnizian reasons that science fiction generally follows traditional canons of representation in the *form* of its texts, even though — or better, precisely because — the *content* being represented is challenging, outlandish, and unexpected: a series of "bizarre fictions."

(Non)-Utopia

"The optimist proclaims that we live in the best of all possible worlds; and the pessimist fears this is true." So writes James Branch Cabell in his fantasy novel *The Silver Stallion* (Cabell 1926). This maxim seems especially appropriate for Leibniz, who both writes that our actual world is the best of all possible ones and clearly believes his own argument. Lardreau insists that — contrary to Voltaire's insinuations — Leibniz is anything but sanguine in the face of catastrophe. Rather, it is precisely by "*facing* the desolating spectacle of the world, confronting it, and not at all by turning away from it, that Leibniz pronounces that all is for the best." Lardreau therefore proposes that we should take Leibniz to be saying, not that the world is marvelous, but rather that it is — given the tragic and constraining circumstances that we actually face — "the least bad of possible worlds" (Lardreau 1988). Things could always be worse, and we are quite skilled in imagining just *how much* worse things could be. Indeed, many science-fictional dystopias, from the mid-twentieth century onwards, do just that: for instance, George Orwell's *Nineteen Eighty-Four* (Orwell 1949), Margaret Atwood's *The Handmaid's Tale* (Atwood 1985), and Carl Neville's *Resolution Way* (Neville 2016). Dystopian visions are also a mainstay of young-adult fiction in the early twenty-first century.

Of course, by the same token, we are also very good at imagining ways that things could be better than they actually are. But Leibniz would warn us that melioristic fantasizing always threatens to lead us astray. Things in the world are too intricately interconnected for us to be able to foresee the ramifying effects of any of our actions. Given our limited power and limited knowledge, we cannot rule out the possibility, or indeed the likelihood, that the changes we institute in order to make certain things better might well, at the same time, make other things worse. There are many familiar narratives, ranging from old fairy tales to modern works like the movie *Bedazzled* (Donen 1967), in which the magical granting of wishes turns against, and frustrates or harms, the very person who makes these wishes.

Leibniz's real point, according to Lardreau, is that we cannot overcome the limitations that are intrinsic to our finitude, and to our confinement in particular perspectives. "One can always *imagine* a better world, Lardreau says, "but one can never *think* it." Similarly, we can logically *explain*, on the basis of God's infinitude, that this world must be the least bad one, but we cannot, in our own finitude, *understand* why this should be so. We can *maintain* the optimist's pronouncement that this world is better than all the other possible worlds, but we cannot ever actually *prove* it (Lardreau 1988).

Here Leibniz seems to anticipate Kant's doctrine of *transcendental illusion*. According to Kant, we can neither escape from metaphysics nor fulfill the demands of metaphysics. There are ideas and ideals that are illusory but to which we are drawn by the very nature of reason itself. We are therefore condemned to

> a natural and unavoidable dialectic of pure reason, not one in which a bungler might be entangled through lack of acquaintance, or one that some sophist has artfully invented in order to confuse rational people, but one that irremediably attaches to human reason, so that even after we have exposed the mirage it will still not cease to lead our reason on with false hopes, continually propelling it into momentary aberrations that always need to be removed.
>
> (Kant 1998)

Though Leibniz never conceives anything like Kant's transcendental dialectic, he remains preoccupied with the way that our finitude once again leads us to the necessity of fictions in philosophical thought. As Lardreau summarizes this side of Leibniz:

> It is in this rupture between explaining and understanding, between maintaining and proving, that is to say finally... between what is accessible to finite comprehension and what can only be grasped by infinite comprehension, that fictions are not only justified, but properly required.
>
> (Lardreau 1988)

This is yet another instance of an *in-between* space that science fiction is uniquely suited to investigate. The gap between explaining and understanding is much like the gap between imagination and knowledge invoked by Donna Haraway, or the gap between completely transparent referents and completely opaque ones posed by Seo-Young Chu. In all these cases, we move beyond what is merely actual, although we never attain anything like a Spinozian comprehension of the whole (and therefore of necessity). Instead, relegated as we are to partiality and contingency, the best we can do is to explore — or at least to open up and wander through — the intermediate spaces of potentiality. The "rupture" that Lardreau describes can never be filled in or repaired. As poetry reminds us, "the Abysm" cannot "vomit forth its secrets," because "the deep truth is imageless" (Shelley 2017). Nevertheless, fictions — and particularly those of the sort that we refer to as science fiction — are able to populate this void with at least partial and tentative images.

Science-fictional images and narratives in general perform a role that is allegorized by one particular science-fictional trope: the wormholes that are often found in the science-fiction subgenre of space opera. Wormholes are shortcuts through the vast distances between stars that otherwise could only be traversed at less than the speed of light, requiring enormous amounts of time. In a similar way, many other science-fictional tropes allow us to traverse the possibility spaces of social and technological change without having to spend long and empty stretches during which nothing new or significant happens. Thanks to these shortcuts, potentialities can be concretized; they congeal or crystallize into narrative events.

These considerations bring us to the question of *utopia*, which is ubiquitous in recent science-fiction scholarship. The utopian dimension of science fiction has been explored by Suvin, Jameson, and especially Tom Moylan (Moylan 2014). Pre-science-fictional expressions of utopian thought, from Thomas More's 1516 book *Utopia* (which introduced the term), all the way up through the early twentieth century, tend to articulate elaborate schemes for regulating every aspect of social life and everyday experience. But Moylan shows that more-recent visionary science-fiction writing, from the mid-twentieth century onwards, is best understood, not as the outline of a perfect social order, but rather as what he calls "critical utopia." In these texts,

> "the subversive imaging of utopian society and the radical negativity of dystopian perception is preserved; while the systematizing boredom of the traditional utopia and the cooptation of utopia by modern structures is destroyed.

Such science-fiction texts, under the influence of the social turmoil of the 1960s and afterwards, "reject utopia as blueprint while preserving it as dream," and "focus on the continuing presence of difference and imperfection within utopian society itself." In rejecting the classical idea of utopia as a blueprint for the perfect society, critical utopias shift their emphasis to the play of multiple human desires, which are inconstant, entangled, and often inconsistent, but which converge upon demanding an alternative to "the immense power of the late capitalist formation to absorb negativity and to congeal unfulfilled desire into commodified objects" (Moylan 2014).

In terms of Moylan's historical schema, it is especially interesting to look at Charles Fourier (1772–1837), whose delightful utopian writings offer us a sort of transition between classical dogmatic utopias and modern critical ones. Fourier pushes rational organization to the point of delirium, and yet at the same time formulates an astonishingly incisive, wholly original, and defiantly non-rationalistic theory of desire. His prodigious account of the manic proliferation of multiple human desires anticipates (or even already exceeds) twentieth-century theories of subjectivity. Fourier imagines a new form of social organization in which every aspect of daily life is libidinally charged to the maximum.

Often Fourier sounds like a proto-science-fiction writer. He rejects mystical and religious formulations, and instead insists upon elaborate technical descriptions of, and (supposedly) scientific and materialist explanations for, all the phenomena described in his texts. His efforts to situate his visions, and describe them in detail, offer us a premonitory form of what we now call science-fictional world-building. For instance, Fourier sets out elaborate rituals and carefully articulated architectural arrangements for the encouragement of polyamory in his ideal society (Fourier 2015). Or to give another example, Fourier envisions the gradual extension of human agriculture into northern areas of the globe. Such increased cultivation will help to warm up the polar regions, which in turn will allow for yet more agriculture. After several hundred years of this synergistic activity, the increasing warmth and fertility will so supercharge the atmosphere that the aurora borealis will expand into a permanent phenomenon. At this point, the aurora's "effusion of creative fluid" will warm up the north polar region still further, and

> will change the taste of the sea and disperse or precipitate bituminous particles by spreading a *boreal citric acid*. In combination with salt, this liquid will give the sea a flavour of the kind of lemonade known as *aigresel*.
>
> (Fourier 1996).

The efflorescence of Fourier's science-fictional imagination is like nothing else in the nineteenth century; it anticipates aesthetic strategies that did not become widespread until much later. Fourier's books were more popular among the surrealists of the early twentieth century than they ever were in his own time. However, Fourier's elaborate descriptions of a new social order unquestionably partake of what Moylan calls the "blueprint" model of utopia. Fourier squeezes all his accounts of proliferating desires, and of biochemical and socio-erotic transformations, into a kind of carefully constructed *tableau*, or what Foucault calls a "grid of empirical knowledge" (Foucault 1971). Every possible human desire, passion, whim, or mania has its proper place in Fourier's grid. Such a form of discourse is far more typical of the seventeenth and eighteenth centuries than it is of any more-recent periods; it was already anachronistic by the time Fourier was writing in the early nineteenth century.

The historical transition from the older blueprint notion of utopia to the newer notion of a critical utopia resonates with (and can be correlated with) a number of other social transitions in Europe and North America during the same time period. In psychology, there is a movement from the understanding of human beings in terms of explicit needs and interests, as was held in the Enlightenment, to the more recent understanding of human beings in terms of desires that resist clear and full articulation. Foucault traces the earlier stages of this transformation, from the seventeenth to the nineteenth century, in *The Order of Things* (Foucault 1971); psychoanalysis codifies this new understanding of human nature in the early twentieth century. We are arguably still in thrall to this picture today. There is also a transition in literary forms, moving from the older sort of philosophical fables (like the writings of Cyrano de Bergerac in the seventeenth century, so much admired by Leibniz, and those of Voltaire in the eighteenth century, which mocked Leibniz), through the "scientific romances" of Jules Verne and others in the later nineteenth century, and on to science fiction as a recognizable literary (or paraliterary) genre starting in the early twentieth century.

Unlike Jameson and Moylan, Guy Lardreau claims in his Leibnizian account of the genre that science fiction is, "by definition, anti-utopian." This follows closely from the way that Lardreau sees Leibniz's "optimism," not as the justification of God's ways that Leibniz wanted it to be, but rather as an attempt to make the best of bad circumstances. Following from this, Lardreau argues that science fiction rejects any notion of static perfection and instead exemplifies the Leibnizian virtue of continual variation. Science fiction is not about abstract possibilities; rather, it is concerned with the ways that developments are compossible with one another. We can only judge a particular state of affairs by grasping the possible world in which it is embedded and then considering the other compossibilties, or affordances, that such a world can offer us. At best, Lardreau grudgingly concedes, science fiction "only offers us utopias in the most *problematic* way." It cannot depict the good life; all it can do is reaffirm the famous slogan from the French rebellion of 1968: "It is always right to rebel" (*on a toujours raison de se révolter*). Lardreau regards this slogan as "radically anti-political," because it refuses to state any positive demands, and therefore cannot be satisfied by any particular changes or reforms (Lardreau 1988).

I want to suggest, however, that Jameson's and Moylan's Marxist critical utopianism is not as incompatible with Lardreau's depressive post-Marxist anti-utopianism as might seem to be the case at first glance. Lardreau's wistful celebration of rebellion for its own sake, without any hope of accomplishment, echoes Jameson's claim that utopian science-fiction writing can only work negatively, "by forcing us to think the break itself, and not by offering a more traditional picture of what things would be like after the break" (Jameson 2005). Both of these formulations value science fiction for its virulent negation of the present, and reject (or at the very least ignore) whatever glimpses it might claim to give of a better future society. Moylan's critical utopianism similarly explores contradictions and alternative outcomes rather than allowing its aims to be dictated in advance. The critical utopia focuses on the human action of struggle that is necessary for social change to happen; and thereby, it also reminds us that a living, breathing utopia would necessarily involve continual human action, and continued struggle, rather than remaining static in some finally achieved state of grace. The critical utopia also acknowledges that utopian longing is not altogether separate from the capitalist society and ideology with which it seeks to break. To the contrary, Moylan reminds us that utopian longing already works

> as the underlying stimulus to the machinery of advertising or, perhaps most strikingly, in those living maps of restrictive pleasure which carry the passive consuming audience along in a totally managed environment, Disneyland and Disneyworld. (Moylan 2014)

Indeed, if capitalism could not call upon this underlying utopian structure of feeling as an alibi, it would never be able to sustain itself or establish consent.

This means that utopian science fiction today is already as "problematic" and inconclusive as Lardreau could ever possibly wish. Moylan's own examples of critical utopias are mostly novels that do not simply depict a singular good society but juxtapose alternative social formations with differing tendencies. The point in every case is that the particular social relations we take for granted today are not necessary and inevitable, but rather are themselves the consequences of multiple, particular historical contingencies. We should say of social history what Stephen Jay

Gould said of natural (or biological) history: if we were somehow able to "replay life's tape," then "any replay of the tape would lead evolution down a pathway radically different from the road actually taken" (Gould 1989).

The texts discussed by Moylan include Ursula K. Le Guin's "ambiguous utopia," *The Dispossessed* (Le Guin 1974), and Samuel R. Delany's "ambiguous heterotopias," *Trouble on Triton* (Delany 1976). These novels portray societies that are in many ways preferable to the one we live in today. But even these better societies are not without their own problems. Le Guin's Anarres is egalitarian and largely non-coercive, but it is also impoverished, under-resourced, and as a result rather grimly utilitarian in its overall values. In addition, Anarres is only able to retain its independence because the opposing forces on its larger neighboring planet Urras are too preoccupied with one another to pay attention to it. Urras is divided (just as Earth itself was divided when Le Guin wrote the novel) between a brutal capitalist society and an authoritarian socialist one. As for Delany's world of Triton, it offers its citizens an astonishingly wide range of lifestyle options, identity formations, and transformations, but the novel also warns us that such freedoms, while desirable in themselves, do not resolve problems of neurotic discontent and personal aggressivity — not to mention the grievances of those privileged people, like the protagonist, Bron Helstrom, whose conceited sense of their own importance is threatened by the extension of similar rights and equal recognition to others.

In such circumstances, the very designation of *utopia* is strained to the breaking point. No utopia is devoid of turmoil or of unresolved issues. And in our actual world, too many people are so hopeless and helpless, and/or so cynical, that they cannot believe in utopia even as a fiction, or as an ideal to strive for. But what is the alternative? As Kim Stanley Robinson points out:

> Utopia has an opposite, dystopia, and also a contrary, the anti-utopia. For every concept there is both a *not-concept* and an *anti-concept*. So utopia is the idea that the political order could be run

> better. Dystopia is the *not*, being the idea that the political order could get worse. Anti-utopias are the *anti*, saying that the idea of utopia itself is wrong and bad, and that any attempt to try to make things better is sure to wind up making things worse, creating an intended or unintended totalitarian state, or some other such political disaster.
>
> (Robinson 2018)

Robinson adds a fourth term to this matrix: *anti-anti-utopia*. Even if we cannot envision a fully realized utopia, we should at the very least reject the "fashionable pessimism, or simply cynicism" that dismisses every effort to make things better: "It's very easy to object to the utopian turn by invoking some poorly-defined but seemingly omnipresent reality principle. Well-off people do this all the time" (Robinson 2018). Anti-utopianism tells us that utopia is impossible; and yet at the same time, it regards utopia as a supreme danger, against which we must remain forever vigilant. Anti-anti-utopianism rejects this self-contradictory double logic, and scorns the complacency of which it is a symptom. Even Lardreau — a former Maoist militant turned transcendental pessimist — vehemently rejects the "lazy" and cynical idea that "we must never change anything, for fear that this will cause everything to collapse, without warning, into horror" (Lardreau 1988).

In short, the concept of utopia remains indispensable and insurpassable — although it is never wholly satisfactory, and never attained in practice. The word or concept that I propose for this situation is *(non)-utopia*. I model this terminology on François Laruelle's *non-philosophy*. Laruelle claims to step away from what he calls "standard philosophy," but without actually critiquing it — because critique itself is still an excessively philosophical gesture (Laruelle 2010, 2013). Utopia, like philosophy, is not rejected or destroyed, but is also not successfully enacted or realized. Rather, it is put into a kind of suspension. Utopia hovers over many science-fiction texts; it appears, and lures us forward, as a prospect in the distance. We never quite reach utopia: just as, walking on the surface of the Earth, we never quite reach the horizon that continually recedes before us as we walk towards it. But we are forced to recognize that, without such a horizon to orient us, we would be truly and utterly lost.

"The Ones Who Walk Away from Omelas"

Ursula K. Le Guin explores the dynamics of what I am calling (non)-utopia in her celebrated short story "The Ones Who Walk Away from Omelas" (Le Guin 2012). The city of Omelas is a place of ubiquitous joy and happiness in a way that is deep rather than superficial. The citizens are "mature, intelligent, passionate adults" who enjoy life to the fullest. They are always free to pursue their own interests, wherever these may lead. Sex, drugs, and fine dining are readily available. Most of the oppressions that we know are explicitly absent: "As they did without monarchy and slavery, so they also got on without the stock exchange, the advertisement, the secret police, and the bomb." Is this all too good to be true? The narrator continually hectors the story's readers, exhorting us and bullying us into believing her — which of course implies that she expects us not to. She withholds certain details, urging us instead to fill in the picture with whatever details we find most pleasing, on the grounds that this will make her overall picture more plausible. She worries that her vision of utopia will not be accepted, because we (her readers) have the "bad habit… of considering happiness as something rather stupid." We suffer from the idiotic prejudice, she tells us, that "only pain is intellectual, only evil interesting." She keeps on badgering us into assenting to her vision: "Do you believe? Do you accept the festival, the city, the joy? No?"

It is only at this point, more than halfway through the story, that Le Guin introduces the twist for which it has become so famous. The narrator hopes that, by giving one more detail about Omelas, her overall description will become "more credible." There is indeed a downside to the city's happiness. A small child is locked away in a windowless closet and relentlessly tortured. The city's utopian qualities, we are told, "depend wholly on this child's abominable misery." If the child's torment were to be alleviated in any way, even slightly, then "all the prosperity and beauty and delight of Omelas would wither and be destroyed." No explanation is given for this, although we are told that, among the citizens of Omelas, "some of them understand why, and some do not." But the crucial point is that none of this horror is hidden. All the citizens of Omelas are continually and oppressively aware that this torment is going on, and that their own happiness entirely depends upon it. In addition, all the city's cultural accomplishments are fueled by the guilt and rage, the "tears and anger," that the inhabitants feel: "It is the existence of the child, and their knowledge of its existence, that makes possible the nobility of their architecture, the poignancy of their music, the profundity of their science."

The title of the story is only explained in the final paragraph. Though most citizens of Omelas come to terms with, and finally accept, the troubling bargain upon which their happiness depends, there are some who reject it: "They leave Omelas, they walk ahead into the darkness, and they do not come back." This act of defection, the narrator says, is "quite incredible," more so than anything she has said about the city itself. Where do these people go? The narrator says that she does not know: "The place they go to is a place even less imaginable to most of us than the city of happiness. I cannot describe it at all. It is possible that it does not exist." The story depicts a utopia/dystopia, and insists on the truth of this representation; but it finds anything outside of this duality to be unimaginable and unrepresentable. Does this mean that there is no actual place aside from Omelas? Is suicide the only way to get outside the city? I am reminded of a line in a story by Maurice Blanchot: "No one escapes the spectacle of happiness" (Blanchot 1995). Even if we only take happiness "as something rather stupid," in addition to being all-too-lucidly aware of how the happiness of some is founded upon the oppression of others, we still find it hard to reject it, or to detach ourselves from it.

On the most obvious level, "The Ones Who Walk Away from Omelas" is a moral allegory. It poses the choice between complicity and conscientious objection. In Omelas, people can only experience their own happiness at the price of causing the misery of someone else. The ones who walk away are those who are unwilling to assent to the torture of a child, no matter how much happiness it brings to themselves and to others. They would rather lose their own happiness than remain complicit with the suffering it causes to somebody else. Much like the trolley problem in analytic philosophy, Le Guin's story offers us an infernal choice between two bad options, and forecloses all other possibilities. The story stipulates that nothing can be done to help the child; indeed, "even if the child could be released, it would not get much good of its freedom," because, as a result of its relentless brutalization, "it is too degraded and imbecile to know any real joy." Also, just as a conscientious objector to the military can do nothing to actually stop the war in which he or she refuses to participate, so in Omelas you cannot change or overthrow the system. You cannot stop the child's exploitation, but only refuse to collaborate in perpetuating it and reject your share of the profits from it. This is not a code of ethics, but a morality without nuance: a morality of Kantian, categorical severity.

The story's hyper-moralism is probably the reason why Marxist critics tend to view it with disdain. Thus Jameson condemns "The Ones Who Walk Away from Omelas" as "counterrevolutionary," a "nasty little fable," and a "decidedly anti-Utopian attack on socialism" (Jameson 2005). But from the perspective of what I am calling (non)-utopia, the story's impasse may be read quite differently. Le Guin is giving hyperbolic expression to the idea that no utopian formulation is ever inclusive *enough*. Due to the finitude of our powers of apprehension and expression, something or someone is always left out of even the most capacious utopian vision. Does Omelas include gays and lesbians, for instance? Does it include trans people or non-binary people? Presumably, if Le Guin had ever been asked about this, she would have replied that it does, at least implicitly. But such people are nowhere explicitly mentioned within the text. The tortured child is an intense figuration of the remainder, the non-inclusion, that haunts any positive formulation of happiness or of utopia. Perhaps because the story was written half a century ago, it does not overtly address contemporary concerns about the need for the broadened representation of multiple identities and subject positions. The virtue of the story is precisely that, rather than pretending to a false universality, it explicitly tells us that something will always be missing, and that totalizing closure is impossible.

A number of other science-fiction authors have written their own revisionist short stories about Omelas, responding to Le Guin's text and exploring the question of what happens to the people who walk away. Sarah Avery's "And the Ones Who Walk In" (Avery 2020) narrates a meeting between Crocus, a young woman who is leaving Omelas, and Paper, a mother with a baby, who is seeking refuge there. Crocus is deeply upset about the way that Omelas works: "After seeing for herself what the blessed city did to win its people their blessings, she did not want to benefit from it a single day longer." Paper suggests that Crocus is way too idealistic in her ideas about life in the outside world. Omelas may be ultimately "ugly and cruel," but the rest of the world is ugly and cruel as well. There are numerous horrors: armies that rape, murder, and pillage; bandits; predatory animals; plagues, earthquakes, and other natural disasters that ravage people's lives. Outside of Omelas, you need money to survive, and you need both "specialized skills" and plenty of luck in order to be able to earn it. People who have left Omelas tend to be smug; they think that they know what is right, and what to do, better than anyone else does. They "grow up soft," and they are too oblivious to realize what an enormous privilege it is to be able to walk away from complicity. But most of the walkers end up betraying their own ideals simply in order to survive. As for the outsiders, Paper has already buried her husband and four of her children. She simply wants her last baby to grow up in an environment where she will be able to flourish. Once the child becomes an adult, she will learn the truth about Omelas, and then she will be free to decide whether or not she is willing to stay.

Erika L. Satifka's "After We Walked Away" considers the fate of a heterosexual couple who leave Omelas. They find themselves instead as poor people in contemporary America (Satifka 2021).

Once they have departed, they are no longer able to remember their past in the city; they no longer know where it is, and they even forget their own names and those of their erstwhile friends. Omelas only remains in their minds as a vague symbol of everything they have lost, everything they can no longer have. They live in a slum. They cannot adjust to American fast food; it continually makes them feel sick to their stomachs. Instead of being haunted by the torture of one child, they encounter the everyday reality of lots of children "squatting amid the discarded condoms and half-rotted rat corpses" and begging for the tiniest morsels of food. The daily reality surrounding them includes "gangs, drugs, beatings," and multiple murders. The woman gets a job dancing in a topless bar, and the man "slings sandwiches at a food cart in the local park." They are worn down by lack and want, and by the ugliness of their everyday lives; they repeatedly quarrel, and eventually they split up. They have exchanged their formerly charmed, albeit guilty and complicit lives for endless rounds of drudgery and misery.

These stories, and a number of other ones, suggest that "The Ones Who Walk Away from Omelas" is not an allegory of utopia and of the dystopian elements that any utopia actually depends upon. More plausibly, Le Guin's story is an allegory of actually existing American capitalism. Despite the continued existence of advertisements and the stock exchange, we middle-class Americans still live relatively privileged and affluent lives by the standards of the rest of the world. We simply ignore the fact that our lives of comfort are only possible thanks to the suffering and exploitation of hundreds of millions of people (or perhaps even more) with whom we never come into contact. The biggest difference between Omelas and America is that only one person suffers in Omelas, instead of the vast numbers that insure our own well-being. And in Omelas, unlike in America, people are fully aware of the injustices upon which their lives are based. Also, America is tied to the rest of the world in a way that Omelas is not. You can walk away from Omelas, if you feel that you must. But you cannot walk away from America, because there is no place else to go. There is no place in the world that is outside of our orbit, free from American power and influence. This also means that there is no place where you can rest and re-establish yourself, finally free from complicity and guilt. In yet another response story, Paul Crenshaw's "AITA: Am I the Asshole for Not Walking Away From Omelas" — rhetorically modeled after the notorious Reddit forum — the narrator concludes by asking his readers: "Am I the asshole for accepting the sweetness that has been given to me? You think you would leave? Then why haven't you left where you are?" (Crenshaw 2023). Anyone with any degree of happiness, comfort, or freedom is in fact living in Omelas, whether they admit this to themselves or not.

The People's Republic of Britain

Carl Neville's 2020 novel *Eminent Domain* is another brilliant exploration of what I am calling (non)-utopia (Neville 2020). This visionary utopian book and its companion dystopian novel, *Resolution Way* (Neville 2016), both take place in Great Britain in 2018, but in alternative timelines, different from one another as well as from the actual one. *Resolution Way* is a dystopia, set in a hyper-capitalist Britain that is closely extrapolated from, but even bleaker and more oppressive than, the actually existing United Kingdom. In contrast, *Eminent Domain* depicts a utopian Britain that is convincingly portrayed, but so radically different from our own world as to be nearly unrecognizable. In the backstory of *Eminent Domain*, the Thatcher reaction that ravaged Great Britain starting in 1979 never happens. Instead, a successful working-class revolution in the 1980s and '90s leads to the abolition of both the monarchy and capitalism. In the present time of the novel, the People's Republic of Britain (abbreviated as PRB) is a cybernetically organized libertarian communist society. It is radically multicultural, and only "minority white." Money has been eliminated. Necessary labor is reduced to a minimum, thanks both to increased automation and to the abolition of what David Graeber calls "bullshit jobs": pointless jobs that seem to have been devised "just for the sake of keeping us all working" (Graeber

2018). Under capitalism, automation and job reduction threaten the livelihoods of many people, but in the PRB, everybody is just granted far more leisure time. Whatever work still unavoidably needs to be done is equally shared by the entire population.

In the PRB, a ubiquitous, but decentralized, computer network keeps the economy running. The novel suggests that, once data gathering is democratized and socialized, digital feedback mechanisms can organize economic production and distribution more effectively and efficiently, as well as more equitably, than capitalist competition has ever been able to do. This is one important aspect of the novel's utopian speculation: it implicitly references the way that left intellectuals have recently returned to, and revised the terms of, the "socialist calculation debate" of a century ago (Morozov 2019). In the PRB, the digital network does not just regulate the economy; it also coordinates human activities on the largest social scales. At the same time, the network functions on an individual or micro-scale: it both provides feedback on people's health and facilitates the realization of a wide range of personal desires. Instead of mobile phones, everybody has an ROD ("Readable Object Device"), a handheld mini-computer that keeps them connected to the network at all times, giving them full access to services, goods, and opportunities.

Eminent Domain quite knowingly pushes against the all-too-common supposition that digital networking and data collection must necessarily lead to totalitarian surveillance. Rather, the novel suggests that such abuse depends upon the distribution of capital, as well as upon the degree of centralization in the state apparatus. A lot of the book is focused upon the state security services, which still exist and still exert a certain degree of power — despite the absence of anything like a central despotic government. But even though there is a certain degree of Machiavellian manipulation and infighting, it is also clear that the power of the security forces is in fact quite limited. Overall, the novel does not present a fully determinate set of power relations, but rather shows these relations in flux, as they are continually being negotiated, debated, and revised. The revolution has developed new institutions, but these institutions are themselves fluid and relaxed, rather than rigorous and petrified. The tradeoff is that the price of increased freedom is increased susceptibility to disruption. The security forces are quite worried about this (rightly, as it turns out), but most people are not. As an individual citizen, you can get involved in policy decisions as much as you want; but you can also just ignore the debates altogether, if that is what you prefer. People are asked to vote on nearly everything; but if you want, you can just delegate the AI in your ROD to do the voting for you, based on what it knows of your opinions and desires.

Medical surveillance is an ongoing issue throughout *Eminent Domain*. People are required to wear patches on their skin that monitor all their vital signs, recommend healthy courses of action, and automatically administer hormones, endorphins, stimulants, and tranquilizers as needed to regulate their moment-to-moment moods and behavior. This is a prospect that other science-fiction writers have found quite horrific; most memorably, perhaps, in Project Itoh's novel *Harmony*, where ubiquitous, mandatory healthcare leads to mind control and the suppression of most of the sensations and feelings that make human life meaningful (Itoh 2010). But *Eminent Domain* refuses to take this approach. The patch is not an intrusion by some alleged "nanny state" (to use a term that I detest, and which does not appear in the novel, but that is unfortunately ubiquitous in public discourse). Rather, the patch is something like an automated form of self-medication (in the same way that you can use the ROD to automate your voting). Some people take their patches off when they do not want to be bothered ("non-compliance" is discouraged, but it does not seem to result in legal penalties), and a wide assortment of pharmaceuticals that you can take on your own recognizance are available. There are even humorous ways in which you can hack your patch:

> You can go into the interface on your ROD and set the sleep mode to the lowest level, 0.25 of a second, so it will knock you out and then wake you up super quick… I heard they use it at parties, *flickering*, you get so tired the patch forces you to sleep

> but you can calibrate it so that you're bouncing in and out of consciousness at an incredible speed.
>
> (Neville 2020)

One of the best things about *Eminent Domain* is its attention to this level of detail. The novel continually fabulates ways in which the overall technologies upon which the society is based can be tweaked, altered, or used to generate unintended, and even bizarre, results. No idealized account of how institutions are structured and intended can give us insight into the multiple and detailed ways that these institutions are actually used and abused. Beyond not only the blueprints of classical utopias but also the dialectical insights of Moylan's critical utopias, we find in *Eminent Domain* a (non)-utopia grounded in the procedures of what Deleuze calls *humor*: taking a principle and stretching and subverting it by "descending towards the consequences" so as to articulate "an art of consequences and descents, of suspensions and falls" (Deleuze 1994).

Beyond these particular issues, *Eminent Domain* offers us a Geertzian *thick description* (Geertz 1973) that powerfully fabulates and renders the textures of life, and the structures of feeling, that characterize the PRB. These are quite different from what we find in most utopian writing. The novel gives us a polyphonic portrait of an imperfect, but still vital and viable, utopia. It is written in short, overlapping fragments that come from multiple points of view. This choppy and discontinuous mode of presentation is the best way to convey the sense of an environment in which both objective practices and institutions, and subjective feelings and states of consciousness, are far different from anything that we are accustomed to. A narrative gradually emerges over the course of the novel. But this is only secondary to the book's kaleidoscopic survey of the new society's experiential textures, stressing its sensuous surfaces and manifold pleasures, but also attending to its defects and its vulnerabilities.

The novel neatly sidesteps both terms of the tiresome "nature versus nurture" debate. It suggests that new social arrangements do not change the shape of so-called human nature so much as they subject its plasticity to different stresses than the ones we are familiar with. The various forms of bourgeois neurosis are still all too common. We encounter the same sorts of unpleasant character types — including passive-aggressive whiners and even treacherous psychopaths — as we do in our experience of the actual world, and in novels set in our actual world or in worse ones. In fact, *Eminent Domain* shares some of the same characters with *Resolution Way*; these characters are close equivalents, but they act somewhat differently in the two books, due to their vastly differing circumstances. For instance, the billionaire entrepreneur Johannes Altborg appears in both books, and in both of them he is overbearing and arrogant. But in the otherwise dystopian *Resolution Way*, Altborg is justifiably beaten into a coma by an angry mob; whereas in the mostly utopian *Eminent Domain*, he is politically powerful enough to initiate a fascist coup.

In any case, *Eminent Domain* depicts a world in which hedonism has replaced labor discipline as the dominant social ethos. Leisure time is plentiful, and mind-altering pharmaceuticals are freely available and widely used. Living in the PRB feels a bit like attending an unending rave, one that goes on 24/7:

> Come with us! they say, if we go fast enough, we can hit the zero temporality in room six and float right through and out the other side… She feels as though her feet come up off the ground and jars loose from her own body, starts to drift, everything seeming to slow and accelerate at the same time, an incredible, dense polyrhythm buffeting her about…
>
> (Neville 2020)

Not everyone partakes in the drugs and the partying; but a psychedelic atmosphere pervades the whole society. Everyone can feel secure in the knowledge that they will be sustained and provided for no matter what happens, rather than fall between the cracks into disaster. This means that taking risks is, well, less risky than it would be in our own society (where alleged risk-taking seems to be possible only for the ultra-rich). But at the same time, the general mood — the *Stimmung* of the society, one might say — is one of thrilling anticipation, with the continuing sense that something wondrous and new is just about to happen. Such excitement is possible because the PRB is serious about eliminating what Herbert Marcuse called *surplus-repression*, or "the restrictions necessitated by social domination," as opposed to the basic level of Freudian repression that is needed for human society to exist and reproduce itself at all (Marcuse 1956).

Eminent Domain thus imagines something like what the late Mark Fisher called *acid communism*:

> The convergence of class consciousness, socialist-feminist consciousness-raising and psychedelic consciousness, the fusion of new social movements with a communist project, an unprecedented aestheticization of everyday life.
>
> Acid communism both refers to actual historical developments and to a virtual confluence that has not yet come together in actuality. Potentials exert influence without being actualized. Actual social formations are shaped by the potential formations whose actualization they seek to impede. The impress of "a world which could be free" can be detected in the very structures of a capitalist realist world which makes freedom impossible. (Fisher 2018)

This is the best description I know of the way that (non)-utopia may emerge out of the cracks that run through the all-too-stable world of what Whitehead calls "settled fact." I have been arguing throughout this book that science fiction is about real potentiality. All social formations necessarily depend upon, and give partial expression to, the very potentialities "whose actualization they seek to impede." This is the underlying mechanism of possible worlds. This is not a process that necessarily brings us salvation, because it works equally well in both directions. Where *Eminent Domain* elaborates upon potentialities that might make for a better world than ours, *Resolution Way* brings forth potentialities that make things worse.

Indeed, this is the great accomplishment of *Eminent Domain*. It fabulates a possible world that is thinkable in practical terms (as opposed to being just an abstract ideal), and that is far from perfect, but which remains clearly much more desirable than our own actual one. The novel gives us an acute sense of everything that is wrong with the PRB — its compromises, its hypocrisies, its unfinished projects, and even its dubious excesses — without suggesting that such problems call the overall social experiment into doubt. For instance, some of the older characters in the novel regret that, during the heady days of the revolution, they gave up their children to collective child-rearing and never had contact with them again. But in counterpoint to this regret, we get the figure of Dominic Bewes, the most villainous character in the novel. Dominic both crassly, cynically manipulates the sentimentality of familial feelings in order to reach his ends and is himself an ideological victim of such sentimental feelings.

Eminent Domain is very far, therefore, from the hoary trope that drives "The Ones Who Walk Away from Omelas": the revelation of a horrific dystopian underside to a seemingly utopian surface. Instead, *Eminent Domain* gives us a sense of the *everydayness* of the problems it shows us. Le Guin's narrator foregrounds the mechanisms of belief (or better, of the fictional suspension of disbelief) by stridently imploring us to accept her extreme fable. This involves building as wide a gulf as possible between the happiness of the city and the misery that fuels this happiness. But *Eminent Domain* adopts a far different strategy. The defects of the PRB do not negate the positive features of the society, but rather are closely intertwined with them. This intimate combination makes the whole structure far more convincing and believable than would be the case otherwise. The PRB is very much a Leibnizian possible world, in a way that Le Guin's Omelas, with its arbitrary dualism, fails to be.

One of the ways that Neville maintains a sense of unactualized possibilities in his two novels is through frequent suggestions that one timeline may bleed through into another. Potentialities are "iterated and reiterated across an infinite number of worlds," but are also twisted in the process, so that from world to world they are "completely different in almost every way." In *Eminent Domain*, there is a monument in Central London called the *Timeline*: a "two metre high grey slab" inscribed with important historical dates. But on occasion, it becomes oddly fluid for just a moment: "A ripple somehow seemed to run through the solid metal and the dates and events shifted" — in this case to an even more utopian world that is nowhere else present in the novel. There is also an area south of the Thames known as the Enthusiasm. This is a spontaneous mass gathering in which the overall tendencies that define the PRB are concentrated and intensified. Large numbers of people converge in the Enthusiasm. They dance, party, and take drugs, but they also seem to be trying "to open up a portal to another world… The Enthusiasm is a site of power, of worlds that slowly grind against others until one collapses." All these alternative social formations — including our own nonfictional, present-day one — seem to be fragile and oddly interconnected. Each of them seems to be on the verge of breaking into and writing over another one; though, aside from the sheer existence of the novels themselves, this never actually happens. (The novel *Resolution Way* exists, and is widely read, in the world of *Eminent Domain*). Neville suggests that social worlds are generated and governed, not by what *Eminent Domain* somewhat ironically calls "the iron laws of history," or "the solid, unalterable path that things have really taken," but rather by an unpredictable series of massive contingencies. Alternative outcomes are never far away (Neville 2020).

Eminent Domain mobilizes contingency and potentiality in order to demonstrate to us that another world is possible — and indeed, a better world than the one Leibniz's God has actually chosen for us. But the novel also warns us not to put excessive faith in contingency and potentiality. A large number of possible worlds are, just as Leibniz warned us, substantially worse than the one we actually live in, to say nothing of the one fabulated in *Eminent*

Domain. In the novel, the main enemy of the PRB is the United States of America, one nation where there has never been a strong socialist movement, let alone a socialist revolution. Throughout the book, the United States actively works to destabilize and destroy the PRB. And we learn over the course of the novel, not only that the United States remains resolutely capitalist, but also that it is on the cutting edge of the celebration of postmodern potentiality.

Eminent Domain conveys the power and danger of the United States in just a few short passages, which I will densely quote from here. The nation is epitomized by its president, Wilhelm Connaught, who seems like some hilarious combination of Donald Trump and Elon Musk, fused together and launched into hyperspace. Connaught gets elected by exploiting "quirks in the electoral system." His speeches utilize nonsense syllables and "twinned puns, partially anagrammatic or based on phonetic overlaps," in order to "activate particular neurological events" in his listeners. Once in power, Connaught rarely appears in public. Instead, he always seems to be "on his ranch in Texas, or in his tower in LA or orbiting the world on his private jet or floating on an airbed in his underwater theme park." He is also often seen playing golf on his private island; his neural and physiological enhancements allow him to get a hole in one on every swing. Connaught embodies, in his own person, the science-fictional process of "meta-human becoming." He lives within "a carapace of nanobots, Connaught himself a shell within that shell, crepe-y yet glistening and reticulated, sustained out and in by this invisible swarm." There are even rumors that he "has gone fully immortal."

Connaught is a figure of fascination and power, precisely because he is totally inaccessible. Unlike other politicians, he does not try to figure out what the voters want. Rather, in America, "life is organized around trying to figure out what HE wants, how to anticipate and satisfy HIS desires." Every American is ordered to "do your duty under this Administration." If anything, the administration's power is only augmented by the inevitable "outraged reactions" to its proposals. Connaught's invulnerability is also secured by the vast historical apparatus of White supremacy. Whether on the golf course or in one of his command centers, he is serviced by

> a teeming profusion of servants and caddies all beautiful deep mahogany shades of brown… available to fuck and kill… a vast class of peoples with whom one could do as one pleased, sub-humans for whom one need have no moral regard.

In philosophical terms, Connaught is the personification of potentiality unleashed — which is also to say that he is, in Marxist terms, "capital personified" (Marx 1993). Connaught glories in "the autopoiesis of the shockwave" and "the mutagenic possibilities of Gaussian randomness." His values are "velocity… impact… volatility… opening up new, unintended, unforeseen possibilities." Connaught appears in *Eminent Domain* as an ever-expanding, charismatic void, whose voracious appetite can never be satiated. It does not seem to matter what particular possibilities are actualized; he devours them and profits from them in any case. This is the force of dire necessity, in comparison to which the novel's vision of (non-)utopia is a slender, fragile hope. The book leaves us with the melancholy fear (or better, the self-reflexive acknowledgment) that in the face of this voracity, "all of this has been a fantasy, a fevered, accelerating dream of a world that is yet to be." And indeed, this is necessarily the case in any depiction of potentiality, which is to say in any work of science fiction.

8. Conclusions

More Than Human

What is science fiction? And *why* science fiction? It is not easy to answer these questions. As I have been arguing throughout this book, the very *fictionality* of science fiction — and specifically the application of fictional strategies to scientific, technological, and sociological questions — is the basic source of its power. Here I echo Istvan Csicsery-Ronay, who eloquently argues for

> the science-fictional imagination's relevance for scientific modeling, critical theory, the deconstruction of the future, the future of religion, the future of nations, the imagination of empire, the construction of aliens, the future of science fiction itself, and the transformation of utopia into mutopia.
>
> (Csicsery-Ronay 2022)

Most of the characteristics that theorists have discerned in science fiction — the sense of wonder, the extrapolation of social and scientific facts, utopia and dystopia, cognitive estrangement and the novum — are consequences of the basic act of envisioning alternatives to the actual state of things in which we find ourselves. If we could not at least entertain different social, economic, and technological arrangements, we would be entirely helpless. We live and die by our ability to imagine. Over the past century, science fiction has been one of our most powerful practices for envisioning alternatives, and the only one to deeply consider the effects of new technologies.

Of course, envisioning alternatives, and realizing how contingent our contemporary conditions of existence actually are, does not in itself lead to changing things for the better. I must confess that I am not Romantic enough, and in particular not Shelleyan enough, "to hope till Hope creates / From its own wreck the thing it contemplates" (Shelley 2017). So it is not on political grounds that I can give my own personal answers to the questions: What is science fiction? And why science fiction? All I can say, really, is that, as I reach the age of seventy, science fiction remains central to my fantasy life, as has been the case at least since I was a teenager. And science fiction has affected me much more in its written or literary form than it has in cinematic or televisual forms — despite my love for Mr Spock and my academic career as a professor of film and media studies. (I am also interested in science-fictional music, but as a non-musician I lack the ability and the training to write as cogently about music as I would wish).

I have had a long and varied career as an academic scholar and critic. But aside from science fiction, the only things I have written about at length in recent years are music videos. I explain this in a way that is too simplistic, but which still contains more than a grain of truth. Science fiction narratives are conservative in form, but radical in content; music videos are conservative in content, but radical in form. Science fiction deals with novel personal and social situations, and it considers how human beings change the world through the technologies they create and are themselves changed in turn by these technologies. But science fiction usually does this in conventional narrative prose. It offers us new wine in old bottles. Music videos, in contrast, are formally adventurous. They experiment with innovative audiovisual techniques: new sorts of images, new sorts of editing, and new sorts of interaction between sound and image. But they do this only in order to convey familiar feelings about sex, love, self-worth, and the persona of the star. They offer us old wine in new bottles. Very few works of art, in any medium, are radical both in form and in content; those that are tend to be challenging, or even entirely inaccessible. I often admire such works, but I usually do not know how to write about them. On the other hand, across media, all too many works of art are conservative both in form and in content; these tend to bore me.

In other words, I seem to be drawn to the sweet spot in between naturalism and experimentation. This is my metaphorical equivalent of what astrobiologists, searching for extraterrestrial life, call the *Goldilocks Zone*: "The range of orbits around a star within which a planetary surface can support liquid water given sufficient atmospheric pressure" (Wikipedia 2023b). In our own solar system, Mercury is much too hot for life to develop, and Jupiter and Saturn are too cold. But of course, the range of the Goldilocks Zone does not exhaustively limit where life might be found. Scientists today are very interested in the possibility of life in the clouds of Venus (as I have already discussed), as well as on certain moons of Jupiter and Saturn. These moons might well harbor life, even if the planets they orbit do not. Although they are far outside the Goldilocks Zone, some of them apparently sustain underground oceans of liquid water as a result of tidal heating.

I recognize similar outliers in science fiction. Doris Lessing, who first became famous for writing political and naturalistic fiction, and who eventually won the Nobel Prize in Literature, wrote a five-book series of what she called "space fiction," *Canopus in Argos: Archives* (Lessing 1992). These novels exhibit the social and political (as well as the psychological) concerns of Lessing's earlier "literary fiction," but they situate these concerns — ranging from individual ethical dilemmas, through gender categories, and on to the global effects of climate change — within a much broader cosmological framework. The five novels in Lessing's series expand outwards from an individualistic concern with how "action in the story impacts the main character or characters" (to use a conventional definition of literary fiction — Dukes 2023) to a profound exploration of the resonances and ramifying effects of events that unfold in and through multiple possible worlds.

More generally, science fiction has an extraordinarily broad scope, because it so often focuses attention upon nonhuman or more-than-human concerns. It is true that in the so-called Golden Age of science fiction (the 1940s and 1950s), the most powerful figure in the genre, John W. Campbell, the editor of *Astounding Science Fiction* magazine, insisted upon stories that depicted "human excellence," and especially ones "in which humans were shown to be superior to aliens." This attitude was itself a lurid projection of Campbell's own racism upon a galactic scale, with human beings standing in for White people and aliens for everyone else (Nevala-Lee 2018). And it is also true that science fiction all too often indulges in the fetishization of technology, and that it is consequently liable to suggest that all problems can somehow be engineered away. Nonetheless, these tendencies do not exhaust the genre.

Science fiction draws upon the general development of scientific rationality in the West over the past several centuries. This is the ultimate source of both its powers and its limitations. Kim Stanley Robinson traces this genealogy of the science-fictional imagination in his novel *Galileo's Dream*, which moves from Galileo's discoveries in the early seventeenth century to thirty-second-century human settlements on the Galilean moons of Jupiter (Robinson 2009). Conversely, John Rieder, in his book *Colonialism and the Emergence of Science Fiction*, traces how the science-fictional imagination is implicated within the ways that Western powers leveraged their scientific and technological accomplishments in order to colonize other parts of the world (Rieder 2008).

In any case, the science-fictional imagination is deeply committed to one crucial achievement of modern science: its relentless decentering of the human. Copernicus showed us that the Earth is not the center of the cosmos, and Darwin taught us that *Homo sapiens* is not the unparalleled crown of creation. Rather, "we are one species among millions on an undistinguished planet circling an undistinguished star that travels along an undistinguished orbit in an undistinguished galaxy" (Layzer 1990). We are no longer able to believe that "man is the measure of all things." We are deeply aware both of the immensity of the universe extending beyond us and of the ways that our short-sightedness has led us to destroy the ecological functioning of our own small planet. Science fiction largely works to extend this awareness.

This broader perspective is even found in what is sometimes called *engineering fiction*. This is a particular, heavily technophilic, subcategory of hard science fiction. It can be characterized by its *can-do* spirit: it depicts its characters, whether human or not, using their technological acumen in order to deal with the affordances and constraints of unfamiliar, harsh, and threatening planetary environments. I often find this sort of approach obnoxious, because it exaggerates the power of technological quick-fixes and reduces everything to the dreary measure of what Horkheimer and Adorno rightly stigmatized as instrumental reason (Horkheimer and Adorno 2002). Nonetheless, engineering fiction also highlights the ways in which the universe is not cut to our measure. For instance, Hal Clement's Golden Age novel *Mission of Gravity* (Clement 1954) is set upon the planet of Mesklin, which is much larger than Earth and has a methane atmosphere. Mesklin's gravitational pull is many times that of the Earth, but also, because of its rapid rotation, it is shaped like an oblate spheroid, and its gravitational pull is much heavier at the poles than at the equator. Clement organizes the novel entirely around these environmental characteristics: he imagines the sentient beings who could have evolved on such a planet, and considers what technologies might be viable in such extreme conditions. Andy Weir's novel *Project Hail Mary* (Weir 2021) offers a more recent example of engineering fiction. The book features interstellar microbes that consume large quantities of solar energy in a number of star systems, including our own, reducing the energy available for planetary life. After many twists and turns, the solution to the problem turns out to involve introducing a second species of interstellar microbe that preys upon the first. In Clement's and Weir's novels alike, human beings must work together with sentient aliens who have an entirely different biochemistry in order to solve problems and maintain viable living conditions for both species.

It is no wonder that so much science fiction, including the books just cited, narrates human encounters with nonhuman forms of intelligence, which are often incommensurate with our own. Sometimes these nonhuman intelligences exist right beneath our noses, like the parrots in Ted Chiang's short story "The Great Silence" (in Chiang 2019). At other times, such intelligences are produced in the course of alternative developments in the evolution of life on Earth, as in the various sections of Adrian Tchaikovsky's novel *The Doors of Eden* (Tchaikovsky 2020). At still other times, alien sentience is the result of human interventions to raise the intelligence of other species, as in Tchaikovsky's Children series (Tchaikovsky 2015, 2019, 2023), which I have discussed in a previous chapter, and in David Brin's six-volume Uplift Saga (Brin 2023). Most of the time, however, alien intelligences in science-fiction narratives evolve on their own, independently of us, and elsewhere than upon our own planet. As a result, they tend to understand the universe in very different ways than we do. Sometimes these intelligences are organic entities; at other times, they are machines that have supplanted their biological creators. In some stories, as in *Project Hail Mary*, the gap between ourselves and the aliens is bridged; but in others, true communication is, and remains, impossible. In Stanisław Lem's *Solaris*, for instance, human beings encounter a whole planet that seems to be a single intelligent entity. The planet displays clear signs of sentience and intentionality, and indeed it seems to be much smarter and more powerful than we are. It is able to "read" human minds to a certain degree, and it sends back to the human characters creepy embodied simulacra of people they have lost but still remember. Nonetheless, the planet's mental processes — even if we can agree to call them that — are so different from ours overall that no sort of meaningful interchange is possible (Lem 2002).

Lem, writing in the twentieth century under the constraints of an actually existing socialist regime, evades the Western (or market-driven) distinction between high and low culture. In the West, however, it seems to me for the most part — and despite the exception of Lessing's "space fiction" — that the exploration of science-fictional themes by writers of so-called literary fiction usually falls flat. This is because literary fiction is just as much a particular genre, with its own set of constraints and expectations, as are science fiction, fantasy, horror, romance fiction, and so on.

Literary fiction is not good at the sort of speculation associated with science fiction, because it dwells too exclusively upon things like individual psychology and interpersonal relations. As McKenzie Wark puts it, something like "climate change exceeds what the form of the bourgeois novel can express." Literary novels usually do not know how to depict the processes of the nonhuman world in itself, let alone its effects upon us and ours upon it. Instead, literary fiction tends to "clog up with what Franco Moretti calls filler, the everyday life of bourgeois society, its objects, decors, styles and habits" (Wark 2017).

For instance, even in a literary novel as thematically focused upon artificial intelligence as Richard Powers' *Galatea 2.0*, the intriguing passages in which the computer speaks are outweighed by the boring details of the narrator's masculinity, his anxieties, and his failed relationship with a woman he completely fails to understand (Powers 1995). And this is not an uncommon problem. As Ken MacLeod puts it, in mainstream literary fiction "the non-human exists… primarily as a metaphor for some aspect of the human condition." In contrast, MacLeod continues, genre science fiction regards "the non-human (the 'scientific fact')" as "an element of interest in its own right":

> Genre SF remains the only form of literature that takes seriously, and takes to heart, the universe of non-human nature that science has discovered. Its readers get from it a particular kick, a bite, that they don't get anywhere else. The world still needs that smack upside the head from the infinite reality beyond human affairs.
>
> (MacLeod 2016)

It is noteworthy that MacLeod himself writes science-fiction novels in which his human protagonists struggle, not always successfully, to grasp nonhuman concerns. His Corporation Wars trilogy (MacLeod 2018) begins in the later twenty-first century, with a war between two tendencies that were actually prominent in the blogosphere in the 2010s, when MacLeod was writing the novels. Though MacLeod doesn't actually use these terms, he is writing about the battle between accelerationists, who seek to push capitalism to the extremes at which it would break down and be transcended by communism (compare Shaviro 2015), and neo-reactionaries, who seek to repeal the Enlightenment and destroy even the vestiges of democracy in order to replace them with a racist, techno-fascist new order (compare Moldbug 2015 and Land 2022). In MacLeod's narrative, both of these groups are ultimately defeated by the corporate-dominated neoliberal state. But thousands of years later, in a different solar system twenty-four light years away from Earth, the digitally preserved minds of fighters from both sides are reanimated in virtual simulations, and are then downloaded into mechanized bodies. They are sent into combat as soldiers for squabbling interstellar corporations, which seek to claim and colonize new planets. But this is also part of the continuing punishment of accelerationists and neo-reactionaries alike: they are condemned by the corporations to fight, to be killed, and to be reawakened, over and over again. The suffering is unending.

Such circumstances create significant problems for the reanimated fighters. MacLeod shows no sympathy for the neo-reactionaries, but he is deeply interested in the fate of the accelerationists. They had initially defined themselves, in the twenty-first century, as Promethean visionaries, rejecting any sort of external constraint upon human self-determination. Their great slogan was "Solidarity Against Nature." But in the course of their renewed existence in the distant future, the accelerationists learn that the struggle for humanity and "against nature" is a catastrophic dead end. Instead, they find that, in order to oppose both large corporations and the neo-reactionaries, they need to ally themselves with intelligent nonhuman agencies such as "freebots" (robots with an emergent self-consciousness who reject their enslavement) and alien life-forms. Even as the accelerationists continue to struggle against submitting to the dictates of a meaningless fate, they find that their militant humanism must mutate into some sort of broader and more inclusive formation.

This exemplifies the way that science fiction, in exploring futurity or potentiality, must necessarily extend itself beyond exclusively human concerns.

The Science-Fictional Imagination

I have been arguing throughout this book that the science-fictional imagination has the power to move back and forth across disparate scales, and even among different ontological registers. The spatio-temporal range of science fiction may be as small as that of quantum events in the subatomic realm, or as vast as that of an entire galaxy over the course millennia. The science-fictional imagination encompasses physico-chemical materiality, biological life processes, technological inventions, historical inheritances, psychological configurations, and sociological structures. What I am here calling the science-fictional imagination is similar to (if even broader than) what C. Wright Mills decades ago called the *sociological imagination*: a mode that "enables its possessor to understand the larger historical scene in terms of its meaning for the inner life and the external career of a variety of individuals" (Mills 1959). Karen Lord cites this passage by Mills in order to articulate what she is doing as a science-fiction writer. Lord calls her own work *sociological fiction*, since it moves between "private troubles, public issues, and historical context," all of which are "considered through overlapping lenses of biography, sociology and history." Her texts give equal consideration to "the personal concerns of the characters, the public issues of their community, and the historical context that has produced both the community and the characters" (Lord 2023). All this pushes against, or at least goes well beyond, the obnoxious (and inexplicably popular) cliché according to which speculative fiction is supposed to express and exemplify "the hero's journey" (Campbell 1949). "More often than not," Lord observes, "the protagonists think and act in ways that won't fit the traditional tropes and don't lead to the usual outcomes" (Lord 2023).

It is on account of this open multiplicity that I continue, throughout this book, to search for definitions of science fiction, even though I maintain that no such definition can ever be complete or fully accurate. When the science-fiction writer James Tiptree Jr. — who had not yet been outed as Alice Sheldon — was asked the question "What *is* science fiction?", she replied as follows:

> What but a staggering, towering, glittering mad lay cathedral? Built like the old ones by spontaneous volunteers, some bringing one laborious gargoyle, some a load of stone, some engineering a spire. Over years now, over time the thing has grown, you know? To what god? Who knows. Something different from the gods of the other arts. A god that isn't there yet, maybe. An urge saying Up, saying Screw it all. Saying Try. To… be… more? We don't know. But *everyone* has made this. Limping, scratching, wrangling, clowning, goony, sauced, hes, shes, its, thems, bemmies for all I know, swooping glory, freaked out in corners, ridiculous, noble, queerly vulnerable in some ways others aren't — totally irrelevant, really.
>
> (Tiptree 2000)

I like this answer because of how messy and indeterminate it is, even as it suggests that things sort of hang together. Science fiction is more than just the sum of its individual parts, more than just a heap of separate texts (or movies or whatever) that have been classed together for marketing purposes. Yet what this *more* might be remains open to doubt; it is proposed in a series of questions rather than definite assertions. The image of "a staggering, towering, glittering mad lay cathedral" suggests a demented modern version of the church construction of the European medieval period, when an enormous edifice was put together with the labor of many separate artisans, all of them working with their individual specialties, few or none of them grasping the ultimate shape of the whole. Science has replaced God in modernity, but the struggle to push beyond our own finitude remains. The science-fictional cathedral might be telling us to proceed and to ascend: "Saying Up… Saying Try." But it also might just be telling us to "screw it all." In any case, Tiptree's language does not imply anything like a fully articulated whole; it suggests a project that is incomplete, and which can never be completed. The cathedral of science fiction is a ramshackle construction, one in which the disparate elements do not necessarily fit together as clearly and cleanly as we might wish. It is internally inconsistent; it is "lay" (not involving hierarchies of clergy) rather than authoritatively religious; and it is directed to a god or gods that may not exist (or at least, that may not exist *yet*). I imagine this cathedral as always tottering on the brink of collapse, even as it grows ever larger, and never entirely crumbling.

One noteworthy aspect of Tiptree's celebration of the "glittering mad lay cathedral" of science fiction is her invocation of all the possible third-person pronouns in English: "hes, shes, its, thems, bemmies for all I know" — where "bemmies" presumably refers to BEMs, the bug-eyed monsters beloved of classical pulp science fiction. This is a formula for multiplicity and radical perspectivism, going beyond the traditional gender binaries. It is fully in Tiptree/Sheldon's spirit that today we have even more sets of third-person pronouns, including *neopronouns* such as ze/zir (Marcus 2021), and my own favorites, the Spivak pronouns e/em/eir (Spivak 1990). Without going into difficult questions about how transgender formations are related to non-binary-gender ones, or about the status of Sheldon-writing-as-Tiptree as a sort of trans author, I think that I can at least say that science fiction has been more open to such new formations than many other literary genres have been. I have especially noted the increasing use of non-binary pronouns in very recent (2020s) science-fiction writing.

Tiptree's sense of science fiction as an edifice that never quite coalesces, but which also never quite collapses or dissolves, may be compared with Philip K. Dick's account of the precarity of science fiction in his 1978 essay "How to Build a Universe That Doesn't Fall Apart Two Days Later" (Dick 1996). Dick says that the aim of all his science-fiction writing is to explore the question "What is reality?", and hopefully to answer it. Dick's own preferred answer to this question is a crackpot one. He tells us that — despite the appearance that he is living in Santa Ana, California, in the year 1978 AD — he is actually living in Judea, ruled by the Roman Empire, in the year 50 AD, when Christians such as he were a persecuted minority. This seems to have been, on some level, Dick's actual, literal belief. Nonetheless, Dick is fully aware that most people will dismiss his claim as crazy, ridiculous, or at best allegorical. In order to preserve his contention, and to shield it from attack, Dick encases it in several layers of defensive irony. This means that he gives it the same status as he gives to people, places, and actions in his fiction. We are asked to accept Dick's claim through the old aesthetic ploy of the suspension of disbelief, while at the same time we remain aware, on a meta-level, that it is fictional.

This strategy, however, brings us back to the unending epistemological twists that drive so much of Dick's fiction. Time and again, in his novels and stories, seemingly self-evident realities turn out to be fake. Appearance gives way to an apparently underlying reality, but then that seeming reality turns out to be yet another false appearance, which gives way to yet another one in its own turn. If Dick's initial readers are sceptical of his claim that it is really 50 AD, he suggests that they should also be sceptical of their own assumption that it is really 1978 AD. In the face of a continual media "bombardment of pseudo-realities," Dick says, "we wind up with fake humans inventing fake realities and then peddling them to other fake humans." This means that the world of consensus reality, which we cannot avoid taking for granted, "is just a very large version of Disneyland" (Dick 1996).

Here, Dick anticipates and parallels the French sociologist Jean Baudrillard, who wrote, only a few years later, that "Disneyland is there to conceal the fact that it is the 'real' country, all of 'real' America, which is Disneyland" (Baudrillard 1994). Of course, if Baudrillard is right in seeing the ongoing Disneyfication of America, then he is wrong in thinking that this process is somehow being concealed from us. To the contrary, Americans are fully aware that things are continually being displaced by their own simulacra. We all know — even if Baudrillard does not know that we know — that all of America is indeed already Disneyland. In Dick's novels, the reign of simulation is not a product of ideological mystification, as it still seems to be for Baudrillard. Dick's protagonists are continually piercing the veil of appearances and discovering what lies beneath. Such demystification does not seem to be all that difficult to do. The real problem for Dick's protagonists (and for us as well, in the actual world) is that the very process of demystification goes on endlessly; no matter how many levels of reality we uncover, there are still additional ones beneath them. Baudrillard writes of "three orders of simulacra" (Baudrillard 1973). But Dick sees no reason to stop at three; he suggests that surely there must be more. Indeed, in the years since Dick and Baudrillard wrote, simulation has only become more ubiquitous, more labyrinthine, and yet more taken for granted. In America today, simulated reenactments of historical events are everywhere, as Katie King tells us (King 2012). Do these simulated reenactments connect us to history, or do they rather displace that history, giving us an alibi for ignoring it? Seeing past historical events in the form of spectacle might well allow us to continue to avoid acknowledging the actual influence of those historical events upon our present.

Dick sarcastically tells us, in the course of his essay, that "I consider myself a spokesperson for Disneyland because I live just a few miles from it." He singles out, for special notice, what he calls the "Lincoln Simulacrum" in Disneyland (Dick 1996). This reminds us that Dick's own novel *We Can Build You* features a simulacrum of Lincoln (Dick 1972). In fact, Dick wrote *We Can Build You* in 1962, two years *before* Disneyland introduced its own "Audio-Animatron®" of Lincoln in 1964 — even though the novel was not published until the following decade (Apel 2014). The very notion of a Lincoln automaton is intrinsically hilarious because of the violent contrast between what we know of the character of our most revered president and the pre-programmed nature of an automaton. Dick is acutely aware of such tensions, even if the Disney imagineers are not. This is why Dick is so ambivalent about world-building. He insists upon the provisional and self-undermining status of his own fictional constructions:

> It is my job to create universes, as the basis of one novel after another. And I have to build them in such a way that they do not fall apart two days later. Or at least that is what my editors hope. However, I will reveal a secret to you: I like to build universes which do fall apart. I like to see them come unglued, and I like to see how the characters in the novels cope with this problem. I have a secret love of chaos.
>
> (Dick 1996)

This sort of dissonance often shadows science-fictional world-building. Dick's contemporary Keith Laumer considers similar issues in his 1968 novelette "Goobereality" (Laumer 2002). The story reflects upon the costs and dangers of creating artificial worlds. The title refers to Mr Harlowe Goober, the billionaire head of Goober Enterprises. He is sort of a Walt Disney figure — or better, he is a Scrooge McDuck figure. He also reminds me of some of our contemporary billionaires, even though many of them were not yet born when Laumer wrote and published the novelette. In any case, Mr Goober seeks to transform the entire world into his own reflection. He sells commodity products named after himself, and he seems to have a monopoly on everything. Walls are made of Gooberplast, and fabrics are made of Gooberlon. You can purchase everything in Goobervendors. You are connected to the public media through Goobervision, Goobertape, and Goobertronics. And you can make video phone calls over the Gooberscope.

After stealing the idea from his ex-employee Barnaby Quale, Mr Goober manufactures the "Goobernetic Goobereality Simulator," an "environmental simulator" that is sort of like a high-powered generator of physically instantiated science-fiction scenarios:

> It assimilates the data introduced, collates, interrelates, extrapolates and, on the basis of up to one hundred billion

> separate informational factors, re-creates the exocosmic matrix implied by the observed phenomena.

The simulated environment thus created is entirely autonomous: a "closed field… segregated from outside influences." It is something like a Leibnizian monad — or better, an operationally closed autopoietic system (Maturana and Varela 1980). Mr Goober hopes to use the simulator for

> market research. With this setup, the advertiser can penetrate right into the innermost secrets of the American scene! No more wondering what brand underarm the typical family uses; just plug in the data, and take a look!

Barnaby is distressed, not only because his idea has been stolen from him, but also because he had hoped that it would "be used for human betterment" and "to make a lasting contribution to human knowledge" — rather than instrumentalized to spy upon people and sell them even more stuff. In order to stop Mr Goober's plans, Barnaby sneaks into Goober Enterprises and enters into the simulation. It appears to be a dense urban area, and is filled with people who talk entirely in advertising slogans and who do not even notice Barnaby's presence. Moreover, it turns out that the simulator does not just mimic a reality that was given to it in advance. Rather, it engulfs whatever external reality it encounters and appropriates that reality for itself. As Barnaby explains it, the simulation field

> developed some kind of self-perpetuating feedback; started cannibalizing everything around, and building itself bigger. Naturally, the apparatus itself was exempt because it was isolated from the field… it simply gobbled up everything it touched.

In other words, the Goobernetic Goobereality Simulator is what complexity theorists call a *dissipative structure* (Prigogine and Stengers

1984). It sustains itself in far-from-equilibrium conditions, and its relation to the world beyond it is not reciprocal. The simulator is "segregated from outside influences," but the outside world is not similarly shielded from its predations. Like all living systems, and many inorganic ones as well, the simulator needs to receive a continual flow of energy in order to function. Mr Goober has made sure that it is connected to the electrical grid; indeed, it has "the whole state's power supply to draw on… it can tap the whole supply for North America — and probably South America too." As long as it continues to be fed by electricity, it also continues to grow, swallowing up whatever it encounters. In this way, the Goobernetic Goobereality Simulator is the ultimate expression of Mr Goober's own effort to transform everything in the world into his own brand, with his own name stamped upon it. Once Barnaby is trapped inside the simulation, he can only escape by short-circuiting the whole system.

One detail from Laumer's novelette is especially worth noting. The world created by the simulator includes Richard Nixon — that is to say, it includes a Richard Nixon automaton, broadcasting a speech in front of television cameras. In his effort to shut down the simulation, Barnaby knocks the Nixon automaton off its seat, but it continues to deliver its speech "unperturbed." Finally, Barnaby bashes the simulacrum's face in. At this point, Nixon gets stuck in a loop, repeating the same phrase over and over: "… The free peoples… The free peoples… The free peoples …" As Barnaby rushes through the simulation, looking for a way to escape or to shut it down, the Nixon automaton shows up again and again, always mouthing the same vapid Cold War slogan.

Where Dick gives us a simulacrum of our most venerated president, Laumer gives us a simulacrum of our most despised president (though I should note that the story was first published in December 1968, when Nixon was president-elect but had not yet assumed office). In any case, the choice between Lincoln and Nixon scarcely matters at this point. For Dick and Laumer alike, the accelerating, all-consuming logic of simulation remains the same: a frenzied orgy of viral replication that transforms the whole world into its own double or makes it retreat into its own image. Science fiction, like any other practice of representation, necessarily moves according to such a simulacral logic. But we may hope, at the very least, that the science-fictional imagination can render this logic so closely, so lucidly, and so precisely as to capture it, isolate it, and suspend it in its naked form as sheer experience and sheer disclosure. Such is the process of what Gilles Deleuze calls *counter-actualization* (Deleuze 1990). Science fiction can register the full horror of the social and physical conditions under which we live, in a way that a non-futural account, one that does not depict potentialities, could not. But science fiction can also register the utopian seeds of hope — the possibilities of difference and transformation — that are also already buried within the present moment. It can nourish these seeds, and allow them to grow, to come to bloom in their full, vibrant, and monstrous glory.

Fictioning and Reality-Testing

I have just discussed three models of science fiction, all of them dating from the New Wave of the 1960s and '70s: Tiptree's ramshackle, mad cathedral, Dick's endless construction of self-discrediting fakes, and Laumer's bulimic environmental simulator. All of these models are powerful, but none of them is definitive. The point is that trying to make a model of science fiction is itself an example of how science fiction tries to make models of a given part of the world — or even of the world as a whole. My focus in this book is on the specific qualities of science fiction, the practices and processes that differentiate it from everything else. But I am *also* placing science fiction within a much wider range of processes and outcomes. In the broadest sense, model-making — which science fiction accomplishes in the three forms of extrapolation, speculation, and fabulation — has a double import. On the one hand, it is an instance of what David Burrows and Simon O'Sullivan call *fictioning*, which they define as

> the writing, imaging, performing or other material instantiation or worlds or social bodies that mark out trajectories different to those engendered by the dominant organizations of life currently in existence.
>
> (Burrows and O'Sullivan 2019)

At the same time, and on the other hand, model-making is also an instance of what therapists often call *reality-testing*. Probing the realities we encounter and constructing avowedly untrue and non-realistic fictions are closely intertwined activities, in ways that we do not always grasp or remember.

Projecting fictions and testing realities is not just something that science-fiction writers do. It is something that all human beings do — and indeed, that other biological entities do as well. All living things arguably engage in reality-testing. As the neuroscientist Björn Brembs notes, in the past several decades biology has witnessed a "dramatic shift in perspectives from input/output to output/input" (Brembs 2015). We are coming to realize that living organisms do not simply react to stimuli from their environment; rather, they actively and spontaneously probe that environment, questioning it, altering it, and soliciting responses from it. When an organism does this, it compares the responses it receives with what can only be called its expectations. If there is a mismatch between expected and actual responses, the organism will seek to correct the imbalance, striving to adjust its own expectations and the surrounding environment to one another. It may do this either by altering the environment to meet its expectations or by altering the model that guides its expectations to better match what it encounters in the environment. Indeed, it may well do both. Biologists and neuroscientists have explored these processes in various ways. Most notably, perhaps, there is Karl Friston's *free energy principle*, which states that "all facets of behavior and cognition in living organisms follow a unique imperative: *minimizing the surprise of their sensory observations*." This means that organisms seek to reduce, as much as possible, the amount of irritation, uncertainty, anxiety, and arousal — or, more generally, the amount of free (unbound) energy — in their sensory-motor systems. Perception and action are thereby closely interlinked (Parr et al. 2022; see also Solms 2021). One of the most elaborate forms that this whole process takes in human beings is the way in which "fictions… involve potential realities to come… fiction as intervention in, and augmentation of, existing reality" (Burrows and O'Sullivan 2019). All in all, the creation of models — or more generally, the production and projection of fictions — is a far more flexible, and ultimately far more accurate, way of referring to the outside world, and also of acting upon it, than a literal one-to-one representation could ever be.

None of this need imply that bacteria or blades of grass are *conscious* in the human sense of the word. Whitehead reminds us that consciousness is only "a very rare component" of organic experience, or even of mental experience (Whitehead 1978). As I have argued elsewhere, *sentience* (or what Whitehead calls *feeling* — using this word as a "mere technical term," but a suggestive one) is a far broader category than *consciousness* (Shaviro 2016a). Even in ourselves, most mental operations, whether affective, cognitive, or both, take place outside of consciousness, and often in ways that are inaccessible to consciousness (Hayles 2017). The explicitly conscious human practices of scientific model-building and reality-testing, and of science-fictional extrapolation, speculation, and fabulation, are particularly sophisticated versions of processes that — in their broader, simpler, and less self-aware forms — are ubiquitous throughout the biological world. Of course, not everything is science-fictional; it is abundantly evident that most life activities and productions are not. But I would still like to claim that *science-fictional becoming* is an actual and even widespread process in the world.

The Antinomies of Science Fiction

To conclude, I would like to turn away from all these attempts to define science fiction as a whole. Instead, I would like to move towards a less exalted level, and to look at some of the tensions and oppositions that seem to be intrinsic to science fiction as it is written and read today. For instance, science fiction is generically oriented towards the unknowable future, but it also tends to reflect and comment upon the actual present moment in which it is written and initially read. In imagining how things might be different from the way they actually are, science fiction moves towards both utopia and dystopia. It emphasizes the power of radical new technologies, but it also considers environmental constraints that limit the power of such technologies, and of human action in general. Science fiction proposes a kind of secular myth, a new Prometheanism for humankind; but it also widens the focus of our attention well beyond the merely human, and directs our attention to the existence of other living entities, as well as nonliving systems. It dramatizes our ambitions to go beyond the limits of our native planet and reach for the stars, but it also suggests a re-dedication to the Earth, against the many ways that we are in process of destroying our own environment. Even in strictly human, twenty-first-century sociological terms, science fiction sometimes expresses the visionary ideals of left accelerationism and of Afrofuturism (Womack 2013). But it also often embodies the cautionary wisdom of movements for ecological care and economic degrowth (Kallis 2017), and the deep, anti-triumphalist warnings of Afropessimism (Wilderson 2020).

All these are tendencies, rather than fixed positions. Each opposing pair is best conceived as a set of extremes, between which a continuum stretches. For instance, a science-fiction text may be more or less utopian, and more or less dystopian; it may be more skewed towards imagining an unprecedented future, or more skewed towards exaggerating, critiquing, and satirizing the conditions of the present. Science fiction writers and artists may locate themselves at particular points along each of these continua. We may also conceive each pair of oppositions as a dimension in possibility space or in phase space, though the number of dimensions makes such a space difficult to visualize.

I find it most convenient, however, to present these contrasts in the form of a table, modeled after Kant's exposition of the four

"Conflicts of the Transcendental Ideas" in his "Antinomy of Pure Reason," in the second half of the "First Critique." Kant divides his pages into two columns; in one he states and proves a series of theses, while in the other he states and proves a corresponding series of antitheses. The proofs of a thesis and of an antithesis evidently contradict one another, and yet both apparent proofs are equally valid. Kant's point is to show how the limits of reason are breached when we take principles that are applicable to particular phenomena, or particular elements in the universe, and endeavor to apply them to the totality of phenomena, or to the universe as a whole. This cannot work, because "the absolute totality of the series" is not itself an element within the series, and the universe as a whole is not an object within the universe (Kant 1998).

Though the tensions inhabiting science fiction are not "transcendental illusions" in Kant's precise sense, they still present a structure of irreconcilable, and yet inseparable, antinomies. I list them here, even though my listing is inevitably incomplete:

Thesis	Antithesis
Envisaging the future	Allegorizing the present
Utopia	Dystopia
Revolutionary technologies	Ecological constraints
Prometheanism	Nonhuman turn
Escape from Earth	Re-dedication to Earth
Accelerationism	Degrowth
Afrofuturism	Afropessimism

Kant rejects the possibility of any sort of synthesis that would resolve the tensions of thesis and antithesis. You cannot get rid of them by jumping to a higher plane or a self-reflexive meta-level. It is as if Kant already foresaw, and blocked in advance, Hegel's dialectic, with its sublation of contradictions and its negation of the negation. Kant is often accused of a static, sterile, and rigid formalism: he keeps his categories strictly in place, never permitting them to promiscuously intermingle and mutually change. But the very rigidity of Kant's categories and schemata allows them to be filled, indifferently, with the most weirdly heterogeneous contents. I think, for instance, that the odd taxonomy cited (or invented) by Jorge Luis Borges (Borges 1999b), and then celebrated by Michel Foucault, is very Kantian in spirit:

> This book first arose out of a passage in Borges, out of the laughter that shattered, as I read the passage, all the familiar landmarks of my thought — *our* thought that bears the stamp of our age and our geography — breaking up all the ordered surfaces and all the planes with which we are accustomed to tame the wild profusion of existing things, and continuing long afterwards to disturb and threaten with collapse our age-old distinction between the Same and the Other. This passage quotes a "certain Chinese encyclopaedia" in which it is written that "animals are divided into: (a) belonging to the Emperor, (b) embalmed, (c) tame, (d) suckling pigs, (e) sirens, (f) fabulous, (g) stray dogs, (h) included in the present classification, (i) frenzied, (j) innumerable, (k) drawn with a very fine camelhair brush, (l) *et cetera,* (m) having just broken the water pitcher, (n) that from a long way off look like flies." In the wonderment of this taxonomy, the thing we apprehend in one great leap, the thing that, by means of the fable, is demonstrated as the exotic charm of another system of thought, is the limitation of our own, the stark impossibility of thinking *that.*
>
> (Foucault 1971)

The objectionable thing about Hegelian dialectics is that its play of negativity and sublation, its strategy of always jumping to a meta-level, is precisely a way of normalizing such a taxonomy, making it fully thinkable after all, placing it safely back within Western thought's "age-old distinction between the Same and the Other."

In contrast, Kant's uncompromising formalism — evident equally in the structure of his three critiques and in his hilarious daily habit of taking the exact same walk at the exact same time every day, regardless of the weather (Heine 2006) — produces a container that can be stuffed with any contents whatsoever without homogenizing them. This is at the root of Kant's proto-science-fictional speculations: in particular, that on the subject of extraterrestrials, which Peter Szendy has discussed at length (Szendy 2013). Kant is able to entertain the thought of sentient beings on other planets precisely because he rejects the closure that would result from the dialectical subsumption and unification of his categories. Just as the conventional form of science-fiction texts (more or less linear narrative) allows them to contain the most startling and unexpected contents, so the rigid form of Kant's architectonics allows them to accommodate the most diverse phenomena. As Foucault puts it, Kant "articulated, in a manner that is still enigmatic, metaphysical discourse and reflection on the limits of our reason." But all this was lost when, with Hegel and other nineteenth-century thinkers, "dialectics substituted for the questioning of being and limits the play of contradiction and totality" (Foucault 1998). As a result, Hegel closes off the Kantian speculation about beings on other worlds and recenters Earth as "the fatherland [*Heimat*] of spirit" (cited by Szendy 2013).

As I have been arguing throughout this book, there is no closure to history. There is no endpoint at which Hegel's "World Spirit" can bind the antinomies together and recapitulate them retrospectively. The real is not rational, and the wounds of the spirit always leave scars. We never return to the Heimat, not even in the beautiful sense that this term is given by Ernst Bloch: "Something which shines into the childhood of all and in which no one has yet been" (Bloch 1995). You can't go home again, not even for the first time. At best, the homeland forever glimmers on the horizon; but it recedes as we try to approach it. This is why the science-fictional imagination, with its continual exploration of potentialities that are real but not actual, remains relevant, and even necessary, for us today.

Works Cited

Adams, Douglas (1979). *The Hitchhiker's Guide to the Galaxy.*

Adkins, Lisa (2018). *The Time of Money.*

Adkins, Lisa, Melinda Cooper, and Martijn Konings (2020). *The Asset Economy.*

Aesthetics Wiki (2020). "Baroque." https://aesthetics.fandom.com/wiki/Baroque

Allen, Barry (2013). "The use of useless knowledge: Bergson against the pragmatists." *Canadian Journal of Philosophy*, Vol. 43, No. 1, 37–59.

Althusser, Louis (1997). "The Only Materialist Tradition: Part I: Spinoza." Trans. Ted Stolze. In *The New Spinoza*. Ed. Warren Montag and Ted Stolze.

Althusser, Louis (2001). *Lenin and Philosophy and Other Essays*. Tr. Ben Brewster.

Amoore, Louise (2013). *The Politics of Possibility: Risk and Security Beyond Probability.*

Anders, Charlie Jane (2010). *The Fermi Paradox is Our Business Model.*

Anders, Charlie Jane (2019). "Why Science Fiction Authors Need to Be Writing About Climate Change Right Now." *Tor*, January 22, 2019. *https://www.tor.com/2019/01/22/why-science-fiction-authors-need-to-be-writing-about-climate-change-right-now/*

Anders, Charlie Jane (2021). *Even Greater Mistakes: Stories.*

Anjum, Rani Lill, and Stephen Mumford (2018). *Causation in Science and the Methods of Scientific Discovery.*

Apel, D. Scott (2014). *Philip K. Dick: The Dream Connection.*

Armstrong, Chloe (2017). "Leibniz and Lewis on Modal Metaphysics and Fatalism." *Quaestiones Disputatae*, Vol. 7, No. 2 (Spring 2017), 72–96.

Asimov, Isaac (1955). *The End of Eternity*.

Asimov, Isaac (1968). *Asimov's Mysteries*.

Asimov, Isaac (2022). *Foundation 3-Book Bundle: Foundation, Foundation and Empire, Second Foundation*.

Asmelash, Leah (2020). "How Karen became a meme, and what real-life Karens think about it." *CNN*, May 30, 2020. *https://www.cnn.com/2020/05/30/us/karen-meme-trnd/index.html*

Atwood, Margaret (1985). *The Handmaid's Tale*.

Avery, Sarah (2020). "And the Ones Who Walk In." *Beneath Ceaseless Skies*, Vol. 319 (December 17, 2020). https://www.beneath-ceaseless-skies.com/stories/and-the-ones-who-walk-in/

Ayache, Elie (2010). *The Blank Swan: The End of Probability*.

Ayache, Elie (2015). *The Medium of Contingency: An Inverse View of the Market*.

Ayler, Albert (1965). *Spirits Rejoice*. Recording.

Babbs, Simon, and Michael Selby (1993). "Contingent Claims Analysis." *https://warwick.ac.uk/fac/soc/wbs/subjects/finance/research/wpaperseries/1993/93-38.pdf*

Bahng, Aimee (2018). *Migrant Futures: Decolonizing Speculation in Financial Times*.

Baily, Martin Neil, Robert E. Litan, and Matthew S. Johnson (2008). "The Origins of the Financial Crisis." *Fixing finance series - paper 3* for The Initiative on Business and Public Policy, November 2008. https://www.brookings.edu/wp-content/uploads/2016/06/11_origins_crisis_baily_litan.pdf

Bains, William, Janusz J. Petkowski, and Sara Seager (2023). "Venus' Atmospheric Chemistry and Cloud Characteristics Are Compatible with Venusian Life." *Astrobiology*, Vol. 23, No. 10.

Ball, Philip (2018). *Beyond Weird: Why Everything You Thought You Knew about Quantum Physics Is Different*.

Ball, Philip (2023). "A New Idea for How to Assemble Life." *Quanta Magazine*, May 4, 2023. https://www.quantamagazine.org/a-new-theory-for-the-assembly-of-life-in-the-universe-20230504/

Ballard, J. G. (1970). *The Atrocity Exhibition*.

Ballard, J. G. (1975). *High-Rise*.

Barad, Karen (2011). "Nature's Queer Performativity." *Qui Parle*, Vol. 19, No. 2, 121–158.

Barbour, Julian (1999a). *The End of Time: The Next Revolution in Our Understanding of the Universe*.

Barbour, Julian (1999b). "The End of Time: A Talk with Julian Barbour." *Edge*, August 15, 1999. https://www.edge.org/conversation/julian_barbour-the-end-of-time

Barbour, Julian (2003). "The Deep and Suggestive Principles of Leibnizian Philosophy." *The Harvard Review of Philosophy*, XI (2003), 45–58.

Barker, Clive (1989). *The Great and Secret Show*.

Baron, Dennis (2010). "A literal paradox: 'literally' generally means 'figuratively.'" *The Web of Language* (October 27, 2010). *https://blogs.illinois.edu/view/25/36843*

Barr, Marleen S. (1992). *Feminist Fabulation: Space/Postmodern Fiction*.

Barthélémy, Jean-Hughes (2012). "Fifty Key Terms in the Works of Gilbert Simondon." Trans. Arne De Boever. In *Gilbert Simondon: Being and Technology*. Ed. Arne De Boever, Alex Murray, Jon Roffe, and Ashley Woodward.

Baudrillard, Jean (1994). *Simulacra and Simulation*. Trans. Sheila Faria Glaser.

Baudrillard, Jean (2017). *Symbolic Exchange and Death*. Trans. Iain Hamilton Grant. Second edition.

Beaumont, Matthew, Esther Leslie, Andrew Hemingway, and John Roberts, ed. (2007). *As Radical as Reality Itself: Essays on Marxism and Art for the 21st Century*.

Becchi, Alessandro (2017). "Between Learned Science and Technical Knowledge: Leibniz, Leeuwenhoek, and the School for Microscopists." In *Tercentenary Essays on the Philosophy and Science of Leibniz*. Ed. Lloyd Strickland, Erik Vynckier, and Julia Weckend, 47–79.

Beckett, Chris (2020). *Two Tribes*.

Benjamin, Walter (2002). *Selected Writings Volume 3, 1935–1938..* Ed. Howard Eiland and Michael W. Jennings. Trans. Edmund Jephcott, Howard Eiland, et al.

Benjamin, Walter (2003). *Selected Writings Volume 4, 1938–1940.* Ed. Howard Eiland and Michael W. Jennings.

Berg, Kirsten, et al., ed. (2019). *Future Tense Fiction: Stories of Tomorrow.*

Bergson, Henri (1911). *Creative Evolution*. Trans. Arthur Mitchell.

Bergson, Henri (1935). *The Two Sources of Morality and Religion.* Trans. R. Ashley Audra, Cloudesley Brereton, and W. Horsfall Carter.

Bergson, Henri (1991). *Matter and Memory*. Trans. Nancy Margaret Paul and W. Scott Palmer.

Berlant, Lauren (2011). *Cruel Optimism.*

Bester, Alfred (1953). *The Demolished Man.*

Bester, Alfred (1956). *The Stars My Destination.*

Bester, Alfred (1997). *Virtual Unrealities: The Short Fiction of Alfred Bester.*

Bhaskar, Roy (1975). *A Realist Theory of Science.*

Bhaskar, Roy (1986). *Scientific Realism and Human Emancipation.*

Birch, Douglas (2013). "The U.S.S.R. and U.S. Came Closer to Nuclear War Than We Thought." *The Atlantic*, May 28, 2013. *https://www.theatlantic.com/international/archive/2013/05/the-ussr-and-us-came-closer-to-nuclear-war-than-we-thought/276290/*

Bird, Kai, and Martin Sherwin (2006). *American Prometheus: The Triumph and Tragedy of J. Robert Oppenheimer.*

Blanchot, Maurice (1989). *The Space of Literature*. Trans. Ann Smock.

Blanchot, Maurice (1995). *Vicious Circles: Two Fictions and "After the Fact."* Trans. Paul Auster.

Bloch, Ernst (1995). *The Principle of Hope*. Trans. Neville Plaice, Stephen Plaice, and Paul Knight.

Bloch, Ernst (2019). *Avicenna and the Aristotelian Left*. Trans. Loren Goldman and Peter Thompson.

Bogost, Ian (2017). "Possibility Space." In *The Edge*, "Annual question: What scientific term or concept ought to be more widely known?" https://www.edge.org/response-detail/27105

Bogue, Ronald (2010). *Deleuzian Fabulation and the Scars of History.*

Boltanski, Luc, and Eve Chiapello (2018). *The New Spirit of Capitalism*. Trans. Gregory Elliott. Updated edition.

Borch-Jacobsen, Mikkel (1991). *Lacan: The Absolute Master*. Trans. Douglas Brick.

Borges, Jorge Luis (1999a). *Collected Fictions*. Trans. Andrew Hurley.

Borges, Jorge Luis (1999b). *Selected Non-Fictions*. Ed. Eliot Weinberger. Trans. Esther Allen, Suzanne Jill Levine, and Eliot Weinberger.

Bostrom, Nick (2002). "Existential Risks: Analyzing Human Extinction Scenarios and Related Hazards." *Journal of Evolution and Technology*, Vol. 9, No. 1 (March 2002).

Bostrom, Nick (2019). "The Vulnerable World Hypothesis." *Global Policy*, Vol. 10, No. 4, November 2019, 455–476.

Bould, Mark, and China Miéville (2009). *Red Planets: Marxism and Science Fiction*.

Bowles, Samuel, and Herbert Gintis (1975). "The Problem with Human Capital Theory – A Marxian Critique." *The American Economic Review*, Vol. 65, No. 2, May 1975, 74–82.

Bradbury, Ray (1980). *The Stories of Ray Bradbury*.

Brassier, Ray (2007). *Nihil Unbound: Enlightenment and Extinction*.

Brembs, Björn (2015). "Watching a Paradigm Shift in Neuroscience." *http://bjoern.brembs.net/2015/03/watching-a-paradigm-shift-in-neuroscience/*

Bresson, Robert (2016). *Notes on the Cinematograph*. Trans. Jonathan Griffin.

Brin, David (2023). "David Brin's Worlds of Uplift." https://www.davidbrin.com/uplift.html

Brown, Gregory, and Yual Chiek, ed. (2016). *Leibniz on Compossibility and Possible Worlds*.

Brown, Jayna (2021). *Black Utopias: Speculative Life and the Music of Other Worlds*.

Brown, Deforrest (2022). *Assembling a Black Counter Culture*.

Brunner, John (1968). *Stand on Zanzibar*.

Brunner, John (1969). *The Jagged Orbit*.

Brunner, John (1972). *The Sheep Look Up*.

Brunner, John (1975). *The Shockwave Rider.*

Brunner, John (1983). *The Crucible of Time.*

Burke, Sue (2018). *Semiosis.*

Burke, Sue (2019). *Interference.*

Burrows, David, and Simon O'Sullivan (2019). *Fictioning: The Myth-Functions of Contemporary Art and Philosophy.*

Burton, James (2017). *The Philosophy of Science Fiction: Henri Bergson and the Fabulations of Philip K. Dick.*

Buskirk, Ruth E., Cliff Frohlich, and Kenneth G. Ross (1984). "The Natural Selection of Sexual Cannibalism." *The American Naturalist*, Vol. 123, No. 5 (May 1984), 612–625.

Cabell, James Branch (1926). *The Silver Stallion.*

Cadigan, Pat (1988). *Mindplayers.*

Cadigan, Pat (1989). *Patterns.*

Cadigan, Pat (1991). *Synners.*

Cadigan, Pat (2018). *AI and the Trolley Problem.*

Calvin, Ritch (2009). "Mundane SF 101." *SFRA Review*, Vol. 289 (Summer 2009), 13–16. https://sfra.wildapricot.org/resources/sfra-review/289.pdf

Campbell, Iain (2019). "Avant-Gardes, Afrofuturism, and Philosophical Readings of Rhythm." In *The Black Speculative Arts Movement: Black Futurity, Art+Design*. Ed. Reynaldo Anderson and Clinton R. Fluker.

Campbell, Joseph (1949). *The Hero With A Thousand Faces.*

Canales, Jimena (2015). *The Physicist and the Philosopher: Einstein, Bergson, and the Debate that Changed Our Understanding of Time.*

Carroll, Jordan S. (2019). "Geek temporalities and the spirit of capital." *http://post45.research.yale.edu/2019/08/geek-temporalities-and-the-spirit-of-capital/*

Carroll, Sean M. (2016). *The Big Picture: On the origins of life, meaning, and the universe itself.*

Carroll, Sean M. (2022). *The Biggest Ideas in the Universe: Space, Time, and Motion.*

Castells, Manuel (2009). *The Rise of the Network Society*. Second edition.

Cathcart, Thomas (2013). *The Trolley Problem, or Would You Throw the Fat Guy Off the Bridge?: A Philosophical Conundrum.*

Cavanaugh, Amy (2011). "Interview: William Gibson." *AV Club*, October 14, 2011. *https://www.avclub.com/william-gibson-1798228056*

Chamovitz, Daniel (2012). *What a Plant Knows: A Field Guide to the Senses of Your Garden - and Beyond.*

Chernaik, Laura (2005). *Social and Virtual Space: Science Fiction, Transnationalism, and the American New Right.*

Cheves, Alexander (2017). "21 Words the Queer Community Has Reclaimed (and Some We Haven't)." *The Advocate*, August 2, 2017. https://www.advocate.com/arts-entertainment/2017/8/02/21-words-queer-community-has-reclaimed-and-some-we-havent

Chiang, Ted (2019). *Exhalation: Stories.*

Christgau, Robert (1978). "Kid Patriarch Makes His Move." *Village Voice*, June 12, 1978. *https://www.robertchristgau.com/xg/rock/johansen-78.php*

Christopher, Roy (2019). *Dead Precedents: How Hip-Hop Defines the Future.*

Chu, Seo-Young (2010). *Do Metaphors Dream of Literal Sleep?: A Science-Fictional Theory of Representation.*

Clarke, Arthur C. (2013). *Profiles of the Future.*

Clarke, Arthur C. (2016). *The Collected Stories of Arthur C. Clarke.*

Clarke, Susannah (2004). *Jonathan Strange & Mr Norrell.*

clipping. (2016). *Splendor and Misery*, album and liner notes. *https://clppng.bandcamp.com/album/splendor-misery*

clipping. (2017). "The Deep." Recording. https://clppng.bandcamp.com/album/the-deep.

Clover, Joshua (2011). "Autumn of the System: Poetry and Financial Capital." *JNT: Journal of Narrative Theory*, Vol. 41, No. 1 (Spring 2011).

Clough, Patricia (2009). "The New Empiricism: Affect and Sociological Method." *European Journal of Social Theory*, Vol. 12, No. 1, 43–61.

Clowes, Daniel (1991). *Lout Rampage!.*

Clute, John, et al. (2015). "Sense of Wonder." In *The Encyclopedia of Science Fiction. http://www.sf-encyclopedia.com/entry/sense_of_wonder*

Clute, John, et al. (2016). "Satire." In *The Encyclopedia of Science Fiction. http://www.sf-encyclopedia.com/entry/satire*

Clute, John, et al. (2018a). "Fabulation." In *The Encyclopedia of Science Fiction. http://www.sf-encyclopedia.com/entry/fabulation*

Clute, John, et al. (2018b). "Fermi Paradox." In *The Encyclopedia of Science Fiction. http://www.sf-encyclopedia.com/entry/fermi-paradox*

Clute, John, et al. (2020). "New Wave." In *The Encyclopedia of Science Fiction. http://www.sf-encyclopedia.com/entry/new_wave*

Collins, John, Ned Hall, and L. A. Hall (2004). *Causation and Counterfactuals.*

Collins, Suzanne (2008). *The Hunger Games.*

Coney, John (1974). *Space is the Place.* Film.

Conway, Philip R. (2019). "The Folds of Coexistence: Towards a Diplomatic Political Ontology, between Difference and Contradiction." *Theory, Culture, and Society*, Vol. 37, No. 3, 23–47.

Cook, Noble David (1998). *Born to Die: Disease and New World Conquest, 1492-1650.*

Coole, Diana, and Samantha Frost, ed. (2010). *New Materialisms: Ontology, Agency, and Politics.*

Coopersmith, Jennifer (2017). *The Lazy Universe: An Introduction to the Principle of Least Action.*

Copeland, B. Jack, ed. (2004). *The Essential Turing.*

Crary, Jonathan (2014). 24/7: *Late Capitalism and the Ends of Sleep.*

Crenshaw, Paul (2023). "AITA: Am I the Asshole For Not Walking Away From Omelas." *Reckon Review*, May 1, 2023. https://reckonreview.com/aita/

Crosshill, Tom (2016). *Fragmentation: A Collection.*

Csicsery-Ronay, Istvan (2012). "Fantastic Mimesis: A Diamond in the Rough, Not the Philosopher's Stone." *Contemporary Literature*, Vol. 53, No. 2 (Summer 2012), 387–405.

Csicsery-Ronay, Istvan (2022). *Mutopia : Science Fiction and Fantastic Knowledge.*

Cytowic, Richard E. (2018). *Synesthesia.*

Davidson, Donald (2001). *Inquiries into Truth and Interpretation*. Second edition.

Davies, Paul (2012). "Time's Passage is Probably an Illusion." *Scientific American*, Vol. S306, No. 1, 8–13 (January 2012). https://www.scientificamerican.com/article/time-s-passage-is-probably-an-illusion/

Davis, Allison P. (2022). "A Vibe Shift Is Coming: Will any of us survive it?." *The Cut*, February 16, 2022. https://www.thecut.com/2022/02/a-vibe-shift-is-coming.html

Dawkins, Richard (2021). "Kafka's Metamorphosis is called a major work of literature. Why? If it's SF it's bad SF. If, like Animal Farm, it's an allegory, an allegory of what? Scholarly answers range from pretentious Freudian to far-fetched feminist. I don't get it. Where are the Emperor's clothes?." Twitter, June 5, 2021. *https://twitter.com/RichardDawkins/status/1401239365678997506*

De Boever, Arne, Alex Murray, Jon Roffe, and Ashley Woodward, ed. (2012). *Gilbert Simondon: Being and Technology*.

Delany, Samuel R. (1975). *Dhalgren*.

Delany, Samuel R. (1976). *Trouble on Triton*.

Delany, Samuel R. (1999). *Shorter Views: Queer Thoughts and the Politics of the Paraliterary*.

Delany, Samuel R. (2009). *The Jewel-Hinged Jaw: Notes on the Language of Science Fiction*. Revised edition.

Delany, Samuel R. (2012). *Starboard Wine: More Notes on the Language of Science Fiction*. Revised edition.

Deleuze, Gilles (1983). *Nietzsche and Philosophy*. Trans. Hugh Tomlinson.

Deleuze, Gilles (1989). *Cinema 2: The Time-Image*. Trans. Hugh Tomlinson and Robert Goleta.

Deleuze, Gilles (1990). *The Logic of Sense*. Trans. Mark Lester.

Deleuze, Gilles (1991). *Bergsonism*. Trans. Hugh Tomlinson and Barbara Habberjam.

Deleuze, Gilles (1992). *The Fold: Leibniz and the Baroque*. Trans. Tom Conley.

Deleuze, Gilles (1994). *Difference and Repetition*. Trans. Paul Patton.

Deleuze, Gilles (1995). *Negotiations*. Trans. Martin Joughin.

Deleuze, Gilles (2000). *Proust and Signs: The Complete Text.* Trans. Richard Howard.

Deleuze, Gilles, and Felix Guattari (1987). *A Thousand Plateaus.* Trans. Brian Massumi.

Derrida, Jacques (1978). *Writing and Difference*. Trans. Alan Bass.

Derrida, Jacques (1982). *Margins of Philosophy*. Trans. Alan Bass.

Descartes, René (1985). *Philosophical Writings*. Trans. John Cottingham, Robert Stoothoff, and Dugold Murdoch.

Dick, Philip K. (1964). *The Three Stigmata of Palmer Eldrich*.

Dick, Philip K. (1969). *Ubik*.

Dick, Philip K. (1972). *We Can Build You*.

Dick, Philip K. (1996). *The Shifting Realities of Philip K. Dick: Selected Literary and Philosophical Writings*. Ed. Lawrence Sutin.

Dick, Philip K. (2012). *The Exegesis of Philip K Dick.* Ed. Jonathan Lethem and Pamela Jackson.

Di Filippo, Paul (1996). *Ribofunk*.

Dixon, Dougal (1981). *After Man*.

Doctorow, Cory (2019). *Radicalized: Four Tales of Our Present Moment*.

Doctorow, Cory (2023). *Red Team Blues*.

Donen, Stanley (1967). *Bedazzled*. Film.

Dukes. Jessica (2023). "What Is Literary Fiction?." *Celadon Books*. https://celadonbooks.com/what-is-literary-fiction/

Edelman, Lee (2004). *No Future: Queer Theory and the Death Drive*.

Edmonds, David (2013). *Would You Kill the Fat Man?: The Trolley Problem and What Your Answer Tells Us about Right and Wrong*.

Egan, Greg (2008). *Incandescence*.

Einstein, Albert (2007). *A Stubbornly Persistent Illusion: The Essential Scientific Writings of Albert Einstein*. Ed. Stephen Hawking.

Ellingham, Lewis, and Kevin Killian (1998). *Poet Be Like God : Jack Spicer and the San Francisco Renaissance*.

Ellis, Warren (2018). *Orbital Operations,* October 7, 2018. *http://www.orbitaloperations.com*

El-Mohtar, Amal, and Max Gladstone (2019). *This Is How You Lose the Time War*.

Emrys, Ruthanna (2017). *Winter Tide*.

Emrys, Ruthanna (2018). *Deep Roots.*

Emrys, Ruthanna, and Anne M. Pillsworth (2015). "Lovecraft's Most Bigoted Story, No Really: 'The Horror at Red Hook.'" *Tor*, March 3, 2015. *https://www.tor.com/2015/03/03/lovecrafts-most-bigoted-story-no-really-the-horror-at-red-hook/*

Engels, Friedrich (2020). *Ludwig Feuerbach and the End of Classical German Philosophy*. Tr. Austin Lewis.

Engels, Kimberly S. (2018). "From In-Itself to Practico-Inert: Freedom, Subjectivity and Progress." *Sartre Studies International*, Vol. 24, No. 1, 48–69.

Eshun, Kodwo (1998). *More Brilliant Than The Sun: Adventures in Sonic Fiction.*

Eshun, Kodwo (2003). "Further Considerations on Afrofuturism." *CR: The New Centennial Review*, Vol. 3, No. 2 (Summer 2003), 287–302.

Eshun, Kodwo (2016). "Drexciya as Spectre." In *Matter Fictions*. Ed. Margarita Mendes.

Faulkner, William (1951). *Requiem for a Nun.*

Fernandez, Tamara Claire (2020). "Semelparity: The great parental sacrifice." *Imperial Bioscience Review*, November 20, 2020. https://imperialbiosciencereview.com/2020/11/20/semelparity-the-great-parental-sacrifice/

Fisher, Anthony (2016). "David Lewis and Science Fiction, Part 1." *The Age of Metaphysical Revolution*. Blog, December 9, 2016. http://www.projects.socialsciences.manchester.ac.uk/lewis/david-lewis-science-fiction-part-1/

Fisher, Mark (2009). *Capitalist Realism: Is There No Alternative?*

Fisher, Mark (2013). "The Metaphysics of Crackle: Afrofuturism and Hauntology." *Dancecult: Journal of Electronic Dance Music Culture*, Vol. 5, No. 2, 42–55.

Fisher, Mark (2016). *The Weird and the Eerie.*

Fisher, Mark (2018). *K-punk: The collected and unpublished writings of Mark Fisher*. Ed. Darren Ambrose.

Fisher, Philip (1998). *Wonder, the Rainbow, and the Aesthetics of Rare Experiences.*

Fleetwood, Steve (2012). "Laws and tendencies in Marxist political economy." *Capital & Class*, Vol. 36, No. 2, 235–262.

Foucault, Michel (1971). *The Order of Things: An Archaeology of the Human Sciences*. Trans. Alan Sheridan.

Foucault, Michel (1998). *Aesthetics, Method, and Epistemology. The Essential Works of Foucault.* Ed. James D. Faubion. Trans. Robert Hurley and others. Second edition.

Foucault, Michel (2008). *The Birth of Biopolitics: Lectures at the Collège de France, 1978-79*. Trans. Graham Burchell.

Fourier, Charles (1996). *The Theory of the Four Movements*. Ed. Gareth Stedman Jones and Ian Patterson. Trans. Ian Patterson.

Fourier, Charles (2015). *Le nouveau monde amoureux*.

Freedman, Carl (2000). *Critical Theory and Science Fiction*.

Freedman, Carl (2002). *The Incomplete Projects: Marxism, Modernity, and the Politics of Culture*.

Friedman, Thomas L. (1996). "Foreign Affairs Big Mac I." *The New York Times*, December 8, 1996. https://www.nytimes.com/1996/12/08/opinion/foreign-affairs-big-mac-i.html

Fukuyama, Francis (1992). *The End of History and the Last Man*.

Fungal Plots (2019). "Lovecraft's Modernist Racism." *https://fungalplots.wordpress.com/2019/03/26/lovecrafts-modernist-racism/*

Galef, David (2001). "Tiptree and the Problem of the Other: Postcolonialism Versus Sociology." *Science Fiction Studies*, Vol. 28, 201–222.

Garber, Daniel (2009). *Leibniz: Body, Substance, Monad*.

Garland, Alex (2018). *Annihilation: The Screenplay*.

Geertz, Clifford (1973). *The Interpretation of Cultures*.

Gehlen, Frieda L. (1977). "Toward a Revised Theory of Hysterical Contagion." *Journal of Health and Social Behavior*, Vol. 18, No. 1 (Mar., 1977), 27–35.

Gibson, William (1984). *Neuromancer*.

Gibson, William (1986a). *Burning Chrome*.

Gibson, William (1986b). *Count Zero*.

Gibson, William (1988). *Mona Lisa Overdrive*.

Gleick, James (1987). *Chaos: Making a New Science*.

Godfrey-Smith, Peter (2016). *Other Minds: The Octopus, the Sea, and the Deep Origins of Consciousness*.

Godwin, Tom (2011). "The Cold Equations." *Lightspeed Magazine*, July 2011. https://www.lightspeedmagazine.com/fiction/the-cold-equations/

Goering, Thomas (2018). "Navy Recruiting Slogans." *Navy Cyberspace*, June 27, 2010. *https://www.navycs.com/blogs/2010/06/27/navy-recruiting-slogans*

Gold, Howard R. (2017). "Never mind the 1% – Let's talk about the 0.01%." *Chicago Booth Review. https://review.chicagobooth.edu/economics/2017/article/never-mind-1-percent-lets-talk-about-001-percent*

Goodman, Steve (2010). *Sonic Warfare: Sound, Affect, and the Ecology of Fear.*

Gould, Stephen Jay (1989). *Wonderful Life: The Burgess Shale and the Nature of History.*

Graeber, David (2014). *Debt: The First Five Thousand Years.* Updated and expanded edition.

Graeber, David (2015). *The Utopia of Rules: On Technology, Stupidity, and the Secret Joys of Bureaucracy.*

Graeber, David (2018). *Bullshit Jobs: A Theory.*

Greenberg, Clement (1965). *Art and Culture: Critical Essays.*

Griffin, Michael V. (2008). "Necessitarianism in Spinoza and Leibniz." In *Interpreting Spinoza: Critical Essays.* Ed. Charlie Huenemann.

Grusin, Richard (2010). *Premediation: Affect and Mediality After 9/11.*

Grusin, Richard (2019). Personal communication.

Gulick, John (2007). *Sociology 450: Sociology of Globalization.*

Gunn, James, Marleen Barr, and Matthew Candelaris (2008). *Reading Science Fiction.*

Haldeman, Joe (1974). *The Forever War.*

Haldane, J. B. S. (1927). *Possible Worlds and Other Essays.*

Hallé, Francis (2002). *In Praise of Plants.* Trans. David Lee.

Halpern, Richard (2023). *Leibnizing: A Philosopher in Motion.*

Hamilton, W. D. (1963). "The Evolution of Altruistic Behavior." *The American Naturalist*, Vol. 97, No. 896, 354–356.

Handwerk, Brian (2013). "Why Some Animals Mate Themselves to Death." *National Geographic*, October 8, 2013. https://www.

nationalgeographic.com/animals/article/131007-marsupials-mammals-sex-mating-science-animals

Hanson, Robin (1998). "The Great Filter — Are We Almost Past It?." September 15, 1998. *http://mason.gmu.edu/~rhanson/greatfilter.html*

Haraway, Donna (1991). *Simians, Cyborgs, and Women: The Reinvention of Nature.*

Haraway, Donna (2016). *Staying with the Trouble: Making Kin in the Chthulucene.*

Harman, Graham (2005). *Guerrilla Metaphysics: Phenomenology and the Carpentry of Things.*

Harman, Graham (2012a), *Weird Realism: Lovecraft and Philosophy.*

Harman, Graham (2012b). *The Third Table/Der dritte Tisch.*

Harman, Graham (2015). *Quentin Meillassoux: Philosophy in the Making*. Second edition.

Harman, Graham (2018a). *Speculative Realism: An Introduction.*

Harman, Graham (2018b). *Object-Oriented Ontology: A New Theory of Everything.*

Harris, Malcolm (2019). "What's Scarier Than Student Loans? Welcome to the World of Subprime Children." *The New York Times*, May 11, 2019. *https://www.nytimes.com/2019/05/11/opinion/sunday/student-loans.html*

Harrison, M. John (2007). *Viriconium.*

Hartman, Saidiya (2008). "Venus in Two Acts." *Small Axe*, Vol. 26 (June 2008), 1–14.

Harvey, David (1994). "The Social Construction of Space and Time: A Relational Theory." *Geographical Review of Japan*, Series B, Vol. 67, No. 2 (December 1994), 126–135.

Harvey, David (2004). "The 'New' Imperialism: Accumulation by Dispossession." *The Socialist Register*, Vol. 40., 63-87.

Harvey, David (2007). *A Brief History of Neoliberalism.*

Hayden, Judy A., and Daniel J. Worden (2019). *Aphra Behn's Emperor of the Moon and its French Source Arlequin, Empereur dans la Lune.*

Hayles, N. Katherine (1999). *How We Became Posthuman: Virtual Bodies in Cybernetics, Literature, and Informatics.*

Hayles, N. Katherine (2017). *Unthought: The Power of the Cognitive Nonconscious.*

Hecht, Hartmut (2016). "Gottfried Wilhelm Leibniz and the origin of the principle of least action — a never ending story." *Annalen der Physik*, Vol. 528, No. 9–10 (October 2016), 641–646.

Hegel, G. W. F. (2018). *The Phenomenology of Spirit.* Trans. Terry Pinkard.

Heine, Heinrich (2006). *The Harz Journey and Selected Prose.* Trans. Ritchie Robertson.

Heinlein, Robert A. (1959a). *The Menace From Earth.*

Heinlein, Robert A. (1959b). *The Unpleasant Profession of Jonathan Hoag.*

Heinlein, Robert A. (1961). *Stranger in a Strange Land.*

Heinlein, Robert A. (1966). *The Moon Is a Harsh Mistress.*

Heller, Nathan (2022). "Is selling shares in yourself the way of the future?". *The New Yorker*, July 25, 2022. https://www.newyorker.com/magazine/2022/08/01/is-selling-shares-in-yourself-the-way-of-the-future.

Henton, Doug, and Kim Held (2013). "The dynamics of Silicon Valley: Creative destruction and the evolution of the innovation habitat." *Social Science Information*, Vol. 52, No. 4, 539–557.

Herbert, Frank (1965). *Dune.*

Higgins, David, and Hugh O'Connell, ed. (2019). "Speculative Finance/Speculative Fiction." *The New Centennial Review*, Vol. 19, No. 1, 1-10..

Hirst, K. Kris (2019). "Did Henry Ford Really Say 'History is Bunk'?." *ThoughtCo*, September 4, 2019. https://www.thoughtco.com/henry-ford-why-history-is-bunk-172412

Hjorth, Daniel (2013) "Absolutely fabulous! Fabulation and organisation-creation in processes of becoming-entrepreneur." *Society and Business Review*, Vol. 8, No. 3, 205–224.

Holden, Steve (2020). "How Dua Lipa and The Weeknd are bringing the 80s back… again." *BBC News*, April 1, 2020. https://www.bbc.com/news/newsbeat-52109397

Hollinger, Veronica (2014). "Genre vs. Mode." In *The Oxford Handbook of Science Fiction*, Ed. Rob Latham.

Horkheimer, Max, and Theodor W. Adorno (2002). *Dialectic of Enlightenment*. Trans. Edmund Jephcott.

Horowitz, Juliana Menasce, Ruth Igielnik, and Rakesh Kochhar (2020). "Trends in income and wealth inequality." *Pew Research Center*, January 9, 2020. *https://www.pewresearch.org/social-trends/2020/01/09/trends-in-income-and-wealth-inequality/*

Hume, David (1969). *A Treatise Of Human Nature*. Ed. Ernest C. Mossner.

Hume, David (1993). *An Enquiry Concerning Human Understanding*. Ed. Eric Steinberg. Second edition.

Hurley, Kameron (2019a). *The Light Brigade*.

Hurley, Kameron (2019b). "The Logic of Time Travel (With Graphs!)." *Kameron Hurley: Welcome to the Hurleverse.* Blog, April 21, 2019. https://www.kameronhurley.com/the-logic-of-time-travel-with-graphs/

Imarisha, Walida, adrienne maree brown, et al. (2015). *Octavia's Brood: Science Fiction Stories from Social Justice Movements*.

Ingram, David and Jonathan Tallant (2022). "Presentism." In *The Stanford Encyclopedia of Philosophy*. https://plato.stanford.edu/archives/spr2022/entries/presentism/

Itoh, Project (2010). *Harmony*. Trans. Alexander O. Smith.

James, Robin (2019a). "Aesthetics and Horizon in Possibilist/Post-Probabilist Neoliberalisms." *It's Her Factory*. Blog, September 2019. *https://www.its-her-factory.com/2019/09/aesthetics-and-horizon-in-possibilist-post-probabilist-neoliberalisms/*

James, Robin (2019b). "Post-Probabilist Neoliberalisms, Orientation, and Sexuality." *It's Her Factory.* Blog, October 2019. https://www.its-her-factory.com/2019/10/post-probabilist-neoliberalisms-orientation-sexuality/

James, William (1983). *Principles of Psychology*.

Jameson, Fredric (1981). *The Political Unconscious: Narrative as a Socially Symbolic Act*.

Jameson, Fredric (1984). "Postmodernism, or the cultural logic of late capitalism." *New Left Review*, Vol. 1, No. 146 (July–August 1984), 53–92.

Jameson, Fredric (1987). "Regarding Postmodernism — A conversation with Fredric Jameson." *Social Text*, Vol. 17 (Autumn 1987), 29–54.

Jameson, Fredric (1991). *Postmodernism, or, The Cultural Logic of Late Capitalism.*

Jameson, Fredric (2005). *Archaeologies of the Future.*

Jameson, Fredric (2015). "The Aesthetics of Singularity." *New Left Review*, Vol. 92 (March–April 2015), 101–132.

Jameson, Fredric (2016). "Revisiting Postmodernism: An Interview with Fredric Jameson Conducted by Nico Baumbach, Damon R. Young, and Genevieve Yue." *Social Text*, Vol. 127, No. 34:2 (June 2016), 143–160.

Janzen, Greg (2011). "In Defense of the What-Is-It-Likeness of Experience." *The Southern Journal of Philosophy*, Vol. 49, No. 3 (September 2011), 271–293.

Jemisin, N. K. (2012). "But, but, but — WHY does magic have to make sense?." *Epiphany 2.0.* Blog, June 15, 2012. https://nkjemisin.com/2012/06/but-but-but-why-does-magic-have-to-make-sense/

Jemisin, N. K. (2015). *The Fifth Season.*

Jemisin, N. K. (2016). *The Obelisk Gate.*

Jemisin, N. K. (2017). *The Stone Sky.*

Jemisin, N. K. (2020). *The City We Became.*

Jemisin, N. K. (2022). *The World We Make.*

Johnson, Kij (2016). *The Dream-Quest of Vellitt Boe.*

Johnson, Mark (1990). *The Body in the Mind: The Bodily Basis of Meaning, Imagination, and Reason.*

Johnson, Micaiah (2020). *The Space Between Worlds.*

Johnson, Samuel (1779). "Lives of the Poets: Abraham Cowley."

Johnson, Steven (2010). *Where Good Ideas Come From: The Natural History of Innovation.*

Jones, Benjamin F. (2014). "The Human Capital Stock: A Generalized Approach." *American Economic Review*, Vol. 104, No. 11, 3752–3777.

Jones, Gwyneth (1991). *White Queen.*

Jones, Gwyneth (1994). *North Wind.*

Jones, Gwyneth (1998). *Phoenix Cafe.*

Jones, Gwyneth (2009). *Spirit, or, The Princess of Bois Dormant.*

Jones, Gwyneth (2017). *Proof of Concept.*

Kallis, Giorgos (2017). *In Defense of Degrowth: Opinions and Manifestos.* Ed. Aaron Vansintjan.

Kant, Immanuel (1998). *Critique of Pure Reason.* Trans. Paul Guyer and Allen W. Wood.

Kant, Immanuel (2000). *Critique of the Power of Judgment.* Trans. Paul Guyer and Eric Matthews.

Kant, Immanuel (2018). *Groundwork for the Metaphysics of Morals.* Tr. Allen W. Wood.

Karabell, Zachary (2018). "What's Stopping Human Capital From Becoming a Security?" *Slate*, November 27, 2018. *https://slate.com/technology/2018/11/mark-stasenko-overvalued-human-capital-market-derivatives.html*

Kauffman, Stuart (2000). *Investigations.*

Kauffman, Stuart (2003). "Molecular autonomous agents". *Philosophical Transactions of the Royal Society A; Mathematical Physical and Engineering Sciences.* June 15, 2003. 361(1807):1089-99. DOI: 10.1098/rsta.2003.1186.

Kenton, Will (2022). "Underlying." *Investopedia.* https://www.investopedia.com/terms/u/underlying.asp

Kessel, John (2017). *The Moon and the Other.*

Keynes, John Maynard (1937). "The General Theory of Employment." *The Quarterly Journal of Economics*, Vol. 51, No. 2 (February 1937), 209-223.

Kincaid, Paul (2003). "On the Origins of Genre." *Extrapolation*, Vol. 44, No. 4 (Winter 2003), 409-420.

King, Katie (2012). *Networked Reenactments: Stories Transdisciplinary Knowledges Tell.*

Knight, Frank (1921). *Risk, Uncertainty, and Profit.*

Koch, Cristof (2009). "A 'Complex' Theory of Consciousness." *Scientific American*, Vol. 301, No. 9 (July 2009). https://www.scientificamerican.com/article/a-theory-of-consciousness/

Koch, Cristof (2019). "Proust among the Machines." *Scientific American*, Vol. 321, No. 6, 46–49. *https://www.scientificamerican.com/article/will-machines-ever-become-conscious/*

Koestenbaum, Wayne (1993). *The Queen's Throat: Opera, Homosexuality, and the Mystery of Desire.*

Koja, Kathe (1991). *The Cipher.*

Kolbert, Elizabeth (2014). *The Sixth Extinction: An Unnatural History.*

Kolbert, Elizabeth (2020). "The Day Nuclear War Almost Broke Out." *The New Yorker*, October 5, 2020. *https://www.newyorker.com/magazine/2020/10/12/the-day-nuclear-war-almost-broke-out*

Konings, Martijn (2018). *Capital and Time; For a New Critique of Neoliberal Reason.*

Kornbluth, C. M. (1997). *His Share of Glory: The Complete Short Science Fiction of C. M. Kornbluth.*

Korzybski, Alfred (1994). *Science and Sanity: An Introduction to Non-Aristotelian Systems and General Semantics.* Fifth edition.

Kress, Nancy (1993). *Beggars in Spain.*

Kubrick, Stanley (1968). *2001: A Space Odyssey.* Film.

Lakoff, George (1987). *Women, Fire, and Dangerous Things: What Categories Reveal about the Mind.*

Lakoff, George, and Mark Johnson (2003). *Metaphors We Live By.* Second edition.

Land, Nick (2022). *The Dark Enlightenment.*

Landon, Brooks (2014). "Extrapolation and Speculation." In *The Oxford Handbook of Science Fiction.* Ed. Rob Latham.

Lane, Nick (2015). *The Vital Question: Energy, Evolution, and the Origins of Complex Life.*

Lapavitsas, Costas, and Ivan Mendieta-Muñoz (2016). "The Profits of Financialization." *Monthly Review*, Vol. 68, No. 3 (July–August 2016). *https://monthlyreview.org/2016/07/01/the-profits-of-financialization/*

Laplace, Pierre-Simon (1902). *A Philosophical Essay on Probabilities.* Trans. Frederick William Truscott and Frederick Lincoln Emory.

Lardreau, Guy (1988). *Fictions philosophiques et science-fiction.* Passages cited in my own translation.

Laruelle, François (2010). *Philosophie non-standard: générique, quantique, philo-fiction*.

Laruelle, François (2013). *Principles of Non-Philosophy*. Trans. Nicola Rubczak and Anthony Paul Smith.

Latham, Rob, ed. (2014). *The Oxford Handbook of Science Fiction*.

Laumer, Keith (2002). *Keith Laumer: The Lighter Side*. Ed. Eric Flint.

LaValle, Victor (2016). *The Ballad of Black Tom*.

Lavigne, Carlen (2013). *Cyberpunk Women, Feminism and Science Fiction: A Critical Study*.

Lawtoo, Nidesh (2017). "The Plasticity of Mimesis." *MLN*, Vol. 132, No. 5 (December 2017), 1201–1224.

Layzer, David (1990). *Cosmogenesis: The Growth of Order in the Universe*.

Lazonick, William, Mustafa Erdem Sakinç, and Matt Hopkins (2020). "Why Stock Buybacks Are Dangerous for the Economy." *Harvard Business Review*, January 7. 2020. *https://hbr.org/2020/01/why-stock-buybacks-are-dangerous-for-the-economy*

Lazzarato, Maurizio (2011). *The Making of the Indebted Man: An Essay on the Neoliberal Condition*.

Leckie, Ann (2013). *Ancillary Justice*.

Leckie, Ann (2023). *Translation State*.

Le Guin, Ursula K. (1974). *The Dispossessed*.

Le Guin, Ursula K. (1976). *The Left Hand of Darkness*.

Le Guin, Ursula K. (2012). *The Unreal and the Real: Selected Stories of Ursula K. Le Guin, volume 2: Outer Space, Inner Lands*.

Leiber, Fritz (1958). *The Big Time*.

Leibniz, G. W. (1969). *Philosophical Papers and Letters*. Ed. and trans. Leroy E. Loemker. Second edition.

Leibniz, G. W. (1989). *Philosophical Essays*. Ed. and trans. Roger Ariew and Daniel Garber.

Leibniz, G. W. (1996). *New Essays on Human Understanding*. Ed. and trans. Peter Remnant and Jonathan Bennett.

Leibniz, G. W. (2007). *Theodicy*. Ed. Austin Farrer. Trans. E. M. Huggard.

Leibniz, G. W. (2011). *Leibniz and the Two Sophies: The Philosophical Correspondence*. Ed. and trans. Lloyd Strickland.

Leibniz, G. W. (2014). *Leibniz's Monadology: A New Translation and Guide*. Ed. and trans. Lloyd Strickland.

Leibniz, G. W., and Samuel Clarke (2000). *Leibniz and Clarke: Correspondence*. Ed. Roger Ariew.

Leinster, Murray (2012). *The Second Murray Leinster Megapack*.

Lem, Stanisław (2002). *Solaris*.

Lessing, Doris (1992). *Canopus in Argos: Archives*.

Levinas, Emmanuel (1981). *Otherwise Than Being: or, Beyond Essence*. Trans. Alphonso Lingis.

Lévi-Strauss, Claude (2021). *Wild Thought*. Trans. Jeffrey Mehlman and John Leavitt.

Levitas, Ruth (1990). "Educated Hope: Ernst Bloch on Abstract and Concrete Utopia." *Utopian Studies*, Vol. 1, No. 2, 13–26.

Lewis, David (1986a). *On the Plurality of Worlds*.

Lewis, David (1986b). *Philosophical Papers: Volume II*.

Lewis, Jeffrey (2018). *The 2020 Commission Report on the North Korean Nuclear Attacks Against the United States*.

Lewis, Michael (2014). *Flash Boys*.

Libertson, Joseph (1982). *Proximity: Levinas, Blanchot, Bataille, and Communication*.

Link, Eric Carl, and Gerry Canavan, ed. (2015). *The Cambridge Companion to American Science Fiction*.

Litt, Carole J. (1986). "Theories of Transitional Object Attachment: An Overview." *International Journal of Behavioral Development*, Vol. 9, 383–399.

Liu, Cixin (2014). *The Three-Body Problem*. Trans. Ken Liu.

Liu, Cixin (2015). *The Dark Forest*. Trans. Joel Martinsen.

Liu, Cixin (2016). *Death's End*. Trans. Ken Liu.

Livingston, Ira (2018). *Magic Science Religion*.

Lord, Karen (2023). "Finding the Space Between Utopia and Dystopia." *Tor*, July 20, 2023. https://www.tor.com/2023/07/20/finding-the-space-between-utopia-and-dystopia/

Lothian, Alexis (2015). "Feminist and Queer Science Fiction in America." In *The Cambridge Companion to American Science Fiction*. Ed. Eric Carl Link and Edward Canavan.

Lovecraft, H. P. (2005). *Tales*. Ed. Peter Straub.

Ludlow, Peter, Yujin Nagasawa, and Daniel Stoljar, ed. (2004). *There's Something About Mary: Essays on Phenomenal Consciousness and Frank Jackson's Knowledge Argument*.

Lukács, György (1980). *The Destruction of Reason*. Trans. Peter R. Palmer.

Lyon, Pamela (2015). "The cognitive cell: bacterial behavior reconsidered." *Frontiers in Microbiology*, Vol. 6, No. 264, article 264, 1-18..

Lyotard, Jean-François (1989). *The Differend: Phrases in Dispute*. Trans. Georges Van Den Abbeele.

Macdonald, Ian (2015). *Luna: New Moon*.

Macdonald, Ian (2017). *Luna: Wolf Moon*.

Macdonald, Ian (2019). *Luna: Moon Rising*.

MacKenzie, Donald (2008). *An Engine, Not a Camera: How Financial Models Shape Markets*.

MacLeod, Ken (2016). "Is science fiction past its sell-by date?." Orbit Books, June 6, 2016. https://medium.com/@orbitbooks/is-science-fiction-past-its-sell-by-date-598403090ba8

MacLeod, Ken (2018). *The Corporation Wars Trilogy*.

Mamatas, Nick (2014). "The Real Mr Difficult, or Why Cthulhu Threatens to Destroy the Canon, Self-Interested Literary Essayists, and the Universe Itself. Finally." *LA Review of Books*, November 24, 2014. *https://lareviewofbooks.org/article/real-mr-difficult-cthulhu-threatens-destroy-canon-self-interested-literary-essayists-universe-finally/*

Mandel, Ernest (1975). *Late Capitalism*. Trans. Joris De Bres.

Marcus, Ezra (2021). "A Guide to Neopronouns." *The New York Times*, April 8, 2021. https://www.nytimes.com/2021/04/08/style/neopronouns-nonbinary-explainer.html

Marcuse, Herbert (1956). *Eros and Civilization: A Philosophical Inquiry into Freud*.

Margulis, Lynn (1999). *Symbiotic Planet: A New Look At Evolution*. Revised edition.

Margulis, Lynn, and Dorion Sagan (1997). *Microcosmos: Four Billion Years of Microbial Evolution*.

Martin (2011). "Is 'now' smeared over time?." Stack Exchange: Physics. *https://physics.stackexchange.com/questions/16688/is-now-smeared-over-time*

Martin, George R. R., ed. (1987). *Wild Cards.*

Massumi, Brian (2011). *Semblance and Event: Activist Philosophy and the Occurrent Arts.*

Maturana, Humberto, and Francisco Varela (1980). *Autopoiesis and Cognition: The Realization of the Living.*

Marx, Karl (1976). *Capital: A Critique of Political Economy*, Volume 1. Trans. Ben Fowkes.

Marx, Karl (1993). *Capital: A Critique of Political Economy*, Volume 3. Trans. David Fernbach.

Marx, Karl (2002). *The Eighteenth Brumaire of Louis Bonaparte.* Trans. Terrell Carver. In *Marx's Eighteenth Brumaire: (Post)modern Interpretations.* Ed. Mark Cowling and James Martin.

Marx, Karl, and Friedrich Engels (1888). *The Communist Manifesto.* Trans. Samuel Moore.

Massumi, Brian (2015). *Ontopower: War, Powers, and the State of Perception.*

Maturana, Humberto, and Francisco Varela (1980). *Autopoiesis and Cognition: The Realization of the Living.*

Maudlin, Tim (2002). "Remarks on the Passing of Time." *Proceedings of the Aristotelian Society*, New Series, Vol. 102 (2002), 259–274.

Maudlin, Tim (2015). "How Mathematics Meets the World." *QSpace*, January 26, 2015. https://forums.fqxi.org/d/2318-how-mathematics-meets-the-world-by-tim-maudlin

Maudlin, Tim (2022). "Einstein didn't think time was an illusion." *IAI News*, November 28, 2022. https://iai.tv/articles/tim-maudlin-einstein-didnt-think-time-was-an-illusion-auid-2317

McFarlane, Anna, Graham J. Murphy, and Lars Schmeink, ed. (2020). *The Routledge Companion to Cyberpunk Culture.*

McKittrick, Katherine, ed. (2015). *Sylvia Wynter: On Being Human As Praxis.*

McLuhan, Marshall (1964). *Understanding Media: The Extensions of Man.*

McLuhan, Marshall, and Quentin Fiore (1967). *The Medium is the Massage*.

McLuhan, Marshall, and Eric McLuhan (1992). *Laws of Media: The New Science*.

McLuhan, Marshall, and Eric McLuhan (2011). *Media and Formal Cause*.

Meillassoux, Quentin (2008). *After Finitude: An Essay on the Necessity of Contingency*. Trans. Ray Brassier.

Meillassoux, Quentin (2015). *Science Fiction and Extro-Science Fiction*. Trans. Alyosha Edlebi.

Mendlesohn, Farah (2019). *The Pleasant Profession of Robert A. Heinlein*.

Merchant, Brian (2018). "Nike and Boeing Are Paying Sci-Fi Writers to Predict Their Futures." *OneZero*, November 28, 2018. https://onezero.medium.com/nike-and-boeing-are-paying-sci-fi-writers-to-predict-their-futures-fdc4b6165fa4

Miéville, China (2002). "Tolkien — Middle Earth Meets Middle England." *Socialist Review*, Vol. 259 (January 2002). *http://socialistreview.org.uk/259/tolkien-middle-earth-meets-middle-england*

Miéville, China (2008). "M.R. James and the Quantum Vampire: Weird; Hauntological: Versus and/or and and/or or?." *Collapse: Philosophical Research and Development*, Vol. IV, 105–128.

Miéville, China (2009). "Cognition as Ideology: A Dialectic of SF Theory." Afterword to *Red Planets: Marxism and Science Fiction*. Ed. Mark Bould and China Miéville.

Miéville, China (2011). *Embassytown*.

Miéville, China (2019). "Silence In Debris: Towards an Apophatic Marxism." *Salvage 6: Evidence of Things Not Seen. https://salvage.zone/in-print/silence-in-debris-towards-an-apophatic-marxism/*

Miller, Melissa B., and Bonnie L. Bassler (2001). "Quorum Sensing in Bacteria." *Annual Review of Microbiology*, Vol. 55, No. 165–99.

Mills, C. Wright (1959). *The Sociological Imagination*.

Moldbug, Mencius (2015). *A Gentle Introduction to Unqualified Reservations*.

Molnar, George (2003). *Powers: A Study in Metaphysics*. Ed. Stephen Mumford.

Montag, Warren, and Ted Stolze, ed. (1997). *The New Spinoza.*

Morgan, Richard K. (2002). *Altered Carbon.*

Morgan, Richard K. (2003). *Broken Angels.*

Morgan, Richard K. (2005). *Woken Furies.*

Morozov, Evgeny (2019). "Digital Socialism?: The Calculation Debate in the Age of Big Data."NLR 116-117 (March/June 2019), 33-67.

Morton, Timothy (2013). *Hyperobjects: Philosophy and Ecology after the End of the World.*

Moylan, Tom (2014). *Demand the Impossible: Science Fiction and the Utopian Imagination.* Expanded edition.

Mumford, Stephen, and Rani Lill Anjum (2011). *Getting Causes From Powers.*

Musser, George (2017). "A Defense of the Reality of Time." *Quanta Magazine*, May 16, 2017. https://www.quantamagazine.org/a-defense-of-the-reality-of-time-20170516/

Nagel, Thomas (1986). *The View From Nowhere.*

Nagel, Thomas (1991). *Mortal Questions.*

Nestler, Gerald (2018). "The derivative condition, an aesthetics of resolution, and the figure of the renegade: A conversation." *Finance and Security*, Vol. 4, No. 1, 126–143.

Nevala-Lee, Alec (2018). *Astounding: John W. Campbell, Isaac Asimov, Robert A. Heinlein, L. Ron Hubbard, and the Golden Age of Science Fiction.*

Neville, Carl (2016). *Resolution Way.*

Neville, Carl (2020). *Eminent Domain.*

Nevins, Jess (2018). "Science Fiction: Defining It, and Pre-Frankenstein Examples of it." Patreon. Blog. *https://www.patreon.com/posts/science-fiction-23049464*

Newton, Isaac (1999). *The Principia: Mathematical principles of natural philosophy.* Trans. I. Bernard Cohen and Anne Whitman, assisted by Julia Budenz.

Nietzsche, Friedrich (1999). *The Birth of Tragedy and Other Writings.* Ed. Raymond Geuss and Ronald Speirs. Trans. Ronald Speirs.

Nietzsche, Friedrich (2001). *The Gay Science.* Ed. Bernard Williams. Trans. Josefine Nauckhoff.

Nietzsche, Friedrich (2005). *The Anti-Christ, Ecce Homo, Twilight of the Idols, and Other Writings*. Ed. Aaron Ridley and Judith Norman. Trans. Judith Norman.

Nietzsche, Friedrich (2006). *Thus Spoke Zarathustra: A Book for All and None*. Ed. Adrian Del Caro and Robert B. Pippin. Trans. Adrian Del Caro.

Nowak, Martin A., Corina E. Tarnita, and Edward O. Wilson (2010). "The evolution of eusociality". *Nature*, Vol. 466 March 10, 2010). 1057–1062.

Nyong'o, Tavia (2018). *Afro-Fabulations: The Queer Drama of Black Life*.

O'Connell, Hugh (2019). "The Novums of Fiscalmancy: Speculative Finance and Speculative Fiction in Ian McDonald's *The Dervish House*." *The New Centennial Review*, Vol. 19, No. 1, 129–154.

OECD (2019). "Under Pressure: The Squeezed Middle Class." OECD Publishing, 2019.

Oliveri, Lucia (2018). "The Logic of the Imagination. A Useful Fictionalism." *https://philosophy.fas.harvard.edu/files/phildept/files/oliveri_the_logic_of_the_imagination_hhw.pdf*

Olsen, Tyler James, and Brian Dorman (2019). "Capitalism Set the Fires in the Amazon Rainforest." *Jacobin*, September 6, 2019. *https://jacobinmag.com/2019/09/amazon-rainforest-fires-capitalism-brazil-bolsonaro*

O'Neil, Denny, and Neal Adams (1970). "No Evil Shall Escape My Sight!." *Green Lantern*, Vol. 2, No. 76, (April 1970).

Ornes, Stephen (2017). "How nonequilibrium thermodynamics speaks to the mystery of life." *PNAS*, Vol. 114, No. 3, 423–424.

Orwell, George (1949). *Nineteen Eighty-Four*.

O'Sullivan, Shawn (2006). "The Aquatic Invasion: A Drexciya Discography Review." *Exchange*. https://ucexchange.uchicago.edu/reviews/aquatic.html

Oyama, Susan, Paul E. Griffiths, and Russell D. Gray, ed. (2001). *Cycles of Contingency: Developmental Systems and Evolution*.

Parr, Thomas, Giovanni Pezzulo, and Karl J. Friston (2022). *Active Inference: The Free Energy Principle in Mind, Brain, and Behavior*.

Pater, Walter (2010). *The Renaissance: Studies of Art and Poetry.*

Patrick, Ryan B. (2019). "Cory Doctorow on Radicalized, the problem with superheroes and writing speculative fiction in a jaded world." *CBC*, April 4, 2019. https://www.cbc.ca/books/cory-doctorow-on-radicalized-the-problem-with-superheroes-and-writing-speculative-fiction-in-a-jaded-world-1.5080939

Peckham, Morse (1979). *Explanation and Power: The Control of Human Behavior.*

Penner, Robert G. (2020). *Big Echo Interviews, 2017-2020.*

Phillips, Rasheedah, et al. (2015). *Black Quantum Futurism: Theory & Practice.*

Phillips, Rasheedah (2018). "Black Futurism and Technologies of Joy." *Schloss*, August 15, 2018. *https://schloss-post.com/black-futurism-technologies-joy/*

Phillips, Rasheedah (2019). "Activating Retrocurrences and Reverse Time-Bindings in the Quantum Now(s)." Exhibition catalog for "Black Quantum Futurism: On the Edge of the Bush / A Long Walk Into the Unknown." January 25–April 20, 2019, Squeaky Wheel Film & Media Art Center, Buffalo, New York.

Pinker, Steven (2011). *The Better Angels of Our Nature: Why Violence Has Declined.*

Plotz, John (2020). "The Realism of Our Times: Kim Stanley Robinson on How Science Fiction Works." *Public Books*, September 23, 2020. *https://www.publicbooks.org/the-realism-of-our-times-kim-stanley-robinson-on-how-science-fiction-works/*

Pound, Ezra (1913). "A Few Don'ts by an Imagiste." *Poetry*, Vol. 1 (March 1913). https://www.poetryfoundation.org/poetrymagazine/articles/58900/a-few-donts-by-an-imagiste

Powers, Richard (1995). *Galatea 2.0.*

prcptm (2020). Reply to thread, "Drexciyan Electro sound design." *Electronauts*, November 2020. https://www.elektronauts.com/t/drexciyan-electro-sound-design/142621

Prigogine, Ilya, and Isabelle Stengers (1984). *Order Out of Chaos: Man's New Dialogue With Nature.*

Public Enemy (1988). "Countdown to Armageddon." In *It Takes A Nation of Millions To Hold Us Back.*

Pullman, Philip (1995). *The Golden Compass.*

Pullman, Philip (1997). *The Subtle Knife.*

Pullman, Philip (2000). *The Amber Spyglass.*

Putnam, Hilary (1973). "Meaning and Reference." *The Journal of Philosophy*, Vol. 70, No. 19, 699–711.

Putnam, Hilary (1975). "The Meaning of 'Meaning.'" In *Mind, Language and Reality: Philosophical Papers, Volume 2.*

Quote Investigator (2012). "The Future Has Arrived—It's Just Not Evenly Distributed Yet." January 24, 2012. *https://quoteinvestigator.com/2012/01/24/future-has-arrived/*

Quote Investigator (2019). "It Is Easy To Predict an Automobile in 1880; It Is Very Hard To Predict a Traffic Problem." October 23, 2019. https://quoteinvestigator.com/2019/10/23/traffic/

Ramsay, William (2019). "Eliminative Materialism." *Stanford Encyclopedia of Philosophy. https://plato.stanford.edu/entries/materialism-eliminative/*

Reesman, Bryan (2021). "'Dynasty,' 'Top Gun' and 'Back to the Future' show '80s nostalgia is totally rad right now." *NBC News*, May 7, 2021. https://www.nbcnews.com/think/opinion/dynasty-top-gun-back-future-show-80s-nostalgia-totally-rad-ncna1266620

Rennix, Brianna, and Nathan Robinson (2017). "The Trolley Problem Will Tell You Nothing Useful About Morality." *Current Affairs*. Blog, November 3, 2017. *https://editor.currentaffairs.org/2017/11/the-trolley-problem-will-tell-you-nothing-useful-about-morality/*

Rescher, Nicholas (2015). "Leibniz as a Critic of Spinoza." *Studia Leibnitiana*, Vol. 47, No. 2, 186–204.

Richmond, Scott (2011). "'Dude, that's just wrong': Mimesis, Identification, Jackass." *World Picture*, Vol. 6 (Winter 2011). *http://www.worldpicturejournal.com/WP_6/Richmond.html*

Richmond, Scott (2016). *Cinema's Bodily Illusions: Flying, Floating, and Hallucinating.*

Rieder, John (2008). *Colonialism and the Emergence of Science Fiction.*

Rieder, John (2017). *Science Fiction and the Mass Culture Genre System.*

Riskin, Jessica (2016). *The Restless Clock: A History of the Centuries-Long Argument over What Makes Living Things Tick.*

Robinson, Kim Stanley (2009). *Galileo's Dream.*

Robinson, Kim Stanley (2017). *New York 2140.*

Robinson, Kim Stanley (2018). "Dystopias Now." *Commune*, November 2, 2018. https://communemag.com/dystopias-now/

Robinson, Kim Stanley (2020). *The Ministry for the Future.*

Rodolfo, Kevin (2000). "What is Homeostasis?" *Scientific American*, January 3, 2000. *https://www.scientificamerican.com/article/what-is-homeostasis/*

Romeo, Nick (2017). "Better Business Through Sci-Fi." *The New Yorker*, July 30, 2017. *https://www.newyorker.com/tech/annals-of-technology/better-business-through-sci-fi*

Rossi, Benedetta (2015). "African Post-Slavery: A History of the Future." *International Journal of African Historical Studies*, Vol. 48, No. 2, 303–324.

Rovelli, Carlo (2018). *The Order of Time.*

Rubin, Mike (2017). "Infinite Journey to Inner Space: The Legacy of Drexciya." *Red Bull Music Academy*, June 29, 2017. https://daily.redbullmusicacademy.com/2017/06/drexciya-infinite-journey-to-inner-space

Ruff, Matt (2016). *Lovecraft Country.*

Rukeyser, Muriel (2006). *The Collected Poems of Muriel Rukeyser.*

Russ, Joanna (1975). *The Female Man.*

Ryman, Geoff, et al. (2004). *The Mundane Manifesto.* https://sfgenics.wordpress.com/2013/07/04/geoff-ryman-et-al-the-mundane-manifesto/

Salmon, Felix (2009). "Recipe for Disaster: The Formula That Killed Wall Street." *Wired*, February 2009. *https://www.wired.com/2009/02/wp-quant/*

Salvage (2015). Journal. https://salvage.zone/

Samatar, Sofia (2017). "Toward a Planetary History of Afrofuturism." *Research in African Literatures*, Vol. 48, No. 4 (Winter 2017), 175–191.

Samatar, Sofia (2019). "How to Get Back to the Forest." In *Tender: Stories*.

Sandifer, Elizabeth (2017). *Neoreaction a Basilisk: Essays on and Around the Alt-Right*.

Sartre, Jean- Paul (1976). *Critique of Dialectical Reason: Volume 1, Theory of Practical Ensembles*. Trans. Alan Sheridan-Smith.

Sassen, Saskia (2017). "Predatory Formations Dressed in Wall Street Suits and Algorithmic Math." *Science, Technology & Society*, Vol. 22, No. 1, 1–15.

Satifka, Erica L. (2021). *How to Get to Apocalypse and Other Disasters*.

Saussure, Ferdinand de (1983). *Course in General Linguistics*. Trans. Roy Harris.

Sawyer, Robert J. (2005). *Mindscan*.

Scalzi, John, et al. (2010). *Metatropolis: Original Science Fiction Stories in a Shared Future*.

Schneider, Eric D., and Dorion Sagan (2005). *Into the Cool: Energy Flow, Thermodynamics, and Life*.

Schoen, Lawrence M. (2015). *Barsk: The Elephants' Graveyard*.

Scholes, Robert (1975). *Structural Fabulation: Essay on Fiction of the Future*.

Schrödinger, Erwin (1944). *What Is Life? The Physical Aspect of the Living Cell*.

Schulze-Makuch, Dirk (2017). "A New Classification System for Water-Based Life." *Smithsonian Magazine*, October 20, 2017. https://www.smithsonianmag.com/air-space-magazine/new-classification-system-water-based-life-180965341/

Schwitzgebel, Eric (2015). "If materialism is true, the United States is probably conscious." *Philosophical Studies*, Vol. 172, 1697–1721.

Schwitzgebel, Eric, and Jacob Barandes (2022). "Almost Everything You Do Causes Almost Everything (Under Certain Not Wholly Implausible Assumptions); or Infinite Puppetry." http://www.faculty.ucr.edu/~eschwitz/SchwitzPapers/InfinitePuppetry-220531.pdf.

Scott, Ridley (1982). *Blade Runner*. Film.

Semley, John (2019). "Cyberpunk is Dead." *The Baffler*, Vol. 48 (November 2019). *https://thebaffler.com/salvos/cyberpunk-is-dead-semley*

Serling, Rod (1962). "The Fugitive." *The Twilight Zone*, March 9, 1962.

Seuss, Dr (1940). *Horton Hatches the Egg.*

Shanahan, Murray (2021). "What is Consciousness?." In *Sound, Image, and Data in Cybermedia.* Ed. Carol Vernallis and Selmin Kara.

Shaviro, Steven (1990). *Passion and Excess: Blanchot, Bataille, and Literary Theory.*

Shaviro, Steven (2003). *Connected: Or What It Means To Live In The Network Society.*

Shaviro, Steven (2009). "The Singularity is Here." In *Red Planets: Marxism and Science Fiction.* Ed. Mark Bould and China Miéville.

Shaviro, Steven (2011). "The 'Bitter Necessity' of Debt: Neoliberal Finance and the Society of Control." *Concentric: Literary and Cultural Studies*, Vol. 37, No, 1 (March 2011), 73–82.

Shaviro, Steven (2015). *No Speed Limit: Three Essays on Accelerationism.*

Shaviro, Steven (2016a). *Discognition.*

Shaviro, Steven (2016b). "Into the Funhole: Kathe Koja's *The Cipher.*" *Genre*, Vol. 49, No. 2, 213–229.

Shaviro, Steven (2017). "Whitehead on Causality and Perception." In: *Rethinking Whitehead's Symbolism: Thought, Language, Culture.* Ed. Roland Faber, Jeffrey A. Bell, and Joseph Patek.

Shaviro, Steven (2020). "Optimism in the Face of Catastrophe: Kim Stanley Robinson's *The Ministry for the Future.*" *Studies in the Fantastic*, Vol. 10 (Winter 2020/Spring 2021), 108–114.

Shaviro, Steven (2021). *Extreme Fabulations: Science Fictions of Life.*

Shaviro, Steven (2022). *The Rhythm Image: Music Videos and New Audiovisual Forms.*

Shelley, Mary Wollstonecraft (1826). *The Last Man.*

Shelley, Percy Bysshe (1988). *Shelley's Prose, or, The Trumpet of a Prophecy.* Ed. David Lee Clark.

Shelley, Percy Bysshe (2017). *Selected Poems and Prose.* Ed. Jack Donovan and Clan Duffy.

Shirley, John (2011). *Bioshock: Rapture.*

Siegel, Ethan (2019a). "Astronomers Debate: How Many Habitable Planets Does Each Sun-Like Star Have?" *Forbes*, October 1, 2019. https://www.forbes.com/sites/startswithabang/2019/10/01/astronomers-debate-how-many-habitable-planets-does-each-sun-like-star-have/

Siegel, Ethan (2019b). "No, Thermodynamics Does Not Explain Our Perceived Arrow Of Time." *Forbes*, November 22, 2019. https://www.forbes.com/sites/startswithabang/2019/11/22/no-thermodynamics-does-not-explain-our-perceived-arrow-of-time/

Simondon, Gilbert (2020). *Individuation in Light of Notions of Form and Information*. Trans. Taylor Adkins.

Slonczewski, Joan (1986). *A Door into Ocean*.

Smith, E. E. "Doc" (1948) *Triplanetary*.

Smith, E. E. "Doc" (1950). *First Lensman*.

Smith, Justin E. H. (2016). "Leibniz's Harlequinade: Nature, Infinity, and the Limits of Mathematization." In *The Language of Nature: Reassessing the Mathematization of Natural Philosophy in the Seventeenth Century*. Ed. Benjamin Hill, C. Kenneth Waters, Edward Slowik, Geoffrey Gorham.

Smith McKoy, Sheila (1999). "The Limbo Contest: Diaspora Temporality and its Reflection in *Praisesong for the Widow* and *Daughters of the Dust*." *Callaloo*, Vol. 22, No.1 (1999), 208–222.

Smolin, Lee (2006). "The Case for Background Independence." In Dean Rickles, Steven French & Juha T. Saatsi (eds.), *The Structural Foundations of Quantum Gravity*. 196–239.

Smolin, Lee (2014). *Time Reborn: From the Crisis in Physics to the Future of the Universe*.

Smolin, Lee (2019). *Einstein's Unfinished Revolution: The Search for What Lies Beyond the Quantum*.

Sobchack, Vivian (2004). *Carnal Thoughts: Embodiment and Moving Image Culture*.

Solms, Mark (2021). *The Hidden Spring: A Journey to the Source of Consciousness*.

Solomon, Rivers (2019). *The Deep*.

Špaček, Jan (2022). "Are Venusians 'life'?." *The Primordial Scoop*, June 3, 2022.

Špaček, Jan, and Steven Benner (2021). "The organic carbon cycle in the atmosphere of Venus and evolving red oil." Venera-D: Venus Cloud Habitability System Workshop, held virtually, November 29–December 3, 2021. LPI Contribution No. 2629, id.4052. https://www.hou.usra.edu/meetings/venera_d2021/pdf/4052.pdf

Spicer, Andre (2020). "Sci-fi author William Gibson: How 'future fatigue' is putting people off the 22nd century." *The Conversation*, January 23, 2020. https://theconversation.com/sci-fi-author-william-gibson-how-future-fatigue-is-putting-people-off-the-22nd-century-130335

Spicer, Jack (1998). *The House That Jack Built: The Collected Lectures of Jack Spicer*. Ed. Peter Gizzi.

Spicer, Jack (2008). *My Vocabulary Did This To Me: The Collected Poetry of Jack Spicer*. Ed. Peter Gizzi and Kevin Killian.

Spiegel, Simon (2008). "Things Made Strange: On the Concept of 'Estrangement' in Science Fiction Theory." *Science Fiction Studies*, Vol. 35, 369–385.

Spinoza, Benedict de (2018). *Ethics*. Trans. Michael Silverthorne and Matthew J. Kisner.

Spivak, Gayatri Chakravorty (1993). *Outside in the Teaching Machine*.

Spivak, Michael (1990). *The Joy of TeX: a Gourmet Guide to Typesetting with the AMSTeX Macro Package*. Second edition.

Standing, Guy (2011). *The Precariat: The New Dangerous Class*.

Stasenko, Mark (2018). "Overvalued." *Slate*, November 27, 2018. *https://slate.com/technology/2018/11/mark-stasenko-overvalued-short-story.html*

Steinskog, Erik (2018). *Afrofuturism and Black Sound Studies Culture, Technology, and Things to Come*.

Stengers, Isabelle (2005). "Introductory Notes on an Ecology of Practices." *Cultural Studies Review*, Vol. 11, No. 1 (January 2005), 183–196.

Stengers, Isabelle (2009). "Thinking With Deleuze and Whitehead: A Double Test." In *Deleuze, Whitehead, Bergson: Rhizomatic Connections*. Ed. Keith Robinson.

Stengers, Isabelle (2010). *Cosmopolitics I*. Trans. Robert Bononno.

Stengers, Isabelle (2011). *Thinking With Whitehead: A Free and Wild Creation of Concepts*. Trans. Michael Chase.

Stengers, Isabelle (2018a). "Science Fiction to Science Studies." In *The Cambridge Companion to Literature and Science*. Ed. Steven Meyer.

Stengers, Isabelle (2018b). "Reclaiming Imagination: Speculative SF as an Art of Consequences." NatureCulture. *https://www.natcult.net/interviews/reclaiming-imagination-speculative-sf-as-an-art-of-consequences/*

Sterling, Bruce, ed. (1986). *Mirrorshades: The Cyberpunk Anthology*.

Sterling, Bruce (2014). *Schismatrix Plus*.

Stevens, Wallace (1997). *Wallace Stevens : Collected Poetry and Prose*. Ed. Frank Kermode and Joan Richardson.

Stevenson, Robert Louis (1886). *Strange Case of Dr Jekyll and Mr Hyde*.

Stewart, George R. (1949). *Earth Abides*.

Stiglitz, Joseph (2011). "Of the 1%, By the 1%, For the 1%." *Vanity Fair*, May 2011. *https://www.vanityfair.com/news/2011/05/top-one-percent-201105*

Strange, Susan (1986). *Casino Capitalism*.

Stross, Charles (2005). *Accelerando*.

Suarez, Daniel (2006). *Daemon*.

Summers, Lawrence H. (2020). "Accepting the Reality of Secular Stagnation." *Finance & Development*, Vol. 57, No. 1 (May 2020). *https://www.imf.org/external/pubs/ft/fandd/2020/03/larry-summers-on-secular-stagnation.htm*.

Suvin, Darko (1997). "On Cognitive Emotions and Topological Imagination." After Postmodernism Conference, University of Chicago, November 14-16, 1997. *http://previous.focusing.org/apm_papers/suvin.html*

Suvin, Darko (2016). *Metamorphoses of Science Fiction: On the Poetics and History of a Literary Genre*. New edition.

Swanwick, Michael (2019). *The Iron Dragon's Mother*.

Swerski, Peter (1991). "Dystopia or Dischtopia? The Science-Fiction Paradigms of Thomas M. Disch." *Science Fiction Studies*, Vol. 18, 161–179.

Syms, Martine (2013). "The Mundane Afrofuturist Manifesto." *Rhizome*, December 17, 2013. https://rhizome.org/editorial/2013/dec/17/mundane-afrofuturist-manifesto/

Szendy, Peter (2013). *Kant in the Land of Extraterrestrials: Cosmopolitical Philosofictions*. Trans. Will Bishop.

Szwed, John (1997). *Space is the Place: The Lives and Times of Sun Ra.*

Taleb, Nassim Nicholas (2010). *The Black Swan: The Impact of the Highly Improbable*. Second edition.

Taplin, Jonathan (2017). *Move Fast and Break Things: How Facebook, Google, and Amazon Cornered Culture and Undermined Democracy*.

Tarde, Gabriel (2012). *Monadology and Sociology*. Trans. and ed. Theo Lorenc.

Tchaikovsky, Adrian (2015). *Children of Time.*

Tchaikovsky, Adrian (2019). *Children of Ruin.*

Tchaikovsky, Adrian (2020). *The Doors of Eden.*

Tchaikovsky, Adrian (2023). *Children of Memory.*

Tenn, William (2001). *Immodest Proposals: The Complete Science Fiction of William Tenn, Volume 1.*

Thacker, Eugene (2011). *In the Dust of This Planet (Horror of Philosophy 1).*

Thompson, Tade (2016). "The Apologists." *Interzone*, Vol. 266 (September–October 2016).

Thornton, Jonathan (2018). "Interview with Pat Cadigan." *The Fantasy Hive*, December 3, 2018. *https://fantasy-hive.co.uk/2018/12/interview-with-pat-cadigan/*

Tiptree, James (1990). *Her Smoke Rose Up Forever: The Great Years of James Tiptree Jr.*

Tiptree, James (2000). *Meet Me At Infinity: The Uncollected Tiptree: Fiction and Nonfiction.*

Toffler, Alvin, and Heidi Toffler (1970). *Future Shock.*

Tolkien, J. R. R. (1954-1955). Lord of the Rings trilogy.

Tomlinson, Gary (2016). "Sign, Affect, and Musicking before the Human." *boundary 2*, Vol. 43, No. 1, 144–172.

Toscano, Alberto (2008). "The Open Secret of Real Abstraction." *Rethinking Marxism*, Vol. 20, No. 2 (April 2008), 273–287.

Tropper, Sarah (2019). "The Importance of Imagination in Leibniz." *Konzepte Der Einbildungskraft in Der Philosophie, Den Wissenschaften Und Den Künsten Des 18. Jahrhunderts*, 25–38.

Uncertain Commons (2013). *Speculate This!.*

Urban Dictionary (2020). "Karen." *https://www.urbandictionary.com/define.php?term=Karen*

Valente, Catherynne M. (2018). *Mass Effect: Annihilation.*

VanderMeer, Jeff (2014a). *Annihilation.*

VanderMeer, Jeff (2014b). *Authority.*

VanderMeer, Jeff (2014c). *Acceptance.*

Vint, Sherryl (2019). "Promissory Futures: Reality and Imagination in Finance and Fiction." *New Centennial Review*, Vol. 19, No. 1., 11-36.

Vint, Sherryl, and Mark Bould (2008). "There is No Such Thing as Science Fiction." In *Reading Science Fiction*. Ed. James Gunn, Marlene Barr, and Matthew Candelaria.

Voltaire (2006). *Candide, or Optimism*. Trans. Burton Raffel.

Vonnegut, Kurt (1963). *Cat's Cradle.*

Vonnegut, Kurt (1969). *Slaughterhouse-Five.*

Walker, Sara, and Lee Cronin (2023). "Time is an object." *Aeon*, May 19, 2023. https://aeon.co/essays/time-is-not-an-illusion-its-an-object-with-physical-size

Walker-Emig, Paul (2018). "Neon and corporate dystopias: Why does cyberpunk refuse to move on?." *The Guardian*, October 16, 2018. *https://www.theguardian.com/games/2018/oct/16/neon-corporate-dystopias-why-does-cyberpunk-refuse-move-on*

Wallace-Wells, David (2011). "Interview: William Gibson: The Art of Fiction, # 211." *The Paris Review*, Vol. 197 (Summer 2011). *https://www.theparisreview.org/interviews/6089/the-art-of-fiction-no-211-william-gibson*

Warhol, Andy (1975). *The Philosophy Of Andy Warhol: From A to B and Back Again.*

Wark, McKenzie (2017). "On the Obsolescence of the Bourgeois Novel in the Anthropocene." *Verso Books Blog*, August 16, 2017. https://www.versobooks.com/blogs/news/3356-on-the-obsolescence-of-the-bourgeois-novel-in-the-anthropocene

Wark, McKenzie (2023). *Raving.*
Watts, Peter (2011). *Crysis: Legion.*
Weinberg, Steven (1992). *Dreams of a Final Theory.*
Weinberger, David (2017). "Our Machines Now Have Knowledge We'll Never Understand." *Wired*, April 18, 2017. *https://www.wired.com/story/our-machines-now-have-knowledge-well-never-understand/*
Weir, Andy (2021). *Project Hail Mary.*
Weir, Erica (2005). "Mass sociogenic illness." *CMAJ*, Vol. 172, No. 1, 36.
Weisman, Alan (2007). *The World Without Us.*
Weisbard, Eric (2021). *Songbooks: The Literature of American Popular Music.*
Wells, H. G. (1898). *War of the Worlds.*
Wells, H. G. (1945). *Mind at the End of its Tether.*
Whates, Ian, ed. (2014). *Paradox: Stories Inspired by the Fermi Paradox.*
Whitehead, Alfred North (1911). *Introduction to Mathematics.*
Whitehead, Alfred North (1920). *The Concept of Nature.*
Whitehead, Alfred North (1922). *The Principle of Relativity With Applications to Physical Science.*
Whitehead, Alfred North (1925). *Science and the Modern World.*
Whitehead, Alfred North (1927a). *Symbolism: Its Meaning and Effect.*
Whitehead, Alfred North (1927b). "Time." *Sixth International Congress of Philosophy*, 59–64.
Whitehead, Alfred North (1933). *Adventures of Ideas.*
Whitehead, Alfred North (1938). *Modes of Thought.*
Whitehead, Alfred North (1948). *Science and Philosophy.*
Whitehead, Alfred North (1978). *Process and Reality: An Essay in Cosmology*. Corrected edition.
Wiener, Anna (2018). "The Complicated Legacy of Steward Brand's *Whole Earth Catalog*." *The New Yorker*, November 16, 2018. *https://www.newyorker.com/news/letter-from-silicon-valley/the-complicated-legacy-of-stewart-brands-whole-earth-catalog*
Wikipedia (2021). "List of *Star Trek* Novels." *https://en.wikipedia.org/wiki/List_of_Star_Trek_novels*

Wikipedia (2023a). "Baroque." https://en.wikipedia.org/wiki/Baroque

Wikipedia (2023b). "Circumstellar habitable zone." https://en.wikipedia.org/wiki/Circumstellar_habitable_zone

Wilderson III, Frank B. (2020). *Afropessimism.*

Willems, Brian (2017). *Speculative Realism and Science Fiction.*

Williams, Evan Calder (2010). *Combined and Uneven Apocalypse.*

Williams, Neil E. (2019). *The Powers Metaphysic.*

Williams, Raymond (1961). *The Long Revolution.*

Wired Staff (2009). "March 17, 1948: William Gibson, Father of Cyberspace." *Wired*, March 16, 2009. *https://www.wired.com/2009/03/march-17-1948-william-gibson-father-of-cyberspace-2/*

Wittenberg, David (2013). *Time Travel: The Popular Philosophy of Narrative.*

Wittgenstein, Ludwig (1974). *Tractatus Logico-Philosophicus.* Trans. D. F. Pears and B. F. McGuinness. Revised edition.

Wittgenstein, Ludwig (2009). *Philosophical Investigations.* Trans. G. E. M. Anscombe, P. M. S. Hacker, and Joachim Schulte, Revised fourth edition.

Womack, Ytasha (2013). *Afrofuturism: The World of Black Sci-Fi and Fantasy Culture.*

Wu, YiBu, Qi Feng, and YiMing Gong (2013). "Blooming of bacteria and algae is a biokiller for mass-extinction of Devonian coral-stromatoporoid reef ecosystems." *Science China Earth Sciences*, Vol. 56, 1221–1232.

Yaszek, Lisa (2020). "Feminst Cyberpunk." In *The Routledge Companion to Cyberpunk Culture.* Ed. Anna McFarlane et al.

Zalasiewicz, Jan, et al. (2021). "The Anthropocene: Comparing Its Meaning in Geology (Chronostratigraphy) with Conceptual Approaches Arising in Other Disciplines." *Earth's Future*, Vol. 9, No. 3 (March 2021), 1-25.

Žižek, Slavoj (2006). *The Parallax View.*

Zuboff, Shoshana (2020). *The Age of Surveillance Capitalism: The Fight for a Human Future at the New Frontier of Power.*

REPEATER BOOKS

is dedicated to the creation of a new reality. The landscape of twenty-first-century arts and letters is faded and inert, riven by fashionable cynicism, egotistical self-reference and a nostalgia for the recent past. Repeater intends to add its voice to those movements that wish to enter history and assert control over its currents, gathering together scattered and isolated voices with those who have already called for an escape from Capitalist Realism. Our desire is to publish in every sphere and genre, combining vigorous dissent and a pragmatic willingness to succeed where messianic abstraction and quiescent co-option have stalled: abstention is not an option: we are alive and we don't agree.